Psychology for the
Third Millennium

Psychology for the Third Millennium

Integrating Cultural and Neuroscience Perspectives

Edited by

Rom Harré and Fathali Moghaddam

Los Angeles | London | New Delhi
Singapore | Washington DC

First published 2012

SAGE Publications Ltd
1 Oliver's Yard
55 City Road
London EC1Y 1SP

SAGE Publications Inc.
2455 Teller Road
Thousand Oaks, California 91320

SAGE Publications India Pvt Ltd
B 1/I 1 Mohan Cooperative Industrial Area
Mathura Road
New Delhi 110 044

SAGE Publications Asia-Pacific Pte Ltd
3 Church Street
#10-04 Samsung Hub
Singapore 049483

Library of Congress Control Number: 2011930454

British Library Cataloguing in Publication data

A catalogue record for this book is available from the British Library

ISBN 978-0-85702-268-4
ISBN 978-0-85702-269-1 (pbk)

Typeset by C&M Digitals (P) Ltd, Chennai, India
Printed in India at Replika Press Pvt Ltd
Printed on paper from sustainable resources

Contents

Notes on the Authors

Christina E. Erneling is Associate Professor at Lund University, Sweden, where she teaches Psychology, Communication and Philosophy of Social Science. She is the author of *Towards discursive education: Philosophy, technology and modern education* (2010), *Understanding language acquisition: The framework of learning* (1993) and co-editor of two books on cognitive science: *The mind as a scientific object: Between brain and culture* (2005) and *The future of the cognitive revolution* (1997). She is currently working on a four-year research project investigating conceptual issues in evolutionary psychology and education: *Evolutionary educational psychology: a biologising of education?*

Vlad P. Glăveanu is a PhD candidate and teaching assistant at the Institute of Social Psychology, LSE. He holds a BA in Psychology from the University of Bucharest and an MSc in Social and Cultural Psychology from LSE (Himmelweit Prize for best overall performance). His main interests are in creativity, the psychology of art and crafts, social representations and qualitative methodologies. His doctoral research, funded by the ESRC, is focused on proposing a cultural psychological understanding of creativity and has been the subject of published work in different journals, among them *New Ideas in Psychology*, *Culture & Psychology*, *Journal for the Theory of Social Behaviour*, *Thinking Skills and Creativity*, *Integrative Psychological and Behavioral Science*, *Theory & Psychology*. He is also founding member and current Editor of *Europe's Journal of Psychology*. (www.ejop.org).

P. M. S. Hacker is Emeritus Research Fellow at St. John's College, Oxford. His main interests are in philosophy of psychology, philosophy of language, the philosophy of Wittgenstein, and the history of analytical philosophy. He has written extensively on the philosophical problems in cognitive neuroscience, including *Philosophical foundations of neuroscience* (2003) and *A history of cognitive neuroscience* ((2008) both co-authored with M. R. Bennett). He is well known for his numerous books on the philosophy of Wittgenstein, including the four volume *Analytical commentary on the Philosophical Investigations* ((1980–96), revised editions of volumes 1 and 2, 2003, 2009), the first two volumes of which were co-authored with G. P. Baker, and *Wittgenstein's place in twentieth-century analytical philosophy* (1996). He published *Human nature: the categorial framework* in 2007, which is the first volume of a trilogy on human nature. He is currently writing the second volume: *The cognitive and cogitative powers of man*.

Rom Harré studied chemical engineering, turning to mathematics and then philosophy of science. Currently he is Distinguished Research Professor at Georgetown University, Washington DC and Emeritus Fellow of Linacre College, Oxford. He has published widely on the ways language and languages impact our ways of being, including our cognitive and emotional skills and propensities (particularly *The Explanation of Social Behaviour* with P.F. Secord). His latest book is *Pavlov's and Schrodinger's cat*, a study of the uses of animals and plants as scientific apparatus.

Sandra Jovchelovitch is Professor of Social Psychology at the London School of Economics where she directs the Masters programme in Social and Cultural Psychology. Her research focuses on how different socio-cultural contexts shape the development and transformation of knowledge, and in particular how different systems of knowing meet and clash in contemporary public spheres. She has a special interest on the genetic and historical methods developed by Piaget and Vygotsky to the study of mind and on the development of dialogical perspectives to the study of knowledge in context. She is the author of *Knowledge in context: Representations, community and culture* (Routledge, 2007), *Social representations and the public sphere: The symbolic construction of public spaces in Brazil* (Vozes, 2000) and *The health beliefs of the Chinese community in England* (HEA, 1998). Her new book, *How communities think* is coming out in 2012.

Fathali M. Moghaddam is Professor, Department of Psychology, and Director, Conflict Resolution Program, Department of Government, Georgetown University. Dr. Moghaddam was born in Iran, educated from an early age in England, and worked for the United Nations and for McGill University before joining Georgetown in 1990. He has researched a broad range of topics, toward developing psychology for and of humankind. Among his recent books are: *The individual and society* (2002), *Great ideas in psychology* (2005), *Multiculturalism and intergroup relations* (2008), and *The new global insecurity* (2010). He is currently writing a book on *The psychology of dictatorship*. For more details, visit fathalimoghaddam.com

Steven R. Sabat is Professor of Psychology at Georgetown University. The focus of his research, published in numerous scientific journal articles has been on the intact cognitive and social abilities, and the subjective experience of people with moderate to severe dementia, as well as on how to enhance communication between people with dementia and their carers. He is also the author of *The experience of Alzheimer's Disease: Life through a tangled veil* and co-editor of *Dementia: mind, meaning, and the person*.

Gordon Sammut is Lecturer in Social Psychology at the University of Malta. His work investigates the psychological study of points of view. His main interests include psychosocial models in the social sciences, attitude measurement and public opinion, the epistemology of representations and phenomena, gestalt social psychology, and issues relating to opinion formation and argumentation. (gordon.sammut@um.edu.mt)

Brady Wagoner completed his PhD at the University of Cambridge and is now Associate Professor at the Aalborg University, Denmark. He has received a number of prestigious academic awards, including the Sigmund Koch Award, Gates Cambridge Scholarship and the Jefferson Prize. His publications span a range of topics, including the history of psychology, cultural psychology, research methodology and the psychology of remembering. He is chief organizer of the Frederic Bartlett Internet Archive. Additionally, he is on the editorial board of four international Journals (*Culture & Psychology*, *Frontiers of Quantitative Psychology and Measurement*, and *Integrative Psychological and Behavioral Science*) and is founding co-editor of the journal *Psychology & Society*. His books include *Symbolic transformation: The mind in movement through culture and society* (Routledge, 2010), *Dialogicality in focus: Challenges to theory, method and application* (Nova Science, 2011), and *Culture and Social Change: Transforming society through the power of ideas* (Information Age, 2012). Currently, he is writing a book titled *Frederic Bartlett in Reconstruction: Where Culture and Mind Meet* (Cambridge University Press).

PART I

Principles and Methods

1

Psychoneurology:
The Program

Rom Harré and Fathali M. Moghaddam

'There is nothing in the universe except meanings and molecules.' (Anon)

As a science emerges from a common-sense understanding of certain kinds of phenomena it only gradually becomes clear what are the fundamental entities of the 'world' under study. Psychology grew out of our everyday reflections on the beliefs and practices relevant to people thinking, acting, feeling and perceiving. The scientific study of these phenomena should, we believe, be built on a common fundamental presumption: that *persons* are the basic beings at the root of a scientific psychology. It is persons who think, act, feel and perceive. Persons are the fundamental entities of psychology.

In a sense a person has no parts, in particular, a person is not a union of a mind and a body. However, while persons have no parts, each person, though a singularity, has a vast array of attributes. Some are material attributes and some are mental capacities, powers and dispositions. Though people are sometimes acted on by outside forces they always retain their status as ultimate agents, at least in principle. Personal agency, we might say, is the default position when we are studying what people do. When people lose their powers to think, act, feel and perceive the world around them and the condition of their own bodies, we take them to be in need of care and perhaps of cure. For example, in the law courts we consider the accused responsible for his or her actions, unless there is a successful plea of insanity.

For more than four centuries psychology was led away from the most fruitful research domain by the widespread assumption that we should treat the material attributes of persons as properties of the human body, a material substance, and the mental attributes of persons as properties of a parallel stuff, the human mind. Persons were taken to be 'miraculous' conglomerates of bodies and minds, a material thing somehow joined to an immaterial thing. In the 20th century this duality assumption subtly influenced the thinking of the majority of psychologists. Even those who rejected the idea of the mental aspects of a human being as attributes of a substantival mind, nevertheless still implicitly subscribed to the *distinction* between mind and body even and especially when they declared that the way human beings think, act, feel and perceive can be understood in material terms. We believe that the next step in the development of psychology, as a human science for the third millennium, will be achieved when the very distinction between minds and bodies is abandoned.

In this book we set out the various ways a hybrid conception of persons as meaning-making embodied agents depending on one another for their very existence as persons can advance the project of a scientific psychology. We will demonstrate the power of this proposal across the traditional domains of psychology, thinking, acting, feeling and perceiving to invigorate the traditional divisions of psychology as a human science.

Wilhelm Maximilian Wundt (1832–1920) was born in the town of Neckarau in Germany, the son of a Lutheran minister. After boarding school he went on to university to study medicine. According to the German custom he attended lectures at several universities, including Tubingen, Heidelberg and Berlin.

In 1857, he began to teach physiology at the University of Heidelberg. From 1858 to 1864 he was assistant to the Heinrich von Helmholtz, the great German polymath.

In 1864, he moved to Leipzig where he began experimental studies of the senses, particularly vision. By 1881 he had gained sufficient confidence to begin teaching a class on physiological psychology, essentially concerned with the correlations between various physiological phenomena and individual experiences of sight, sound and so on. In 1879, Wundt claimed that he had founded an independent *science* of psychology. The fame of his laboratory soon spread, attracting students from across the world, including E. B. Titchener and G. Stanley Hall.

According to Wundt, psychology was the study of conscious experience. A person was surely the best observer of his or her own experience, so introspection became the major experimental method, as a rigorous and highly disciplined research method, by which elementary sensations were extracted from the complexities of actual experience without imposing interpretations. Together with the intensity and duration of sensations went attention to the qualities of the feelings that accompanied them. The combination of sensations and feelings is what constitutes our mental functioning.

Later in life Wundt began a very different kind of psychology – *Volkerpsychologie* – something very like the cultural psychology we recognize today. Wundt set out to show by the accumulation of examples of cultural phenomena of all kinds, that key aspects of human life could not be accounted for by the attention to individual consciousnesses. They were distinctive in kind and origin, requiring the hypothesis of collective mental processes. Wundt never quite arrived at the current idea of how such processes are possible through the use of language and other symbolic systems to generate interpersonal psychological processes. He died in 1920.

This project is not new. In the 19th century Wilhelm Wundt directed a program of experimental researches to the study of the correlations between the elements of conscious experience and the physical stimuli which brought them about. However, he also undertook a vast study of the cultural side of human psychology and published an enormous 10-volume treatise on *Volkerpsychologie*, commonly translated as 'folk psychology' (Wundt, 1916). Here Wundt's focus was on the form that human activities take by adherence to norms rather than by responding to events or states as causes.

Another version of a two-pronged psychology was proposed by William Stern at the beginning of the 20th century. Philosophers such as Ludwig Wittgenstein (1953) and psychologists such as Lev Vygotsky (1978a) and Jerome Bruner (1986) anticipated the idea of such a hybrid. It is being rediscovered in the 21st century. Stern coined the phrase 'unitas multiplex' to capture the idea that though persons are the fundamental unanalyzable units of the science of psychology each has a complex and unique manifold of attributes (Stern, 1938). Psychology must somehow blend our knowledge of meanings and our knowledge of molecules. While seeking universal features of the human form of life, psychology must acknowledge the individuality of each human being. During the latter part of the 20th century there emerged a robust literature representing psychology as a normative science, for example, as reflected by developments in cultural psychology (Cole, 1996), socio-cultural psychology (Valsiner & Rosa, 2007), as well as various other emerging normative research traditions (Moghaddam, 2002, 2005, ch. 20).

William Stern (1871–1936) was born in Berlin into a middle-class family, the only child. His father had a modest business designing wall paper. After high school he entered the University of Berlin in 1888 to study philology but soon changed to philosophy and psychology. He realized that psychology could not be fruitfully developed according to the methodology of the natural sciences as presented by the positivists. In 1899, he married Carla Joseephy with whom he began their famous diary recording the development of their three children. After his doctoral studies in Berlin he moved to the University of Breslau in 1897 to work under Herman Ebbinghaus, staying until 1916. Though he invented the Intelligence Quotient (IQ) as a ratio of mental to chronological age he soon became sceptical of the uses to which it had been put.

His importance to the advent of hybrid psychology was his emphasis on the distinction between things and persons, and his realization that persons were to be understood as individuals. He came to this insight from his work on differential psychology. It is not a great step to realizing that acknowledging the importance of differences between people implies that each person is in many respects unlike any other. His conception of critical personalism came from the further insight that people are active agents capable of evaluating a huge variety of thoughts and actions. The person is a simple entity with complex attributes. For this he coined the phrase 'unitas multiplex'.

In 1916, he moved to Hamburg where he helped to found the university in 1919. He continued in Hamburg until the Nazi regime banned anyone of Jewish origins from university teaching. In 1934 he moved to Duke University in the United States. He died in Durham, NC, on 27 March, 1938.

Under the principle of unitas multiplex our research will involve the study of 'bodily' aspects such as the running of molecular machines and 'mental' aspects such as the unfolding of sequences of meanings within the constraints of the norms of our local ways of life. The results of the study of each such aspect will reveal the tools and instruments with which people manage their lives.

Scientific Methodology and the Two Concepts of Causality

In order to understand the way a scientific psychology *should* develop we need to understand the basic principles of scientific research thoroughly. Unfortunately, through a series of misunderstandings, a good deal of the psychological research of the last half century has been profitless, based on a flawed philosophical account of the nature of scientific explanations.

Human beings long ago became aware of the world around them and of their own lives as a flux of change. Though most change is smooth and continuous the human way has been to chop up the flow into sequences of events, happenings. The first step in a scientific research program is to develop a classification system for the happenings that are the focus of research. Sometimes events seem to defy all pattern and order, but more often regular sequences are discernible among types of happenings. We observe and catalogue sequences of changes, both continuous and discrete.

How can regularities in the flux of events be explained? Pairs of sequential events are picked out in terms of the concepts of 'cause' and 'effect'. To bring about a desired state of affairs one makes the cause happen, and then, all else being equal, we can expect that the desired effect will occur. We boil the oatmeal and the porridge thickens. But what mediates the transition from cause event or state to effect event or state, from the raw to the cooked? As a general rule when we first notice a regularity among pairs of events or states we have no idea what the intervening process might be. We soon turn to speculations about unobservable processes that link cause events and states with their effects. Alternatively, we ascribe some sort of efficacy, power or agency to something that seems to be the efficacious cause. Already we have the source of a long-running duality in how people understand causality.

Agency explanations abounded in the 17th and 18th centuries, particularly in physics and chemistry. They were matched by an equal abundance of hidden mechanism explanations. While Isaac Newton filled the universe with forces and powers, Robert Boyle filled it with invisible corpuscles or molecules. Though we can observe the effects of the action of forces, the forces themselves remain hidden. The same is true of the consequences of rearrangements of the minute parts of material things. We can observe the outcome of a chemical reaction but we cannot observe the interchanges of atoms among the invisible intangible molecules.

However, if we think that knowledge must be certified by observation then speculations about forces and powers as well as hypotheses about invisible atoms ought not to be included in the realm of scientific certitude. In an influential study published in 1787(1962), David Hume argued that the only legitimate meaning that could be given to the concept of causation among events and states must be limited to the fact of regular sequences in like pairs of events. Any idea of efficacy or power to bring about changes must be put down to the psychological effects of observing many such regularities. Our sense of the necessity of a causal process is nothing more than a tendency or habit to expect an event of the effect type when we have observed one of the cause type. No connection can be observed between them. To establish the existence of a causal sequence all we can do is to turn to statistical analyses of lots of similar cases. The danger of crossing the boundary between certitude and speculation precludes our seeking the active powers or the hidden mechanisms that bring about the effects in which we are interested. In the 20th century this point of view was revived in the influential writings of the positivists (see Ayer, 1978), the philosophers of the Vienna Circle. Intent on ridding the world of ungrounded metaphysical speculations and of the other-worldly fantasies of religion, they managed to eliminate most of science as well. The effect of these ideas diffusing into psychology was disastrous. Unfortunately, under the influence of James B. Watson and the behaviorists, psychologists abandoned agent-causality completely and took up the Humean or positivist version of event-causality, without the underpinning of hypothetical causal mechanisms. In the intervening years various attempts to make up this deficit have been proposed, such as the computational model of cognition. From our point of view agent-causality is the appropriate concept for cultural/discursive studies of human thinking and acting, while a kind of event-causality that is based on hypothetical generative mechanisms is the appropriate concept for neuroscience and related programs.

There is no place for the Humean regularity of sequence concept in any science. This point of view became a kind of dogma despite the fact that the sciences had advanced by the very route that Hume would have forbidden them, by developing hypotheses about the causal powers of natural agents such as magnetic poles and electric charges and about the hidden mechanisms that brought about orderly change in the world. The mechanism of the solar system explained eclipses, the seasons, the phases of the moon and so on. This mechanism was held together by the force of universal gravity and the kinetic energy and momentum of the moving planets. What was there not to like in this magnificent Newtonian analysis of the solar system?

Drawing on the triumphant success of the natural sciences we have two kinds of causality available for the psychology of the third millennium, each with its proper domain of application and each with its attendant implications. Agent-causality focuses on beings with powers to act, which are shaped and constrained by all sorts of environmental conditions. Event-causality focuses on hierarchies of hidden mechanisms which underpin the patterns of meaningful actions agents bring about. How to link these two causal modes into a coherent non-reductive hybrid is an important part of the approach to psychology we take in this book.

Cultural psychology is the study of active people carrying out their projects according to the rules and conventions of their social and material environments. Thus it is normative. It conforms to the principle of agent-causality.

Neuroscience is the study of the mechanisms which active people use to carry out their projects and plans. It conforms to the principles of hierarchical event-causality. Neuroscience does not reach to the depths of the physical processes on which neuro-events ultimately depend, and where agent-causality re-emerges among the basic electromagnetic groundings of the universe.

We can see the pattern of explanation formats in Figure 1.1.

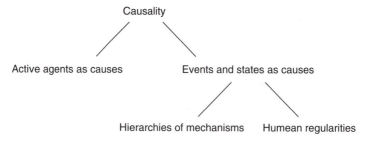

Figure 1.1   Varities of causality

When we are dealing with cognitive phenomena, with social actions and relations, with emotional states and displays, with motives and with problem-solving abilities and much more, the causal mode we need is agent-causality. When we are dealing with the activities of the brain and nervous system the causal mode we need is hierarchies of mechanisms. If we want to create a science of the powers of human thought, feeling, action and perceptions, we never need Humean regularities except as the starting point for beginning a search for genuine causal explanations.

At present, and for the foreseeable future, both neuroscience and normative or cultural/discursive psychology are developing vigorously. In this text we will show ways in which various links can be established whereby the integrity of each paradigm is maintained, and how they can inspire each other.

Despite the rapid developments in normative psychology, the mainstream 'introduction to psychology' texts remain true to an event-causality model appropriate to neuroscience but wholly inappropriate to studies in the meaning-dominated realm of human thought and actions, and completely neglect the 'second psychology' based on persons as agents. Traditional Humean event-causality psychology is well represented by Kalat's highly popular introductory psychology text, in which he states:

> One of the key points of the scientific approach is seeking the immediate causes of an event (what led to what) instead of the final causes (the purpose of the event in an overall plan). That is, scientists act on the basis of determinism, the assumption that everything that happens has a cause, or a determinant, in the observable world ... The assumption that behaviors follow cause and effect seems to work, and anyone planning to do research on behavior is almost forced to start with this assumption. (2005, pp. 5–6)

In line with the approach described by Kalat, traditional introductory psychology texts follow a strictly Humean approach to discussing the psychology of human beings, in a wide range of topics. An irony of the persistence of this kind of psychology is that it is based on an almost total misunderstanding of the nature of the method and metaphysics of the natural sciences. A major feature of this text is the way it demonstrates to students that neuroscience and cultural psychology exemplify the same paradigm of scientific method. Though the range of topics to follow will shadow those of traditional general psychology books, each topic will be presented as a hybrid, with its neuroscience aspects and its cultural aspects integrated into a coherent story.

The Domain of Psychology

People are actively producing streams of thought and action, both public and private, embedded in a flux of bodily feeling. We routinely and unthinkingly partition this stream in all sorts of ways. We express *a* belief, we claim to have *a* memory, we make *a* decision, and we have *a* temper tantrum and so on.

Psychologists cannot but make use of these everyday partitions of the stream of human behavior, for they define the subject matter of their studies. If we could not tell a temper tantrum from a memory claim there would be no psychology, indeed no human life at all as we know it. This picture is filled out by the idea that we should think of our lives as narratives, lived and told stories that are not only expressed in what we do, but, at the same time, shape what we do. The metaphor of life as narrative is one of the most important organizing concepts of the discursive method for many new-wave psychologists, for instance Bruner (1986), the Loughborough School (Billig, 1999; Edwards & Potter, 1992) and many others.

The Act-Action Distinction

Can we find a general principle to partition the stream of private and public, individual and social human activity in the most psychologically illuminating way? We could say that 'actions' are what people do intentionally, while 'acts' are the meanings of such actions in some specific context. A nod is an action, which, in the appropriate circumstances, can mean that one agrees with what has been proposed. In other circumstances the very same action can mean something else; for example, a greeting, or a bid at an auction, as far as public recognition goes, mean nothing at all. Acts not only constitute narratives, but are constituted by the storyline that the narrative realizes. In the garden of Gethsemane a kiss is a betrayal. In greeting the Pope or the Grand Ayatollah it is a mark of submission and respect. Behavior without meaning is psychologically empty.

The cultural/discursive approach to psychology involves the following main theses:

(a) **We produce both public and private streams of meaningful acts in carrying out a huge variety of projects, ranging from practical work with the hands to highly abstract symbolic work with the relevant regions of the brain.**
(b) **Some acts are conveyed verbally and some non-verbally, by gestures, postures, diagrams and so on.**
(c) **Public and private, verbal and non-verbal acts fall under the same general system of categories, both analytically and explanatorily. Acts are the meanings of actions, determined in time and place by the identity of the actors and the nature of the cultural context.**

Mind as Discourse

The choice of 'discourse' as the leading metaphor for human thought and action is intimately related to the idea that the flow of intentional actions is the very 'stuff of mind'. Having a mind is to be master of certain discursive practices, for example, remembering, intending, regretting and so on. All sorts of practices fall under this heading. Some are linguistic, some are not. All involve meanings according to local lexicons, and all are subject to standards of correctness and propriety. The sort of practice with which cognitive activities are being carried on, linguistic or non-linguistic, will determine the choice of methods for the conduct of research into those patterns of acts and their sustaining actions. For example, if the practice is resolving a dispute we might try to discern the points of view of the opposing factions, their sense of their moral positions among rights and duties, religious affiliations and so on.

According to the 'discursive' point of view as sketched above, psychology is primarily the study of practices and their outcomes – streams of human actions and interactions, which can be understood in terms of their meanings for the actors and interactors and the norms and traditions that are generally accepted by the people involved and which shape their actions. Many of these streams of meaningful actions can be made sense of as lived narratives, storylines well known to people who share the culture. Within this general scheme, conversation is the most useful, but not the only model for analyzing such streams of action. Adopting this model for a research program invites the researchers to treat all that people do collectively and individually, privately and publicly, as if it were a kind of conversation, that is, consisting of meaningful exchanges constrained by a local normative framework, including, of course, the method of research itself.

There are many different conversational jobs that language can be used for. We use words to give orders, to make apologies, to issue invitations, to express our hopes and fears, as well as to describe and explain matters in our environments.

How is it possible for a person to do all these things? Each human being must have acquired a body of knowledge, appropriate to the local culture. This is a resource for getting the performance right. Rarely is this body of knowledge accessed consciously. Mostly it is immanent in the activities of the actors, as habits of mind and action.

This leads directly to the study of what people must know and what skills they must possess to be able to produce the required actions. Complementary to each mode of collective action there must be a repertoire of individual skills and dispositions. One of the most difficult questions faced by psychologists is what form this knowledge takes. Is the common metaphor of a 'store of knowledge' of any value? How should we analyze the concept of a skill or disposition? This question will occupy us in later chapters.

Ludwig Wittgenstein (1889–1951) was born in Vienna on 26 April 1889, into a cultivated and wealthy family. Young Ludwig was brought up as a Catholic, and despite a 'metaphysical' scepticism, retained a strong attachment to Christianity as a way of life. Until he was 14, he studied at home with various tutors. He attended the Realschule at Linz from 1903 until 1906. By a curious chance, he was a classmate of Adolf Hitler.

The intellectual and musical elite of Vienna, then in its heyday as a center of European civilization, were often visitors to the Wittgenstein 'palace'. After finishing his secondary education Ludwig attended the Technical Hochschule in Berlin, studying the science and mathematics needed to equip himself as an engineer. In 1909, he began research at Manchester University into the design of aircraft propellers. However, by 1911, he had begun to interest himself in the foundations of mathematics. He was advised to consult Bertrand Russell at Cambridge if he wanted to pursue this interest further.

For the next two years he continued an intense and often emotional conversation with Russell and came to realize that Russell's views on logic were deeply unsatisfactory.

At the outbreak of the First World War in 1914, he volunteered for the Austro-Hungarian Army, serving with distinction on the Eastern Front. He exulted in exposure to danger in battle, as a test of character. Throughout the war he continued to write on logic, completing his first important book, the *Tractatus logico-philosophicus,* while a prisoner of war in Italy.

He thought that the perfect language worked out in the book would bring all philosophy to an end. What mattered in life, personal relationships, religion, art and music, could not be adequately expressed in language, if it was expressible at all. All that was left for him was a life of service.

(Continued)

In 1929, he returned to Cambridge where he began to forge a new approach to philosophy, the main thrust of which was his realization that the medium of cognition is not the formal algebra of logic, concealed within the word forms we use, but the language itself. It is both the instrument for living a human life, and at the same time full of pitfalls and temptations to error. He wrote extensively during these years but his *Philosophical investigations* (1953), in which he presented his later point of view, was not published until after his death on 29 April 1951.

Continuing the 'discourse' metaphor, we will find Wittgenstein's concept of a 'grammar' helpful. We have already referred to the idea of clusters of rules, implicit and explicit, which shape what we do, say and think in certain contexts. Sometimes a person is consciously following an instruction. This is one sense in which the word 'rule' can be taken. However, the word 'rule' can also be used as a metaphor for cases in which a person or group of people act in an orderly way by habit, custom, convention and so on, where no one is paying attention to explicit rules. Shweder (1991a) refers to such shaping principles as 'contingent universals'. He finds such principles implicit in the customs of cultures other than our own, and of course they can be found in ours too. These seem to be just the sort of principles that would be found in a Wittgensteinian grammar. Shweder illustrates the idea of 'contingent universals' with some of the taken-for-granted conventions for living one finds in a small town in India. It would be unthinkable to eat fish on the day of one's father's funeral, or to have one's hair cut for two weeks thereafter. People would no more dream of calling these 'rules' into question than we would cast doubt of the practical utility of the principle that two distinct things cannot be in the same place at the same time. Of course, dear reader, you have already been thinking of the kinds of things that would violate this rule! It is universal for some kinds of things, but not for others, just as the funeral customs of an Indian town are universal for some kinds of people, the Hindus who live there, but not for others, their Muslim neighbors.

The final step in a psychological study of a cognitive procedure, for instance, remembering or classifying, after the analysis of the streams of activity in which the procedure is carried on into elementary actions and acts, would be the proposal of a 'grammar' or 'grammars' expressing the norms that are evident in what people are doing. There are both tacit and explicit grammars. Garfinkel (1967) and Polanyi (1958) have pointed out that in order to use any explicit technique one must make use of a repertoire of tacit knowledge. When such knowledge is formulated explicitly the use of that knowledge as an explicit guide to thought and action will depend on yet another corpus of tacit knowledge. What was explicit in one context may be tacit in another.

In sum, standards of correctness for the uses of all sorts of tools in the performance of all sorts of tasks can appear either as explicit instructions for correct performances, or as rules expressing different kinds and levels of implicit norms displayed in the orderliness of what people do and how they comment on, correct and criticize the activities of others and themselves. In many cases habits acquired by following instructions come to be 'second nature', and are carried out without thought. They mimic the forms of cause-effect patterns of event-causality and stand in need of hypotheses about the neurological structures and processes that have thereby been established.

The Grammars of Psychologically Relevant Discourses

Everyday psychological discourse has been ordered by many different clusters of rules and conventions. However, every one of them has been shaped around some local version of the concept of 'person'. By a person we mean an embodied self-conscious being, which is taken to be morally protected, that is, as a general rule, persons must be preserved and their welfare taken into account. Of course, in every culture there have been exceptions to various details of this prescription. For example, the retention of the death penalty in some parts of the United States appears to be such an exception. However, arguments to justify this practice cite higher order personal values, such as the protection of the innocent from the depredations of evil people, that reinterpret a seemingly anomalous practice in person-preserving terms.

Attempts at establishing a psychological science on the model of the natural sciences has evolved two more distinct grammars – that of the discourse of organic evolution and that of molecular biology. Let us look at these clusters of explicit and implicit rules in more detail. In neither is event-causation Humean.

A Soul or S-grammar

In much of the world outside contemporary Western Europe, there is a powerful grammar in common use. The basic categories recognized in this grammar are God, the soul, sin, redemption and the like. Modernity theory would suggest that this grammar, as an acceptable and unquestioned way of shaping one's thoughts and actions, should have disappeared and where it still exists is confined to certain rather restricted tribes and regions, for example, the Mormon community in Utah. One notices, however, that by many measures (such as church attendance) religiosity is still high in the United States. Religious terminology is still in widespread used for rhetorical purposes, for example, in the speeches of candidates for the United States Presidency. Also, the rise of religious identity, as reflected in a resurgence of Islamic, Christian, Jewish and Hindu fundamentalist movements in association with globalization (Moghaddam, 2010), suggests that S-grammar is very much alive in most of the world, though it no longer plays a part in the grounding of academic and therapeutic psychological discourses.

A Person or P-grammar

In using the discourse categories and rules of the P-grammar, persons are presumed to be the basic individuals and originating sources of activity. This grammar comprises the rules for the use of the tribal dialects and idiolects of everyday life. Among some of the specialized dialects of this generic grammar are the idioms of the courtroom, Freudian psychotherapy, the linguistic conventions of cookbooks, academic jargons, the ever-changing discourse conventions of the internet and so on.

A main feature of P-grammars is the way that responsibility is dealt with. This is particularly important for a philosophy of psychology, since the transition from the infancy to maturity of a being that has native agentive powers and acts teleologically, occurs along the dimension of growing responsibility for what it does. Shaver (1985) has proposed an analysis of responsibility dimensions that will do very well as a working analysis for much of the P-grammar of current English language folk psychology.

The attribution of responsibility according to Shaver runs as follows:

> A judgment made about the moral accountability of a person of normal capacities, usually but not always, involves an agentive connection between the person being judged and some morally [approved or] disapproved action or event. (Shaver, 1985, p. 66)

Accountability of persons would then be an important feature of cultural/discursive social psychology in which persons are the basic agents.

However, responsibility also appears as an important feature of cognitive activities. The use of the P-grammar in ordinary cases of remembering, and bearing in mind that only people remember, not their brains, includes person responsibility for memory talk. To say 'I remember...' is to claim some kind of authority as to the verisimilitude of what has been said or otherwise indicated, to commit myself to what I assert about the past. It involves my moral standing as a person.

Playing tennis is another example. The exchange of shots is constrained by conventions of meaning: 'On the line is in', and of procedure: 'Change ends after four games'. Scores accrue to people and it is people who play shots, good and bad, for which they are responsible, and so on.

The priority of persons in the study of psychology can be linked to Wittgenstein's notion of the role of 'taken for granted' practices in a culture and the concepts with which they can be described. Many of these practices have that duality of material and cognitive aspects that Wittgenstein called 'Language games'. These involve tacit adherence to 'taken-for-granted' practices.

An Organism or O-grammar

Current Western discourses make use of a third grammar, that in which the basic entities are organisms. While it has its natural domain of application in discussions about animals it has some important uses in discourse about the biology of human beings as homonids. The O-grammar is the vehicle for introducing biology into psychology. In the last two centuries treating human beings as organisms and adopting the O-grammar for this kind of discourse has taken the existence of human beings and their societies to be the products of processes of Darwinian evolution, introducing genetics and ethology into psychology.

A Molecular or M-grammar

In discourse shaped by this grammar, molecules and molecular clusters are the basic particulars and originating sources of activity. Among the dialects shaped by M-grammar is molecular biology. This will play a major part in the hybrid psychology of the emotions. Discourse framed in this grammar includes such attributions of agency to molecules as the power (alleged) of melatonin to put one to sleep, reflux of stomach acid as the cause of heartburn, deficiency in the quantity of serotonin in the synapses as a cause of depression and so on. There are many other examples of the influence of this grammar and its discourse of molecules and molecular states and processes as causes; for example, eating a banana during a tennis match, using cortisone to reduce the inflammation in a cartilage and so on. Causes in this context invoke hierarchical generative mechanisms.

We have a loose cluster of grammars that set the standards of proper discourse for the human domain, the S-, the P-, the O-, and the M-grammars. Each has variants, and in certain circumstances they fit together into hierarchies, and, in other circumstances, they complement one another. However, S-grammar has an insignificant role in modern psychology as an academic discipline.

These grammars include taxonomies, classification systems for categorizing the sorts of entities that comprise their domains. A user of the P-grammar must presuppose that there are intended actions, classifiable into various types that can be identified in the flow of human activity. The O-grammar user presupposes that there are bodily forms and behaviors, also classifiable into types, and found amongst the behavior of pets and wild animals too. When someone uses the M-grammar to describe some aspect of their life, for example, Chronic Fatigue Syndrome, the sufferer talks about organo-phosphates damaging the immune system – the reality of molecular exchanges in organ systems and the hierarchical clustering of molecules is presupposed.

The four grammars must also include principles of sequence and order among basic and dependent particulars. For many people the S-grammar is the fundamental discourse mode for almost everything that they do. Think of such categories as sin and redemption, sanctity of people and places in relation to social behaviors and so on. In P-grammars these include semantic and syntactic rules, narrative conventions and moral imperatives, all of which are used to shape sequences of meaningful actions. Thanks to the work of the ethologists we now see the lives of many animals teleologically in terms of repertoires of actions directed towards maintaining their forms of life. This would be reflected in the O-grammar, if we came to understand the existence of these routines in Darwinian terms, serving some reproductive advantage. A complicated neurological causality is presumed in the uses of O-grammar in psychology. In M-grammar, discourse sequences of chemical phenomena are understood to be shaped by causal processes and described by causal laws. Only in the M-grammar do we have the means to provide event-causal explanations of the conventional 'efficient causation' sort, in which some prior state of the system brings about a present or future state. We note, however, that this explanation schema is not Humean. It presumes that efforts will be made to develop hypotheses of further levels in a hierarchy of generative mechanisms. The O-grammar is teleological, framing reproductive advantage in the theory of genetic mutation. In the P-grammar discourse it is persons who are credited with agentive powers, all else being equal.

The everyday discourses of contemporary Western life seem to be shaped by the same four grammars as are revealed in studying 'psychology as discourse'. To illustrate this feature of our lives consider the field of uses of the phrase 'red wine', as a non-psychological example or model for the use of the four grammars we have selected for psychology. In the thinking and acting shaped by the S-grammar the meaning of 'red wine' is determined by its part in the ceremonies of the Christian churches – from a literal understanding of the 'blood of Christ' among Catholics to a potent symbol of Christ's sacrifice among Protestants. The P-grammar includes rules for the uses of words and phrases where persons as conscious and discriminating judges are presumed – 'red wine' is an object of aesthetic significance in the discourse of wine-buffs. However, almost everyone has been made aware of the liquid that is the referent of the phrase 'red wine' as a health-giving supplement to an ordinary diet, that is, in relation to the good of the human organism. Finally, we can hardly miss the emphasis on biochemistry in discussions of the value of this substance as we talk about its role in eliminating 'free radicals' from our bodies thanks to the 'anti-oxidants' it contains.

The point is not whether the people whose talk is shaped by these four 'grammars' understand the theology or the science – rather that they manage to make use of these ways of shaping their lives discursively by drawing on all four. The labels on the bottles and packets in the supermarket display a discourse mode that draws on all of P-, O- and M-grammars, but not the S-grammar in the Western world. However, in shops attached to cathedrals the S-grammar is in daily use. People manage most aspects of their lives with the triad as a kind of hybrid, and it never occurs to them that there may be some contexts in which they are incompatible.

How is fruitful and coherent hybridization managed? Can we achieve the same level of hybridization that we encounter and manage in everyday life for the four grammars that have shaped psychology as a science over the last millennium?

Anna Wierzbicka (1938–) was born and educated in Poland. She is Professor of Linguistics at the Australian National University. Her work has become very well known in recent years for her creation of the 'Natural Semantic Metalanguage' together with her Australian colleague Cliff Goddard (Goddard & Wierzbicka, 2002). This proposal, based on the empirically established intersection of all sampled natural languages, has important consequences for psychology. The central hypothesis is that this metalanguage corresponds to the innate and universal 'lingua mentalis' – the hardwired language of the human mind, and that the small lexicon of this metalanguage constitutes the 'alphabet of human thoughts' once envisaged by Leibniz. This intersection between neuroscience and language is of great significance for the project of this book.

She is also very well known for her studies of emotions in their cultural and historical diversity. Most recently her book, *Experience, evidence and sense: The hidden cultural legacy of English* (2010), opens up the fundamental question of how far the current lingua franca shades the psychology of most of humanity.

'Mind-body' Ties: Two Links Between P-, O- and M-Discourses

We are now in a position to deal with one of the most persistent problems in the foundations of a scientific psychology – the relation between mind and body. We seem to be forced to admit the truth of two incompatible theses. Mental and material phenomena seem to be radically different in kind. For example, thoughts are weightless, quite free of the power of gravity. Limbs are locked in the gravitational field of the earth. Yet mental processes, such as deciding to throw a ball, seem to lead to material processes, the hand and arm moving in such a way as to project the ball into something like the trajectory the thrower intends. Injuries to the body seem to be the cause of painful sensations. Molecules of acetyl-salicylic acid, aspirin, seem to be effective in eliminating the pain of a headache. And so on, through a huge catalogue of ways that the mental aspects of a person's being are interrelated with the material aspects. Mental and material phenomena seem to be correlated with one another by simple event-causality. If they are radically different in kind, how could such causal relations possibly exist? Not only must there be regularity in the pattern of these happenings, but there must also be a generative process, observed or hypothesized, between the occurrence of the one and the occurrence of the other. But if there are only meanings and molecules in the universe the generative mechanisms would have to be either a sequence of meanings or a sequence of molecular transformations. The problem simply reappears when we think of how meanings and or molecular happenings could be related to either kind of mechanism.

The situation seems irresolvable. It is easy to see how philosophers of psychology could be driven to adopt one or other extreme solution denying the reality of one or the other of the poles of the distinction between mental and material phenomena on which the existence of the problem depends. If there are only material phenomena there is no fundamental problem. If there are only discursive phenomena there is no fundamental problem either.

Breeding a Viable Hybrid

The project of setting up a hybrid science, in which the symbol using capacities of human beings are brought into a unified scheme with the organic aspects of members of the species *Homo sapiens*, demands the *dissolution* of the mind-body problem, somehow setting it aside as an illusion, based on mistaken presuppositions. The possibility of a unified cognitive science depends on shifting the focus from entities to discourses. We have already encountered the metaphor or leading idea with which the unification of the whole field of psychologically relevant discourses is to be accomplished, the metaphor of cognitive tasks and neural tools. It is not the only candidate for a unifying principle. In this section some other possibilities are examined, each having a role in the total project.

Having shifted the focus of our enquiries from the misconceived puzzle about how two wholly disjoint substances, mental and material, could interact, and avoiding the complementary pitfall of the attempt to build a human science on the basis of one or other of these alleged substances exclusively, we can turn to examine ways in which the person-based discourse, the organism-based discourse, and the molecule-based discourse are related to one another. There are at least three ways in which links are in fact established between these ways of talking that currently dominate the discourses of the human form of life *and* its scientific investigation. There is the task-tool metaphor by which tasks defined in terms of the P-discourse are accomplished by tools described in terms of the O- and M-discourses. For example, the task may be to recall as accurately as possible the events of yesterday, a task for which such bodily organs as the hippocampus and the entorhinal cortex are the material means. Then there is the way in which dispositions and powers defined in the P-discourse are grounded in structures, states and processes described in O- and M-discourse terms. Ability to respond to the individuality of a face is grounded in the structure of the parvo-cerebral tract, linking the visual cortex with the frontal lobes. The third interrelation appears in the way that classificatory systems applicable to the entities, states and processes describable in the O- and M-discourses are dependent on classifications of beings which are identified as belonging to types defined in the P-discourse. For example, only if we can already identify an emotion as anger or grief or jealousy, can we try to locate the regions in the limbic system that are activated when that emotion dominates someone's thoughts and feelings. We now turn to examine these strategies in more detail.

The Task-Tool Metaphor

The idea that cognitive tasks often require the use of material tools introduces the metaphor of 'brain-as-tool'. First, consider the way we human beings carry out certain cognitive tasks, such as adding up a bill. We are accustomed to think of a pocket calculator as a tool for doing sums. But since that gadget is a prosthetic device, accomplishing cognitive tasks formerly performed by our brains, it seems entirely appropriate to apply the same concept to the brain, or a relevant region of it, when we are engaged in performing the cognitive task without using a prosthesis. A certain electronic device is a 'calculator' only in relation to the task it is used to perform. Similarly, a certain region of the brain is the organ of calculation only in relation to the task we use it to perform.

Material tasks also engage persons as agents. There too we make use of material tools. Some of these are prostheses for other body parts than the neurological. For digging we need spades. They are prostheses for hands, to which, in the absence of spades, we are obliged to have recourse, even now. Pieces of iron are 'spades' only in relation to the task they are devised to perform.

There are some tools which far outstrip their prosthetic ancestors, for both cognitive and material tasks. Bulldozers are spades of a sort, but of another order altogether when the task in hand is shifting earth. The same is true of computing machines when the task in hand is arithmetical or the reliable storage of vast amounts of data.

Finally, there are cognitive tasks for which we use cognitive or symbolic tools, for instance, reasoning carried on with propositions. At this point the simple task (P-grammar)/ tool (M-grammar) scheme seems to be in need of further development. To produce a statement, expressing a proposition, which is to serve as a tool in the task of solving a problem, is to engage in a task using a material tool, one's brain. Here we seem to have the use of a tool to produce a tool. This, too, is a metaphor with a familiar origin in industry. Every engineering works depends on the skill of the tool makers.

What advantages does the task/tool metaphor have over other ways of expressing the role of O- and M-entities and states as enabling conditions for P-activities? People do not generally talk of their brains as tools. However, the point of introducing a metaphor is to extend the power of the existing language to cope with new insights and situations. Boundaries that seem to be impenetrable need to be re-examined. The metaphor of body parts as tools seems unproblematic in such a piece of advice: 'If you can't find a trowel, use your hand to scoop out a hole to plant the seedling'. The idea of 'tool and task' seems already to be fully formed in the common injunction to someone stuck in some problem: 'Use your loaf!', meaning 'Use your head [brains]'. 'Brain as a tool' is the scientifically innovative or creative concept that comes from the extensions of the 'Use your ... ' metaphor, inviting us to look on our brains in a new way. Philosophical justification can be found in the prosthesis argument, set out above. Since the calculator, electronic organizer and even one's pocket diary are tools for cognitive tasks, though there are cognitive skills required to use them, we can also use our brains as prostheses for prostheses, stand-ins for 'extrinsic' cognitive tools, for example, by trying to remember the appointments recorded in a mislaid diary. The brain or one of its modules is functionally equivalent to something which it is not at all controversial to classify as a tool.

The Taxonomic Priority Principle

We now turn to the classificatory technique by which neural states, structures and processes are identified as relevant to cognitive processes, emotional displays and social acts.

By the use of the Taxonomic Priority Principle, the proper tools can be picked out from among all the available material things as just those relevant for the tasks in hand. The molecular bases of memory, for instance, can be identified only if they are picked out in relation to acts of remembering performed by the people whose brain states and processes are being investigated. Similarly, we can only identify certain features of people's brains as abnormalities if we have a way of identifying abnormal kinds of speech or conduct. Unless we could identify cases of people having word-finding problems we could never identify a tangle of plaques as the relevant abnormality for Alzheimer's Condition, nor damage to the immune system as the relevant abnormality for Chronic Fatigue Syndrome.

In general, the criteria of identity for states, processes and structures of the P-discourse exercise 'taxonomic dominance' over the criteria of identity for neural states and processes relevant to psychology, that is, for the M-discourse. Relevant neural states and processes are picked out by attention to the cognitive states and processes that are occurring. This is the way we will be using the Taxonomic Priority Principle. It has the effect of making the relation between mental states and processes and the relevant brain states and processes conceptual, not empirical. This is an important point that needs spelling out. If the relation were empirical each 'side' of it would have to be able to be picked out independently of the way the other is identified. Then research might reveal that there was a correlation between them. In medicine there are plenty of examples of this kind of discovery. For instance, we identify coffee drinking according to certain criteria, and we identify Parkinson's disease by another and different set of criteria. These sets of criteria have nothing to do with each other. Research has established a very good correlation between coffee drinking and a low incidence of developing Parkinson's disease. However, if we use a PET scan, a method of research discussed in Chapter 3, to pick out the parts of the brain that are activated when someone is reading, the criteria for identifying these parts include the criteria for knowing whether someone is reading. It is a matter of logic that these are parts of the 'reading machine'. This way of picking things out has been called 'top-down' classification.

There are ways in which such taxonomic relations, once established, are protected against disturbance. The most important has a central role in the establishment of empirical research projects in neuroscience. Here is how it works: suppose we do an experiment on a subject using a PET scan, while the subject is performing some cognitive task, for example, calculating. The Taxonomic Priority Principle allows us to identify what is revealed in the PET scan as among the relevant neural processes for calculating. Imagine that we repeat the experiment on the same subject on another occasion and find a different neural process seemingly showing up in the PET scan when the subject is performing the same task. Do we abandon the thesis? No. We save it by the hypothesis that there is a so-far unobserved neural process common to both occasions, and then we set about trying to find it. The case is somewhat different if we repeat the experiment on a different subject and get a different result. In that case we tend to partition the population into groups, for each of which the TPP holds. For example, the finding that men and women read with different parts of their brains is not permitted to upset TPP. The problem is resolved by partitioning the human population into two groups by gender with respect to the common P-discourse defined skill of reading. Thus we have men readers and women readers as two P-discourse categories, each with their relevant but different brain mechanisms, though apart from the early years, the reading abilities (P-grammar) of the sexes are identical.

Psychology as a Hybrid Science

Having looked at three ways in which the P-, O- and M-grammars can be bound together into a comprehensive conceptual system fit to serve as the basis of a science, what kind of science will it be? Since doing psychology is a human activity, the same principles should apply to it, as to any other pattern of action which realizes well-established storylines. If psychology is a cluster of narrations: what are the relevant grammars? It would surely be unacceptable to most psychologists to describe their professional activities in the O- and M-grammar. Only if presented in the frame of the P-grammar could credit be claimed for a successful research project. Only in a frame in which the concept of 'person' picks out the basic active beings, professors and their students, does the concept of responsibility have a place, and hence the concept of credit.

There is, in a sense, only one stream of action. As described in the P-grammar it displays such phenomena as 'emotions', 'attitudes', 'memories', 'items of knowledge', 'performance of athletic feats', and so on. Using the metaphor of a stream we might think of these phenomena as eddies, whirlpools, froth and waves in the continuous flow that dries up only on the brain death of the actor. Some are ephemeral and others more enduring.

It seems that the basic type-hierarchy that has evolved in psychology in recent years has two main branches, one material and one discursive.

The first branch consists of the agents that produce material processes, in the environment and in the bodies of organisms. The active entities are molecular clusters of a huge variety of types. For this branch we have recourse to a discourse-style shaped by the molecular grammar. The mode of action of M-entities is causal in the sense that it is explained by the discovery or supposition of hierarchical generative mechanisms.

The first branch includes those agents to whom we assign goal-seeking capacities, and for our purposes the basic agents are predominantly whole organisms. For this branch we have recourse to the O- or organism-grammar. The mode of action of O-entities is teleological, seeking practical goals, such as the bear that looks for honey.

The second branch consists of the agents who produce discursive patterns, normatively regulated streams of meaningful actions, the psychological practices of human beings, singly and in groups. The active beings are people as intentional agents. For this branch we have recourse to the P- or person-grammar and agentive causation. The mode of action of P-entities is intentional, that is, by recourse to meanings and 'rules' in the carrying out of projects.

As singular sources of action and the embodied centers of perceptual fields people are centers of discursive activity. They produce complex private and public intentional and ever-changing and evolving structures of discursive acts. Those that are private we are inclined to call mental, thoughts and feelings, but *qua* intentional acts they differ not at all from public acts, except in so far as the interactor whose uptake completes the action as a meaningful act, is, in the case of private acts, oneself. We produce our own minds with the connivance of others (Vygotsky, 1978a), just as we produce conversations, tennis matches, orchestral performances, ditch digging and so on with others.

Lev Semionovich Vygotsky (1896–1934) was born on 17 November 1896, in a prosperous middle-class family in Orsha, a small town in Byelorussia. The family moved to the larger town of Gomel, where his father had a senior position in a bank. The town was completely destroyed in the Second World War, but a good deal of Vygotsky's early life has become known through the stories of his friend, Semen Dobkin.Young Lev was educated at a private Jewish secondary school. He seems to have owed a great deal to a tutor, Solomon Ashpiz, who developed his mind through searching conversations, rather than through formal exercises.

He entered Moscow University just before the First World War, in the medical faculty. He enrolled at another university, the unofficial but influential Shanyavskii People's University, to study psychology and philosophy. He graduated in 1917, an ominous year in Russian history.

Lev Semionovich returned that year to Gomel, where he spent the next seven years as a teacher. The setting up of a psychology laboratory in the local Teacher Training College, in relation to his teaching, furthered his interest in experimental psychology. While teaching, he read widely – poetry, fiction and psychology. The idea came to him that there could be a new psychology that would transform the human race, a psychology that centered around historical change and the centrality of language as a major instrument in the life of human beings.

Shortly after he came to Moscow in 1924 he met Alexander Romanovich Luria and Alexei Nikolievich Leont'ev, the founder in later years of activity psychology. These friendships matured into a famous collaboration. Their key ideas had some antecedents in the West, for example in the writings of William James, but they took a form that owed a great deal to Vygotsky himself. The principles of the cultural/historical/instrumental method are simple to state but profound in their consequences.

The first idea was that the social life of human beings was the source of their individual psychological traits and capacities. The second idea seemed to lead away from the individual as the locus of psychological reality to the history of languages, cultures, material practices and so on that went into the formation of individual minds. The third idea was that human beings acquired a repertoire of skills, including linguistics capacities, which should be looked on as instruments in the management of life. This was the cultural/historical/instrumental method.

Throughout these years, until his death from tuberculosis in 1934, he conducted a vigorous research program. There can surely be no doubt that the frenetic pace of his life was a response to his realization that tuberculosis was sure to claim his life very soon, and yet, at the same time, his response to this intuition was hastening the end. After a serious hemorrhage, he entered the Serebryani sanatorium on 2 June 1934, and died a few days later. As S. E. Toulmin rightly said: 'Vygotsky was the Mozart of psychology.'

There are no hidden mechanisms in the P-domain, according to the point of view being developed here. The program of scientific psychology is not to be fulfilled by postulating an imperceptible realm of unobservable mental mechanisms, as Freud did in introducing the unconscious mind. Scientific ideals in psychology are achieved by making use of the Task/Tool metaphor in proposing neural mechanisms as among the devices that people use for accomplishing their P-grammar tasks. The workings, but not the roles, of these tools are described and explained in the M- and O-grammars. Their domains are tightly woven together in that O-processes are routinely accounted for by recourse to hypotheses about hidden molecular processes. Since at least some M-processes are observable in principle, the proposal of a hidden mechanism explanation can often lead to a research program in an effort to verify the verisimilitude of the working model of the mechanisms on which the hypothesis depends.

Neither component of the hybrid psychology we envisage can colonize the other. Human beings in the molecular ontology are machines with no moral attributes. Brains in the person ontology are tools for use in tasks set discursively by people who are morally responsible for what they do with them. Giving priority to the P-grammar preserves the outlines of human life as a moral world while finding the place for our brains as tools for morally constrained tasks. However, if we were to prioritize either O- or the M-grammar, people as a category would disappear from the world of psychology, taking the moral universe with them.

Psychology is about the life-long activities of human beings and their relations to one another in a huge variety of social formations. As such it cannot help but be a moral science (Brinkmann, 2010). The admiration due to the natural sciences, their methods and their discoveries must not blind us to the fact that cultural phenomena are also fit subjects for the application of scientific method, *properly understood*. One of the main aims of this book is to show how the method of honest and accurate description and the building of explanatory models, common to both the natural and cultural sciences, can be the core of working hybrid science. We must resist the temptation into which our predecessors fell – they insisted that we were less than we are for fear we might think we were more than we are. Our modest aim is to display human beings just as they are.

Conclusion

We can approach the development of a hybrid psychology, fit for the third millennium, by setting out the insights we have tried to present in this introductory chapter in relation to some important basic concepts, dispositions, powers, skills and capacities. The hybrid we are seeking is reached by linking these psychological concepts to their material groundings. Thinking of human beings and their lives in these terms leads us far from aiming at the explanation of human cognitive and social life exclusively in terms of event-causation of either kind, Humean or hierarchical.

People have *powers* to act, they have *skills* for performing tasks properly, and they have *capacities* for undertaking projects of many kinds. In each case the common feature of all these P-grammar attributes is the conditionality of the relevant performance on the existence of situations appropriate for their display. So for every power, skill and capacity and so on, we can offer a dispositional formulation in 'if … then … ' terms, to express the conditional aspect of the attribute (Ryle, 1949).

This formulation captures only the minimal sense of these terms, since each has further implications. For instance, the exercise of a person's powers is not just conditional on the coming to be of certain states of affairs, but on the person as the active source of the behavior. 'Jim has the power to jump that fence' implies that if Jim is so minded he will successfully negotiate the obstacle. But Jim must be so minded. If he jumps it is his act, and not the effect of some extrinsic stimulus. Even as he is being chased by a bull he must very quickly estimate his best strategy for self-preservation.

Cognitive capacities, powers and skills are grounded in brain states, structures and processes. Here we have another way of binding the P-grammar to the O- and M-grammars. For example, cognitive skills are described in terms derived from the P-grammar. It is persons who decide wisely, tot up accounts correctly and so on. These skills are grounded in permanent neural states and patterns of dendrites in the brain. When brains are damaged cognitive skills are affected, even lost. 'Grounding' here can mean only that the *instrument* by which a person performs the skillful activity is made up of neural states and processes, that is, it is describable in the M- and O-grammars. Other instruments could be used for many of these tasks.

Though it is an obvious truth that the brain must be in a certain state for cognitive activities to be performed, one has to be cautious in assuming that that is also a sufficient condition. All sorts of other conditions must be in place. For example, the presence of other people in active conversational engagement with the thinker is sometimes required. One must also be cautious in how one interprets the many studies on loss of cognitive skills by virtue of brain damage. One would think it would be obvious that because a certain psychological skill cannot be exercised if a certain part of the brain is damaged, that when the person is exercising the skill, that part of the brain is the module that is the tool in question. If the bike chain breaks the bike no longer provides transport, but a bike chain alone will not afford locomotion. A moment's reflection tells us that the lesion that stultifies the proper exercise of the skill may be just one aspect of the whole mechanism, and indeed perhaps a minor part at that. The battery of my mini-laptop runs down but all else is in order.

The disposition–grounding link and the task-tool link are connected in that powers exercised in tasks are grounded in neuro-physiological mechanisms which are thereby the relevant tools, or parts of the relevant tools. There is no place for attempts to find evidence for the hybrid relation. All we can do is to assemble a complex array of metaphors to characterize the nature of a unique relationship between the findings of neuroscience relevant to psychology and the findings of research into the cultural discursive forms of actual psychological functioning. Our task of assembling such metaphors of which the Task-Tool image is one, can never be completed. New insights are sure to emerge.

2

Methods of Research:
Cultural/Discursive Psychologies

Rom Harré

The difficult thing to do here is not to dig down to the ground; no, it is to recognize the ground that lies before us as the ground.

For the ground keeps on giving us the illusory image of a greater depth, and when we seek to reach this, we keep on finding ourselves at the old level. (Wittgenstein, 1953, § 31)

Methods of research in the cultural/discursive psychology that partners neuroscience in hybrid psychology are focused on the way people use symbolic systems in thinking and acting. We now know that such systems are also involved at a very fundamental level in the way people feel and what they perceive in other people and in the world around them. The most deeply studied of these systems is language.

There is a great diversity of languages and each is the bearer of core features of the culture in which it is used as a major instrument for managing everyday life. Each language is the bearer of a distinctive psychology. The way the users of particular languages think, act, feel and perceive is shaped by their cultural inheritance, of which a major component is their mother tongue.

In the first part of this chapter, we look closely at the implicit psychology of one widely used language, leaving the examination of the fine details of dialect and technical uses for more specialist studies. Our choice of a vernacular as the object of study is English. We could have chosen any one of a great variety of languages to illustrate the methods by which implicit psychologies can be abstracted from everyday use. Our choice of English reflects the fact that not only is it spoken and written very widely but it is the most widely used language in the sciences, commerce and other international activities. These factors are important for a textbook such as this, which is intended for an international audience.

As we set out the implicit psychology of one form of English, roughly middle-class Anglo-American, we will draw attention to some of the ways other languages differ from it in their implicit psychologies. It is not our intention to privilege English as a source of cognitive standards and proper social relations in any way except as the most useful place to start our studies. There will be some very general concepts that find a representation in every language (Wierzbicka, 1992), but local variants will often be important psychologically.

In the second part of the chapter, we turn to cultural psychology where we focus our attention on some of the approaches that have been developed to understand how cultures develop unique ways of being. Particularly important are the narratives or storylines that shape the fourfold ways we live, as thinkers, actors, beings sensitive to feelings in ourselves and of others, and perceivers of the world around us and of our own bodily states.

In the third section, we set out the basic principles of positioning analysis. This is a procedure by which some aspects of the moral background to thinking, acting, feeling and perceiving can be revealed and their influence on how we act, think and feel disclosed. By means of positioning analysis we can elaborate our understanding of human behavior by bringing to light the interplay between what a person can do, what that person believes it is correct or proper to do, and what a person does. The richness of everyday life is partly due to the fact that what people actually do is not determined only by what they can do but what they think they should do. This applies not only to public actions but also to personal thoughts and feelings, and in some circumstances even to what we can perceive.

What are the products of these research techniques? We need to recognize two levels of research products. There are the bodies of knowledge and beliefs that people draw on in thinking, acting, feeling and perceiving. These include lexicons of meanings and systems of rules and conventions expressing the norms within which people carry on their activities. At a second level, we should be able to specify the skills that people need to acquire and to make use of the systems of knowledge that underlie their culture. Some of these skills might also be displayed by people in very different cultures – but some may be indigenous and local.

The study of the discursive activities of people, whether alone or in a group, calls for the identification of situated meanings, and the rules and conventions that express the norms that are realized in the practices of speakers and actors as they try to realize their projects. Human activities are usually carried on in highly structured and often distinctive local contexts.

The concepts of neuroscience must conform to the semantics of vernacular psychological concepts – or we are not studying the same subject matter. How that conformity is achieved is no simple matter as we have explained in Chapter 1. This conformity allows for a reciprocal influence. Evidence for neurological processes that are not explicitly represented in the vernaculars of a particular culture might emerge and so call for modifications of that vernacular. This does not alter the requirement that all psychological research must begin with vernacular concepts which identify the field of interest and the psychological processes that comprise it. At the same time, it is evident that whatever we do as human beings within a cultural context, involves the use of bodily organs. As material mechanisms the understanding of these systems calls for concepts from natural science, natural agents and hierarchical generative mechanisms. The plot of this book is the reconciliation of the two modes in a higher order synthesis, hybrid psychoneurology.

The methods of qualitative cultural psychology provide one way of extracting the meanings and rules that shape the meanings of human activities. Discourses and their grammatical and narratological foundations are the targets of research. Our task is to display and illustrate methods for the discovery of the cultural matrices of human thought, feeling, perception and action. This chapter does not include a separate section on ethnographic and anthropological research. Results from these well-established research programs are scattered throughout the book, as they bear on understanding different ways of thinking and acting. Cross-cultural research, in so far as it transports Western methods and concepts to attempt to understand alien life forms, has little to offer a hybrid scientific research program (Cole, 1996).

The format for a psychological investigation of some cognitive or social practice within the general framework of cultural psychology includes the following aspects:

1   We must identity an agent or group of agents having intentions or purposes in some local context, and having a mastery of a language or languages. The kind of material technology they use may also be relevant.
2   These people behave in orderly ways which can be assessed with respect to local standards of correctness and propriety. Sometimes these standards are already expressed as explicit rules, or implicit in criticisms, advice and so on. Sometimes they exist only as patterns of taken-for-granted practices.
3   People carry on their activities by the use of a wide variety of symbolic and material means.
4   Contexts of human action are hierarchical – universal, tribal, and local.

These are the targets for any investigation. Who are the agents and what are their projects? What devices and tools do they use to accomplish these projects? What are the standards of correctness and propriety (rules and conventions) in accordance with which they undertake their projects? What contexts do they recognize or otherwise take account of?

Grammatical Analysis

Language in use is the major tool for cognition and social interaction. What do words for psychological processes and states such as 'knowing', 'believing' and 'remembering' and so on, as used in ordinary everyday discourse, mean? We will follow Gilbert Ryle's dispositional analysis of one part of the psychological vocabulary of one vernacular, namely English (Ryle, 1949). However, the analyses we find in Ludwig Wittgenstein's *Philosophical Investigations*, originally in German (Wittgenstein, 1953), suggest that Ryle's analysis has a rather wide cultural scope.

Gilbert Ryle (1900–1976) was born in Brighton, England, in 1900. He was educated at Brighton College, and in 1919, he went up to the Queen's College, Oxford, initially to study classics. He was quickly drawn to philosophy. He graduated with first-class honours in 1924. He was appointed to a lectureship in philosophy at Christ Church Oxford, shortly becoming a Tutorial Fellow. He continued to teach at Christ Church until the Second World War.

A capable linguist, he joined the Intelligence Service during the Second World War. After the war, he returned to Oxford and was elected to the Waynefleet chair at Magdalen College. His most famous book, *The concept of mind*, was published in 1949. He was very active in the development of philosophy as a profession, and influential in the staffing of university departments all over the world. He was president of the Aristotelian Society from 1945 to 1946, and editor of *Mind* from 1947 to 1971. Ryle died on 6 October 1976 at Whitby in Yorkshire.

His point of view in philosophy and the methods he devised for resolving philosophical problems such as the puzzle of how a material body could influence and be influenced by an immaterial mind were often misunderstood. It was not that 'ordinary language' had some sort of priority over the languages of the professions or of the sciences. Rather, the classical problems that troubled philosophers had their origin in misunderstandings of the way words were actually used by people in everyday life. More recondite problems had their origins in misunderstandings of the way words were used in technical languages. Some of these issues had distorted attempts to found a scientific psychology.

Dispositions and Occurrences

According to Ryle, there are two basic patterns of psychological concepts that we use in everyday life. Words have an *occurrent* use for ascribing actual, then and there states to a person – for example 'Joe is tall' or 'Ethel is angry'. She is angry here and now. Words have a *dispositional* use for ascribing propensities, capacities, competences or skills to someone. For example, 'Joseph is liable to get upset,' or 'Margaret is very good at managing the office', or 'Mary is an excellent mathematician.' We ascribe these attributes to people when they are not upset, not managing anything nor solving problems. To lay out the meaning of dispositional attributions fully we can express them as conditional statements: 'If Mary were to be given an algebraic problem she would solve it quickly.' Dispositional words are appropriate for ascribing qualities of intellect and character that are displayed only from time to time. Often we use 'modal' words like 'can' and 'might' rather than the conditional 'if … then …' form to explain the meaning of a dispositional ascription. 'Fred is strong' can mean 'Fred can carry a heavy bucket.' 'John is irascible' can mean 'John might blow up for no good reason'.

It is useful to identify several varieties of dispositions.

Capacities and Competences

These comprise a dispositional ascription plus a presumption of agency on the part of the person to whom the disposition is ascribed. Not only that, but many performance verbs associated with the display of dispositions signify not just the occurrence of actions but suitable or correct actions – achievements. For example, 'spell', 'solve', 'find', 'persuade' and so on suggest that a task has been brought to a satisfactory conclusion, or at least an attempt has been made to do so. So from the dispositional ascription 'She is good at spelling' we expect that when asked to spell 'diarrhoea' she will spell it correctly herself.[1]

Liabilities, Tendencies, Propensities and Pronenesses

These are used to ascribe dispositions but without the implication of agency. They hint at an expectation of failure, or a less than adequate coping. 'He is liable to get lost if he is in the woods by himself,' 'She has a tendency to weep for no reason,' and 'George is prone to fits of depression.'

Ryle warned against mistaking dispositional ascriptions for description of occurrent states. For example, the word 'intelligent' does not describe an occurrent state of a person, but is used to ascribe a generic cluster of related dispositions (see Chapter 11). We tend to slip into treating dispositions as if they referred to occurrent states, and so set off on worthless quests to find these states. Whatever in the here and now distinguishes a clever student from a stupid classmate it is not a matter for psychologists to discover. Ryle held that it was a mistake to look for something mental behind cognitive and practical skills. This is not to suggest that these skills are ungrounded. Rather, such dispositions as an ability to play a musical instrument or to think four-dimensionally should be occasions for a hybrid research program. What can neuroscience tell us about the workings of the main instruments of cognition – the frontal lobes, the hippocampus and so on? There are plenty of opportunities for hybrid research programs focused on skills and competences, liabilities and propensities, identified by cultural/discursive criteria, such as solving problems, remembering names, becoming giddy when high up, and so on. To say that someone knows the names of all the American Presidents or can ski or remembers how to get to Santa Fe is clearly dispositional talk. Neuroscientists with a combination of methods can be challenged to demonstrate how these skills are materially grounded. Yet, these skills do not reduce to their material groundings – to identify which skill it is requires attention to history and context. We doubt that any description of the content of a memory in terms of O- and M-grammatical concepts alone, will enable us to distinguish between remembering how to get to Santa Fe from remembering how to get to DesMoines.

Psychologic

The way words are used involves many layers of psychological concepts and implicit generalities. For example, we use the concepts of knowledge and belief in various ways to highlight differences in the confidence with which we declare something to be the case. We do not need to carry out psychological research to show that a belief claim is weaker than a knowledge claim. This is a matter of how words are used – in Wittgenstein's phrase, a matter of 'grammar'. There are many such grammatical relations in the vernaculars of our human cultures that masquerade as factual truths and yet carry important psychological distinctions. Jan Smedslund has given the name 'psychologic' to this kind of linguistic study (Smedslund, 1988). We do not need to carry out research to know that an agent is someone who acts intentionally. That is what 'agent' means. Here is another example: 'Surprise follows the occurrence of something unexpected.' It looks as if this statement expresses a discovery about people's reactions. But we can only use the word 'surprised' to describe someone's psychological state if that person has encountered something they had not been expecting. Discourse analysis preempts experimental psychology in this and other cases.

Speech Acts

Language is used for a great many more purposes than just the description and reporting of supposed matters of fact. Without troubling ourselves too deeply about the ultimate significance of truth and falsity we recognize fact-stating as a mode of language use in which the words 'true' and 'false' are routinely used, along with a very large related vocabulary. In the 1950s, J. L. Austin (1962) began a study of the ways words are used to perform social acts – he labeled these 'performative speech acts'. These are linguistic forms that play a large part in social interactions. Their study should be a key element in social psychology.

We do not ask whether a promise is true, but whether it is sincere or genuine. These uses are of the utmost social psychological relevance when we see how they can be used to create and disrupt social bonds, to seal bargains, to make commitments, to raise and lower the emotional temperature etc. To understand the social processes that are being carried through in the course of an ordinary conversation as well as by means of a formal discourse such as that of a court of law, even of a medical diagnosis, an analysis in terms of speech acts is highly relevant.

Psychologists can learn from Austin's insights into the social uses of language and his categories of speech acts. We need three technical terms to get started. The locutionary aspect of an utterance is what it might be taken to mean in the absence of any specific social context and storyline, for example, 'the crowd is getting restive' as a description of a street scene. The illocutionary force of an utterance is the social force it has when uttered by a certain person in a specific context and usually with a definite intent. The watcher at the window of the presidential palace turns to the beleaguered head of state and says, 'the crowd is getting restive,' meaning to warn him that an attack is imminent. The stage hand at the gap in the curtain says to the stage manager, 'the crowd is getting restive,' meaning to urge him to get the cast on stage. The perlocutionary effect is the cluster of consequences that arise from the illocutionary force as it is then and there taken up by the other people on the scene more or less as intended by the speaker. The president comes out on the balcony and announces his resignation; the stage manager bangs on the star's door and so on.

Austin sketched two features of performative speech (and writing) that are particularly psychologically relevant.

Just as descriptions can succeed or fail, that is, be true of false, so performatives can succeed or fail – be felicitous or infelicitous. The right thing must be said by the right person in the right place at the right time and in the presence of the right people. These conditions can be set out as the protocols for formal ceremonies in which the social efficacy of the ceremonial speech acts is formally defined. Doing and saying certain things on the lawn of the White House in the presence of certain people transforms a person into the President of the United States, affecting the behavior of thousands of others, profoundly altering the performative force of what he or she says.

Austin proposed a classification of speech-acts into several classes of performatives. *Verdictives* are speech acts which make something so, such as the foreman of the jury as saying 'not guilty' acquits the prisoner. *Exercitives* are speech acts with which we exercise what powers we may have to change the social status of a person. For example, the Pope can excommunicate a villainous priest. *Commissives* commit the speaker to a future course of action, for example, in promising, undertaking, guaranteeing, betting, espousing and so on. *Behabitives* are speech acts used to express an attitude to another person with respect to something that has been done by the speaker or interlocutor. For example, saying 'I'm sorry' expresses contrition.

Pronoun Systems

Pronouns play several roles of importance in the psychological processes carried through by our uses of language. In learning our culture we learn among many other things, the significance of choice of pronouns. This is just the kind of repertory item which it is the task of discursive/cultural analysis to bring to light explicitly. The word 'I' in English is an indexical, that is, its significance on any given occasion is determined by one or more attributes of the speaker who is using it. Where the speaker is and when he or she speaks is tied in to the meaning of what has been said by the use of the first person. In this respect the use of 'I' is similar to the uses of 'here' and 'now'.

In almost all contexts the use of the first person singular is a way of taking responsibility either for the veracity of what has been said or for the social act that has thereby been performed. If someone says, 'I have just heard a nightingale,' the truth of the statement would rarely be questioned, even if it had been said at the International Polar Station, so long as it was uttered by a respected person. If someone says, 'I will do the dishes,' the force of this statement would not be questioned unless the speaker were known to be unreliable. The use of the first person is a way of taking responsibility.

We know from studies of diverse language systems that the first person does not always have the same personal responsibility-taking force. Japanese indexicals are more complex than Indo-European first-person expressions in this aspect (Mühlhäusler & Harré, 1990). Japanese has a variety of first-person expressions, nearly all of which are sensitive to relative social status but which also serve to diffuse commitment from the actual speaker to the group indexed by the pronoun form. For example, 'watachi' is a word used by those who take themselves and are taken by others to be socially superior, while 'uchi' is a word literally meaning 'my house', and tying the speech-act to one's family. 'Boku' is another first-person pronoun having the sense of the speaker being someone who is part of a powerful group – the word is said to be favored by gangsters and radical feminists.

The second person too is of social psychological significance. If one is in France one needs to judge whether one should use 'tu' or 'vous' in addressing someone – the French size up the social relations between one another in a flash.

English has a very simple system with only one word, 'you', for the many possible second-person pronominal relations, to self and others. Only one word, 'we', suffices for all the many kinds of plurality that could exist among persons and are recognized in other languages.

French and Spanish have two words for second-person singular, though derived from different grammatical sources. 'Vous' comes from the plural, a frequent indicator of respect, while 'Usted' comes from the honorific 'Vuestra Merced', roughly, 'Your Honor'.

In those languages that have preserved functionally distinct forms of the second person, the use of a pronoun expresses social relations between speaker and hearer, of which the speaker must take account. The basic relations have been summed by Brown and Gillman (1960), as the T (tu)/V (vous) system. They called their dimensions 'power' and 'solidarity' but it would be better to identify them as in Figure 2.1.

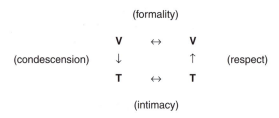

Figure 2.1   The social grammar of the second person

Maori is an ergative language, that is, unlike Indo-European languages which are based on word classes such as feminine/masculine or concrete/abstract, Polynesian languages are based on the distinction between agents and patients, active or passive beings. Pronouns are inflected for marking this distinction. A Maori speaker must know whether an entity is active or passive in choosing a pronoun, just as speakers of French must know the social status of a person to be addressed or their gender in order to use the correct inflection of the pronoun.

Finally, there is the use of pronoun shift as discourse strategy in a small-scale competition for hegemony in a conversational episode. In Shakespeare's *Love's Labours Lost* four young women and four young men engage in a complex game of semi-serious flirtation. At that time, English retained the T/V second-person system, particularly used to display intimacy though not necessarily affectionate, while the V form expressed formality or social distance. For example, one of the young men tries to move to a more intimate relation with one of the women by adopting the 'thou/thee' pronoun form, but is quickly put in his place by her staying with the 'you/ye' form (Adams & Harré, 2003, ch. 11).

This sample of psychologically significant linguistic forms illustrates the way that 'grammatical' analysis (where 'grammar' refers to the explicit formulation of rules and conventions) brings to light the psychology that is implicit in the very act of speaking and writing. It also enables us to identify local cultural variations of putative universals as well as revealing aspects of the psychology of speakers of a language which are indeed local. There is much less cognitive work required in using the second person in English since the speaker does not have to take account of the social relations implicit in the T/V system.

Discourse Analysis: Narratology

As J. S. Bruner (1986) and others have emphasized, 'narrative' can be adopted as a working concept for understanding how patterns of the big four of psychological science – thinking, feeling, acting and perceiving – are orderly, repetitive and display local aspects as well as universal features. The idea of 'discourse' appears in three roles in narratology. It serves as a characterization of what people are doing as they act, think, feel and perceive. It opens the way for treating the flow of thoughts, actions and feelings as stories that are 'told' or 'lived' or both. Does it fill the place that generative mechanisms occupy in patterns of explanation drawn from the natural sciences? Not really – because it identifies the kind of performance that human agents are seen to be doing in the framework of cultural/discursive psychology, namely, conforming to storylines as ideal forms for thinking, acting, feeling and perceiving.

Basic Principles of Narratological Research

Certain psychologically relevant properties of discourses are carried by the stories that unfold in the telling or living of a story or stories, which in the simplest case everyone engaged in the activity already knows.

Stories can be classified as follows:

'Chronicles' are descriptions of sequences of events in the order in which they occurred, without explicit interpretation or assessments of their significance.

'Narratives' are stories recounting sequences of events with some social or psychological purpose and with some explicit interpretations of their significance for the point of the tale. There are several varieties of narratives:

'Picaresque' are stories ordered like a chronicle but told to show development or deterioration of character, and thereby sometimes to make some social point. For example, *one* point of the story of the misadventures of Don Quixote is to display a certain kind of character and to ironize romantic longings for the long defunct chivalry of the Middle Ages. The story might have any number of other readings. However, at any particular time and place, these readings can often be ranked in various orders of significance depending on the point of view from which the story is being told or heard.

'Narratives proper' or 'storylines' are descriptions of sequences of events which are ordered in terms of their significance – the most important event may often be told first, for example, in autobiographies and obituaries. The achievements of the deceased appear in the first paragraph with date and place of birth coming later in the story.

We can begin by setting out some general features of narratives.

The storyline determines the meanings of the events and vice versa. In the course of story living and story telling, persons are created as beings of a certain sort whose activities can be seen as roles, histories and displays of aptitudes, from one of a possible multitude of points of view. The same discursive 'creation' can be applied to and used in acts of self-definition by families, other small to mid-sized social groups such as clubs and business enterprises, even nations. Sometimes the 'creation' comes from us the onlookers – sometimes it is the product of a deliberate and managed policy by those involved.

These creations are realized in the beliefs of others about the person, group etc. and also in the self-beliefs of the personal entities involved and realized in books, plays, sports events, movies, TV dramas and soaps, operas, court reports, citations for war heroes, spy stories, and so on. What we believe as psychologists and literary critics, sport commentators and judges *can be expressed* in explicit form as plots, roles and events.

Narratives have plots and a cast of characters. Plots are rarely improvised. They exist and persist in cultures, through oft told stories, the forms of monuments and war memorials, and nowadays, through the patterns of action displayed in the electronic media. They reappear in folk tales (and in 'urban myths') and in fairy stories such as Cinderella and Little Red Riding Hood – these tales show us how life should go. They are recreated in TV dramas, plays, for example, *Hamlet*, novels such as *Gone with the Wind* or *Moby Dick*, and movies, for example, *Star Wars*. These often show us how life *should go*.

The basic premise of narratology is that we live our lives in an orderly manner, and in often repeated patterns. We can use the metaphor of 'acting in accordance with schemata', that are verbal expressions of the narrative conventions of our cultures, without any particular commitment as to how those conventions exist. For example, even in the 21st century, some Indian men leave home, family and profession to seek enlightenment as bodhisattvas, a pattern of life initiated by Gautama himself and reproduced in various forms since then. How do these seekers know what to do? The culture repeats the story of the search for enlightenment over and over again.

Jerome Seymour Bruner (1915–) was born on 1 October 1915 into a well-off middle-class family in New York. 'Jerry' was the youngest of four children. He describes his family as 'nominally observant' in religious matters. Born blind, he was not able to see until the age of two when his sight was restored surgically. Later, the consequences of the death of his father when he was 12, led to constant disruption in his schooling. However, he succeeded in entering Duke University in 1933.

Completing the undergraduate courses early, he began graduate work with animal experiments in William McDougall's laboratory. Having to choose between animals and people as the places where 'psychology' happened, he chose Harvard and people, over Duke and animals, largely under the influence of the writings of *Gordon Allport*. He began his graduate studies in 1938 on the power of propaganda broadcasts to influence public opinion.

Throughout the Second World War he worked in a variety of offices concerned with the management of information. Returning to Cambridge, Massachusetts after the war, he completed his doctorate in 1947. He stayed at Harvard until he moved to Oxford in 1972.

A grant from the Carnegie Corporation enabled him to join with George Miller in the setting up of the Center for Cognitive Studies. However, as Miller remarked, mainstream psychologists looked askance at the revival of the use of mentalistic concepts. Many of the most important members of and visitors to the center were from outside psychology as such.

In 1972, he was elected to the new Watts chair in psychology at Oxford. At that time Oxford was the preeminent center for language-oriented philosophy and philosophy of mind, a sibling to Bruner's increasingly narratologically grounded psychology. This environment was congenial to him.

Returning to his home town in the mid 1980s, Bruner began a new academic career at the New School for Social Research in New York, and later at New York University. It gave him a chance to set about completing the project begun in the 1950s. How did narrative shape thought and action?

There are three basic principles which express the psychological significance of narrative:

1 'Narratology is that part of qualitative psychology that is concerned with the self', the qualities that are attributed to people and that people attribute to themselves (Parker, 2002).
2 'People narratarize their experience of the world and their own role in it' (Bruner, 1986).
3 'The interpreter has to grasp the narrative's configuring plot to make sense of its constituents' (Bruner, 1986).

Thus who we are and what we are doing is both shaped by and expressed in narrative form as we live through the episodes of everyday life and relive these episodes in story form as we tell the tale. It is worth bearing in mind that keeping to the plot may be as much a matter as hints and pressures from other actors as the realisation of knowledge of a plot by one of the actors alone.

The Form of Some Standard Plots

Plot analysis has been a major preoccupation of discursive psychologists and literary analysts, many of whom should be considered to belong to both groups. Here are several useful way of analyzing a plot to reveal the dynamics of certain kinds of social episodes. Kenneth Burke's scheme, 'Pentad', has the following components:

(a) Act [meaning of action], scene [setting of action], agent [active entity], agency [instrument], purpose [intention of the unfolding events].
(b) Ratios: scene in relation to act; scene in relation to agent; scene in relation to agency; and scene in relation to purpose, and so on through all 24 possible combinations. In practice, the 'scene' ratios are often the most enlightening.

Hamlet's efforts to shame his uncle and prove him to have been guilty of the former king's murder, by putting on a play in which a king is murdered, set going an episode the plot of which includes the act (an accusation that his uncle has murdered the old king), scene (the Court at Elsinore), agent (Hamlet himself), agency (the play) and purpose (to elicit an unmistakable sign of guilt).

On a grander scale, the First Iraq war could be seen as the unfolding of a plot and analyzed in terms of Burke's Pentad. As an example of a 'ratio' we could take 'act in relation to purpose', where the 'act' is the attack on occupied Kuwait following the invasion of Kuwait by Saddam Hussein's military which led to the First Gulf War of 2003. The 'agency' is the army, the 'purpose' is to restore Kuwaiti sovereignty. This is one storyline. There are others in the media to make a different sense of this piece of history.

Other proposals for an analytical scheme more or less echo Burke's Pentad. Tavetan Todorov (1975) identified the dynamics of a storyline in terms of the disturbance and restoration of equilibrium.

In any episode, large or small, ephemeral or long running, there is a cast of characters. Vladimir Propp (1968) devised a scheme for the classification of the dramatis personae of folk tales. It is easy to see that it has applications in a great many real-life situations, fictional dramas and so on. We have the hero, the villain, the donor, the helper, the victim, the dispatcher (who sends the hero on a quest), and so on.

Algirdas Greimas (1990) proposed an analytical scheme that focuses on the dynamics of episodes regarding relations between the main sources of activity in the story. Greimas pays explicit attention to the relations between pairs of *actants*. These are the axes of the narrative:

1   Axis of desire [Subject – Object]: Anthony wants Cleopatra for his lover.
2   Axis of power [Helper – Opponent]: Ted Kennedy helped Barack Obama in his campaign to become presidential candidate, while Hillary Clinton opposed him as an alternative candidate.
3   Axis of transmission [Sender – Receiver]: Whistle blowers like Wikileaks transfer hidden knowledge to the public domain.

Narratology as a Key Aspect of Cultural/Discursive Psychology

(a) A person 'understands' what someone else (other people) or him or herself is doing or has done, because that person knows explicitly or implicitly a possible plot that might be unfolding.
(b) When living out an episode, social or cognitive, for example, deciding a course of action, thinking about plans and hopes for tomorrow and so on, the sequence of 'decisions' on how to act is determined by a known plot but not necessarily consciously – that is why there is a psychological research program to find out or propose: a 'best plot explanation', and to source the plot in the culture. For example, to understand the Kamikaze phenomenon at the end of the Second World War we can turn to the Japanese cult heroic failure – making the alien emotional context less strange (Morris, 1975). In his remarkable book Morris proposed a 'best plot explanation', grounding his claim for the central storyline in a detailed cultural history of Japan.

The criterion for successful narratological research is whether the storylines revealed make the events more intelligible. Do they link up with an existing repertoire of narratives? There are no 'mechanisms' to be discovered – rather, sequences of meanings and the 'scripts' and 'conventions' which express the norms to which they seem to be sensitive. As in all kinds of qualitative research, the ultimate aim of a study is to propose a relevant body of knowledge that people must share to be able to understand and take a proper part in the unfolding of an episode which seems to realize a possible storyline. The idea of a shared body of knowledge links narratology with the approach of social representations (to be presented in some detail in Chapter 9).

Positioning Theory: Moral Aspects of Thought and Action

All thinking, expression of feeling in emotional and other displays, and social actions take place within shared systems of belief about the moral standards in use in a community and about the distribution of rights and duties to think, speak and act in certain ways among the people in that community. Moral presuppositions appear as long-term patterns of speech and action in the roles people are assigned or take up. They also appear momentarily in the unfolding of local short-term episodes such as family gatherings, friends planning a trip, committee meetings, and so on. Every social group has a moral order or orders implicit in their form of life, some aspects of which are made explicit from time to time.

The distribution of rights and duties among a group of people depends on:

(a) **The story line or lines that the actors take themselves to be living out.**
(b) **The meanings of the actions (including speech acts) that the actors perform singly or jointly that seem to be shared by the participants, or, if not shared, disputed and negotiated.**
(c) **Beliefs about the attributes of the people involved in an episode, particularly their powers and vulnerabilities, held by those engaged in an episode.**
(d) **These become salient in so far as they are matters of rights and duties in relation to the project under way and the alleged attributes of the actors.**

A cluster of rights and duties as expressed in the discourses of a certain community relevant to the actions of a person or group of people from that community is a *position*.

There are social-cognitive processes carried by discourses by means of which people and groups are *positioned*, that is, have been assigned or ascribed positions by someone or some group in that community, or have taken up positions themselves as theirs. An assignment or ascription of a position may be refused, disputed, declared illegitimate (for example, that no such position exists in that culture corner) and so on. These are then second-order social-cognitive discourses. Their efficacy will depend on the positioning of the person or persons who dispute positions and those with whom they contest them.

The attributes a person has that are relevant to some social action or episode is a '*preposition*' and the attribution process '*prepositioning*'. For example, I attribute physical strength to you, so prima facie prepositioning you as one who has a duty to help me lift a log. In prepositioning moves there is a basis from which positions are assigned, resisted, refused and so on, often on grounds of alleged matters of fact. I preposition you as conscientious, so grounding my positioning of you duty bound to take care of the club's money. However, prepositioning is a cognitive-social discursive process and involves accepting or refusing the attribution of strengths and weaknesses, agreeing with or denying the occurrence of biographical events relevant to this prepositioning, and so on. Who has the right to assess my capacities in relation to your needs? A person may make claims about his or her attributes in order to avoid being positioned in a certain episode, for example, duty to give blood is deleted if the person has had malaria. Or help may be refused by a claim to be 'too busy at the moment'. This too is prepositioning. But not everyone has the right to perform such an act in a particular context, so this depends ultimately on a relevant positioning move.

Positions are related to storylines and to speech act types, and these connecting nodes mutually influence one another. Positioning is then a necessary component of narratology and of speech act analysis. We can present these relations in a triangle of mutual influences (see Figure 2.2).

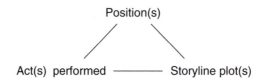

Figure 2.2 The positioning triangle

We must remember that the events in any life episode are capable of multiple interpretations, some more salient to the unfolding of larger strips of life than others.

Recent research directions have involved a close study of the fine structure of the discursive processes by which people are positioned and position themselves (Harré & Dediać, 2011).

Also of importance in practice is the question of the authenticity of presumed positions. It is one of the issues that can be raised by someone who refuses to acknowledge a claim to a right, and by someone refusing to accept a duty.

How far are positions local? Other cultures differ from ours in many ways, but always to some extent in the moral systems that are taken for granted. This raises the question of whether there are any trans-cultural or universally acknowledged positions. The answer to this question must await the accumulation of a wide repertoire of studies revealing local moral orders in local positioning practices.

Here is an example of the use of positioning analysis to track the social cognitive processes that were involved in the unfolding of the Terri Sciavo case. How is the right to end the biological life of a victim of catastrophic brain injury decided? In a recent case that attracted a great deal of public interest it was possible to follow the discursive process by which a decision was reached in the interplay between the positioning moves by the two main interested parties, the family of the victim and the husband (Grattan, 2008, ch. 8).

Each party claimed, as it were, a natural right to determine the issue. Parents have a prior right and duty of care for their children while a spouse has an acquired pattern of rights and duties generally supported by the law. As Grattan showed in her analysis of the discursive acts of the parties, the structure of their contrary discourses rested on powerful efforts at prepositioning each other. The parents were prepositioned by the husband, as motivated by financial interests. He was prepositioned by the parents as self-interested and callous. Each party introduced evidence on which their respective prepositionings were based. The husband declared that he had taken a course in the nursing of the brain injured while the parents of the victim asserted that he had spent the insurance money on things other than the immediate care of their daughter.

As Grattan shows, these discursive strategies were aimed at a higher authority, the legal officers of the state who had both the right and the duty to decide if any of the disputants had the right to switch off the support system. Both parties claimed the duty to make the decision: the parents insisting that the machine not be turned off, and the husband claiming the right to terminate the life support. The husband ultimately was granted the superior right.

From the point of view of psychology in tracing the long history of this case, we are studying a cognitive process, but one which is occurring in the public-social world of a particular version of American culture.

Products of Cultural/Discursive Psychological Methods

Bodies of Knowledge

In the course of this chapter we have become acquainted with a variety of methods for the analysis of psychological phenomena, understood in the mode of Vygotsky and Bruner as sequences of meanings, carried by a great variety of bearers and aimed at the successful performance of all sorts of tasks. The results of these analyses can be interpreted as the content of bodies of knowledge and the norms that are displayed in the ways they are used. In short, instead of the vain search for a hierarchy of mechanisms to sustain the empty sequences of Humean event causality we are trying to bring to light what someone or some group of people must know to live their lives satisfactorily with others. Life should go by without bringing personal distress on one another, without minor or major social disasters and without the breakdown of social order. According to the principles of cultural/discursive psychology, displays of emotions are also shaped and legitimated and interpreted in conformity to storylines and meanings.

We note that a body of knowledge that is complete for practical purposes may be available in the resources of a single individual, or it may be common to whole populations in that each member has more or less the same resources as every other. However, and this is probably the most common situation, each person in a community has some of the resources needed to accomplish a correct performance, which can only be successfully completed if each member of the relevant group contributes his or her bit to the whole procedure.

Displaying a Body of Knowledge

Having completed an analysis of a form of life and episodes of importance within it, how can we best record our findings?

Presuming that both analyst and actors share a common body of linguistic knowledge, the analyst proposes hypotheses as to the possible projects the actors are undertaking, remembering that the actors may be undertaking more than one project at the same time by the use of the very same words, gestures and so on. The analyst proposes interpretations of the text as the means by which each possible project is accomplished.

A lay out such as that in Table 2.1 represents actors' tacit body of knowledge. However, we must remember that individuals may not have all of it or some idiosyncratic version of it. Storylines will appear among rules and schemata for unproblematic action.

Table 2.1

Situation	Actor	Rules and schemata	Available meanings
S1	A1	R1	M1
S2	A2	R2	M2
etc.			

A first-order study does not involve asking how we come to have these items in our repertoires for living, nor how they could change or be changed. It has proved possible to apply these methods to other eras of our own culture (Stearns & Stearns, 1988) and with caution to other cultures than our own (Wierzbicka, 1992). Examples of this amplification of discursive psychology will appear here and there throughout the chapters devoted to narrower topics.

Conclusions

Cultural/discursive psychology is by no means the first proposal for methods for a psychological science that will truly reflect the nature of the material being studied. Though Wundt's *Volkerpsychologie* opened up the possibility of agent-oriented psychology, the variety of qualitative methods that evolved in the 20th century were usually developed for medical and psychiatric purposes. Grounded theory (Glaser & Strauss, 1967), ethnomethodology (Garfinkel, 1967), and phenomenological psychology (Giorgi & Giorgi, 2008) have all found favor with some people in some places. The idea that these methods should be the methods of choice to displace the 'experimental' methodology of the old psychology for studies of cognition, emotion, social action and perception, was rarely contemplated by the majority of psychologists working in academia. In recent years a number of very fine manuals for research in the style of qualitative psychology have become available, for example, *Qualitative psychology: A practical guide,* edited by Jonathan Smith (2008) and *Interpreting qualitative data* by David Silverman (1993).

In accordance with the spirit of this text we do not intend to spend time retelling how mainstream experimental psychology has drifted away from the rigorous standards and powerful methods of the natural sciences. It is these standards that animate the proposals laid out in this and the following chapter.

Summing up the results of the discussions in this chapter we can say that the final product of qualitative research is a catalogue or lexicon of the meanings people give to beliefs or to situations and to their own and other's actions within those situations. Such meanings may be common to a great many people, a small group or even to one person alone. Coupled with catalogues of meanings there are systems representing hierarchies of rules, conventions, customs and habits which shape the actions of human agents in carrying out their situated projects. Again we note that the agent might be a single person or a group that is organized in such a way as to be capable of joint action. How do these catalogues, lexicons and hierarchies exist? There is no single answer to this question. They might be ingrained habits, the product of training to act in accordance with rules. They might be among individuals people's beliefs. They might exist as social representations. *The basic explanatory format is agent-causation.*

Note

1   This word baffled several contestants in a recent spelling competition!

3

Methods of Research: Neuroscience and Genetic/Evolutionary Psychology

Rom Harré

The brain adapts to the tasks a person uses it to perform. (Anon)

In this chapter we turn to the approaches that have been developed to investigate the mechanisms of the material tools (many of which are parts of the human body) that people use to accomplish culturally defined tasks. As we have argued in the previous chapters, the results of studies using the cultural/discursive methodologies have enabled us to determine what kinds of dispositions, capacities and skills etc., we need to carry on our lives successfully. These powers and skills are possible because we have been born with or have acquired the mechanisms necessary to exercise them. The possession of such mechanisms endows a person with the locally relevant powers, capacities and skills.

The discourses by which research programs along these lines are proposed, managed and their results presented, are shaped by the O- or organism grammar and the M- or molecular grammar. In the first part of this chapter, we describe methods of research that presuppose that human beings are organisms which have evolved according the processes of organic evolution. In the second part, we outline some research programs in which people are treated as sites for chemical reactions relevant to thinking, acting, feeling and perceiving.

Research Framed by the O- and M-grammars

Since Pierre Jean Georges Cabanis (1757–1808) first clearly enunciated the thesis that the brain is the organ and the only organ of thought, the instrument by means of which people think, the project of grounding the psychology of human beings in mechanisms that involve states and processes in the brain has been pursued with more or less success. The project is formidable and was dogged for centuries by the mereological fallacy – assigning to brains and their organs functions, powers, capacities and skills that were defined only in relation to people. Legs are important organs of bipedal locomotion, but despite what Nancy Sinatra had to say about her boots, it is people not their legs or their boots who walk all over someone!

This ever-present temptation to error means that we have to be extremely careful in how we lay out the program of neuroscience in relation to psychology. For the most part investigations of the neural correlates of psychological phenomena, that is, the management of meanings within normative frameworks, adds little to our understanding of what people are doing when they are thinking, feeling, acting and perceiving.

However, when we are faced with disorders in our ways of living, with a decline in or failure to manage the means by which we think, act, feel and perceive, psychoneurology comes into its own. The task-tool metaphor provides the generic frame for research programs that are aimed at understanding and remedying deficits in our capacities and skills, relative to what are presumed to be local norms. There are some failures that seem to disrupt human life at all times and places. Someone who loses the capacity to find the words for what he or she wants to say – someone who has great difficulty in creating and maintaining the kind of social relationships we take to be normal – someone who can no longer distinguish one melody from another – it is not unreasonable to suppose that the neural tools for accomplishing these tasks are defective. They may never have developed to the level of functioning that would enable a person to fulfill the demands of their culture. They may have declined from what they once were. Using the Taxonomic Priority Principle, TPP, we can identify possible sites where the tools of thinking and acting have broken down.

The contrast between neuroscience as a kind of psychology and as a part of medicine has been very well put by H. W. Shipton.

> ... pioneer EEGers hoped that the study of the small electrical changes in the brain would throw light on brain function, and thus, by extension, help with the understanding of mental processes ... most progress in EEG has been in medicine ... empirical correlations between disease processes [epileptic attacks] and the electrical activity of the brain have firmly established the technique in the clinic. Attempts to use EEG as a means for understanding mental processes ... have been much less successful. (1975)

The Human Animal and its Organs

Here we describe research methods that have been presented in research discourses that exemplify the O-grammar. By constructing research discourses in this form the research methods and results require the presupposition that human beings are organisms in order to be intelligible. The relevance of the results of these research methods to the project of hybrid psychology is determined by the use of the Taxonomic Priority Principle, TPP, and the Task-Tool metaphor, TT, in setting up research programs and interpreting their results.

Until recently it was impossible to study the living brain of a person going about a cognitive or practical task, or who was experiencing or expressing an emotion, or seeing, hearing or touching something. At the same time, a succession of conceptions of the way that the human brain worked as a tool for personal projects drew on whatever happened to be the latest technology of the era. In the 17th century it was hydraulics, in the late 19th century it was the telephone system and in the latter part of the 20th, the computer. There are 10^{11} neurons linked in a dense network of synapses, much the most complex thing in the universe as we know it. The difficulty of carrying out studies of the workings of living brains and the speculative character of models of brains in action add up to a formidable scientific problem indeed, if we are bent on finding out what is happening in the brain when a person is thinking, acting, feeling and perceiving. It must be reiterated that what is happening in the brain is not thinking, feeling or perceiving! Only people can do that!

We have argued that in fact much genetic and neurological research is shaped by the metaphor of the brain as a tool-kit. Here we draw on the discussion in Chapter 1 in which we introduced the Task-Tool metaphor as a way of bringing cultural/discursive studies of people thinking and acting into a fruitful coherence with neuroscience research into what is going on in someone's body and brain when they are thinking and acting in certain way. Just as we need ballistics and the physics of elastic strings to understand how the tools of tennis, the racquets, courts and balls function, while the game and the playing of it is a cultural phenomenon, so we need neuroscience in its various forms to understand how the relevant body organs with which these cultural tasks and projects are accomplished function when people are making use of them. In carrying out this project we must learn to avoid the mereological fallacy – brains do not decide or compose music – people do.

Neuroscience and the Brain as a Mechanism

We begin by explaining the methods by which the relevant features of the brain as a tool-kit can be discovered. Here our thinking is shaped by the M-grammar. Then we turn to questions of how this set of tools evolved. Genetics and evolutionary psychology form a pattern of research methods shaped by and expressible in discourse ordered in accordance with the O-grammar. Discourses of this kind depend for their intelligibility by tacitly presupposing that people are organisms for the purposes of the research in hand.

Lesion/Deficit Methods

The idea that the brain is the organ of thought and the only organ of thought remained largely schematic until the middle of the 20th century. Various areas and regions of the brain had been mapped during the 19th century, for example, Paul Broca (1842–1880) had shown that an area in the lower part of left frontal lobe was the seat of one aspect of language capacities, the ability to use words in an orderly manner. Carl Wernicke (1848–1905) located an adjacent region of the brain which seemed to be the seat of the capacity to organize language according to local semantic rules. However, the understanding of the brain as a living organ and the tracking of the processes by which cognition was accomplished was rudimentary.

The first major step towards this understanding came when Alexander Luria (1902–1977) adapted some of the techniques he had developed to deal with war casualties to a study of the neurology of cognition. Luria's method of brain research was based on the principle that when some part of the brain is damaged or destroyed, that is there is a 'lesion' at that location, and when there is a correlated disturbance of some psychological function, we can infer that that part of the brain when intact, played a role in the neurofunctional system with which the higher order cognitive function was performed.

Alexander Luria (1902–1977) was born in the ancient town of Kazan, east of Moscow. In the aftermath of the Revolution the universities were in chaos. Luria more or less educated himself, following a wide reading program that was particularly oriented to German experimental psychology.

(Continued)

He graduated in 1921, and began his medical studies. However, Luria's enthusiasm for a 'new psychology' led him to begin to work with Alexei Leont'ev, focusing on the interplay between verbal/practical activities and emotion. Luria built up a research program on real-life emotions in studies of the emotional states of criminals, during and after arrest, while on trial and after sentencing.

In 1924, he met Lev Semionovich Vygotsky, whose conception of cultural/instrument/historical studies as an ideal psychology, went much further than Luria's more modest studies of the role of language in the management of labor. Luria organized two expeditions to Uzbekistan, to study the effect of literacy programs on the cognitive powers of people who had hitherto been largely illiterate. There were distinctive cognitive styles and patterns of thought among illiterate Uzbeks, unlike anything found among literate Russians.

Shortly after the German attack in 1941, Luria was commissioned to open a hospital in the Urals for the treatment of soldiers with brain injuries. He undertook the mapping of cognitively significant regions of the brain that were essential to the integrated activities of the higher cognitive functions. His method of research was based on the deficit/lesion/function pattern of reasoning that had been used in the 19th century by neurologists like Paul Broca.

Luria's studies were unsystematic, in the sense that they depended on the kinds of brain injuries and the kinds of motor and cognitive deficits that were presented by the patients who came his way, both during and after the Second World War. For him, research became diagnosis. The testing of diagnostic hypotheses was carried out by trying out various curative regimes suggested by the kind of brain injury associated with the correlated defect. One important result from Luria's vast range of such 'tests' was his realization that more than one region of the brain is involved in any one motor and cognitive process, as identified by the use of concepts from the P-grammar. 'It should be apparent that if the operation of intellectual processes is thought of in terms of functional systems instead of discrete abilities, we have to reorient our ideas about the possibility of localizing intellectual functions [in the brain]' (Luria, 1979, p. 141).

In diagnosing the sources of some disruption to a higher order cognitive function or complex motor function, one has first to find out which links in the normal system of the working constellation of brain zones' are disrupted. Once that is achieved, the work of finding alternative linkages can begin. Underlying this methodology is a deeper principle: the relevant constellation of brain zones' can be discovered step by step by identifying the *various* regions where damage disrupts a specific cognitive or motor function.

In defining the project of neuropsychology that grew out of his wartime work, Luria pointed out that this research necessarily involved two quite different modes of enquiry:

On the one hand, I had to move from brain structure to a deeper understanding of the neurophysiological mechanisms that were operating these structures. On the other hand, our psychological analysis of higher cortical functions was by no means complete, and we needed improved psychological analyses as well. (Luria, 1979, p. 157)

Here Luria is clearly enunciating the two principles we have put forward as the basis for the psychology of the future. The Task-Tool metaphor is tied to the 'neurophysiological mechanisms' by the Taxonomic Priority Principle which provides the link between higher cortical functions as revealed by 'improved psychological analyses'. And by that is meant the kind of discursive analytical studies that had been pioneered by Lev Vygotsky.

Scanning Methods

The use of scanning techniques to identify the regions of the brain that are active during the performance of tasks by an experimental participant has become the major research tool of our era. Three methods have been developed.

Electroencephalography

This was first 'scanning' technique to be introduced early in the 20th Century. It consisted in recording the electrical activity of the brain as a whole, by means of an array of electrodes spread over the scalp. The patterns of activity of the brain when the person is in a certain broadly defined state are revealed by correlating the input from each of the electrodes which display a changing pattern of different frequencies. These turned out to be associated with being asleep and being awake, and with different phases. They are not characteristics of these states as they are experienced by human beings and discussed, classified and so on in the P-grammar. The criteria for whether someone is asleep or awake do not include the patterns of the electrical activities of their brains; the alpha, beta, theta and delta rhythms. One does not have to have an electrocardiogram to know whether one is awake.

However, we note the use of this technique in psychopathology, to determine whether someone in a coma or though catastrophically paralyzed, is still believed to be conscious.

Recently, Suppes and Han (2000) have revived the research possibilities of EEG studies by first obtaining correlations between the patterns of whole brain activity of a group of people reading words and sentences. Then, after abstracting wave forms combining a small number of sine waves from the EEG data, they tested to see whether by identifying these patterns among new EEG data they could tell which words were being read. The results were encouraging, in that for the most part the identifications were correct. How far this method can be extended to many more words is the question the authors leave us with.

Positron Emission Tomography

The PET (positron emission tomography) method traces neural activity in the brain by means of radioactive markers attached to molecules taken up from the blood stream at sites where cellular activity is above a certain resting threshold.

The physics behind PET scanning technology is fairly simple, but the engineering needed to create working machinery is very complex. At places where increased neural activity is taking place there is an increase in the amount of glycogen taken up. The original method made use of the fact that it is possible to produce short-lived radioactive fluorine atoms which can be attached to the molecules of a glycogen analogue. These molecules are taken up at active sites in the same way as glycogen is. In decaying, radioactive fluorine atoms emit positrons carrying a positive electrical charge opposite to that of the negative electron. After a very short time and close to the place of its emission a positron

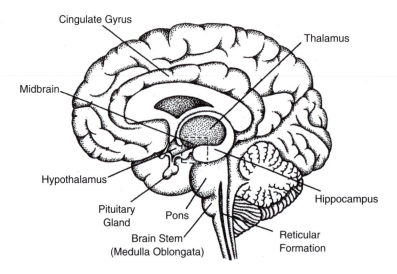

Cingulate Gyrus

Thalamus

Midbrain

Hypothalamus

Pituitary
Gland

Pons

Brain Stem
(Medulla Oblongata)

Hippocampus

Reticular
Formation

Figure 3.1

will encounter an electron. They mutually annihilate one another. The energy of the former two particles is emitted as a pair of gamma rays in opposite directions. The object being scanned is surrounded by a halo of gamma-ray detectors. The information from these devices is fed into a computer. The computer is programmed to compute the location from which the pair of gamma rays was emitted and hence to identify the nearby location where the original positron was produced in the decay of a radioactive fluorine atom. A picture of the active sites in each slice is created as the object being scanned moves step by step through the machine. The result is the familiar representation of brain activity as shown in Figure 3.1.

Functional Magnetic Resonance Imaging (fMRI)

The principles on which various Magnetic Resonance Imaging methods are based are fairly simple – but the technical details are formidable. We believe that psychologists need to understand only how the scanning system works in a general way, without delving deeply into the physics or the engineering that is involved in the design and production of the machines.

Jezzard, Matthews, and Smith condense the basic physics into an admirably clear description:

> Imaging the location of a resonating molecule in a sample (e.g. protons in water molecules in the human brain) is made possible with the use of small magnetic field gradients which are superimposed on the larger homogeneous static magnetic field of the imaging magnet … the relative positions of molecules along the smaller gradient field are measured simply from the differences in resonance frequency as the resonance frequency for a nucleus (e.g. hydrogen ion) in a compound (e.g. water) is proportional to the applied field strength (the sum of the large static field and the smaller field of the gradient coil). (2010, p. 5)

The further 'down' the gradient of the smaller magnetic field, the weaker the resonance frequency of the photons emitted when the smaller magnetic field is turned off and the hydrogen ions (protons) in the relevant molecules return to the orientations that they had under the influence of the large static magnetic field. This is the simple two field sketch of how molecules are located along one dimension, that of the gradient of the smaller magnetic field.

The ability to create three-dimensional images of the locations of clusters of molecules is the result of the elaboration of this simple system into magnetic fields in three dimensions. Locating a molecule along each of the three dimensions of space will show where it is in the topography of the brain. The development of computational methods of integrating the information so obtained has made possible visible images of contrasting tissue structures.

Research into the brain activation patterns of many cognitive processes using MRI devices are troubled by the high level of noise coming from the machine itself. The devices for producing both the high Tesla primary field and the magnetic gradient field are both noisy. The ambient noise creates problems for studies of hearing, be it speech or music. Various techniques of auditory shielding and software systems for controlling the equipment and presenting material for the participants have been developed. There is a useful survey of both solutions in Okada and Nakai (2003).

One successful MRI research method is based on the physiological phenomenon of the 'hemodynamic response'. When there is a level of neural activity above the resting threshold in any region of the brain more glucose and oxygen is required to sustain it. This results in an increase in oxygenated hemoglobin over deoxygenated hemoglobin. Neural activity shows up as Blood Oxygen Level Dependence or BOLD. There is a change in the ratio of diamagnetic oxyhemoglobin, which is weakly repelled by a magnetic field, to paramagnetic deoxyhemoglobin, which is weakly attracted to a magnetic field. When there is a higher level of neural activity in some region of the brain, more oxygenated hemoglobin will be drawn there to sustain the increased levels of glycogen consumption. The magnetic resonance response of the pre-activity ratio of the two forms of hemoglobin is detectably different from the response when neural activity is taking place. The difference is small, so generally many repetitions of the cognitive task, thought pattern or elicitation of the feeling is required for the success of an experiment using the BOLD response to find the region in the brain where the relevant activity is occurring. Statistical analysis is routinely used to deal with random variations in response.

Important data is revealed when the graded field is shut down and the atoms oriented by the graded field return to their original state since the time they take to return to their original orientations is related to their molecular environment. In the case of BOLD, the relaxation time is related to the ratio of the difference in the magnetic susceptibility of oxygenated and deoxygenated hemoglobin.

Magnetic methods can also be used to display the density of water molecules and their rates of diffusion in soft tissues using the magnetic properties of protons, the cores of hydrogen atoms. Neuroscientists are thus able to 'see' the structure of the living brain and to detect any features that may exist there. This can range from tumors to a decline in the integrity of the white matter of which the brain is largely made up. We will be illustrating the power of the hybrid methodology with a study in which relative diffusion rates of water molecules in the white matter of the brain was detected and measured by means of the Magnetic Resonance phenomena, enabling abnormalities in the structure of the white matter of the brains of people with declining memory abilities to be mapped.

Here is how it works: for the sake of simplicity of exposition let us suppose we are studying a long line of water molecules, in each of which are hydrogen ions, protons. Each proton is rotating and so has a magnetic field oriented in relation to its axis of rotation but these magnetic fields are randomly oriented overall. Now we apply a powerful external magnetic field to the line of protons. The individual magnetic fields are roughly oriented in the same direction by this field. Then we apply a weaker graded magnetic field to the sequence of protons that lines up their individual magnetic fields more precisely. The further down the gradient, the smaller is the effect of this secondary field. Now we send a radio-frequency pulse into the array. The protons resonate to this pulse, that is, they send a return pulse the strength of which depends on how much they were affected by the graded magnetic field. Detecting these pulses allows us to determine the location of protons along the line of the graded magnetic field. The weaker the response, the further down the line is that proton.

Here is an example of the use of MRI technology to infer the anatomical structure of regions of the brain by mapping the diffusion rates of water molecules through the white matter of an elderly person's brain (Howard & Howard, in press). While the research is interesting and important itself, in this chapter it is the implicit principles of the discursive practices with which the research is described and how these are integrated with the planning of the scanning program and its results that is our focus.

The project that the Howards have undertaken exemplifies the use of the two main linking principles of the hybrid paradigm – TPP, the Taxonomic Priority Principle, and TT, the Task-Tool metaphor. It is important to bear in mind that in developing research programs there is a constant back and forth between vernacular or P-grammars and technical or O- and M-grammars, each enriching the other.

The context and focus of the research is briefly described in the P-grammar:

> Moving to a new home or job can be stressful and tiring because we cannot fall back on routines. But gradually we adapt to the novel physical and social surroundings . . . This adaptation involves implicit learning . . . [which] contrasts with the more explicit and elaborate way we learn the names of the new people we are meeting . . . (Howard & Howard, in press)

The reader learns the meaning of 'implicit learning' from the already meaningful P-discourse with which the presentation opens. For example, 'learning' is a P-grammar concept. 'Implicit learning' in this context is linked to already existing P-grammar determined kinds of displays of growing competence in some everyday practice, though the authors do not spell this out.

Equipped with the concept of 'implicit learning' alone, innumerable research programs could be set up to explore it further. The authors go on to work with their own fruitful addition to the taxonomy 'of multiple forms of' implicit learning – the 'aging of implicit learning'. The program develops by bringing to light 'age related deficits' in 'task-dependent patterns of aging', which are now in need of explanation. The project is aimed ultimately at investigating 'brain function' and so will require at some point the utilization of the Task-Tool metaphor to link the performances of the participants to the brain structures and processes that they use to perform these tasks.

A simple taxonomy of tasks distinguishes situations in which different kinds of implicit learning might take place. The research is carried out on an analytical model of the phenomenon of interest rather than on the phenomenon itself – a familiar technique in the natural sciences (Harré, 2006).

The first model for event-sequence learning mixes patterned sequences with random. The second model makes use of repeated and novel spatial configurations. The tasks are implicit in the models. These are models because they are abstractions from the tasks that people would normally undertake and so analogues of patterns of ordinary life.

In a direct application of the Task-Tool metaphor, Howard and Howard (in press) turn their attention to changes that might have occurred in the mechanisms by which people perform implicit learning tasks. The shaping of their research discourse by TT is explicit. 'We propose that the task dependent patterns of age differences reflect different aging in the MTL and striatal-based *learning systems*'. Now the research task can be specified in the O-grammar – 'the two types of implicit learning might prove to be sensitive … indicators of brain function.' This proposal makes sense under the implicit shaping of the discourse defining the research project by the Task-Tool metaphor. Other metaphors are possible and so other research programs of very different characters could branch out from here.

As the research progresses, the shaping grammar shifts from O- to M-. The weakening of the striatal learning system is to be explained in an M-grammar discourse (2011, p. 13). 'The dopamine transporter gene DAT1 regulates synaptic dopamine levels, particularly in the striatum'. Here the talk is of molecules.

The next step involves a proposal using the O-grammar again to reshape the research discourse to make use of Magnetic Resonance Imaging to determine how far 'white matter integrity in the relevant neural tracts is relevant to the distinction between two types of implicit learning. The results showed very clearly that white matter integrity, declining with aging, was correlated with deficits in task performance' (Howard & Howard, in press). Here the discursive presentation of the results make use of the TT metaphor backwards, that is to say, to disclose the fault in the tool that accounts for the decline in the standards of the results of using it. If the commutator in the motor of the drill is scratched or worn the drill may only work intermittently.

To understand how information about the structure of the white matter of a living person's brain was ascertained we need to look a little more deeply into the principles behind the investigative method. Water molecules diffuse through the brain tissue. Diffusion is the spread of one kind of molecule within an environment of molecules of a different kind without the application of any external force, such as stirring the water into which a drop of ink has been added. It comes about because of the random impact of molecules on one another. However, when water molecules are diffusing through brain tissue they progress at different rates depending on the orientation of their tracks to the line of the nerve fibers of which the tissue is made up. These fibers are bundles of neurons each wrapped in a myelin sheath. Crossing a fiber, diffusing water molecules encounter a series of obstacles, while diffusing along a fiber their passage is relatively free. It is easy to see that measurements of the difference of diffusion rates across and along nerve fibers will enable the investigator to map the layout of the constituents of the tissue.

Not only is this an example of a high quality piece of research in neuropsychology, it displays the way that the research discourse, which was used to create and shape the research procedures, depends on implicit shifts in grammars from P-grammar to O-grammar to M-grammar and back to P-. *Our* analysis displays implicit features of Howard and Howard's research-shaping discourse as *they* display implicit features of the performances of their aged participants.

All three examples of neuroscience studies in research into the mechanisms by which certain psychological functioning is accomplished exemplify the two basic principles which we identified in the first chapter.

Ethology: Evolutionary Paths to Useful Tools

The second question that the idea of persons as animals prompts is simply, 'How did we get the brains and their mechanisms that have been revealed by the research described in the first part of the chapter?' One answer might be – by divine creation. If that were the accepted answer nearly all the research so far described would have gone forward. However, the popular answer in the 21st Century is Darwinian. We got this equipment as the result of organic evolution as first described by Charles Darwin and Alfred Russell Wallace and greatly elaborated upon since their pioneering writings.

Ethology, the study of animal behavior in naturalistic settings, has revealed that some fixed routines or patterns of behavior are the result of evolution by natural and sexual selection, such as the anatomical and physiological attributes of living creatures. Other patterns of behavior depend on the evolution of skills or capacities that are put to use by the animal in various ways in different circumstances. These too have a basis in organic evolution.

The 20th century saw a rapid growth in studies of the Darwinian evolution of behavioral patterns, inspired by the pioneering work of Konrad Lorenz (1903–1989), Nikko Tinbergen (1969) and many others. Their researches have shown that there is a complex matrix of inherited routines and capacities which, with acquired skills, are involved in the survival of individuals and in the reproductive lives of animals and birds. These include: the marking out of territories; the struggles to establish and maintain a place in the local social hierarchy; the rituals of the mating season; and many more. Natural selection clearly plays a part in the establishment of inherited routines and also in the background organic conditions, such as neural networks, that make the learning of cultural practices, such as bird song or simple tool using, possible. At the same time this development, when generalized to human beings, has posed the age-old 'nature or nurture' question more sharply, and in a very much complicated way than previously.

Animals have been used in moral tales at least since Aesop collected his fables. In these stories their behavior reflected their natural dispositions to some extent. However, their main role was as illustrations of human vices and virtues. The industrious ant is contrasted both morally and practically with the feckless grasshopper. Darwin himself inaugurated scientific ethology and emphasized the existence of a behavioral continuum with his wonderful study of the display of emotions in animals and man (Darwin, 1872).

Konrad Lorenz (1903–1989) was born in Vienna, the second son of the prominent surgeon Adolf Lorenz. He was able to build a huge house outside the city in the village of Altenberg, close by the river Danube. Here young Konrad spent a good deal of his childhood, commuting to school in the city. In his Nobel autobiography, Lorenz gives a very detailed and lively account of his childhood obsessions with all sorts of animals and birds. His family indulged his hobby and encouraged his projects.

He entered the medical faculty of the University of Vienna. There he came under the influence of Ferdinand Hochstetter, a distinguished embryologist and comparative anatomist. During his time as an assistant in Hochstetter's laboratory, Lorenz continued his comparative studies of the behavior of animals and birds. He had encouraged jackdaws to establish a colony in the attics of his father's house at Altenberg, and there some of his most illuminating work was done. The writings of Oskar Heinroth had a great influence on his own ideas, as did the work of Wallace Craig who persuaded Lorenz to give up the idea of patterns of behavior as 'chain reflexes', in favor of the theory of von Holst, that the origin of behavioral routines was the disinhibiting of pre-existing neural activity.

In discussions with Nikko Tinbergen, in 1936, the key ideas of ethology, namely innate releasing mechanisms and fixed action patterns, were clearly formulated. In 1939, he took up the chair of psychology at Königsberg where he had the opportunity for vigorous discussion on philosophical matters with his idealist colleagues in philosophy.

After the Second World War, during which he served as a doctor on the Eastern Front, he was able to set up a small research station at Altenberg. However, the conservative stance of the Austrian Ministry of Education precluded any hope of a job in Austria for so dedicated a Darwinian as he. He was offered a research station in Germany which became the Max Planck Institute, at Seewiesen, where he remained for the rest of his academic career.

He shared the Nobel Prize for 1974 with his colleagues and friends, Nikko Tinbergen and Eric von Frisch. He continued active work, particularly in developing the application of ethological principles to human behavior.

In 1974, Konrad Lorenz, Nikolaas Tinbergen and Otto Von Frisch shared the Nobel Prize for their revelations of how animals, birds and insects lived in natural surroundings. This work was firmly grounded in Darwinian evolutionary theory. Whatever routines could be shown to be inherited, must have an explanation in terms of their contribution to reproductive success and individual survival.

Not long afterwards, the idea that human beings too might display some of these patterns of thought and action began to be suggested in popular literature (Morris, 1967). The tradition of Aesop was reversed. Now human beings were to be exemplars of at least some of the behavior patterns observed in animals, suitably remodeled for the world of *Homo sapiens*. Though Lorenz contributed to this development, he was always careful to emphasize how different human beings were from even their nearest animal relatives.

What was the influence of ethology on the psychology of the latter part of the 20th century? There were direct influences on social psychology, particularly to be seen in the rise of sociobiology according to which almost all of human life was the product of selection pressures. Perhaps more important in the long run was the legitimating of evolutionary psychology, as a more moderate and less proselytizing doctrine. This has led to innumerable studies of the alleged relationship between genetic endowment and psychological and social attributes of the mature human being (see Chapter 6).

If Darwin was right, the extension of natural selection from anatomical and physiological aspects of organic beings to behavioral routines meant that these patterns should display certain characteristics. They should be activated without having been learned. They should be able to be shown to be adaptive for successful breeding. How far can the Darwinian account of complex behavioral routines be applied to human beings?

Lorenz advocated three major principles or prescriptions for such an extension:

1   The whole range of relevant phenomena had to be comprehended. A fully developed human science must be a hybrid enterprise involving the study of the human organism and the subjective experiences of which such a being is capable.
2   All such studies must be historical, in the sense that Darwinian biology is historical. 'For, if we ask why a particular organism is structured in one way rather than another, the most important answers will be found in the history of the species concerned' (Lorenz, 1977, p. 34). This applies to human beings as much as to other primates, but in the human case the dominant historical force is cultural.
3   Finally, Lorenz took an 'emergentist' view of the status of higher order capacities. An organism ' . . . acquires a number of system characteristics in its evolution' (Lorenz, 1977, p. 33). Life, for him, was 'an eminently active enterprise aimed at acquiring both a fund of energy and a stock of knowledge, the possession of the one being instrumental to the acquisition of the other' (Lorenz, 1977, p. 27).

Naturalistic description must come before any attempt to probe further by active experimentation, an application of our TPP or Taxonomic Priority Principle to animal behavior.

How should we balance the effect of natural selection on behavioral patterns against the effect of the acquisition of rules and customs, the content of ever-changing cultures? E. O. Wilson remarks that genetic evolution of human traits occurred 'over the five million years prior to civilization . . . by far the greater part of cultural evolution has occurred . . . [in the last] 10,000 years . . . The behavior [explained genetically] should be the most general and least rational of the human repertoire . . .' (Wilson, 1978, pp. 34–35). This leaves a great deal of human psychology to be accounted for by cultural factors, evolving symbolic systems that have developed over hundreds of thousands of years, perhaps millions of years.

It seems that humans live in disjoint worlds, and yet are capable of managing meanings as well as transforming the material environment causally. Biological and cultural evolution fit together neatly with the hypothesis that the neural mechanisms which have evolved as the bases of symbolic skills became established under other imperatives. Though we are not evolved to ride bikes, the balance maintaining mechanisms we use for that skill could have arisen in the course of the evolution of bipedalism as a biological advantage in the savannah. We are not evolved to solve differential equations but the ability to count could have had a selectionist origin. Matt Ridley's recent discussion of the balance between biological sources and cultural origins of personal characteristics, competences, capacities and skills is a welcome corrective to the speculations of journalists (Ridley, 2003).

There is a tendency among evolutionary psychologists to slide over the gap between the genesis of a neural mechanism by natural selection and the innovations that are necessary for the employment of such a mechanism in all sorts of culturally defined tasks. Some are everyday, such as cooking or gardening or mending clothes. Others are highly sophisticated, for instance, doing organic chemistry or designing a high-speed train or writing a sonnet. A passage from Hampton's introductory textbook on evolutionary psychology illustrates the temptation to elide the sources of tools with that of tasks. ' . . . our minds are a collection of specific adaptations shaped by natural and sexual selection to solve problems of survival and reproduction' (Hampton, 2009, p. 32). No doubt! But the invention of '0' is essential to sophisticated solutions to some of the problems of 'survival and reproduction', as well as accountancy, space travel and differential calculus. It surely did not arise as a specific adaptation shaped by natural and sexual selection! Did it spread because those who picked up its use from Aryabhata, who found themselves using zero, were thus enabled to have more offspring? On the contrary – it was because Aryabhata's innovation was copied by more and more mathematicians, book keepers and so on, over the ages.

Human Beings as *Homo Sapiens*

In this chapter, our purpose is to illustrate the methods that have been used by neuroscientists and evolutionary psychologists – reporting the results of their researches only by the way. We are not concerned with whether gossip is the cement of social order but how Robin Dunbar (2000) came to this conclusion. The method in evolutionary psychology is only experimental in a limited way. It involves balancing the plausibility of homology between human cognitive and social behavior and animal ethology against the plausibility of treating this relation as no more than analogy. As homology, psychology is just human ethology. As analogy, there are similarities and differences of significance between human psychology and animal ethology. In addition, inferences about the ways of life of ancient populations are drawn from observations of the way hunter-gatherer tribes live nowadays or at least within the record of recent anthropology. Essentially, evolutionary psychology follows the example of Newton and Darwin in the use of fragments of data in the here and now to create a conception of life processes as a thought experiment.

Starting with the observation that the ratio between the size of the neocortex and the rest of the brain increases as we examine various primate species roughly laid out in order of apparent cognitive and social sophistication, we find that the ratio increases to reach 4:1 in *Homo sapiens*. Correlating this ratio with the observable group size among the other primates, the preferred human group ought to have about 150 members. Robin Dunbar has presented a good deal of anthropological and historical evidence for the reality of this estimate. His research is a good example of a thought experiment, setting out a network of analogies and homologies.

Grooming is a powerful cohesive practice among chimps and other non-human primates. What would the corresponding intimate social practice be for people? Grooming unites four or five primates into a social unit. What could unite 150 human beings? It can't be grooming, so the conclusion is not to be found in a homology between apes and people. Dunbar's conclusion is that it must be language, in short, gossip. So we follow Dunbar as he spells out an impressive analogy. His conclusion is not the result of an empirical study.[1] Social psychologists have argued that gossip is a powerful way of reminding the members of a group of the conventions that shape the life of their tribe (Sabini & Silver, 1981). So not only does conversation make possible the favored group size, but also sustains the norms that make the group cohesive.

When did the necessities for this use of language become salient as an evolutionary pressure – perhaps in the Paleolithic era? It seems reasonable to say that our psychology was fixed as far as its biological component goes in that era. All subsequent change has been driven by cultural phenomena. But how does Dunbar know that? Here we meet the second phase of the thought experiment, the projection of our knowledge of contemporary or near contemporary hunter-gatherer societies back through millennia to the societies of Paleolithic times.

Computational Modeling: Persons as Machines

Descartes made a sharp distinction between human beings possessed of immaterial minds and so of immortal souls, and animals, nothing but machines. In the 20th century this idea was revived in the development of computational models of human cognition. Alan Turing's speculations (Turing, 1950, pp. 433–450) about the possibility of conceiving thinking as a kind of computing can be expressed in a simple formula:

Brain/Thinking as Computer/Computing

Taking 'computing' to mean roughly, running a program, we have the makings of a research paradigm. Can we express a cognitive problem in computational terms, that is, as a computable function, run it on a computer and read the result as the solution to the problem? If we can get somewhere near this, two subsidiary research problems emerge.

How like is thinking to computing? Here we need to be able to give a formal expression to the cognitive process of interest as a computational problem, that is, as a representation of the moves that might be made in dealing with a problem *by thinking*. This was the project undertaken by Alan Newell and Herbert Simon (1972). They recorded the steps that people declared that they were taking as they tried to solve a problem. They expressed these steps in a suitable form so that they could be used as input and output to a computer to test a hypothetical set of rules they supposed that people could be using for solving such a problem.

How like is an active brain to a computer in structure and mode of working? We can easily know how a computer is structured and its activity organized. After all, it is a human artifact. If we think the brain or some organ of the brain is like a computer in the way it works and how it is built we can infer that the structure and mode of operation of the relevant brain region is somewhat like that of the computer which mimics it. The original exploration of this question was based on the assumption that the computing machine was a device that realized Turing's basic machine – that is, it performed computations sequentially, step by step. Brain architecture and activity did have aspects of these desiderata, but the limits of this layout for a computational model soon emerged.

However, a different conception of computing developed, actually foreshadowed by some speculations of Turing himself – connectionism. The machine would consist of a network of many simple computational devices connected in parallel arrays, functioning rather like the neurons in a real brain, firing or not firing when they received input from several adjacent neurons depending on a set threshold. Instead of imputing a program, a set of rules for computations, a neural net can be 'trained' by changing the properties of the nodes and the connections between them so that net eventually outputs the correct result for an operation on a chosen input. Suitably coded, '2 + 2' is given to the input surface of the net, and then the net is 'run', that is, the properties of nodes and connections are changed, until the output surface yields '4'. Linking these artificial neurons into nets analogous to real brain structures, connectionist models have been created which can be made to perform some of the functions of the brain components that they model.

Notice that the problem which the net is to be trained to solve is formulated in discursive/cultural terms. What is the result of adding two and two? If we can get our connectionist net to give the 'right' output we can infer, so the method suggests, that the region of the brain which is the tool we use for calculations is structured like our trained net. This is a very simple example – but there has been considerable success in using this method for quite sophisticated cognitive processes. For example, McLeod, Plunkett, and Rolls (1998) have succeeded in producing a working connectionist model of the relevant structures of the hippocampus involved in long-term remembering. The pattern of reasoning employed in this piece of research is particularly clearly set out and makes an admirable exemplar for the technique.

The Human Body as a Site for Chemical Reactions

Here we describe research methods that exemplify the M-grammar, which presupposes that the human body is a site of complex chemical processes. TPP and TT are used to link these research methods and the results of using them to psychological phenomena that are expressed in discourses shaped by the P-grammar.

In this chapter, we are describing actual research methods in a certain amount of detail. Of course, each such example will include the results of the research program it has been used to carry through. However, our purpose is not to report scientific discoveries, but to illustrate the methods by which they were reached and to identify any limitations and difficulties with method and interpretation in actual cases. For example, it is interesting to learn of the recent advances in our understanding of the role of the neurotransmitter dopamine in many aspects of our lives. However, the description of recent dopamine-oriented research to follow is aimed at showing how the results were arrived at, method rather than outcome.

In the study of 'synaptic chemistry', the focus of research is on neural networks and the role of neurotransmitters, the molecules that occur in the synapses between neurons, and are instrumental in the transmission of neural impulses across the synaptic cleft. These are the chemicals involved in passing signals among cells in the brain. Neural signals move along nerve fibers as waves of potential difference between the inside and the outside of the fiber. Neurons meet at synapses. At the presynaptic end of the nerve cell or neuron the arrival of a signal stimulates the production of a neurotransmitter. This substance transfuses through to the synaptic end of a connected neuron, often carried by a 'transport' molecule, where it stimulates the beginning of a wave of potential difference that transmits a signal along the axon in the adjoining cell. In this way the neurotransmitter passes the neural impulse across the synapse, to the dendrites of the next cell in the network, and so on. At each junction there are receptor sites for each type of transmitter molecule on the post-synaptic surface of the next cell. Differences in the number of such sites can affect the effectiveness of a neurotransmitter such as serotonin.

Studies of the relation between different levels of concentration of these molecules and psychological states people experience have shown that neurotransmitters are psychologically relevant. Of course, overlaying the simple correlations between the concentrations of molecules such as serotonin and dopamine and felt emotional states and moods is the complex web of criteria through which people give meanings to their experiences. This complex pattern of linkages across the apparent gap between chemistry and meaningful experience is important in psychopathology. The instrument for managing life events could be malfunctioning, just as a blunt saw is not an ideal tool for high-quality cabinet making. Moreover, the instrument may be in order but the interpretative system may be awry. One may see a smile on the face of a friend and in one's paranoiac way see it as a patronizing smirk.

Here is an example that illustrates an experimental program of active intervention in the chemistry of the brain. Ethical problems about experimenting on people were overcome by using mice as a model for human psycho-biochemistry, with attendant difficulties of assessing the viability of the analogies between mouse and human biochemistry and between mouse and human psychological states.

Serotonin and a Mouse Model

Serotonin, or 5-hydroxytriptamine, is a neurotransmitter very widely distributed in the body. The popular press enthusiastically but often recklessly transfers the results of research on mice by analogy to draw conclusions about people. According to Mark Henderson, a *Times* science correspondent:

> A gene that may explain why some people are more likely to suffer depression has been discovered by scientists, paving the way for improved treatments of mental illness that strikes one in five people . . . Though the mutation has so far been identified only in mice, the findings have excited mental health researchers . . . (*The Times*, 9 July 2004)

Of course, considered scientifically, this is reckless extrapolation. Delving into the story to try and find a nugget of respectable scientific research we find two analogical links. They illustrate the methodology of research into the complex pattern of linkages between gene endowment, neurochemistry and *human* experience. A certain gene, about which more later, influences the production of serotonin in mice. This neurotransmitter is known to be implicated in various aspects of human psychology. Drawing on an analogy between the neurochemistry of mice and that of people, it has been suggested that the corresponding gene in human beings might also influence the production of serotonin. The second link in the pattern of reasoning behind this research method is more tenuous. Does a certain kind of behavior in mice match a corresponding psychological condition in human beings? Only if that link is secure is there any virtue in the mouse model as an analogue for drawing conclusions about the nature and sources of different styles of human experience and activity in relation to different levels of serotonin.

The relevance of serotonin to human psychology is based on a strong correlation between low levels of serotonin and a tendency to depression, seemingly independent of distressing life events. This is direct evidence that serotonin plays some role in the biology of people who have that kind of lowness of spirit we nowadays call 'depression'. It should also be born in mind that there is no way for measuring the amount of serotonin the synapses of the neural nets in the brain directly. Measures are confined to the concentrations of serotonin in the blood. It seems to be a reasonable assumption that high and low levels of this neurotransmitter in the blood reflect high and low levels in the brain.

However striking such correlations might be, they do not give the slightest support to the idea that depression is a chemical phenomenon. This would give rise to the illusion that in the end all we *really know* about depression is chemical. However, biochemical correlations do make a great deal of difference to the treatment of depression if it becomes part of the catalogue of human disorders, though it was not always so.

The chemistry is interesting because it shows how serotonin 'therapy' could be developed to treat 'depression' as a disorder. It is transported across the synapse by a transport protein. Serotonin is produced by and reabsorbed into the presynaptic terminal. This cycle can be affected by 'serotonin reuptake inhibitors' which target the serotonin transport protein. If the transport protein is inhibited then more serotonin will remain in the region of the synapse. In this way a deficit will be made good. Indirect evidence for the correlation comes from the effect of Prozac and similar drugs on people's sense of well-being. These drugs prevent serotonin being reabsorbed and so effectively increase the amount available as a neurotransmitter.

The relevant enzyme that limits the rate of serotonin uptake is tryptophan hydroxylase. Its expression in the brain derives from the gene Tph2, via a complex chain of events.

To follow the reasoning that leads to suggestions about human psychological states in relation to concentrations of serotonin we must first let us look at the *biological* analogy between man and mouse. Zhang, Besaulieu, Sotnikoa, Gaitnetdinov, and Caron (2004) showed that a variation in the gene Tph2 affects the production of serotonin in mice. Mice with the variant gene produce very much less serotonin than normal mice. These data provide direct evidence for a fundamental role of Tph2 in brain serotonin synthesis. What we don't know yet is whether this difference is displayed in the behavior of mice or in the feelings and thoughts of people, that is, whether it has any relevance to psychology.

The mouse not only provides a model for rodent and human biochemistry but also for the second stage of the research program, the step from mouse behavior to human psychology. Luigi Cervo, Canetta, Calcagno, Burbassi, Sacchetti, Caccia et al. (2005) found that when mice are immobilized by a stressful event, such as being put through a 'forced swimming test', those with the variant that is expressed in less tryptophan hydroxylase remain immobile longer than normal mice. They took the immobility to be a behavioral expression of 'mouse depression'. Once the mice were 'depressed', administering an antidepressant, citalopram, made no difference to how long they remained immobile. But if tryptophan was administered before the stressful event, thus bumping up the amount of available serotonin in the depression-prone mice, the antidepressant worked. This showed that the lack of success with the administration of the antidepressant, citalopram, to reduce immobility time in the mice with unremedied lower levels of tryptophan is attributable to the genetic variation. But, what about people?

We now have two bridges to cross. One leads from mouse biology to human biology. The other runs from 'mouse depression' to human depression. Could it be shown that there were similar variants of 'Tph2' that resulted in differences in the amounts of serotonin produced in human beings? Van Den Bogaert, Sleegers, De Zutter, Heyrman, Norrback, Adolfsson et al. (2006) suggested a possible bridge across the species gap. Shorn of technicalities, the research, which was conducted in northern Sweden, showed that two groups of people, one group with simple depressive tendencies and the other with a tendency to manic-depression (now often called 'bipolar disorder') shared a deficiency in serotonin production. Comparing these people genetically with a control group who did not have either of these depressive tendencies, the research showed that variant Tph2 was associated with depressive disorders in sufferers of northern Swedish descent. So far so good, but there is a long way to go before a truly general claim can be substantiated.

Here we have a beautiful example of the hybridization of three psychological research methods – even if in the end the results have to be qualified. 'Depression' and its varieties are discursive categories, that is, they are components of a classification system for experiences having its roots in the common ways of speaking of local cultures. The correlation of the expression of depressive moods with concentrations of serotonin in the neural networks that provide the mechanisms of thought and action leads to the question of the origin of significant neurochemical differences between people. Variants of a relevant gene seem to complete the story very neatly.

In this story it is taken for granted that 'depression' refers to an undesirable state of mind. Depression should therefore be 'cured'. If we turn to the psychology of the renaissance we find the discursive aspects of this story to be very different, only partially fitting our current interpretations of these moods.

In the renaissance, the generic category for 'low moods' was 'melancholia'. The word appears the title of one of great works of psychiatry, Burton's *Anatomy of melancholy* (Burton, 2000[1621]). Burton distinguishes between *atra bilis,* an undesirable mind set, and *candida bilis,* a kind of melancholy that is conducive to deep and creative thinking, not only in the composition of poetry but also for scientific and mathematical thought. Other low states of mind were also identified and examined at that time such as *accidie.* This is a historical descendent of *acedia,* a mood that descended on religious people when their devotions palled. Regimes for the cure of *atra bilis* were matched by regimes for the induction of *candida bilis.* Shakespeare probably gave the most subtle descriptions of depression in any literature, DSM IV notwithstanding. The discoveries about serotonin make no difference at all to the psychological meaning of 'depression' if we think about Hamlet's predicament, or to our understanding of Milton's famous poem 'Il penseroso'. He begins with a passionate greeting: 'But hail thou Goddess sage and holy, Hail divinest Melancholy'. Later in the poem (lines 85–92) he sketches a moment in the life of the scholar thus:

> Or let my Lamp at midnight hour,
>
> Be seen in some high lonely Tower,
>
> Where I may oft out-watch the Bear
>
> With thrice great Hermes,[2] or unsphere
>
> The spirit of Plato to unfold
>
> What Worlds, or what vast Regions hold
>
> The immortal mind that hath forsook
>
> Her mansion in this fleshly nook.

Don't we all somewhere in our souls hanker for at least an interlude of scholarly melancholy?

Even if the neurochemistry of serotonin had been available at that time to track the concentrations of neurotransmitters, the biological research projects emerging from the local ways of understanding 'low moods' would have been radically different.

Conclusion: Breeding the Hybrid

By reshaping the discussion in terms of language, words and their uses and the schemata that shape those uses, we can see more exactly how the hybridization of the discourse of neuroscience comes about by linking the requirements for the relevance of biological and chemical researches to the vernaculars from which our basic concepts of psychology as the study of thinking, feeling, acting and perceiving must have come.

Here we make further use of the proposals of Ludwig Wittgenstein – in this context the idea of the field of family resemblances. When we find a word (in the sense of a vocable or an inscription, a spoken or written word or sentence), used in a variety of contexts, we are tempted to think that there must be something in common to the contexts which will account for this broad band of usage. This presumption is supported by the old idea that all words are names and that their meanings are ultimately what people use them to denote. Thus we slip into the idea that if there is one word in play in a certain culture, in the sense of 'word' above, then there must be one 'something' that accounts for the use of this word in all meaningful contexts. Wittgenstein's examples were rather hum drum – for instance, the fields of use of the word 'rule' and of the phrase 'being guided'. We are tempted to think there must be some essential meaning to each of these expressions that accounts for their being used in the diverse contexts in which they appear. Closer to our interests would be the uses of words like 'memory' or 'anger' which appear both in the English vernacular, in neuroscience and in particular, in neurochemistry. Bemused by the idea that only chemistry, physics and biology are truly sciences, we slip into thinking that vernacular uses of key psychological terminology are either covert ways of referring to neurological phenomena or that the natural science concepts should prevail as the only respectable uses of words for a scientific psychology.

We have been trying to show that psychology will only be progressive as a science by acknowledging that both neuroscience and discursive/cultural psychology are respectable scientific disciplines, *with the latter taking conceptual priority over the former*. What should be our model for hybridization? The uses of key words are embedded in fields of family resemblances and no one use can have such priority over all others that it must displace them as expressing what something truly is. 'Implicit *memory*' when used in reporting priming studies where it is shown how what someone says, sees, thinks or does is influenced by a previous experience of which they were not conscious resembles 'my *memory* of a summer at the beach'. It also resembles the use of the word in 'granny's *memory* is affected by plaques disrupting the relevant brain region'. But the use of the word in verb form, as in 'can you *remember* the French word for "tortoise"?' has less in common with either of the above uses than they have with each other, though it belongs in the same field of family resemblances. And it is well to remember that the use of the word in neuroscience and its use in describing reminiscences are of equal significance as psychology.

The remarkable power of the joint method of linguistic, psychological and neurological research can be illustrated by the successful attack on understanding the neurological basis of the fundamental linguistic distinction between the paradigmatic dimension of word use and the syntagmatic dimension. This distinction was introduced by Ferdinand de Saussure. The paradigmatic dimension of the use of a word is the category of beings referred to. Thus the paradigmatic dimension of 'bread' includes 'cake', 'biscuit', and so on, that is, it belongs in the category of farinacious foodstuffs. The syntagmatic dimension of the word is its sequential relations with others in an endless variety of sentences, such as 'Fetch me some bread', 'I prefer cake to bread', and so on, uses that often involve using the word in question to fulfill our intentions or satisfy our wants. Our ability to use the word to mediate thought and action requires mastery of both dimensions of meaning.

Luria and his team found that lesions in the forward part of the left hemisphere in Broca's area impair fluent speech production, leaving categorization relatively intact.

Patients could name single objects but could not construct complex sentences. However, patients who had lesions in the rear of the head, Wernicke's area, though speaking fluently, could not manage semantic relationships between individual words (Luria, 1979, pp. 169–170). Of course, Luria recognized very well that an undamaged left hemisphere is a necessary but not a sufficient condition for mastery of the productive skills of word use and of language comprehension. This insight has largely stood the test of time. More powerful scanning techniques have shown that there is some involvement of both areas in both speech production and comprehension.

We can look forward to many further hybrid research projects of this kind with a broadening and deepening of our understanding of how human beings go about their lives. Provided, of course, that our research projects are framed in the twin principle of the taxonomic priority of vernaculars and the understanding of the role of the brain in our actions on the metaphor of task and tool.

Notes

1   He did find that the total recipients of the Christmas card blitz from any one family is about 150 persons!
2   Hermes Trismagistus, a mythical mathematician, astronomer and alchemist.

4

The Brain and Consciousness

P. M. S. Hacker

What is important about depicting anomalies precisely? If you cannot do it, that shows that you do not know your way around the concepts. (Ludwig Wittgenstein, 1977, p. 72)

Bogus Mysteries and Bogus Questions

It seems a truth universally acknowledged that consciousness is a mystery. Francis Crick (Nobel laureate) and his colleague Christhof Koch (a neuroscientist) inform us that consciousness is 'the most mysterious aspect' of the mind/brain problem (Crick & Koch, 1992, p. 111). Eric Kandel (Nobel laureate) and his neuroscience colleagues T. D. Albright, T. M. Jessel, and M. I. Posner announce that 'Perhaps the greatest unresolved problem . . . in all of biology, resides in the analysis of consciousness' (Albright, Jessel, Kandel, & Posner, 2000, p. §40). An eminent physiologist Ian Glynn concurs: 'Consciousness has always been a mystery' (Glynn, 1999, p. 193). Psychologists join the chorus. John Frisby writes that consciousness 'remains a great mystery, despite considerable advances in our knowledge of perceptual mechanisms' (Frisby, 1980, p. 11). Philosophers add their voice: Daniel Dennett has remarked that consciousness 'is the most mysterious feature of our minds' (Dennett, 1989, p. 160), and David Chalmers asserts that 'Conscious experience is at once the most familiar thing in the world and the most mysterious' (Chalmers, 1996, p. xi). So, it may indeed be 'universally acknowledged' – but what is acknowledged is no truth. Moreover, with this acknowledgement begins the path to error and confusion. Consciousness is no mystery. The only mystery is that neuroscientists, self-styled cognitive scientists, psychologists and philosophers have persuaded themselves and the educated public who are at their mercy that consciousness *is* a mystery.

Among the many who view consciousness as a mystery it is generally acknowledged that consciousness is a property of the brain. In addition, it is widely held there are two great scientific problems concerning consciousness. The first, which is sometimes alleged to be the greatest problem facing cognitive neuroscience, is: What are the neural correlates of consciousness? The second problem is addressed to evolutionary theorists. It is: What are the evolutionary advantages of consciousness? It is commonly assumed that there could be creatures just like us in every behavioral respect, but lacking consciousness. (These fictitious beings are referred to as 'zombies'.) So what advantage does consciousness confer on us if there could be creatures just like us, but without it? What is consciousness for? Finally, there is alleged to be a deep question for metaphysics: How is the mysterious phenomenon of consciousness reconcilable with our scientific view of the universe? How could something like consciousness emerge from mere matter? Given what we know about the physical universe, how is consciousness possible? – But, despite 'truths universally acknowledged', consciousness is not a property of the brain. The quest for *the* neural correlate of consciousness is a chimerical one, the question about the evolutionary justification of consciousness is misconceived, and the metaphysical question, like all metaphysical questions, is not a question in need of an answer, but a question in need of probing questions. The purpose of this chapter is demystification. The mysteries are all of our own making.

Francis Crick (1916–2004) was born in Northampton in England. He was educated at Northampton Grammar School and Mill Hill School in London. At University College London, he studied physics, graduating in 1937. In 1940, he married Ruth Dodd. Their marriage was dissolved and he later married Odile Speed. During the Second World War he worked on methods for the protection of shipping from magnetic and acoustic mines.

After the war he moved to Cambridge, eventually joining the Medical Research Council Unit led by M. F. Perutz. In 1951, he met James Watson, with whom he collaborated in the work that led to the discovery of the double helical structure of DNA, for which he and Watson, with Maurice Wilkins, received the Nobel Prize in 1962. He continued to work on the understanding of the genetic code, particularly with Sidney Brenner for some years.

In 1976, he moved to the Salk Institute in La Jolla, California and began an intensive study program around the nature and origin of consciousness in collaboration with Christof Koch. While acknowledging the existence of qualia, elementary sensory experiences that do not have anything obviously material about them, he began a program of research aimed at discovering the neural correlates of conscious experiences. He became the de facto leader of a movement to try to establish the non-spiritual nature of consciousness. The publication of his consciousness studies in *The astonishing hypothesis* in 1994 caused something of a stir because of its uncompressing reductionism. "'You', your joys and your sorrows, your memories and your ambitions, your sense of personal identity and free will, are in fact no more than the behavior of a vast assembly of nerve cells and their associated molecules'. Not surprisingly this blunt claim has attracted a good deal of criticism.

He died in San Diego, California.

Traditional Confusions about Consciousness

In order to demystify consciousness and to break the spell that scientists, psychologists and philosophers have woven round it, we must briefly explore the origins of the term 'consciousness' and the history of the roles allocated to it by philosophers and psychologists since its introduction. The English word 'consciousness' and its cognates are of 17th-century origin. So is the French *la conscience* when used to signify a faculty of inner sense. The German *Bewusstsein* is 18th-century coinage, introduced to translate what was by then well-established English and French philosophical usage. I shall defer consideration of the ordinary use of the words 'conscious', 'conscious of' and 'consciousness' until later in the chapter, and focus first upon the introduction of the term into philosophical thought in the 1640s.

The familiar and well-worn Latin verb *conscius*, which meant 'knowing together with another' or just 'knowing well' was transformed by Descartes. It was harnessed to a new yoke, and made to carry the burden of *knowledge of our own current mental operations*. The pivotal notions in Cartesian metaphysics were the transparency of the mind, and the infallibility and indubitability of one's current 'thoughts' (*cogitationes*). *Thought* was construed to signify not only thinking, but also seeming to perceive, feeling sensations as if in the body, feeling passions, imagining and willing. For these mental operations seemed to be such that they cannot occur without being known to occur. It is, according to Descartes, impossible for one to think and not to be conscious of one's thought. The occurrence of such operations of the mind seemed indubitable. One cannot, Descartes held, doubt whether one is or is not thinking whatever one is thinking. Moreover, one cannot be mistaken in taking oneself to be thinking whatever one is thinking. One's consciousness of one's thoughts is infallible.

Although Descartes did not use the expression 'inner sense' to characterize consciousness of one's mental operations, it rapidly came into use.[1] Arnauld and La Forge in France and Cudworth in Britain all explained that to be conscious of what passes in one's mind is to know one's 'thoughts' or 'mental operations' *by means of an internal sense*. Locke, writing half a century after Descartes, characterized consciousness not epistemically, in terms of indubitability and incorrigibility, but psychologically, in terms of 'the perception of what passes in a Man's own Mind' (*Essay*, II-i-4: 125). We cannot perceive without perceiving that we perceive (ibid., II-xxvi-9). It was in order to translate the phrase 'perceiving one's perceptions' into French that Leibniz coined the technical French term 'apperception'. The notion of *apperception* was duly Germanified and transmitted to Kant. However, Thomas Reid, writing at the same time as Kant, sharply differentiated consciousness from perception, and denied the analogy between consciousness of one's mental operations and one's perception of the material world by means of the senses. '*Consciousness*', Reid wrote, 'is a word used by Philosophers, to signify that immediate knowledge we have of our present thoughts and purposes, and, in general, of all the present operations of our minds' (Reid, 2002[1785], p. 24). Strikingly, it was only in the 19th century that the word 'to introspect' (also of late 17th-century provenance) was corralled into philosophical service for the purpose for which Leibniz had coined the verb 'to apperceive'. At the end of the 19th century, William James wrote apropos the methods of investigation in psychology:

> Introspective observation is what we have to rely on first and foremost and always. The word introspection need hardly be defined – it means, of course, the looking into our mind and reporting what we there discover. Everyone agrees that we there discover states of consciousness. (James, 1890, vol. i, p. 185)

He betrayed the Cartesian origins of this confused notion in his addendum 'That we have *cogitations* of some sort is the *inconcussum* in a world most of whose other facts have at sometime tottered in the breath of philosophic doubt' (ibid.).

What is of capital importance is not that Descartes introduced the idea of consciousness into early modern philosophy, but that he revolutionized philosophy of psychology by reference to it. For it was Descartes who created the modern conception of the mind and of mental phenomena.

The scholastics, working in the tradition of Aquinas and Aristotle, conceived of the mind as the powers of the intellect and rational will. Accordingly, sensation, perception and appetite, which we share with animals, were not conceived to be distinctive of the human mind at all. What is distinctive of the mind and is a mark of the mental is sensitivity to reasons and to reasoning. The mind was not conceived to be an immaterial substance, but an array of rational powers of the human agent. Powers are studied by observing their exercise. The intellect and the rational will are properly exercised in human behavior and interaction. So they are best studied not by introspection but by observation of what human beings say and do in the circumstances of their lives.

Descartes swept this tradition away. He forged a novel conception of the mind as a mental substance causally linked to the human body. The essence of the mind, he argued, is thought (in his extended sense of the term). Thought, he defined as whatever passes in our minds such that we are conscious of it. Accordingly the mark of the mental is *consciousness*. This conception was destined to dominate European philosophy for the next four centuries. It holds our intellect in a vice to this very day. In the 19th century, philosophy of mind, physiology and physiological physics gradually gave birth to psychology. Psychology, at its inception, was conceived to be the study of the nature of the human mind, that is: *of consciousness*.

It is helpful to have an overview of the conception of consciousness characteristic of Cartesian philosophy and its heirs. This can be given in the form of 10 theses:

1 **Consciousness is the general form of operations of the mind.**
2 **Consciousness is an inner sense.**
3 **The deliverances of consciousness are indubitable.**
4 **The deliverances of consciousness are infallible.**
5 **The objects of consciousness are limited to the operations of the mind.**
6 **The objects of consciousness are limited to the present.**
7 **The objects of consciousness are privately owned (e.g. no one else can have my pains).**
8 **The objects of consciousness are epistemically private (the subject has privileged access to his own mental operations).**
9 **Consciousness of what passes in one's mind requires possession of ideas or concepts of mental operations. These ideas or concepts have no logical relationship to behavior, since they are applied to the objects of inner sense without reference to behavior. To possess such ideas or concepts requires no more than consciousness of the mental operations of which they are ideas, or private ostensive definition.**[2]
10 **Consciousness of the operations of the mind is conceived to be self consciousness – that is, consciousness of how things are with one's self.**

Note that this is a Galtonian picture. Leibniz and Kant acknowledged that there are 'minute perceptions' that fall below the threshold of apperception. In the early 20th century, Freud was to make the idea of *unconscious* mental operations central to psycho-analysis. Reid denied that consciousness is a kind of sense, insisting rather that it is a natural form of immediate knowledge of the contents of the mind. In the 19th century, Spencer and Compte denied that the deliverances of consciousness are infallible or indubitable, insisting that they are on the same level as outer perceptions. Locke denied that consciousness is limited to the present, insisting that memory is consciousness of the past. Mill denied that consciousness is precisely contemporaneous with its object, insisting that it involves memory of what has just occurred in the mind. Nevertheless, this Galtonian picture captures well the received conception of consciousness in the Cartesian and empiricist tradition. And every single thesis is radically mistaken.[3]

The inspiration for the introduction of the concept of consciousness into philosophy was the seemingly straightforward question: How does one know what passes in one's mind? The conviction that one *does* know rested on the idea that one *cannot doubt*, or be mistaken, about the warranted self-ascribability of a certain range of mental attributes. Moreover, it was held, one *cannot be ignorant* of the warranted self-ascribability of such mental attributes either. If one is in pain, one cannot be ignorant of the fact that one is, cannot doubt that one is, and one cannot be mistaken either – one cannot mistake a pain for a feeling of delight. One cannot mistake thinking that *p* for thinking that *q*, or wanting an X for intending to V. And so on. Of course, perceiving in all its variety is fallible. It may seem to one that one sees an X, or hears a Y – and yet one may be mistaken in thinking that one saw or heard anything. So acts of perception are not acts of thought. But *seeming to perceive* (its visually seeming to one just as if there is a dagger before one, for example) is an indubitable and infallible act of thought of which one cannot be ignorant. In short, what defines the mind was held to be consciousness. Of its contents, one has indubitable and infallible knowledge by means of consciousness (apperception, introspection).

However, the whole Cartesian picture, with its epistemological (and metaphysical) motivation, is radically misconceived. The very question that lies at its center is misguided. For insofar as there are certain attributes the self-ascription of which *cannot* be doubted or mistaken, those self-ascribed attributes *are not objects of possible knowledge at all.* For insofar as it is true that one cannot doubt that one is in pain when one is, cannot be mistaken that one thinks that *p* whenever one does, cannot doubt that it visually seems to one that *q*, that is not because the justifications for certainty exclude doubt, and indisputable grounds of correctness exclude error. It is rather because *it makes no sense* to doubt or be mistaken in such cases. Were someone to announce that perhaps he has a headache, perhaps he doesn't, but he is uncertain which, we would ask him what he meant. Were someone to say that he was under the impression that he thought that *p*, but maybe he was mistaken, we would not understand him. *Such doubt and mistake are excluded by grammar – we have given no sense to such forms of words.* But the Cartesian and empiricist tradition confused the logical exclusion of doubt with the presence of justified certainty, the logical exclusion of mistake with the presence of indisputable correctness, and the logical exclusion of ignorance with the satisfaction of the criteria for knowledge. But it is precisely because ignorance, doubt and error are *logically* excluded that knowledge, certainty and correctness are likewise logically excluded. After all, outside philosophical seminars, no one has ever heard another say 'I am certain I am in pain' or 'I am sure I am right in thinking that I am in pain'. And if anyone has ever heard the utterance 'I know I am in pain' it would be no more than an exasperated emphatic assertion that the speaker is indeed in pain and doesn't have to be reminded of the fact. One does indeed say such things as 'I know what I want!' – but that, if it is not merely an emphatic insistence that one really does want what one has previously avowed one wants, is closer to an exclamation indicative of having made up one's mind or a report of having come to a conclusion than to an epistemic claim. 'I don't know *what* I want!' is not a declaration of *ignorance*, but of *indecision*. Such indecision is not remedied by 'introspective scrutiny' of one's desire, but by reflection on the relative desirability of the available options.

So, the very question that gave rise to the Cartesian-empiricist philosophical concept of consciousness was misconceived. 'When I think that *p*, how do I *know* that I think that *p*?' should be answered 'You don't *know* that you think that *p* – but, of course, *neither are you ignorant* of your thinking that *p*'. The construal of consciousness as a faculty of inner sense was indeed predicated upon the assumption that one *knows* by means of consciousness (apperception, introspection) how things are with one 'inwardly'. But there is no such thing as a sense faculty without any sense organ. There is no such thing as a sense faculty the exercise of which is not dependent upon observation conditions. And there is no such thing as a cognitive faculty that is immune to doubt and error. True, when we are thinking, we can say what we're thinking. ('A penny for your thoughts!') When we think we perceive an X, we can describe what we take ourselves to perceive. When we want an X, we can ask for or request one. It was characteristic of the whole post-Cartesian tradition to confuse the ability to say with the ability to see (introspect).

Of course, there is such a thing as introspection, but it is not a kind of 'inner sense', it is a form of reflection. One's ability to say *that* one perceives and *what* one perceives, one's ability to say what one thinks or believes, one's ability to characterize one's feelings and attitudes, are not the upshot of reflection. The introspective person, like Proust, is one who dwells on his feelings, thoughts, attitudes, motives and reasons for action, who thinks about his character traits and dispositions, and wonders about their origin, and so forth. Being able to say that one has a headache and wants a glass of water, being able to say that one is tired and intends to go to bed, is not the upshot of introspection and not the mark of an introspective person.

It should be noted how the Cartesian/empiricist conception of the mental not only extended the boundaries of the mind and of the mental far beyond anything that would have been countenanced by the Aristotelian scholastics, but that it simultaneously contracted or distorted it in ways that their predecessors would rightly have found strange. For while they incorporated (apparent) sensation and perception, as well as the reproductive imagination into the domain of the mind, they had either to exclude or give a grossly distorted account of belief, memory, understanding, wanting and the rational will, since these are not mental phenomena (appearances or experiences). But the empiricists characteristically represented them as such – construing belief and memory as feelings, understanding as a mental state, wanting as felt desire, and the will as a combination of the belief-feeling and the feeling of desire.

The Analysis of the Concept of Consciousness

Given the historical confusions, it is worth pausing to remind oneself of what consciousness is, and what it is to be conscious of something. There is no mystery here, and we need but bring to mind how these expressions are used. For the ordinary concept of consciousness evolved at much the same time as the misconceived philosophical/psychological concept, and with much happier results. For while the philosophical employment of the term led to a morass of incoherence, the common or garden use of the term evolved into an important and highly useful set of *specialized* instruments in our conceptual toolkit.

We may start by distinguishing transitive from intransitive consciousness. Transitive consciousness is consciousness *of* something and consciousness *that* something is so. Intransitive consciousness is contrasted with being unconscious. It is something one loses when one is knocked out, intoxicated or anaesthetized and subsequently regains or recovers when one wakes up.

Transitive consciousness may be dispositional or occurrent. Dispositional transitive consciousness is exemplified by being class-conscious, money-conscious, or safety-conscious. These expressions signify a disposition to be struck by matters of class, a tendency to be occupied with the cost of things, and a propensity to be concerned with considerations of safety.

Occurrent transitive consciousness belongs to a small group of verbs of *cognitive receptivity*.[4] Other members of the family are being aware, realizing, and noticing. All are *cognitive* verbs, that is: they signify forms of coming to know or of knowing something.[5] Hence they are *factive* verbs. So, for example, if one is conscious of something or that something is so, then it follows that it is present or that things are as one is conscious of them as being. Nevertheless, although they are all cognitive verbs, they are not *achievement* verbs or *success* verbs. They do not signify the achievement of knowledge (as do such verbs as 'detect', 'discern', 'discover', 'find out') which may be the successful upshot of endeavor. Rather, they indicate the *reception of knowledge* – the manner in which knowledge is *given* one, by something's striking one, dawning on one, or catching and holding one's attention. To become conscious or aware of something, to notice or realize something, is not a matter of attaining knowledge as a result of one's efforts. One cannot try or attempt to become conscious or aware of something, or to realize or notice something (although one may make an effort to note something). One cannot intend or decide to become conscious of something, nor plan to realize or resolve to notice something. For these are not *acts* or *activities* that one might perform voluntarily, intentionally, deliberately or on purpose. That is why one cannot be ordered or forbidden to become or be conscious of something. (Consequently any account of consciousness as second-order thought (thinking about one's thinking) is mistaken.)

Although transitive consciousness, unlike mere attention, is generally a form of knowledge, it is a very specific one. One can know something well (e.g. Latin), thoroughly (e.g. physics), intimately (e.g. Jill), or in detail (the history of St John's College), but one cannot be conscious of something well, intimately, thoroughly or in detail. For to be conscious of something is neither to exercise a skill, nor to be an expert in a given domain of knowledge. One cannot be trained to be conscious of things, only trained in greater *receptivity*. One cannot be skillful at becoming conscious of things – although one may be more *sensitive* and hence receptive to certain things. One can be good at learning, discovering, detecting and finding out that things are thus-and-so, but one cannot be good at becoming or being conscious of things. One can find out that one knows something (e.g. the way from Kensington to St Albans, the dates of the English monarchs), but one cannot find out that one is conscious of something (as opposed to finding out what has caught one's attention). One may ask 'How do you know?', but not 'How are you conscious of … ?' Rather, one asks 'What made you conscious of … ?' There are sources of knowledge (perception, inductive evidence, reason, hearsay, authority), but no sources, as opposed to causes, of what one is conscious of.

Occurrent transitive consciousness has three faces:

1   Having one's attention caught and held by something;
2   Something's weighing with one in one's current deliberation;
3   Something's occupying one's mind and knowingly coloring one's thoughts, feelings and manner of behaving.

The classical philosophical supposition that what one is conscious of is limited to the current operations of one's mind, is wholly mistaken. Transitive consciousness may take many different kinds of object:

(a) What one perceives – both objectually and factually, that is to say, both objects, properties and relations, and things being perceived to be so, events and processes. This we may call 'perceptual consciousness'.
(b) Facts previously learnt and that are currently occupying one's mind, weighing with one in one's deliberations, and coloring one's thoughts and behavior.
(c) One's actions.
(d) What one feels or feels to be so, that is to say, a *subset* of traditional 'mental operations'. This may include sensations, felt inclinations, felt desires and urges, intimations, felt emotions. This by no means includes the whole range of the 'contents of the mind'. And ironically, it is precisely here – in part of the range that so obsessed Descartes – that any talk of *knowing* is either misplaced or non-epistemic.
(e) Self-consciousness – which is not a form of consciousness of a self, or of how things are 'inwardly' with oneself.

I shall elaborate:

Perceptual consciousness is a matter of having one's attention caught and held by something one perceives. Because one *becomes* and then *is* conscious of something, what one is conscious of (unlike what one notices) must pre-exist one's becoming conscious of it, and must last for a time. (One may notice a flash of lightening, but one may become and then be conscious of its raining outside.) One cannot be conscious (unlike being aware) of many things at a time, for one cannot attend to many different things at the same time. One cannot remain conscious of something that no longer holds one's attention, although one may remain aware of it.[6] One cannot either be or fail to be conscious of something to which one is *intentionally* paying attention, any more than one can unintentionally lie, discover something one already knows, or detect something one has already found out. Consequently perceptual consciousness is commonly a matter of peripheral attention.

Because perceptual consciousness is not only a form of attention (a passive form) but also a form of knowledge (a form of reception of it), merely having one's attention caught and held by something is not sufficient for being conscious of it. One must also *realize* what it is that has caught one's attention. One may have one's attention caught by something one perceives, yet *not* be conscious of what one perceives because one misidentifies it (as when one mistakes a shadow in the bushes for an animal). To be perceptually conscious of something is not to apperceive – for what catches and holds one's attention is what one perceives, not one's perceiving what one perceives.

Factual consciousness: the cognitive receptivity of perceptual consciousness includes consciousness of perceived fact. But not all consciousness of fact involves either perception or cognitive receptivity. It can equally well be a matter of knowledge *already possessed* coming to mind, occupying one and affecting one's thoughts, deliberations and feelings, as well as one's behavior. Hence, one may be conscious of the honor being done one, of the fragility of the economic recovery, or of the gravity of the situation. This is not a matter of one's attention being caught and held, but of information of which one is already well aware being before one's mind and weighing with one in one's deliberations, as when one is conscious of the dangers facing one. But it need not be something affecting deliberation and decision. It may be information that colors one's thoughts and affects the manner of one's behavior, as when one is conscious of the grief of one's widowed friend.

Consciousness of one's actions may take either of two forms: agential or spectatorial. One is conscious of one's actions qua spectator when one suddenly becomes aware of something one is doing and realizes it – as when one becomes conscious that the joke one is telling in a lecture is one that one already told last week. One is conscious of what one is doing qua agent when one 'consciously and deliberately' does something.

Consciousness of what one feels or feels to be so (in the extended sense of the term that includes hunches, intimations, occurrent emotions, felt attitudes and inclinations) is the form of consciousness that obsessed the post-Cartesian philosophical tradition. As we have noted, it was inflated by them to incorporate *all* the 'operations of the mind', and misrepresented by them as a form of perception (apperception or introspection) and as a mode of indubitable and infallible knowledge. But consciousness of what one feels is not a mode of perception at all. Far from being a paradigm of certain and indubitable empirical knowledge, if it logically excludes ignorance, doubt and error, it is not a form of knowledge at all. The ability to *say* how things are with one in the relevant respects does not rest on having *found out* or *come to know* anything. No one other than those corrupted by bad philosophy would speak of being conscious of seeing, hearing, tasting or smelling something, as opposed to being conscious of what one sees, hears, tastes or smells. Blindsight, *pace* Weiskrantz, is not a case of seeing without being conscious of one's seeing, and consciousness is not an internal monitor that 'scans' one's 'visual sensations' converting them into 'visual perceptions' (see Hyman, 1991). Nor would anyone uncalloused by philosophy say that they became and then were conscious of knowing, recollecting, thinking or believing this or that. If someone were to express his opinion by saying 'I think that inflation will rise before the end of the year' and were asked whether he was conscious of so thinking, he would not know what was meant or what to say. Of course, he would not say 'no', since that would seem to imply that he opined thus but was ignorant of so opining, and *that* he would not wish to say.

What is the connection between consciousness of what one feels and other forms of consciousness? Sensations are not perceptibilia. But they do catch and hold one's attention. Hence the propriety of saying that one became conscious of the increasing pain in one's back, of one's cramped position, or of one's great weariness. We may also become and then be conscious of our affections, and changes in our affections – of our rising irritation as the speaker drones on, of our feeling of jealousy as our spouse flirts with another. So too we may become and be conscious of our moods, our depression or cheerfulness. Affective consciousness typically takes the form of realization, rather than captured attention – for it often dawns on us that we are feeling jealous or irritable, and we sometimes dwell on our feelings of depression. Consciousness of the attitudes we feel, of our likes and dislikes, approvals and disapprovals are likewise typically the upshot of realization, the object of which then occupies us. We can become conscious of the misgivings we feel, of our feeling that it is time to go, or of our feeling inclined to take another drink – if these cross our mind and we dwell on them prior to resolving what to do. It is interesting that 'being aware of' fits more comfortably here than 'being conscious of'.

Self-consciousness, in one of the common or garden senses of the phrase, is a form of perceptual consciousness. It is a matter of one's attention being caught by others' eyes being upon one (or of thinking that they are), and of this causing one to feel embarrassed and to behave unnaturally. In another innocuous sense, we speak of self-conscious artists or writers who reflect at length upon their work – by contrast with spontaneous artists or writers. What they do is then done 'consciously and deliberately', rather than intuitively and spontaneously. What self-consciousness is certainly *not* is a cognitive source of the ability to express one's sensations, perceptions and affections. It takes time for a child to master sufficient language to say 'I have a tummy-ache', 'I can see pussy in the garden' or 'I like biccies'. But when it does, this achievement does not betoken the dawning of self-consciousness, let alone of self-knowledge.

More Conceptual Disasters: The Sorry Tale of Contemporary 'Consciousness Studies'

Two important shifts in the prevalent conception of the mind occurred in the post-war years. The first was the increasing tendency among both scientists and philosophers to *identify* the mind with the brain and mental states with brain states. The second was a reaction against cognitive psychology and functionalism in the philosophy of mind, which duly affected theoretically minded psychologists and cognitive neuroscientists. These two complementary changes led to ever-growing confusions concerning the nature of the mind, and contributed further to the mystification of consciousness.

Whereas the great pioneers of modern neuroscience, such as Sherrington, Adrian, Eccles and Penfield, were dualists, the third generation of 20th-century cognitive neuroscientists were adamant monists. They rightly denied the existence of mental substances. However, in so doing, they tumbled from the frying pan into the fire. For they labored under the illusion that the fundamental error of the Cartesian conception of man was its dualism. This, they thought, could easily be remedied by identifying the mind with the brain. (This is rather like realizing that the horse-power of a car does not consist in invisible horses, and jumping to the conclusion that it is identical with cylinders.) Abandoning the Cartesian predilection for the 'ethereal', neuroscientists, as well as psychologists and philosophers, *identified the mind with the brain*, sometimes even making use of Noam Chomsky's oxymoron – the 'mind/brain'.[7] Apart from that, they left the rest of the Cartesian account of the mental intact. Where the Cartesian/empiricist tradition was prone to ascribe all mental predicates to the mind, our contemporaries ascribe them to the brain. So the brain is now said to think, believe, perceive, understand, know and remember. Dualists had characterized *the mind* by reference to consciousness, our contemporaries hold that consciousness is a property of *the brain*. Brain-body dualism displaced mind-body dualism; or, to put it less ironically and more technically: substance monism replaced substance dualism, but the *structural* dualism of the prevalent tradition was retained intact.

In mid-20th-century Gilbert Ryle's *Concept of mind* (1949) launched a critical onslaught on the Cartesian conception of the mind and the mental. Ryle explained belief, thought and motivation in dispositional terms, but he did not attempted to reduce sensations (e.g. pain) or mental images to behavior and behavioral dispositions. However, Central State Materialism (the 'Australasian Heresy'), pioneered by U. T. Place and J. J. C. Smart, attempted such a reduction by arguing that sensations and mental images are in fact contingently identical with states of the central nervous system. Within a decade, the subtle and refined Rylean analyses were brushed aside by D. M. Armstrong in favor of *global* type-identity of *mental states* and brain states. This, however, was rapidly abandoned, partly due to difficulties associated with *type*-identity. It was replaced by functionalism (H. Putnam and D. Lewis), which seemed more in tune with the new cognitive (or more properly: computational) psychology pioneered by such figures as Jerome Bruner. Functionalists thought to characterize what they called 'mental states' in terms of informational inputs, behavioral outputs and causal relations with other mental states. The dominant analogy was with the machine table of a Turing machine. The contingent 'realization' in humans of any given mental state was held to be a token neural state. This conception of a mental state won a considerable following in the USA and Australia.

Daniel Dennett (1942–) was born in Boston the son of an historian by the same name. He studied at Harvard and received his BA in 1963. He then went to Oxford to work with Gilbert Ryle, under whose supervision he completed the D Phil in philosophy in 1965 on the topic of 'The Mind and the Brain'. Returning to the United States, he taught at U.C. Irvine from 1965 to 1971, when he moved to Tufts, where he has been ever since. He has held a number of visiting posts at Harvard, Pittsburgh, Oxford, and the École Normale Supérieure in Paris. He gave the John Locke Lectures at Oxford in 1983, the Gavin David Young Lectures at Adelaide, Australia, in 1985, and the Tanner Lecture at Michigan in 1986, among many others.

His first book, *Content and consciousness*, which appeared in 1969, was widely read and was followed by further explorations in the philosophy of psychology. The best known have been *Brainstorms* (1978), and *Consciousness explained* (1991). His most recent publication on the consciousness theme, *Sweet dreams: Philosophical obstacles to a science of consciousness*, was published in 2005.

He lives with his wife in North Andover, Massachusetts, and has a daughter, a son, and three grandchildren.

It was on the back of this bizarre scientism that science fiction entered the debate. Functionalism seemed to have all the virtues of behaviorism without denying the traditional causal role of the mental, and it fitted the emerging computational psychology of the time. On the other hand, it seemed *to have eliminated experience itself*. The position for which it argued was compatible, it seemed, with the thought that there could be 'zombies', in other words, creatures who behave exactly as we do, with the same inputs and outputs and causal relations between inner (computational) states, but without *any experience* whatsoever – there is, as it were, *darkness inside!* But, it was argued, *we* are not 'zombies' – we are *conscious beings*, we have *conscious experiences* – there is, so to speak, *light inside!* It was this response to a misconceived doctrine that led to the emergence of the new conception of consciousness, and the new wave of consciousness theorists among philosophers and, in due course, also among psychologists and cognitive neuroscientists.

It began with a seminal paper by T. Nagel (1974), entitled 'What is it like to be a bat?', which sowed the seed of fresh confusions.

Nagel argued that conscious experience is such that there is something which it is like for its subject to have it. For surely, there is something it is like for one to be in pain, to see or hear, to love or lust, and so forth. A conscious creature, unlike a 'zombie', is a creature that *has consciousness experiences*. This 'something which it is like for the subject', the 'phenomenal feel' of experience, was denominated the 'qualitative character of experience'. *Every* experience, it was argued, has a unique qualitative feel. Knowing what it is like for one to have the experiences one has is denominated 'phenomenal consciousness'. Moreover, there is something that it is like for a conscious creature to be the creature it is. There is not something it is like for a jet-ink printer to be a jet-ink printer, but for sure, there is something it is like for us to be humans, or for a dolphin to be a dolphin. Indeed, there is something which it is like for a bat to be a bat, even though *we* cannot in principle know what it is like. For one can know what it is like for a creature to undergo a certain experience or what it is like for a given creature to be the creature it is, only if one occupies the same 'point of view' as it, or can imaginatively do so. But we cannot occupy the point of view of a bat or even imagine what it is like for a bat to be a bat. And finally, there is something it is like for me to be me – although it may well be quite impossible for me to tell anyone exactly *what* it is like, since no one can share my 'point of view' upon the world (share my 'subjectivity', as some enthusiasts put it).

Just as the Cartesians extended the notion of *thought* to include sensation, perception and emotions (which are not forms of thought), the new wave of consciousness studies extended the notion of *experience* to include such things as believing, thinking, and understanding (which are not forms of experience). Just as the Cartesians and empiricists defined the mind in terms of conscious thought (conceived as the field of apperception or introspection), so the new wave defined the mind in terms of conscious experience (conceived as the field of phenomenal consciousness).

This mesmerizing doctrine caught on like wildfire. It spread from philosophy to psychology and cognitive science, and thence to cognitive neuroscience. What was a mere ripple in 1974 had reached tsunami proportions by the new century. There is overwhelming consensus among members of the self-styled 'consciousness studies community' that consciousness is to be defined in terms of the 'what-it's-likeness' of experience.[8] It was on the back of these intellectual aberrations that all the 'deep mysteries' emerged. Since zombies were held to be possible, what was the point and purpose of consciousness? What is its evolutionary advantage? How is phenomenal experience related to the brain? How can the subjective qualities of experience emerge from cortical tissue? What are the neural correlates of conscious experience? How is the phenomenon of consciousness to be rendered compatible with all that we know about the physical universe? And so forth. But the mysteries are rooted in illusions. Remove the illusions and the mysteries vanish.

The Logic of Illusion: The 'What-it's-likeness' of Experience

It is true that one cannot ask an ink-jet printer what it is like to print a page. One can't ask an ink-jet printer anything! One cannot ask a dolphin what it is like to eat its favourite fish, but it is evident from its behavior that eating herrings is enjoyable for dolphins. The question

'What is it like for an X to V?' can arise only for sentient creatures that exhibit hedonic (and anti-hedonic) attitudes towards their experiences and the objects of their experiences. That is news from nowhere. We may ask someone 'What is it like for you to V?', and the answer takes the form of a hedonic (or anti-hedonic) predicate, for example 'It's delightful (charming, most enjoyable)' or 'It's very painful (revolting, horrible)'. Note two crucial points.

First, it is not true that everything one does, undergoes or experiences is such that there is an answer to the question 'What was it like for you to V?' – Reflect on the following questions addressed to normal people under normal circumstances: 'What is it like for you to look at the buttons on your shirt?', 'What was it like to walk past the lamp post?', or 'What is it like for you to see the tree in the quad?' – The answer can only be – 'What *do* you mean?' For such experiences are neither pleasant nor unpleasant, neither interesting nor boring. They normally have no qualitative character at all, but are quite indifferent. The vast range of experiences are qualitatively neutral.

Second, *if* for some reason one wishes to engage in second-level existential generalization (existential quantification over predicates) with respect to answers to the question 'What is it like for you to V?', the form it takes is *not* 'There is something it is like to V', but rather 'There is something that it *is* to V'. If you are asked 'What was it like for you to smell the roses?', the answer may be 'It was wonderful (heavenly)', but not (save in California) 'It was like wonderful (or: like heavenly)'. So the existential generalization is 'There is something *that it was* for you to smell the roses, namely wonderful', and not 'There was something it was like for you to smell the roses, namely wonderful'. So it is doubly mistaken to suppose that every experience is such that there is something it is like for one to undergo it. For not every experience has a qualitative character, and for no experience is it true that there is something that it is like to have. In fact, the latter expression is not even English.

It is true that one can ask someone what it is like for them to be a tinker, a tailor, a soldier or a sailor. Their answer will describe the joys and sorrows of the role as they have fulfilled it. The general form of the question is 'What is it like for an X to be a Y?' (e.g. 'for a woman (as opposed to a man) to be a soldier?' or 'for a woman to be a soldier (as opposed to being a sailor)' or, more personally, 'What is it like for you to be a Y?' (e.g. 'What was it like for you to be a soldier?' (as opposed to something else you may have been or might have been).) What makes no sense is a question of the form 'What is it like for an X to be an X?' or 'What is it like for you (a human being) to be a human being?' For nothing other than an X *can be* (as opposed to *become*) an X, and if 'X' is a covering sortal noun, then of course, there is nothing else an X *could possibly be* other than an X. It makes no sense to ask 'What is it like for you to be a human being?' (unless you are an avatar or Jesus Christ). It makes no sense to ask 'What is it like for a human being to be a human being?' – the most one can make of this misbegotten question is 'What is human life like?' – the answer to which is not problematic ('Nasty, brutish and short' or 'Full of hope and fear', 'Much sorrow and occasional joy' and so on). Hence too the question 'What is it like for a bat to be a bat?' is a senseless question, unless it amounts to no more than 'What is the life of a bat like?' And the answer to *that* question is wholly unproblematic: for example, 'bats sleep all day, hanging upside down in caves; they have leathery wings, and can fly fast; they locate themselves by means of echo-location, they feed off insects or fruit, and have a particular liking for . . . and so on'. So not only is it not true that there is something which it is like for a bat to be a bat, for a human to be a human, or for me to be me – the very phrases make no sense.

The new wave of consciousness studies became obsessed with the idea that all experience is from a subjective point of view. Science, it was argued, is an endeavor to see the world from an objective point of view, but it is of the essence of human experience, and so of human consciousness, to involve a subjective point of view. But this involved a misuse of the term 'point of view'. Although I may look at something from a specific viewpoint, you may occupy exactly the same place as I. There is nothing private about viewpoints. But one does not see, or more generally, perceive, something from a point of view, but from a position in space. One does not feel pain, or feel tired, from any *point of view*. One may pass judgment or give one's opinion from a point of view, for example, from a political, economic, or cultural point of view. One may judge things from one's own point of view, to wit, from the point of view of one's interests, preferences or concerns. *This* might be said to be a *subjective judgment*. But a judgment passed from a political, economic, or cultural point of view is not in any sense *subjective* – it is a judgment that takes into account a limited range of relevant *objective* factors, such as political, economic or cultural ones. Most judgments (e.g. 'It's going to rain today', 'Prices are rising in the shops', 'Jack is in London') are not made from any point of view. Moreover, experiences are not enjoyed from any *point of view* – after all, I don't have a headache or enjoy Mozart's music from a point of view!

Finally, while scientism and science fiction mix well, science fiction and conceptual clarity do not. The idea of zombies could only seem intelligible when viewed from the perspective of functionalism. But functionalism was an incoherent doctrine. It needed direct refutation. But what it received was embroidery with mystery. Consciousness was super-added to the putative functional correlation of neural inputs, behavioral outputs and causal relations between functional states that were alleged to define mental states. It seemed to be a mysterious emanation from the brain, that accorded ill with 'everything we know about the physical universe'. This, as we shall see in the next section, is wholly mistaken. But before tackling that, it is worth pointing out that the very idea of zombies is incoherent.

Beings who behave exactly as we do in similar circumstances of life have exactly the same experiences we have. If they respond to visibilia as we do, then they see as we do. If they did not actually see, there would not be 'darkness inside', there would be darkness *outside*! They would be falling over things and would be unable visually to discriminate as the sighted can. If they bleed as we do, cry out as we do, flinch as we do – then they suffer as we do. If they respond to questions as we would, draw conclusions as we would, reason aloud as we do, then they think as we do. But still, members of the self-styled 'consciousness-studies community' will object, they lack consciousness, there is nothing it is like for them to have experiences! – Really? There is nothing *it is like* for us to have the experiences we have either. Rather, there is something which it *is* to have certain experiences – to wit: enjoyable, dull, exciting, boring. So too, if these beings patently enjoy playing cricket, but are evidently bored playing football, then there is something which it *is* for them to play cricket, to wit, great fun, and something which it is for them to play football, namely boring. Why speak in this funny way? Well, I agree with you. I didn't introduce it. All I mean is that to the question 'What is it like for these people to play cricket?', the answer – if they are always eager to play, say what fun the game was, express disappointment when rain stops play, and so forth – is: 'They enjoy it very much'. Zombies belong to the Looking Glass World of Lewis Carroll.

Consciousness and the Brain

The mind is no more identical with the brain that the horsepower of a car is identical with its cylinders or eyesight is identical with the eye. The mind is not seven inches tall, and it does not weigh three pounds – but not because it is taller and heavier, nor because it is short and lighter. The mind is not a *thing* (an 'entity') of any kind – just as horsepower and eyesight are not things of any sort. They are *powers*. The mind is an array of distinctive powers to engage in activities that characterize humanity. These are predominantly powers consequent upon or corollaries of mastery of a language and possession of concepts. They are, for the most part, linked to acts and activities, responses and reactions, involving or associated with, reasons and sensitivity to reasons for thinking, feeling and acting. To possess a mind is *to be able to do* various things, and to use one's mind is to *engage* in those acts and activities. The mind is not located in one's head, any more than the horsepower of a car is located under its bonnet – it is not located anywhere. There is nothing mysterious about this. Abilities are not located anywhere, but attributable to the creatures that possess them. The exercise of an ability is located wherever possessor of the ability is when he exercises it. So one does not think *in* one's brain, but in one's study, and one does not think *with* one's brain in the sense in which one sees with one's eyes and walks with one's legs. In that sense, the brain is not the *organ* of thought, any more than it is the organ of locomotion – although, of course, one could not think or walk but for the normal functioning of the brain.

Consciousness is *not* a property of the brain. It is a property of living organisms. It is human beings who are conscious or unconscious, who lose and regain consciousness, who fall asleep and later awaken. To ascribe consciousness to the brain – like ascribing thought, belief, understanding, interpreting, perceiving and feeling sensations to the brain – is to commit a *mereological fallacy*. To ascribe attributes to a part of a whole that can properly be ascribed only to the whole of which it is a part is a mereological fallacy. Aeroplane engines do not fly – it is aeroplanes that fly (which they would not do but for the proper functioning of their engines). The fusée of an antique table clock does not keep time, it is the clock that keeps time (which it would not do but for the proper functioning of its fusée). So too, we would not be able to think, believe, understand, interpret, perceive or feel pain but for the normal functioning of our brains, but it is *we* who think, believe, understand, etc. – not our brain.

So too, it is not the human brain that has its attention caught and held by something it perceives. For the brain does not attend to anything, and it does not perceive anything either. It is the human being that attends to things, that may have his attention caught and held by things, and that may realize what it is that has caught his attention. Perceptual consciousness is not a property or capacity of the brain, but of the living organism. So too, it is not the brain that learns things and remembers what it has learnt – it is the human being. And it is not the brain, but the human being, who can bear a previously learnt fact in mind, be affected by it and take it into account in deliberation. It makes no sense to ascribe any form of transitive consciousness to the brain, although of course, no living being could become and be conscious of anything but for the proper functioning of its brain.

These considerations shed light upon the vexed question of the neural correlates of consciousness. The quest for the neural correlates of consciousness is misconceived, since there is no one thing called 'consciousness', but many different things. Moreover, the many different things are not related as species to genus, but in much more complex and irregular ways. Of course, it makes perfectly good sense to search for the neural correlates of intransitive consciousness, as well for the neural correlates of states intermediate between being conscious and being unconscious, such as epileptic automatism, fugue, somnambulism, and so forth. Indeed, neuroscientists have made great strides forward in their research on these matters. But when it comes to searching for the neural correlates of the various forms of transitive consciousness, matters become much murkier. In the case of perceptual consciousness, one would have to search for the neural correlate of the conjunction of (1) perceiving something or other in a given perceptual mode, (2) having one's attention caught and held by what one perceives (as opposed to voluntarily attending to it), and (3) realizing, and hence knowing, what caught one's attention. It is far from clear (a) whether we are remotely close to being able to do this, and (b) why on earth it is interesting. Were we further to engage in a quest for the neural correlates of factual consciousness, other difficulties would arise. We should have to search for neural correlates of the conjunction of (1) being aware of some piece of information antecedently acquired, (2) taking this piece of information into account in one's current thought and deliberation, and (3) having one's thoughts, feelings and decisions colored by the information. Again, would a neuroscientist know even where to begin? Taking a piece of information into account is neither a mental event nor a mental state. Having one's thoughts colored by a piece of information that one is bearing in mind is not something that *could* be correlated with neural events. And again, why should this quest be of any interest? I leave it to the reader to go through parallel exercises with regard to the other three forms of transitive consciousness examined above.

The moral of the tale is that the idea of a quest for neural correlates of consciousness was predicated upon *gross* misconceptions of *what consciousness is*. Once the idea of the alleged qualitative character of all experience is dismantled, once the fiction of the 'what-it's-like-ness' of experience is deconstructed, once the thought that consciousness is a mysterious 'inner light' associated with functionally correlated inputs (neural stimulation) and consequent outputs (bodily movement) is abandoned, then all interest in neural correlates of consciousness *in general* simply evaporates. As long as one thinks of consciousness in a primitive manner as an inner scanner of mental states, then the quest for the neural correlate of consciousness appears exciting. It seems to be the key to the understanding of the functioning of the conscious brain. It then seems as if the re-entry pathways in the cortex must be part of the 'scanning mechanism'. But this is predicated upon a complete misunderstanding of what transitive consciousness is. It involves a neuroscientific correlate of the venerable philosophical confusion of the ability to say with the ability to see. What is left behind after these egregious confusions have been swept away is some perfectly decent and *unmysterious* research into the neural correlates of intransitive consciousness and various forms of aberrant borderline cases of being conscious.

Demystifying Bogus Mysteries

It should by now be obvious that the puzzlement over the evolutionary advantage of consciousness is a puzzle of our own making. For it too was predicated upon the assumption that consciousness is either a self-scanning mechanism in the mind/brain that enables us to introspect and so know of our own mental operations, or that it is the qualitative character of all experiences to which each of us has privileged access – but which zombies would lack. Once these confusions are extirpated, the question ceases to be puzzling.

To ask after the evolutionary advantage of consciousness properly conceived is either silly, or the answer is obvious. 'What is the evolutionary justification of being conscious as opposed to unconscious?' seems to be a silly question. To ask for the evolutionary advantage for being awake as opposed to asleep is foolish. But there is a genuine question lurking in the background, namely, what is the purpose, and evolutionary advantage of, sleep? To this, as far as I know, there is no clear answer as yet. It is obvious that we need sleep and cannot function if deprived of it, but it is not obvious why that is so.

The evolutionary advantage of perceptual consciousness is too obvious for it to be worth asking – the evolutionary value of peripheral perception and the susceptibility to having one's attention caught and held by what one peripherally perceives is patent.

To ask after the evolutionary advantage of factual consciousness or of consciousness of those operations of mind that can be deemed *feelings* is confused. Both modes of consciousness are largely spin-offs of mastery of a language. The evolutionary advantages of language for group-survival are patent – the rest is the history of a rational animal. Whether rationality, or the degree of rationality of which we are capable, is of evolutionary value is becoming more and more doubtful as the 21st century proceeds. It seems very doubtful whether we, as a species, will achieve the survival record of the dinosaurs, who certainly could not have their attention caught by, or reflect on, their emotions, inclinations, or intimations, and surely could not have their previously acquired knowledge color their thoughts and deliberations.

There is no biological *mystery* about consciousness, only biologists' muddles about consciousness.

Finally, what of the 'metaphysical problem' of consciousness? How can something as strange and unique as consciousness be compatible with everything we know about the physical universe? How can consciousness emerge from mere matter? The questions betoken sore confusion. What is wonderful, but no longer mysterious, is *life*. We do have a rough idea of how it might have emerged from an appropriate primaeval 'soup' of chemicals. What is even more wonderful is the emergence of sentient organisms. Here too we have a rough idea of the evolutionary tale. It would be absurd today (as opposed to 400 years ago), to think that there is any incompatibility at all between what we know of the material universe and the existence of conscious beings. Consciousness, to be sure, does not 'emerge from mere matter'. It is not an emanation. And it is not a property of 'mere matter' anyway. It is a property of living organisms. How sentient creatures first evolved from insentient micro-organisms is no doubt something we will learn more about in due course, but the advantages of primal tactile sensitivity, the benefits of taste responsive cells at the ingress of primitive digestive tracts were already obvious to Aristotle. There are no metaphysical mysteries – only metaphysical confusions.

Notes

1   The idea was an ancient one. It was mooted by Plotinus, and was prominent in Augustine.
2   It should be remarked that theses 7–9 unwittingly commit those who embrace this conception of consciousness to the intelligibility of an intrinsically private language. This, Wittgenstein showed to be incoherent. The matter will not be discussed here. For a discussion accessible to psychologists and neuroscientists, see Bennett and Hacker (2003), ch. 3, sections 3.3–3.9.
3   This critical assertion cannot be fully justified here. For more detailed treatment, see Bennett and Hacker (2003), chapters 9–12.
4   See A. R. White (1964), Chapter IV, to which I am much indebted.
5   Save in cases such as being conscious of the worsening of the pain in one's back, where the concepts of knowledge and of ignorance alike are excluded.

6   Everything one is conscious of one is also aware of, but one is aware of much more than one is conscious of. One may have to be reminded of something one is already aware of, but one cannot be reminded of something one is already conscious of. What one is aware of may be what has been filed away for future use, what one is conscious of is on the table.

7   This has as much, and as little, sense as the 'sight/eye'.

8   This misbegotten phrase is becoming common among adherents. See Bayne, Cleeremans, and Wilken (2009) passim. Virtually every entry about consciousness characterizes conscious experience in terms of there being something it is like for the subject to have it, and conscious creatures as creatures such that there is something it is like for them to be what they are.

PART II

Applications and Illustrations

5

Perception

Rom Harré

> The earlier students of nature did not speak well in supposing that there is nothing white or black without sight, nor flavour without taste. For in one way they spoke correctly and in another not: for 'sense' and 'sensible object' are ambiguous terms, i.e. may denote potentialities or actualities. The statement is true of the latter, false of the former. (Aristotle quoted in Everson, 1997, p. 111)

The psychology of perception has always followed the hybrid format, analyzing the character and content of what we can see, hear, touch, taste, smell and know of our orientation in the world of space and time as expressed in our various everyday and technical vocabularies, and studying the means by which we are able to do so.

So far as we know every language has words for the major sensory modalities – 'seeing', 'hearing', 'touching', 'tasting', and 'smelling' – and phrases for expressing the sense of the location and motion of the body in space. For example, Sanskrit, the mother of many languages, has *vilokana* (looking), *srotra* (hearing), *sprsa* (touching), *asvade* (taste), and *ghsana* (smelling). Swahili seems to have a very refined vocabulary for the perceptual modalities, in which *uwezo wa kuona* is not just sight but visual power and *kusikea* the power of hearing. Taste, *ladha*, and smell, *harufa*, are attributes of things or places, while touch, *mgusa*, is a sensation.

Within each modality there are extensive vocabularies for describing and referring to the character of things and events given by looking, tasting and so on, such as the color, shape, and distance for things we see with the power of vision; The loudness, pitch and timbre for sounds we hear and so on, (see Chapter 4). We need to note that people do not usually say 'I see a loaf of bread' or 'I touch a toad.' We usually express the contents of the world as seen in expressions like 'There is a car in my parking space!'; 'Toads are dry!' The 'I see …' form is likely to be used when the issue is problematic or a question is asked. I am in the reeds by the lake and I tell my less well-placed companion 'I can see a heron.' This cluster of vocabularies must be the starting point for any psychological study of perception, the place of the Taxonomic Priory Principle. Perhaps the earliest experiment we all do in coming to have elementary theories of perception is covering our eyes so that we cannot see and covering our ears so that we cannot hear and so on. This is the moment that the Task-Tool metaphor becomes a fundamental conceptual principle that underlies our taking for granted that the eyes are the instruments for seeing, the ears for hearing, the tongue for tasting and the nose for smelling – though as research has progressed these simple applications of the TT principle have suffered substantial modifications. The eyes are the core of the instrument I use to explore my material environment, to manage actions and to gather information for reports.

The psychology of perception fullfils the pattern of a well-established Hybrid Psychology. The taxonomies of sensory processes and their deliverances are determined in the first instance by the categories of the vernacular, while the tools or instruments for performing the tasks of becoming acquainted with the material environment are already evident in the role of the sense organs.

Given this seemingly universal starting point, the first scientific probe must be into *how* the sensory organs serve to display the attributes of our environments. The 17th century was rich in analyses of sensory experience and there were many attempts to apply the newly resurrected atomism to the task of understanding how the interaction between material world and human experience via the sense organs could be explained. The two principles that define a hybrid psychology – the Taxonomic Priority Principle and the Task-Tool metaphor – are evidently presupposed in all these writings, for example, in the works of Descartes (1596–1650). The conceptual formations in his *Passions of the soul* (Descartes, 1650) are derived from the everyday vocabulary of the French of the time as they describe and comment on the life around them. For example, in Article 23 he writes of *le son du cloche* (translated as 'sound') and *la lumière* (translated as 'light') *d'un flambeau*.

New departures in natural science, particularly evolutionary biology, have shown how the sense organs evolved in relation to the successive environments inhabited by evolving animals. Plants also respond to material conditions in the world. Until recently, animal models have played a minor role in the psychology of perception – after all, we do not share a vocabulary with animals though commonalities in behavior are obvious. Von Békésy did his investigations on human corpses; nevertheless, some important discoveries have been made using animal sense organs. For example, Kepler replaced the back of an ox's eyeball with a piece of egg shell and so discovered that the image on the retina was reversed. Here was research into the way that the 'seeing tool' worked – even though it seemed to present a puzzle. It seems to be a puzzle only because we have not been thinking of the eye as a seeing *instrument*.

By the 21st century huge advances in knowledge of the anatomy and physiology of human sense organs and associated neural systems had been made. Some ideas about the sites of brain activity correlated with perceptual experiences have been under test. However, at this point we run up against an apparently insoluble conceptual problem – a description of a state or process in the brain and nervous system that scarcely more than records the location, duration and intensity of a physiological process that is correlative to the description that a human being who is conscious of that process or state would give. We will discuss these systems in terms of a technical concept from physics – 'transduction'. Transduction is the process by which a signal carried by one physical process, for instance, a pressure wave, stimulates a transducing device, to initiate a new physical process, for instance, an electric current, by which an analogue of the original signal is carried further into the system.

Not only is there transduction in the organs of sense from a physical input, such as the amplitude of a sound wave, to sequential neural impulses, but there is a transduction of another kind between activity in the auditory cortex and the experience of sounds as speech and as music. The double transduction pattern is evident in each sensory system.

So, at the core of any hybrid account of the psychology of human perception lie two sequential links of transduction. Signals of the first type, originating outside the body of the perceiver and propagated in one kind of medium, for example, electromagnetic radiation, instigate signals in a different medium in a different material system, signals in neural pathways. This is the first transduction and is such that several formal properties of the signals of the first type are reproduced in the signals of the second type. Signals of the second type activate another system, and instigate phenomena in the domain of conscious experience, sights, sounds, feelings and so on. The phenomena that appear through the second transduction have some properties analogous to the relevant properties of signals of the first type. 'Relevance' is determined by the role of the perceptual system in the life form of the animal (or even plant). It is easy to fall into the mereological fallacy at this point. People see and hear; their organs for seeing and hearing do not (see Chapter 4).

In animal perceptual systems, including that of human beings, the first transduction links physical signals propagated from the environment and received by a sense organ to neural signals that enter pathways in the brain. The second transduction links consequential states and processes in the brain with people's experiences of seeing, hearing, touching, tasting, smelling, and a sense of the spatial location of the body and its parts. While the link that occurs in the first transduction is mediated by an observable mechanism, such as the hair cells in the cochlea and the rods and cones in the eye's retina, no such mechanism has ever been found to mediate the second transduction. This may be the final and *ungrounded* link that has evolved with the development of visual, auditory and tactile skills and powers. It limits the possibility of using animal models to study audition though there have been many important animal-based studies of the first transduction, using bats, rats, cats and other creatures.

We will follow the hybridization of the psychology of perception in detail in only two sensory/perceptual systems, seeing and hearing. In both cases the cultural contexts of seeing and hearing play an important role in how people experience their environments.

The Perceptual World

When a human being is awake there is a colorful and ever-changing field of related things experienced by each person (and higher animal) in a three-dimensional array centered on the bodily location of the perceiver. Colored and shaped things, sounds, substances with various tastes, the way things feel to the touch etc. are there to be observed by almost everyone, though some may lack sensitivity to certain color differences, to some pitch relations and so on. There are things to be seen and touched, melodies to be heard, tastes to linger over. What is the relationship between the sensory properties of things and the ordered and structured entities *we* perceive? It seemed to many philosopher-psychologists of the 17th century and since that 'conscious experience', that is, the sensations of which they were aware when they were awake, were private and personal, while the world in which they lived and which we unreflectingly claim to know, is public and available to almost everyone. (See Chapter 4 for further discussion on the way such a picture is liable to mislead us.)

It seems obvious that while each person has his or her own pains, the color of the rose and its scent are common attributes reappearing in almost everyone's world. Though this distinction is important in the practices of human life, it plays almost no role in the psychology of perception. We will be concerned with research into the nature of the two transductions.

Attempts to understand how people perceive the world around them, and the states and configurations of their own bodies, go back into surviving texts from the ancient world, including Indian and Chinese writings on perception. There are detailed discussions of the senses in the work of Aristotle in the fourth century. For a detailed account see Everson (1997). In his account, Aristotle's focus on perceptual powers or capacities that are linked to the kind of objects that these powers enable us to perceive is more in keeping with the position we take in this chapter than the 'cluster of sensations' view that dominated this branch of psychology for so long. The details Aristotle presents in *De anima* are sometimes bizarre. In the 17th century, the philosopher-psychologists of the era, such as Rene Descartes and John Locke (1632–1704) took for granted that sensations were mental entities impressed on the mind; the effects of emanations from material things interacting with the sense organs. According to the 'official' doctrine of the era, one group of sensations were primary, such as the geometrical shapes of material things. As a human experience, the shape of a patch in the visual field resembles the 'real' qualities of material things, attributes things would have in the absence of any creatures to perceive them. Another group of qualities such as taste and color, were said to be secondary. According to this analysis, the sensation of red a person has when viewing a ripe apple does not resemble the state of the apple that caused the experience of the color in the simple Humean, event to event or state sense of 'cause'. Locke simply declares that a surface of such a molecular configuration has the *power* to produce such and such a sensation, and leaves it at that.

This basic distinction was challenged in the 18th century by George Berkeley (1685–1753) and by Thomas Reid (1719–1796). They made the first systematic attempts to use the geometrical configuration of the movements of the eyes to analyze the source of our ability to see objects as three-dimensional things. These pioneering studies secured the dominance of the sense of sight in the research programs of psychologists and philosophers, to the neglect of touch, hearing, taste, smell, pains and other bodily sensations, and the sense of the movement and position of limbs, trunk, head and so on.

In the early 20th century the psychology of perception was still oriented to vision. The starting point was the work of the German psychophysicists. Their work was concerned with the relation between physical stimuli, including neural impulses, and the corresponding sensations experienced by individuals. Gustav Fechner (1801–1887), Professor of Physics at Leipzig, showed that the intensity of a sensation was proportional to the logarithm of the intensity of the stimulus. This was already a hybrid project since the sensations were reported by the people who were experiencing them, necessarily in words from the German language. Johannes Müller (1801–1858), who worked in Berlin, proposed the 'law of specific energies', that each sensory nerve produces its own characteristic sensation. While these ideas seemed to cast the human perceiver in a passive role, Hermann von Helmholtz (1821–1894), argued that perceiving was an active process. It was not the passive reception of stimuli at the sense organs but result of explorations of the material world.

The German psychophysicists had unraveled some of the relationships between physical stimuli and sensations to which a person can attend, that is, the relationships between events and states at the beginning and the end of the double transduction, but we do not perceive just sensations. We can attend to colored patches no doubt, but we see a three-dimensional world of things. We are aware of sounds but we hear articulate speech, rhythms and melodies. We are not aware of pressure patterns on the surface of the skin but we are aware of differences of textures. What is the relation between bodily sensations and perceptions? The brain and the neural components of the perceptual systems must play a crucial part, but so must learning what our culture tells us is in the world and our language provides us with a vocabulary that predetermines to a large extent what sorts of attributes are salient for us.

Double Transduction Systems

Following the Task-Tool metaphor as the general guide to research in perception, we turn to report what has been discovered over many hundreds of years of study of the instruments or tools with which a person comes to perceive the material environment. Eyes and the parts of the brain to which they are connected by neural pathways make up the instrument of vision, ears and the parts of the brain to which they are connected make up the instrument of hearing, and so on for the other sensory modalities.

Seeing

The visual system is sensitive to several features of the material world in which a person is engulfed. The first transduction occurs when the retinal cells, stimulated by receiving light of differing wave lengths and intensities, send neural impulses through a complex pattern of nerve fibers into the brain. As Sir Arthur Sherrington showed a century ago, there are both afferent and efferent neural pathways linking the brain with the peripheral systems of the body including the visual system. The visual system is not wholly a passive receptor of stimuli from an external source.

Not only that, but the brain is organised three-dimensionally. Hubel and Wiesel (1959) found that all the cells in a column at right angles to the surface of the visual cortex respond to simple objects in the same orientation, while those in adjacent columns do not. The same is true of the primary auditory cortex, though Hubel and Wiesel studied only vision. Each column of cells responds to the neural impulse from a sound of a specific pitch 'picked up' by frequency-sensitive hair cells in the cochlea. If we can generalize these findings to all human perceptual systems no doubt the same would be found in the tactile systems with which we recognize shapes and textures by touch.

In the visual system, the first transduction transforms features of light such as intensity and wave-length into neural signals. This process occurs in the eye and its complex network of dedicated nerve cells and their interconnections. The resulting neural signals pass down the optic nerve to the lateral genticulate nucleus to the visual cortex where the second transduction occurs. Just as the primary auditory cortex is arranged with columns of cells mapping the layout of the cells along the cochlea, which are differentially sensitive to wave length and amplitude of the induced pressure waves in the cochlea fluid, so too the cells in the lateral genticulate nucleus are laid out as a map of the retinal cells that are involved in the first transduction in the contralateral hemifield of vision. Signals from the right side of each eye reach the left region of the visual cortex via the left portion of the lateral genticulate nucleus. Signals from the left side of each eye reach the right region of the visual cortex and the right

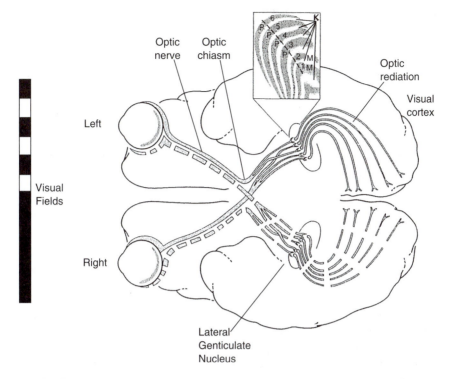

Figure 5.1 The visual pathways

Source: This diagram, reproduced from Frishman (2001, p. 55) by kind permission, shows the general layout of neural connections from the eyes to the visual cortex.

portion of the lateral genticulate nucleus. The point at which these cross overs occur is the 'optic chiasma'.

The cells of the lateral genticulate nuclei on each side of the brain are arranged in six layers, in such a way that each layer is a 'map' of the retinal cell layout in the contralateral hemisphere of the opposite eye. In effect, the patterns of activity of the cells of the lateral genticulate nuclei are representations of the stimulation patterns of the retinal cells.

In the visual system as a whole, the 'processing' of visual signals seems to follow two broad paths, along the upper or dorsal surface of the brain and along the under or ventral surface. The two streams receive signals from different regions of the lateral genticulate nuclei. It has been suggested that the dorsal stream is concerned with the perception of place and motion and the ventral with objects and their properties (Figure 5.1).

Let us look more closely at the processes that occur in the retina in the course of the first transduction, from photons to neural signals. The shapes, colors, relative sizes and arrangements in space of the objects in the nearby environment at least must be represented digitally.

Each feature of an environmental scene is 'encoded' in some physical property of the light that enters the eye from that scene. The variety of retinal cells matches the variety of salient properties of the light. The most prominent types are rods and cones. The eyes have about 100 million rods and five million cones altogether. Rods are sensitive to light of low intensity while cones detect light of higher intensities and are the basis of color vision. Cones have either red, blue or green sensitive pigments in their outer regions, while rods have only a general light sensitive pigment.

The first transduction involves the effect of photons on the visual pigments. Chemical changes occur with the absorption of even a single photon and very few are required to activate a retinal cell to emit a signal. Rods require fewer photons to emit a signal than do cones. These signals are combined in various ways by a complex network of axons and dendrites within the retina, finally exiting the eye via the optic nerve bundle.

The neural impulses reach the lateral genticulate nucleus where they activate the multi-layered system of neurons that reproduces the pattern of activation of the retina. The retinal image is now reproduced deep in the brain.

Research on the activity of the visual system has disclosed a fundamental process that seems at first sight to be an anomaly – the 'dark current'. Receptor cells produce a current in the dark that in turn produces a continuous release of neurotransmitter, glutamate. The interruption of the dark current when the cell absorbs photons reduces the amount of neurotransmitter and in this way signals the arrival of light at that point in the retina (Hagins, Penn, & Yoshikami, 1970).

The second transduction does not occur at the lateral genticulate nucleus. Pathways lead from these nuclei to as many as 30 different regions of the brain. The second transduction, from patterns of neural impulses to visual experience of shape, color, distribution in space and so on as a unified visual field, is accomplished over a widely scattered assembly of activations. The second transduction is a brute fact of psychoneurology, with no hint at all how it is accomplished. However, thanks to it, a person can use their visual apparatus to explore and enjoy that aspect of the environment that emits light.

With these termini for the neural signals from the eye we come full circle. Our vernaculars must be used to begin the identification of the many aspects of sight that are the topics of neurological research. However, when we reach the scattered termini of the output from the pair of lateral genticulate nuclei in many parts of the brain the second transduction returns us to the environment we started out with. Necessarily we return to the language we began with – for example, English. Some minor modifications to vocabulary and grammar may have come from the hybridization of the psychology of vision, but in a certain sense we could delete the intermediary system that leads from the first to the second transduction.

Hearing

The double transduction system and the role of the Taxonomic Priority Thesis in the exercise of perceptual skills is particularly clear in the case of hearing and the perception of sounds as speech and as music. The unraveling of the complicated anatomy and physiology of the primary transduction system of the sense of hearing is to be credited to Georg von Békésy (1899–1972). Pressure waves in the air are characterized by distinct frequencies, often complex patterns that can be represented as superpositions of simpler sine waves, and of a certain energy or amplitude. When these impinge on the eardrum the main physical properties, wave form, frequency and amplitude, of the sound waves are transmitted through the ossicles, minute bone linkages, to the oval window, a membrane at the entrance to the cochlea. This is a process of transmission, not at this stage, transduction.

The vibrations of the oval window send a pressure wave through the fluid in the cochlea exciting the sensitive hair cells arranged in rows along the basilar membrane which runs the length of the cochlea.

The hair cells are arranged in inner and outer clusters. Depending on the physical properties of the pressure wave, hair cells at different locations along the basilar membrane are activated. Neural impulses from the hair cells are integrated in a complex network of neural connections, resulting in neural signals sent via the auditory nerve bundle to the primary auditory cortex, one of the three layers of cells that make up the paired regions of the auditory cortex in the left and right temporal lobes. The cells in the primary auditory cortex are arranged in columns. Each column is sensitive to a particular frequency, that is, they are tonotopical. The tonotopical organization of the primary auditory cortex has been confirmed by recent experiments using fMRI scanning techniques (Musick & Burns, 2007). Auditory experiments by MRI methods are particularly difficult because of the noise of the equipment which is difficult to screen out. However, recently, 'silent' MRI methods have been developed. They tend to show that though absolute values of excitation are different in the noisy and the silent environments, the relative difference between excitations is preserved.

The sequence of impinging sound wave, to cochlea pressure patterns, to neural signals, is the first transduction terminating in the neural excitation of the columns of cells in the primary auditory cortex. Unlike the neural network that links the visual system to the brain, the left and right halves of the auditory system are cross-linked in complex ways.

Neural signals from the primary auditory cortical regions located on the temporal lobes are conveyed deeper into the brain, finally activating the secondary and tertiary auditory cortical regions that surround the primary cortex. There are also connections to sites in other brain regions. When this mode of activation occurs, a person hears sounds of different pitches, loudness, harmonic and melodic relations, and timbres. This is the second transduction. And from those sounds a human being hears the words of many languages and phonetic systems, and music of many genres and scale systems.

Appreciating the pattern of regional neuronal activation requires not only an understanding of the basic principles of scanning techniques (see Chapter 3) but a grasp of the way regions of the brain are described. Geographically, so to speak, we have the lateral, dorsal, ventral, sagittal and occipital regions. From the point of view of function, the main features relevant to the neuroscience of perception are cortical sites, particularly regions relevant to auditory experience, the temporal lobes and Herschel's gyrus, and for visual experience the visual cortex regions. For these we need also to understand ipsilaterality. The way this terminology works can be best seen in a schematic diagram (see Figure 5.1).

Thanks to von Békésy, we understand the first transduction very well, but as in the case of the visual system, we must simply accept the existence of the second transduction as a basic feature of the universe. A pattern of activity in several regions of the brain can be detected by scanning devices, but neural activity is not pitch, melody, harmony, timbre or loudness, however well correlated the neural activity and the experience might be.

Research into the anatomy and physiology of the auditory system must begin with the analysis of hearing speech and listening to music, the most sophisticated uses people make of their auditory systems. The form that the human auditory system takes and the processes that are possible in that system no doubt have a Darwinian explanation, as the accumulation of advantageous mutations have refined and extended its functions. The *psychology* of vision and audition begins with the incorporation of human visual and auditory experience as the starting point of research. However, study of the double transduction perceptual systems moves in the opposite direction. Having identified the relevant aspects of the material world by the use of the Taxonomic Priority Principle, musicology and linguistics providing the conceptual resources enabling us to identify relevant features of the physical sources of perceptual experience, we then trace the causal links that take us back through the double transduction to the final stage, human visual and auditory experience. In music, the basic harmonic experience occurs when listening to intervals of thirds, fifths and octaves. These are singled out for musical and aesthetic reasons. Psychologists and neuroscientists gradually discovered the relations between these experiences and the ratios of the frequencies of sound waves, then traced the mechanism of cochlea and hair cells by which these ratios give rise to distinct patterns of neural impulses, the first transduction. With the help of fMRI scanning we can trace these impulses to their destination in the auditory cortex and elsewhere (Engelian, Yang, Engelian, Zonana, Stern, & Silberweig, 2002). Then, consonant with neural activity in these regions, the experimental participant reports hearing something consonant or dissonant, a melody or a jumble of unrelated pitches; words, sentences and songs, or mere noise. This is the second transduction.

Touch, Taste and Smell

Similar systems have been found to enable the first transduction between the stimuli that come from contact of various kinds of things with the surface of the body, with the molecules that provide the material basis for the senses of taste (the gustatory system) and smell (the olfactory system). Each system has its characteristic features with the general framework of the double transduction pattern. We will describe a series of famous experiments undertaken by J. J. Gibson on the perception of shape by touch that showed the importance of the proprioceptor cells in the skeletal joints to the ability people have to detect shape by running a hand over an object.

What Tasks Do These Systems Perform?

From this basis we must now ask what tasks the perceptual systems perform in creating a material world with its many dimensions of reality, its colors and its sounds. The first comprehensive hybrid system in modern times was developed by the German psychologists, Max Wertheimer (1880–1943), Kurt Koffka (1886–1941) and Wolfgang Köhler. James Gibson showed how these systems automatically search the energy flux within which an organism is living to extract invariances. On Darwinian grounds we would expect such invariances to be advantageous to the organism. However, our ability to perceive solid objects, stationary and moving, is not enough. We perceive telephones, trains, cabbages, fires and so on. Richard Gregory suggested and put forward some strong evidence to support the idea that the secondary role of perceptual systems is to test hypotheses.

Köhler and the Gestalt Hypothesis

The experimental program of the Gestaltists began with the study of perception. It seemed clear that it was impossible for meaningful and structured perceptions to be synthesized from meaningless, atomic constituents. The two key requirements for a theory of perception were to account for the *meaning* and the *organization* of what is seen or heard or touched.

Wertheimer made the point forcibly:

> When we are presented with a number of stimuli we do not as a rule experience 'a number' of individual things, this one and that. Instead, larger wholes separated from and related to one another are given in experience. (Wertheimer, 1938 [1923], p. 78)

Wolfgang Felix Ulrich Köhler (1887–1967) was born in Reval, now Tallinn, the capital of Estonia, then a part of the Russian Empire. Köhler's father was headmaster of a school for the children of the German community in Tallinn. In 1893, the Köhler family returned to Germany.

In 1905, he began his university studies, moving from one university to another, as was the custom in Germany. He eventually settled in the University of Berlin where he studied the natural sciences and mathematics intensively. In 1909, he was awarded his PhD for work in the psychology of audition, with particular reference to music. His mentor in this work was Carl Stumpf (1848–1936), well known for his work in the psychology of hearing.

His first academic post was at Frankfurt University. Here he came into contact with Max Wertheimer (1880–1943) and Kurt Koffka (1886–1941). In 1914, Köhler took up an invitation from the Prussian Academy of Sciences to direct the work of a primate research center to be established on the island of Tenerife in the Spanish Canaries. This led to his classic work *The mentality of apes* (1921), in which he described the ability of chimpanzees to solve problems by making use of available material resources in the environment.

Interference by the Nazis in his own institute led to his finally leaving for the United States in 1935. He quickly found a position at Swarthmore College in Philadelphia. After his retirement from Swarthmore in 1958 he joined MIT where he inaugurated their graduate program in psychology, working there from 1960.

From about 1950, Köhler began to teach again in Germany at the Free University of Berlin. He was elected President of the American Psychological Association for 1958–1959. He married twice. In his later years he retired to a farm in New Hampshire, dying there on 11 June 1967.

Various rules of structure were discovered in the Berlin Institute, such as the law of similarity, that similar things will be grouped together. Other laws included the law of completeness, that incomplete but symmetrical figures will be seen as complete. Köhler argued that these could all be seen as consequences of a general law, his Law of Pragnanz, that experiences will take on the 'best' form that is possible in the context. Köhler was insistent that there was overwhelming experimental evidence that the structural properties of organized wholes were not insertions by the mind, but objective attributes of the wholes in question:

> Up to the present time there has been a tendency to regard the remarkable properties of wholes, especially the possibility of transposing their translocal properties [such as the sameness of a melody in different keys] as the achievement of 'higher' processes. From the view point of *gestalt* theory sensory organization is as natural and primitive a fact as any other side of sensory dynamics. (Köhler, 1938, p. 216)

Perhaps even more important were the experimental demonstrations of the way that perception of such matters as shape and motion were dependent on context (Köhler, 1938, pp. 8–15). An influential experiment revealed the way in which two black bars, separated by a small distance, were seen depending on the times at which they were presented. If there was only a small difference between the times at which each was shown, they were seen to appear simultaneously. If the interval was lengthened, an observer would see a single bar moving across the screen. To avoid any predisposition to explain the phenomenon as 'apparent motion', Wertheimer and his colleagues called it the 'phi phenomenon'. They insisted that the motion was not an illusion but an observable fact. 'Illusory contours', such as the completion of an incomplete figure, for example 'shadow letters', were treated in the same way. The seeing of completed figures was not an illusion. Structure is as much an objective feature of what is seen as colors and other sensory items.

Studies of the differences in visual speed when objects moving with the same physical velocity are presented in differently structured contexts were also used to demonstrate Gestalt principles. For example, large circles moving across a large aperture in a screen are seen to be moving more slowly than small circles of the same velocity, moving across a small aperture. This is not an illusion, but the perception of a structural property of the set-up, namely certain relations of proportionality between circles and apertures.

Köhler cited the figure/ground distinction, as identified by Rubin, as another example of the role of Gestalt patterns in perception. The shape that is seen as the figure usually stands out from the ground in a third dimension. The familiar fact that objects are more or less easy to identify depending on their surroundings was another phenomenon for which Gestaltists provided careful empirical tests. For instance, Köhler investigated the conditions that facilitated identifying the expression of a face presented upside down. The gravitational field becomes part of the conditions of perception.

The attempt to develop a hybrid psychoneuroscience of perception within the Gestalt point of view led Köhler to propose that analogues of the structures that were perceived were present in the brain. In his Page-Barbour Lectures of 1938 (Köhler, 1938, ch. 2), he describes the development of Gestaltist *field theory* in detail, consciously aiming at a hybrid perceptual psychology. The fact of the internal relation between elements and patterns suggests a field concept, that is, that we should view each perceptual element as having an influence at places distant from its actual location, thus contributing to an organized or structured perception. This is the basic principle of field physics. Indeed,

Köhler explicitly cites Michael Faraday as a source of field concepts (Köhler, 1938, p. 65). How could there be fields of influence displayed in perception unless there were processes in the brain that had a field-like character? It was a short step to hypotheses as to the actual existence of such fields, and suggestions as to the neural mechanisms by which they might be realized. In this way, not only would there be structured groups of entities in experience, but there would be corresponding or *isomorphic* structures of neural representations in the brain, the influence of each element spreading throughout the structure.

The first transduction led through the sense organs and the neural networks that emanated from them to a kind of reverse transduction as structures appeared in the substance of the brain. The second transduction from brain-state structure to percept structure was a mysterious isomorphism.

This idea appealed to no one and with its demise the Gestalt approach faded from view as a general theory of perception. Nevertheless, the ability to perceive structure is a major component of the capacities that people employ in coming to perceive sounds as music.

Perceptual Systems as Devices for the Extraction of Invariants

As a person moves through a material environment, the substantial things that fill it continue to be perceived as three-dimensional objects, even though the stimuli that reach the brain via the retina are continually changing, and the retina itself is two-dimensional. The basic idea of perception as the experience of invariance under transformation is at the root of J. J. Gibson's understanding of the psychology of perception, and the school of 'ecological perception' that his work inaugurated.

Rather than conceive of the perceiver as passive and the mind as a blank slate on which sensations are impressed and somehow organized into shapes and arrangements of things, some of which are in relative motion, Gibson thought of perception as the upshot of active exploration of the streams of energy that fill the environment and impinge on the sense organs. The perceptual systems such as lens, iris, retina, optic nerve, visual cortex, or pinna, eardrum, basilar membrane, hair cells, primary and secondary auditory cortex, skin and finger and wrist joints, explore the energy flux in search of invariant relations. 'The animal and the environment make an inseparable pair' (Gibson, 1966, p. 8). 'When the senses are considered as channels of sensation' Gibson (1962, p. 3) remarked, 'one is thinking of the passive receptors and the energies that stimulate them … it does not explain how animals and men accomplish sense perception'. That is, it does not explain seeing a world of permanent things, hearing sounds as melodies or speech, discerning the shapes of things by touch. What is missing from the passive receptor theory? The stimuli that affect the sense organs are changing continually as the animal moves about an environment. It follows that whatever it is that is the source of the experience of the permanence of things must be something in the flow of stimulus energy other than the causes of sensations. There are geometrical features of the material environment which are present as higher order invariants in that flow. The key idea is that these invariants do not change as the patterns of stimulus on the retina change. 'These invariants correspond to permanent properties of the environment.'

James Jerome Gibson (1904–1979) was born in the small town of McConnelsville, Ohio. The family were strict Presbyterians, and James was brought up in the religious atmosphere of the times. After attending the local high school, he began his university education at Northwestern University, later transferring to Princeton University. He completed his PhD in 1928, working on the relation between learning and memory.

In 1928, immediately after receiving his PhD, he joined the faculty of Smith College, a highly regarded all-women college. His meeting with the well-known gestalt psychologist, K. Koffka, at Smith, had a profound influence on his way of looking at the phenomena of perception. The gestaltists had emphasized the supreme importance of structure in perception. In 1932, he married Eleanor Jack, who had come to teach at Smith in 1931. When the Gibsons moved to Cornell in 1949, she took up a post in the psychology department. She was involved in most of his subsequent work on the psychology of perception, though she received less credit than perhaps was her due.

From 1941 Gibson became director of the USAF unit in aviation psychology. How the pilot experiences the world became for him a working model for visual perception in general. 'The world with a ground under it – the visual world of surfaces and edges – is not only the kind of world in which the pilot flies; it is the prototype of the world in which we all live' (Gibson, 1950, p. 60).

With the publication of *The senses considered as perceptual systems* in 1966, Gibson's ecological theory of perception with its array of brilliant supporting experiments became widely known. However, the shift from conceiving of the perceiver as a passive receptor of stimuli to an active explorer of the energy flux emanating from the material environment required the abandonment of deeply entrenched presuppositions.

The Gibsons made several extended visits abroad, but their connection with Cornell continued after Jim Gibson's retirement in 1972 until his death in December 1979.

Gibson's radically new theory, already well articulated in his first book of 1950, was based on the hypothesis of an active organism. The active observer gets invariant perceptions despite varying sensations. How does this come about? The answer to this question was fundamental: the organism explores the energy flux. The movements of the eyes, mouth, and the hands seem to keep on changing the input of sensation, just so as to isolate over time the invariants of the level of input at the level of the perceptual system. Somehow as perceivers, we 'pick up' the invariants in relations between changing sensations, and these form the basis of the experience of permanent structures in the environment. The agency of active exploration of retinal, auditory and tactile images can be a property of the perceptual system itself, as in the saccadic movements of the eyes (rapid shifts of point of attention of which we are unaware), or the exploratory movements of the hand in perceiving a shape, or a movement of the whole organism, such as the pilot bringing a plane in to land. The key point is the idea of an activity in the course of which, for example, the sensory image on the retina is changing, the perceptual system abstracting higher order invariants from the changing point of view such as the point of touch down on an airfield or the trajectory of a tennis ball.

A new theory requires new terminology to express the new insights on which it is based. Part of the explanation for the slow acceptance of Gibson's ecological theory of perception was the way he expressed his radically different point of view. He used the word 'pickup' for the process by which invariants in the stimulus energy were taken in by the active organism. His choice of term for the process as a whole, 'direct perception', was unfortunate, suggesting, as it did, that the passage from stimulus to conscious experience was not mediated by anything. The point was that what an organism perceived was neither the result of the imposition of order on fleeting sensations, nor was it the result of inferences drawn from sensory data. It was neither sensory nor cognitive. The invariants were fundamental, sensations clothing them in color, texture and so on. Information pickup was not information processing.

The other important Gibson terminological innovation was the word 'affordance'. To emphasize the priority of the uptake of invariants, Gibson asked his readers to think of the environment as a rich resource of possibilities of action. In perceiving a knife as something sharp one *saw* that it afforded cutting. In hearing a sound as a tone above the tonic, one heard that it afforded resolution. The environment is the source not only of sensations, but affords the experience of permanent things, and, in a general kind of way, what can be done with them. The relation between environmental states and conditions and the two components of perception, sensations like color and pitch, and visual invariants such as shape, and auditory invariants such as tonic and dominant, the first and fifth notes of a scale, are radically different. Sensations are caused via stimulus of the retina, hair cells of the cochlea, and so on, but invariants are abstracted from the energy flux by active exploration, for what it will afford to an organism with its specific organs of sense, and, in the case of human beings, its deeply engrained cultural expectations.

The phenomenon that is at the heart of the ecological view of perception is easily replicated. When one moves one's head from side to side the sensations one is experiencing related to the pattern of stimulus on the retina are changing, while the world continues to be experienced as stationary, for example, a book on the table. However, when something passes by a stationary head, for example, the book is moved, the visual sensations are very similar to those one experiences when one moves one's head. Yet, the book is seen to move and the head becomes the stationary frame against which the motion is perceived. There must be another ingredient in the process of perception, part of which is an unattended awareness of the movement of one's own head. One is aware of the book, stationary or moving. In the ordinary course of events, as one walks around the desk, one is not aware of the state of motion of one's own head.

Gibson once remarked that he hoped that his new concepts would '… never shackle thought in the way the old terms and concepts have done'. On the old sensationalist view it had to be presumed that one learned how to organize sensations into perceived things or imposed a prior schema that existed independently of visual, auditory or tactile sensations.

We can follow Gibson's brilliant program of experimental tests and elaborations of the theory best with one of the great experiments in the history of psychology, the experimental study of the perception of shape by touch (Gibson, 1962). Gibson needed to show that sensations produced by touching the skin with objects of different shapes did not result in accurate perceptions of those shapes if there was no movement between the test object and the surface of the body. If this were so, then there must be more to tactile perception of shape than sensations of touch on the surface of the skin. The second step would be to show that if the hand, for example, could be used in active exploration of the shape, by moving the hand over the object, then accurate perception of shape did occur. The stimulus objects were common kitchen cookie cutters.

Using a simple device to make sure the pressure with which the cookie cutters touched the hand was the same in all the experimental conditions Gibson carried out three studies. In the first, the stimulus objects were pressed on a stationary hand. The shapes were correctly identified in only 29 percent of the trials. However, when the shape was actively explored by moving the hand over the stimulus object, the wrist, fingers, palm and so on, changing their relative orientations to the shapes, they were correctly identified in 95 percent of the trials. In a third experiment the hand was stationary and the cookie cutters moved over the surface of the palm. In this condition, the shapes were correctly identified in 72 percent of the trials. The exploratory movements allow for the identification of shapes as invariants in the relations between the edges, angles and corners of the objects. The role of the finger and wrist joints in the perceptual process is remarkable. It showed that it was not only the tactile sensations that yielded invariants, but also kinesthetic neural impulses that were not registered in consciousness as such, but only indirectly in the awareness of shape.

Summing up his discoveries, Gibson (1966, p. 160) remarks:

> Tactual perception corresponds well to the form of the object when the stimulus is almost formless, and less well when the stimulus is a stable representation of the form of the object … the role of the exploratory finger movements in active touch would then be, to isolate the invariants … in the flux of sensation.

Among a plethora of observations and experiments on visual perception the 'stake in the field' experiment has the beauty of simplicity. If perception is based on the retinal image, then a distant object should appear smaller than it is, because the image in the retina will be smaller. Choosing a very long flat field, Gibson planted a stake at increasing distances, at each distance asking one of his participants to estimate its height. He reports that 'the judgments of the size of the stake did *not* decrease, even when it was ten minutes walk away and becoming difficult to make out. The judgments become more *variable* with distance but not smaller. Size constancy did not break down.' The implication was that 'certain invariant ratios were picked up unawares by the observers and that the size of the retinal image went unnoticed … no matter how far away the object intercepted or occluded the same number of texture elements in the ground. This is an invariant ratio' (Gibson, 1966, p. 160).

Gibson lists the main invariants in visual perception as 'optical structure under changing illumination' and 'under change of point of observation', invariance of structure 'across sampling of the optical array', and 'local invariants of the ambient array under the local disturbance of its structure' (Gibson, 1966, pp. 310–311). The retinal image is explored for invariants, for example, the ratios of the lengths of sides of a cube as its image on the retina changes during the rotation of the object in real space. These are what we see.

Instead of thinking of the image changing and moving relative to the retina, we must think of the retina moving with respect to the image, and thus *exploring* its geometrical features.

By making another shift in our way of thinking about the psychology of perception Gibson's discoveries and his interpretation of them becomes clearer. Thinking in terms of 'information', rather than in terms of the contents of states of conscious awareness, enables us to think of perception in terms of the information that eventuates in a conscious experience, but may not itself be wholly conscious. Some of the information that is implicit in perception is not given as sensation, but is the result of a process of geometrical analysis performed by the perceptual system as it is used to explore the environment. Some of this information flows to the brain from proprioceptors, nerve endings in the joints and muscles, information that is almost never represented directly in states of conscious awareness. This information is directly represented in what is perceived, mediated neither by hidden cognitive processes nor past experience.

Getting the conceptual tools in order is one of the most important aspects of scientific research. The puzzle about the perception of motion and rest, the fact that the pattern of stimulus on the retina may be the same when the head moves past an object and when that same object moves past the head is readily resolved if one gets one's concepts right. Motion *of* the retinal image is a misconception ... motion *in* the retinal image, change of pattern, is not displacement with reference to the retina. In perceiving visually, the retina is displaced *over* its image, exploring it for invariances in the relations between the sensory elements as their disposition on the retina changes. The eye is constantly in motion, the point of attention changing with great rapidity. These are referred to as the 'saccadic' eye movements, rapid jumps or saccades from one point of fixation to another. The perceiver is not aware of these movements. According to the thesis of ecological optics it is the invariants in retinal image that are maintained as the image is constantly changing that are 'picked up' by the brain, and are what we see.

How does it come about that the perceptual systems behave in this way? It is not learned, nor is the structure of percepts inherited. The *perceptual apparatus* of an animal species evolves with the environment. There is reciprocity of animal perceptual capacities and the key features of the environment in which it is evolving.

Perceptual Processes as the Testing of Hypotheses

This general approach to understanding the psychological processes on which perceptual experience depends was given particularly cogent form by the work of Richard Gregory. 'In ideal conditions,' says Gregory (1998, p. 2) 'object perception is far richer than any possible images in the eyes.' While agreeing with Gibson that 'the added value must come from dynamic brain processes' Gregory eschews a biological or even a mathematical explanation, since he claims that the process of perception involves 'employing knowledge stored from the past, to see the present and predict the immediate future' (Gregory, 1998, p. 2).

For Gregory, the prime historical source for his way of conceiving perception was the work of Hermann von Helmholtz. According to Helmholtz, perception is a species of unconscious inference, from sensory data as premises to hypotheses as to what there might be in the environment. Unlike inferences proper, from propositions to propositions, the conclusions of these inferences manifest themselves to us as something essentially pictorial. At first sight this conception of what is seen, heard, touched and so on seems to run counter to common experience. We perceive things rather than representations of things. Propositional expressions of the natures of the things that are in the environment seem to be quite different from perceptions. However, it is clear that the electro-chemical signals which enter the visual cortex from the complex neural structures of the retina are digital rather than analogue. There is nothing in the least pictorial about what enters the visual cortex. Yet, what we see can be physically matched and compared to representations which are pictorial, such as photographs, diagrams, models, sculptures and paintings, all of which are extended in space as are what they represent.

Just as Gibson developed a special vocabulary appropriate to the intuitions and insights he wanted to share with his readers, so too have Gregory and the cognitivists. 'We now think of the brain as representing, rather as the symbols of language represent characteristics of things …' (Gregory, 1998, p. 5). He goes on to say that the typical cognitivist concepts of meanings and rules 'seem necessary for processes of vision; though its syntax and semantics are implicit, to be discovered by experiment'. This approach can soon come to seem very puzzling. The objects of perception, things, events and so on, those things, events which we perceive, do not seem to be the least like symbols, nor does it make sense to suggest that what one perceives is a representation of something in the environment. It *is* something in the environment. The cognitivists face a problem that the advocates of the direct pickup view do not face, namely, if the relevant states and processes in the brain are symbolic transformations according to rule, how is it that the person in whose brain these processes are going on, sees trees, hears bells, touches fur and so on? We will not get an answer to our question, from either Helmholtz or Gregory. Does this matter?

Richard Langton Gregory (1923–2010) was born the son of C. C. L. Gregory, the leading astronomer at London University. He went to King Alfred School, Hampstead, and in 1941 into the RAF, serving in the signals until 1947. He then went up to Cambridge to read philosophy and experimental psychology. From 1950 to 1953 he worked in the Medical Research Council Unit in Cambridge, spending part of the time seconded to the navy to improve the methods of escaping from submarines. From the MRC unit he went on to a lectureship in Cambridge and to a fellowship at Corpus Christi College. From 1970 until his retirement in 1988 he held a professorship in the Medical School at the University of Bristol.

In later years he was actively engaged in promoting the public understanding of science.

Gregory says explicitly that sensory signals are not adequate for direct or certain perceptions; so, he argues, intelligent guesswork is needed for seeing objects. By contrast, Gibson would agree that sensory signals are not adequate, so, he argues, the active organism must explore retinal images for higher order properties, invariant relations, for example, geometrical structures preserved under transformation. The brain of higher organisms carries through these explorations automatically, because it is built to do just that. For Gregory the brain is actively involved in the process of perception, but as an inference machine, drawing conclusions from premises. The retinal image is the source of the premises of the inferences, but it is the conclusions of these inferences that we see.

Gregory makes much of a parallel he sees between perceptions and the predictive hypotheses of the sciences. In the sciences, hypotheses not only refer to what is to be expected in the future, but also to dispositional properties of material systems, what they would do if certain conditions came about. Visual images, like experimental data, are of little use in practical activities, 'until they are read in terms of significant properties of objects' (Gregory, 1998, p. 10). Any pattern of visual stimuli can be interpreted in an infinite number of ways. What we do depends on the interpretation we have given to the pattern. 'Seeing objects involves general rules, and knowledge of objects from previous experience, derived largely from hands-on exploration' (Gregory, 1998, p. 11). What is the basis for this powerful claim?

The methods of PET scanning and fMRI show very clearly that diverse areas of the brain are active when someone is perceiving something. But what is the brain doing? The rather coarse-grained images of distributed patterns of brain activity do not answer that question. Is the brain automatically performing complex mathematical analyses in search of invariants, as Gibson would have it? Or is it performing logical and conceptual operations, below the level at which such activities are experienced by a conscious being? Is it analyzing formal properties of the sensory flux, or is it reasoning, applying past knowledge to a problem of interpretation? Key areas of the brain that receive fibers from the optic nerves receive more fibers from the higher centers than from the eyes themselves. Clearly seeing involves higher level brain activity. Is it cognitive or is it analytical?

Gregory has supported his Helmholtzian theory of perceptions as knowledge-based hypotheses by a wide variety of observations and experiments investigating or inducing visual abnormalities (Gregory, 1998, ch. 8). People blind from birth have usually accumulated a considerable body of knowledge about how things would look, from what they know about how things feel, as extended in space. Having sight newly made possible as adults, people seem to be ready to identify things visually only in so far as they have plausible conjectures as to how things would appear visually, a kind of hypothetical knowledge. Though babies can see objects of special interest from birth, such important visual perceptions as the permanency of objects during times in which they have been hidden from the infant have to be acquired. This still leaves open a Gibsonian interpretation, but the phenomenon of visual agnosias (Sacks, 1983), not knowing what it is one sees, seems to indicate the role of knowledge based on past experience for the uses and meanings of things in the act of perceiving them.

Another source of support for the Helmholtzian theory comes from the problem of accounting for illusions. The size-weight illusion is easily reproduced. If two material things of the same weight differ markedly in size, the smaller feels heavier than the larger. Gregory claims that this is a *cognitive* illusion. 'The muscles are set for *expected* weights. As larger objects are usually heavier than smaller objects, the smaller weight calls for less muscle force – so it seems surprisingly heavier than the larger weight' (Gregory, 1998, p. 198). The illusion, so Gregory affirms, depends on one's *knowledge* of objects. To make clear the force of the Helmholtzian thesis, Gregory uses the distinction between 'top-down knowledge' and

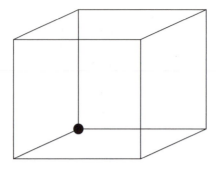

Figure 5.2a   Necker cube with inside/outside spot

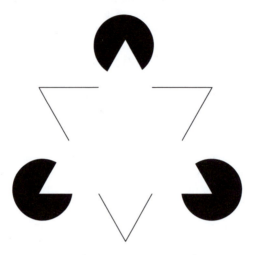

Figure 5.2b   Kaniza triangle

'bottom-up signals' to separate out the components that go into such illusions as ambiguous figures.

In reviewing a great many ambiguities, distortions and illusions of perspective, Gregory makes use of hypotheses from both 'directions' as it were. The key experiments that he believes establish the priority of the top-down component are based on the phenomenon of the Necker cube and Kaniza triangle (Figure 5.2a and b). Focusing our visual attention on one vertex or another, we can see it as if looking down on the top surface or as if looking upwards into the under surface of the top. Let us call the change of perspective 'flipping'. The physical components of the drawing or the wire frame do not change. Yet, in flipping from seeing one face at the front becoming the back, the cube can be seen to change from a regular right-angled cube to a truncated pyramid, if there is sufficient 'depth' in the cube. In some cases there are no bottom-up depth cues in the way the retinal image would look, so sometimes scaling relations between a quadrangle seen as the smaller top of a truncated pyramid or the perspectively reduced back of a regular cube, must be 'downwards' from knowledge assumptions, how we are accustomed to expect things to look. The top surface of a truncated pyramid is smaller than the base, just as the back side of a cube is seen as smaller than the front by reason of perspective.

A simple argument for 'top-down' knowledge involvement in perception is the phenomenon whereby we see a certain figure as a completion of an incomplete figure. Everyone is familiar with the three dimensional appearance of shadow letters. Kanizsa's triangle is an example of the way perception goes beyond the sensory given as knowledge-based expectations seem to be involved in how things look. Similar auditory illusions can be produced by sounding only part of an established pattern of notes when a note that has not be sounded can be heard.

Gregory has never shirked the issue of the evident disparity between material states of the brain and the experiences a person has somehow 'on the basis' of the existence of those brain states. He admits that we have not the faintest idea how to provide an explanation of the fact that, as such pioneers as La Mettrie pointed out in the 18th century, the flow of brain activity is accompanied by a stream of thoughts and feelings which bear no qualitative resemblance whatever to the neurophysiological processes now observable in the brain itself. This is the second transduction.

Perception as Computation

What is happening in the optical, auditory or tactile systems as the analysis of the structure of images proceeds? David Marr, following the Gibsonian line, and realizing the complexity of the processing broadly sketched by James Gibson, began to think in computational terms, as if the brain was a computing machine. According to Marr, the next step must be to go further into the question of how the extraction of invariants is accomplished and that is 'an information processing problem', invoking the 'computational model of mind' (Marr, 1982, p. 30). According to Alan Turing, any and every higher order process ought to be expressible in a computable function, and 'run' on a computer. It was indifferent whether the hardware was a pattern printed on a silicon chip or a pattern of neural networks among the 10^{11} cells of the human brain. Marr's project is based upon the AI or Artificial Intelligence reading of Turing's analogy between brain and computing machine. By creating a program that would simulate certain aspects of perception when run on the input from a video camera into a computing machine, Marr hoped to model what was happening when a brain dealt with the input from an eye.

An underlying and now contested presumption of Marr's project is that the brain processes inputs in the same or at least in a very similar way to the processing of binary representations in the registers of a traditional computer. This has now been replaced by the more sophisticated notion of a neural net. It seems possible that Marr's project might still be happily realized by a connectionist model.

However, a preliminary stage of Marr's project was to develop a set of geometrical figures which might be necessary and perhaps sufficient as the constituents of all possible three-dimensional figures as perceived. Even if the computational aspects of the project fall victim to a better understanding of the brain/computer analogy, the analytical parts of the project might be recovered. In a way it is a recovery of some of the ideas of the Gestaltists.

Here is how Marr's model of the perceptual process worked. Vision, he argued, 'can be thought of as a mapping from one representation ... [as] arrays of image density values as detected by the retina' to another representation but now in terms of items of a radically different kind (Marr, 1982, p. 31). To reach a Gibsonian invariant several steps are required. 'At each level the primitives are qualitatively similar symbols – edges, bars, blobs and terminations or discontinuities – but they refer to increasingly abstract properties of the image' (Marr, 1982, p. 91). Once a computational theory for a process has been formulated, that is, a proposal including basic elements and rules for their combination and manipulation, 'algorithms for implementing it may be designed, and their performance compared with that of the human visual processor' (Marr, 1982, p. 331).

The project reflects the basic principle of computational modeling in psychology: there is a mathematical description, there is a piece of the retina, and there is a silicon chip. All three are similar at the most general level of description of their function. According to the computational point of view, if the running of the program parallels the neuropsychological process, the scientific problem of perception has been solved. Marr (1982, p. 354) summarizes his project with the thesis that 'perception is the construction of a description'. However, here, once again, the gap between neuropsychology and experience opens up. I see a tree, not a description or representation of a tree. One has to admit that the most fundamental question that is raised by the psychology of perception, namely how is visual *experience* possible, is not solved by Marr's proposal. Of course, as we have been hinting throughout this chapter, the very idea that there is such a question may be the result of a fundamental misunderstanding of the sequence of sensory and perceptual transductions.

Conclusion

Perceptual systems provide ways through which people become acquainted with the state of the world around them and various kinds of things that populate it and how they are arranged. Human beings are aware of what is around them, but the attributes of the world as revealed by our perceptual systems are not always of the same kind as those of the objects in the world that initiated the first transduction. Electromagnetic waves are not colors. Nor are we conscious of the processes by which our perceptual systems reveal the environment to us. There is a double transduction. The first transduction links physical processes with neural signals in a consistent way. This transduction is now fairly well understood. Then there is a second transduction which associates activity in distinctive brain regions with perceptual experiences. This is the basic transduction upon which acquaintance with the world depends. We believe that there is no process mediating the second transduction corresponding to that of the first transduction.

6

Becoming a Person

Rom Harré and Christina E. Erneling

A child has hurt himself and he cries; and then the adults talk to him and teach him exclamations and, later, sentences. They teach the child new pain-behaviour. (Wittgenstein, 1953 § 244)

Nothing could be more obvious than the differences between newborn human beings and mature adults. Human infants are more helpless than the young of most other animals, yet under normal circumstances and within a few years, the infant has acquired its native language, a remarkable ability to deal with its environment and a complex set of beliefs about both the physical and social world and other people. The child has developed both physically and psychologically. It has become a person.

A variety of research methods powered by very different theories of development have been adopted by psychologists. On the one hand, there are methods for the study of the development of psychological attributes such as cognitive skills, moral sensibilities and personality traits, and on the other, the study of biological or physical maturation. Obviously, genetics has a part to play in both. And so does culture. Japanese foot binding and Victorian wasp-waist corsetry radically changed the final form of the developing female skeleton, with profound psychological consequences. The natural sciences aim at the discovery of universals, but, as we have pointed out throughout this book, it is often a misleading desideratum for psychological research. The variety that is evident in the domains of culture, geography, climate, history and so on must be taken into account in developmental psychology as elsewhere in the human sciences.

At the heart of any developmental psychology there must be a theory of how the inevitable crises that arise from the clash between biological drives and the demands of cultural conventions trigger developments in the level of cognitive, social and motor skills.

A central demand on any such theory must be to provide an account of how the infant comes to master the discursive practices of its surroundings. In particular, how the infant acquires a grasp of the repertoire of symbols and the rules for their manipulation that amplifies its natural abilities to act purposefully into intentional action appropriate to its cultural setting. Only one of the developmental psychologies we will present in this chapter realizes the ideal of the hybrid format in full – the historical/cultural/instrumental approach of Lev Vygotsky. All, to some extent, achieve a synthesis of gene-driven biological bodily maturation and culture-driven intellectual, social and personality growth.

Varieties of Human Maturity

There are many ways to reach maturity and many ways of being an adult – some valued and some not, different in every culture and perhaps even in each family. To some extent we make the sort of people we want. Families, societies, and historical epochs differ in what the people of these groups take to be the ideal fully developed human being. Both the paths of transformation and the processes of person creation may turn out to be different in so far as the goals are different.

Developmental psychology is dominated by work done in the Western world. Can we assume that development is directed towards the same ideals of maturity and follows the same patterns in non-Western cultures? Do differences in the ideals of cognitive competence and moral sensibility show up when we follow the infant to adult transition in different historical epochs, different cultures, different social classes and perhaps even different families? It is a commonplace that what are taken to be desirable character traits and acceptable personality dispositions differ widely historically and geographically.

One solution to the problems of the researcher who aims to meet the traditional requirements that a scientific theory ought to cover more than just one case, in the face of the historical, cultural and even familial fragmentation of concepts of maturity, is to abstract from particular cases step by step until a level of generality is reached that will be realized in all human developmental transitions, no matter what the cultural differences in the outcome. Whether you want your children to be scholars or to be adventurers it may be that the same general method of managed development is called for. It might require a common pattern of stages, or a common motivational force or a common process of transition from infancy to adulthood, though the content might be different. However, as in the natural sciences, too high a level of abstraction can leave us with a bare schema which needs to be filled out for every application.

In developmental psychology the clash between claims for the natural maturing of adult characters and claims for the overriding power of cultural norms surfaces again and again. According to psychodynamics, the mature human being exhibits a productive resolution of the conflict of forces between id and superego. In Vygotskian psychology, mature or higher cognitive skills are the result of the shaping of the natural activity of the nervous system by the acquisition of symbolic skills, particularly the mastery of language. Evolutionary psychology ties cognitive, social and moral development very tightly to adaption to physical and social environments encountered in the history of humankind, thus seeing both cultural and bodily maturation as an expression of biological adaptation.

Development as Passage through a Hierarchical Sequence of Stages

The famous slogan 'ontogeny recapitulates phylogeny' expresses the powerful idea that throughout the living world investigators will encounter sequences of stages ordered in various ways. Some sequences will be marked by ever greater complexity. Others will be marked by a neater fit to ecological niches. These are phylogenetic stages, seeing historically changing populations of mature organisms as ordered series. The slogan above, originally due to Ernst Haeckel, points to the possibility that each individual organism will go through a similar sequence of stages as those that mark the historical sequence of its biological ancestors. Embryology seems to support this idea, at least in a general way.

Applied to the psychology of human development it comes to this: the development of each individual human being should display the same stages as the development of thought patterns in the history of the human race. Primitive ways of thinking have been succeeded by more sophisticated patterns of reasoning. The cognitive and moral development of a child should display a similar transition.

Stage Theories of the Development of Cognitive Skills

Cognitive staging theories began with the distinction, originally drawn by James Baldwin (1861–1934), between assimilation of new experience into existing schemata (habit) and accommodation of existing schemata to new experience by taking on new forms, 'Consciousness constantly tends to … show itself receptive to that which in any way conforms to its present stock [of schemata]' (Baldwin, 1895, p. 308). This is 'assimilation' or 'habit'. 'Accommodation is the principle by which an organism comes to adapt itself to more complex conditions of stimulation by performing more complex functions' (Baldwin, 1895, pp. 478–479). 'Assimilation/accommodation' is the hypothetical mechanism by which stage transitions are brought about. The process repeats itself '… and the organism acquires a habit of accommodation at a higher level' Baldwin, 1895, p. 486).

Underlying these processes there is a native capacity for imitation. At first there is only 'organic imitation', a stimulus initiates a motor process which produces an effect which is the focus of a new imitation. Eventually, conscious imitation appears, and initiates the assimilation/accommodation process at a symbolic cognitive level (Baldwin, 1906).

Very detailed observational studies were undertaken, particularly by Jean Piaget on his own children, to establish the reality of cognitive staging as the core of human development. Piaget followed in minute detail the gradual maturing of concepts, for example, time, space and number (Gruber & Vanèche, 1977). Lawrence Kohlberg (Kohlberg, 1984) turned his attention to the stages of moral reasoning, setting out a ladder of levels, based on the idea of 'justice' as the mark of maturity.

Jean Piaget (1896–1980) was born near Lake Neuchatel in the French-speaking region of Switzerland. His father, Arthur Piaget, was a university professor. Piaget declared that 'his mother's poor mental health' led him to take a (temporary) interest in psychiatry, but he preferred the study of normality.

While still at high school he began publishing on the subject of the classification of molluscs. From this precocious childhood he brought into adult life a respect for science as a protection against the temptation to engage in ungrounded speculation. About this time he decided that his life work should be the search for a 'biological explanation of knowledge'.

(Continued)

He completed a doctorate on molluscs in 1918. Generalizing the biological point of view, he formulated a principle that dominated the rest of his life work: that there are emergent totalities that impose their form on their parts. He worked in Bleuler's clinic in Zurich, before moving to Paris. Young Piaget was offered the job of developing a French version of the English tests in Alfred Binet's school/laboratory. However, he soon turned from merely collecting children's answers to the prescribed test questions, to discussing with them their reasons for what they had written or said. For the rest of his life, he developed his ideas about how children reasoned by talking to them and following their thoughts in both natural and contrived situations. The focus on children's cognition was not the result of an interest in pedagogy or even developmental psychology as such. It was part of a much larger project: the project of genetic epistemology. How did knowledge grow?

In 1921, he returned to Switzerland to the Institut Rousseau, where he began systematic studies of the reasoning powers of school children. He married one of his students, Valentine Châtenay, in 1923. Their three children became the focus for an intensive study, the results of which appeared in book-length monographs.

For the rest of his career he moved from one important job to another, becoming more and more involved in the public uses of psychology. He was successively director of the International Bureau of Education, director of the Psychology Laboratory at Geneva, and eventually a professor at the Sorbonne. He died in Geneva on 16 September 1980.

Associated with the temporal progression, there is a progression in levels of sophistication of the skills of the developing individual. They are assumed to be more or less the same across the population. Stages cannot be skipped – each stage is a necessary precondition for the transition to a higher level of cognitive functioning. There is a subsidiary hypothesis – that children move from an egocentric point of view, in which the child is the focus of its own thoughts and actions, to a more advanced stage in which the possibility of other points of view becomes salient.

A stage *theory* proposes several hypothetical more or less coherent groups of norms that are supposed to explain the observed reasoning performances of children of different ages. We might treat clusters of norms on an equal footing, each having an appropriate use in the thinking with which we manage our lives. To treat a cluster of norms as a *stage* in a hierarchical sequence of such clusters, as both Piaget and Kohlberg do, suggests that the norms relevant in explanations of acceptable patterns of reasoning differ both in content and scope, and that there are criteria by means of which the clusters can be ranked. There is an invariant order in the modes of thinking displayed in individual patterns of development, each mode of thought is a structured whole, and higher stages displace or integrate lower stages.

Piaget's ladder begins with the Sensory-motor stage (0–2 years). Then comes the Pre-Operational stage (2–7 years) in which symbolic thinking has not yet appeared. Thinking at this stage is dominated by local demands on the actor. At the Concrete Operations stage (7–14 years) symbolic thinking appears but it is carried on by the use of concrete images. Finally, there comes the capacity to carry out Abstract Operations in which arbitrary symbols are put to use in thinking about almost any topic and in solving almost any problem (Formal Operations at age 14).

Transition between stages is not an inevitable consequence of biological maturation. It is brought about by a sequence of adaptations of an existing level to new information inconsistent with at least some of the components of the cluster of rules then dominating the child's thinking. At first, information that is not coherent with the current stage of development is 'assimilated', that is, made to fit the cognitive paradigms typical of that stage. Eventually assimilation can give way to 'accommodation', when the cognitive paradigms are changed to accommodate novel input.

It is important to bear in mind that this is a theory. We do not 'see' assimilation/accommodation going on, but we do realize that Little Mary, who last year was confusing the volume of a liquid with the height of the container, no longer makes that mistake.

We do not 'see' egocentricity disappear. We realize that Suzy and Billy are taking account of each other's wishes and points of view, both literal and metaphorical, in ways that they had not done before.

The staging theory of moral development was deliberately designed to track the staging theory of cognitive development. It was a theory of the development of powers of moral reasoning, that people made moral decisions through reasoning rather than intuition or feeling. The highest form of moral reasoning took account only of the most abstract and universal moral principles for the guidance of our conduct. Kohlberg set out his theory in his *Philosophy of moral development* (1981). Kohlberg, Levine, and Hewer (1983, p. 5) describe the project of the study of the psychology of moral development as the 'rational reconstruction of the ontogenesis of justice reasoning'. Kohlberg emphasizes the theoretical character of the stages.

Kohlberg's stages are as follows:

At the 'Preconventional' level, moral decisions are based on patterns of punishment for disobedience. At the second or 'Instrumental' stage, right actions are those that satisfy one's needs and sometimes those of others.

The 'Conventional' level defines good behavior as that which pleases or helps others, and the need to maintain social order by doing one's duty and respecting authority.

Finally, we reach the 'Postconventional' level. At this stage we find concepts like the 'Social Contract', according to which moral worth is decided by tacit agreement of the whole society. At the highest moral level, people are able to make moral judgments by making use of universal ethical principles, such as justice and human rights.

The theory is explicitly tied to a certain Anglo-American presumption, that morality is concerned predominantly with justice. We know that there have been great and subtle civilizations based on different moral codes. The most obvious alternative to the justice-oriented morality of our day is the morality of honor.

Difficulties abound that have limited the acceptance of staging theories. Studies by Kitwood (1980), have shown that the style of moral reasoning a child chooses in dealing with a problem is determined not by a supposed level of cognitive development but by the demands of the situation in which the problem has arisen. This shadows the generally correct principle that the level of cognitive competence deployed is related more to the problem situation than it is to a 'level' of development. This criterion used in Kohlberg's researches is discussed in more detail in Chapter 14.

Doubts have also surfaced at the conceptual level with the appearance of seeming inconsistencies between the theories and later observations of patterns of thinking. Children seem at first unable to see that the volume of a liquid has been conserved when it is poured from a wide container into a narrow one. According to staging theory, children who make this mistake lack the concept of conservation of volume. Later research has shown that saying that there is more water in the long narrow container than in the broad and shallow one from which the water was transferred comes from requiring the use of two different mensuration principles simultaneously – one, that liquids do not suddenly change their volume, and the other, that length is a good measure of quantity (Bryant, 1984, pp. 251–260). Staging is more learning to operate and prioritize a multitude of principles in the same problem field than acquiring new rules for measuring volume.

The thesis of egocentricity was upset by Margaret Donaldson's experiments (Donaldson, Grieve, & Pratt, 1983, pp. 246–250) which showed that whether or not a child displayed egocentricity depended on the context and the way a problem was set.

Stage Theories of the Development of Personality, Temperament and Character

Looked at from the point of view of observable behavior it is evident that neonates have distinctive personalities. Some are more vociferous than others. Some sleep much longer than others. Some are more responsive to interactions with other people. Gender differences in personality are claimed to be discernible in the nursery, long before they are displayed in the school playground. Human beings seem to have stable personalities, temperaments and characters throughout the age span, until the once stable and acceptable personalities sometimes decay in old age. However, like every other aspect of human life we ought to discern growth and change here too.

Sigmund Freud (1856–1939) was born in Frieberg in the province of Moravia, in the Austro-Hungarian Empire. His mother, Amalia, was Jacob Freud's third and much younger wife.

He received a good elementary education, though he was wracked by the shaming poverty of the family. Amalia was a powerful influence in his life, and his affection for her was tinged with darker emotions, as he himself later confessed.

Freud entered the Medical School of the University of Vienna in 1873 where he was drawn to physiological research. He worked in the physiology laboratory under Ernst Brücke, who was one of the earliest promoters of the strict materialism that later flourished in Vienna among the philosophers and physicists of the Vienna Circle. Organic life is a matter of chemical and physical forces. Psychology, conceived biologically, would be a study of the transformations of energy in the human system.

In 1885, young Dr Freud set off for a year in Paris where he met Jean Charcot, whose practice was largely concerned with hysteria, the presentation of distressing physical symptoms which had no evident physiological causes.

In 1886, he married Martha Bernays, and set up a neuropsychiatric practice in Vienna with a well-established practitioner, Joseph Breuer. Just as in Paris, hysteria was a problem of prime concern to Breuer and his assistant. Hypnosis proved ineffective as a permanent cure, but Breuer's habit of encouraging the patients to talk freely about their early lives sometimes led to the relief of the symptoms.

Freud came to the conclusion that the ultimate source of the symptoms must be a traumatic event which had been forgotten but was still exercising a malign influence on the health of the patient. If the event could be recalled and confronted the patient would be cured.

The next crucial insight that led to the Oedipus complex and his theory of personal development, was his realization that the stories of childhood seductions that some of his women patients had told him were significant but not literally true.

In 1923, Freud was finally forced to acknowledge that he had developed a 'growth' in the back of his mouth. For the next 15 years, he fought a long battle against cancer.

The publications of the early years of the 20th century propelled Freud into worldwide fame. In his own home country his work was generally rejected, and even condemned as scandalous. Freud gathered a small group of disciples around him, the members of the Psychoanalytic Society, for regular meetings. Dissent from the views of the master generally led to expulsion.

Hitler came to power in Germany in 1933. On March 12 1938, the German army entered Austria, to bring about the unification of the two Germanic nations. Freud's apartment was searched a few days after the Anschluss, but Freud himself was unmolested. His friends began a concerted effort to bring him to England. He left Vienna on 4 June 1938. He died in London on 23 September 1939.

Psychodynamics

Psychodynamics began as a theory to account for adult neuroses. Sigmund Freud believed that the sources of neurotic problems were to be found in the early life of the sufferer. This meant that of necessity it became a theory of the development of adult personalities, both mature and distorted. At the heart of the various versions of the general theory are hypotheses about the processes by which infantile thinking and feeling is transformed into the psychology of the adult.

Psychodynamics as developmental psychology is well described by Anna Freud (1982, p. 6):

> At any time during his [sic] moves to maturity the child can be shown to be under pressure. Internally, his maturing higher functions battle with his primitive drive derivatives and try to limit satisfaction and wish fulfilment. Externally, the loved persons on whom he is dependent urge submission to the demands of reality. From step to step the child has to reconcile these influences and has to find solutions which are acceptable in the inner as well as the outer world.

It is an important principle in developmental psychodynamics that the child makes use of the same psychic procedures of resolution of conflicts as does the adult.

The foundation of psychodynamics is the theoretical principle that the flow of psychic energy, personified as the id, is transformed, redirected and elaborated by the influence of social norms, personified as the superego. The id represents the ever-present urge for sensual gratification. The theoretical status of Freud's id and superego are emphasized by Anna Freud:

> Our knowledge of the id … can be acquired only through derivatives which make their way into [conscious systems]. If within the id a state of calm and satisfaction prevails, so that there is no occasion for any instinctual impulse to invade the ego in search of gratification … we can learn nothing of the id contents. (Freud, 1982, p. 5)

Similarly, 'the superego, like the id, becomes perceptible in the state which it produces with the ego, for instance when its criticism evokes a sense of guilt' (Freud, 1968, p. 6).

The influence of the superego on the id appears in the course of two major transitions. The first transition is a shift in the bodily location of the major source of sensual gratification. The second is a shift in the patterns of sexual feelings between the members of the nuclear family.

According to the theory of psychodynamics, infants and very young children pass through three phases or stages defined by the location in the body of sources of sensual gratification. These are the oral, anal and genital stages. In the first phase, the mouth provides the main source of sensual gratification achieved by sucking. In the second phase the anus is the most important region of gratification achieved by defecation. In the third phase the genitals assume paramount interest achieved by manipulation. Deficiencies and latencies in the transition from one phase to another in the life of an infant can have life-long effects on the personality. Thus development is not a straightforward progression, as Piaget conceived cognitive development to be.

A version of this is incorporated in everyday thinking in the distinctions between oral, anal and genital personalities, of which the anal is much the most common in folk psychological talk. Meticulous, pernickety and grasping – this sums up the anal personality for many.

Psychodynamic theory includes another phase transition, which, if successfully accomplished, leads to a normal, well-adjusted character and personality. This is the famous doctrine of the Oedipus complex. This too is a theory, in that it is built around hypotheses as to the existence and forcefulness of events and states of mind of which people are not generally aware.

According to the psychodynamic point of view, the family is the site of intense psychosexual feelings, not confined to the parental adults but active even in very young children. The theory posits that boys develop a strong sexual attraction to their mothers. At the same time, they are jealous of their fathers whose relation to the mother they may wish to usurp. Since these feelings can hardly be publicly displayed in their true form they fuse into a hidden pattern, the Oedipus complex. This may appear in consciousness as fantasy. Boys are afraid that their fathers will castrate them, but gradually this threat wanes. Maturity is marked by a growing solidarity with the father and a shift of interest from the mother as an actual person to an interest in the female sex generally. Girls are envious of the males in the family seeing the penis as a source of power, an organ which they lack. However, they resolve this lack by realizing that female power resides in their capacity to produce babies. After these transitions are successfully accomplished, there emerge mature and stable men and women.

It must be emphasized that psychodynamics is a cluster of *theories*. The hypothesis of the oral–anal–genital transition is not the result of a program of close observation of the behavior of children. Nor are the Oedipus complex and penis-envy states of mind confessed to by boys and girls. These are explanatory hypotheses to make sense of the advent of psychopathologies, such as hysteria, as deviations from what should be the normal relatively contented life of human beings. The psychoanalytic movement soon generalized these hypotheses as universal theories of the pattern of personality development.

Development as Progressive Expression of Genetic Endowment

According to this point of view, psychological characteristics of adults derive ultimately from the human genome. The path of this 'derivation' is complex. Genes are expressed as proteins in the processes of life. Proteins have very specific characteristics that determine how they will be assembled into the constituents of complex bodily organs such as the brain or the pancreas. The way they are assembled determines how that organ functions. Much of this story is taken for granted in psychobiology. Perhaps all we need to say is that biopsychology presumes there is a route from protein to practice!

There are two strands in the history of attempts to explain the direction and goal of human development biologically. One theory comes from a simple generalization of processes known to occur in the developmental progression of infant animals and baby birds towards adult maturity. This theory has been associated with Konrad Lorenz (1903–1989), John Bowlby (1907–1996) and Mary Ainsworth (1913–1989). This is the 'ethological theory'.

The other strand of theory, evolutionary psychology, comes from the thesis that the genetic endowment of modern human beings is a direct descendent, with only minor changes, of the genetic make-up of our Palaeolithic ancestors. Developmental processes are once again sequences of patterns of gene expression but they terminate in adult characteristics that were evolutionarily advantageous in the Stone Age. This theory has been associated with the biologist Edward Wilson (1998), and more recently with the psychologists Cosmides and Tooby (1997).

Ethology

Ethology appeared as a reaction to behaviorist accounts of animal behavior. Ivan Pavlov had discovered the conditions under which animals could be trained to respond to stimuli, basing his research on the conditioning of natural responses to arbitrary environmental events. The forms of animal behavior, however complex, were seen as chained sequences of stimulus-response pairs which were either natural or established by conditioning.

This theory had its origin in laboratory studies of animal behavior. When the lives of animals and birds were studied in their natural habitats it became clear that there were long running patterns of behavior, routines that seemed to be run through from beginning to end in a way that suggested that there was an innate template realized in the routine. Where could such a template come from? The best place to look for an explanation was the role of the routine in the life of the organism. Thinking in Darwinian terms led to the general principle that all such routines existed because they were advantageous to the reproductive process. As such, the genetic basis for them would have been established by natural selection in a very straightforward way. Those organisms that began to behave this way would be more successful reproductively and so if there were genes or gene-complexes at the root of the behavior they would have been preferentially selected.

The story becomes more complex with two further discoveries. A routine had to be triggered by something in the environment. There had to be a releasing mechanism. Was this learned or was it inherited? Research seemed to show that like the format for the routine, the dancing and prancing of male birds for example, the releasing mechanism was also innate. This too proved too simple. Some bird-song was brought to life by innate releasing mechanisms, but in other species songs had to be learned and differed from place to place – almost as if there were cultures of bird song. A chance rediscovery of a phenomenon that came to be called 'imprinting' led to further refinement of the theory. It turned out that some releasing mechanisms that initiated innate routines were established by infant experiences during certain sharply bounded periods in the life of the young. Konrad Lorenz was able to imprint young jackdaws with a pattern of choosing flying companions that favored crows, but was unable to imprint them with a pattern for choosing mates other than jackdaws (Lorenz, 1970).

Ethology was quickly generalized from animals and birds to human beings as a comprehensive theory of development. Developmental psychologists began to look for routines and innate releasing mechanisms and to see whether there was any evidence for the existence of imprinting in human development.

As John Bowlby (1997–1998, p. 30) put it:

> Built-in [species-specific] patterns of behavior seem to remain as important for mediating the basic biological processes [for example, reproduction] of mammals as they do for other species … it would be odd if [human beings] … were not to share some at least of these behavioral components.

In short, we should apply ethological concepts, such as 'social releasers' and 'social inhibitors' to understanding human development as an alternative to an exclusive reliance on either learning theory or on psychodynamics.

One of the most striking patterns of inherited behavior, according to John Bowlby and Margaret Ainsworth, is explained by the hypothesis of a powerful and inherited bond between mother and child (Bowlby, 1997–1998, pp. 37–43). This is displayed in the phenomena of attachment. The attachment bond shows up very early in a child's life, in the signs of distress when separated from the mother. This is an ethological theory in that the patterns of attachment behavior are inherited via the passing down of certain genes. This genetic endowment exists because of the advantage those so endowed have in the process of reaching reproductive maturity and so contributing to the gene-pool of the next generation.

The theory came to prominence when John Bowlby used the idea to account for the troubled minds of children whose attachment bond had been disrupted by the exigencies of the Second World War. Complementary to the concept of 'attachment' there is the concept of 'separation anxiety'. These are theoretical concepts, the content of hypotheses that are offered to account for the behavior of children and their mothers.

The theory, like all theories in developmental psychology, is teleological. It postulates a desirable end-state in the character and personality of adults, the 'healthy personality'. This concept is based on the idea of a 'trusted person' or 'attachment figure'. Thus, the healthy personality 'reflects … an individual's ability to recognize suitable figures willing and able to provide him [her] with a secure base … and [an] ability to collaborate with such figures in mutually rewarding relationships' (Bowlby, 1997–1998, p. 104). It is not difficult to see the relationship between the smiling infant and the responsive mother as the ethological foundation for the 'healthy personality'.

John Bowlby (1907–1990) was born in London. His father, Sir Anthony Bowlby, was surgeon to the King's household. His nanny, to whom he become very attached, left when he was four, an event which he later described as being as painful as a bereavement. At the age of seven, he was sent to boarding school. He found the experience 'terrible'. Not only did these childhood experiences shape his later studies, but they imbued him with a particular sympathy to the sufferings of children.

At Trinity College, Cambridge, he studied psychology and pre-clinical sciences. He completed his medical qualifications in 1930 at University College Hospital in London. While doing his clinical training he joined the Institute for Psychoanalysis. He continued to develop his interests in psychiatry at the Maudsley Hospital. By 1937, he had qualified as a psychoanalyst. In 1938, he married Ursula Longstaff, herself from a medical family.

The development of his famous theory of the power of separation of children from their mothers came about partly through his experiences in the aftermath of the Second World War when he saw the psychological devastation among homeless children, and partly through his studies with Mary Ainsworth. She was a Canadian psychologist who came to England to work with Bowlby. She developed her own version of attachment theory in Africa and later at Johns Hopkins University she put it to a systematic empirical test.

After the war, he became deputy director of the Tavistock Clinic which was dominated by the Freudian point of view. Bowlby aroused the wrath of the Freudian circle by his theory of childhood neuroses as having their origin in actual separation from their caretakers.

He died 2 September 1990, at his summer home on the Isle of Skye. Scotland.

It was also applied by Mary Ainsworth in her experimental studies of attachment behavior, leading to her theory of the three types of personality (Ainsworth, 1978). These appeared in the responses of infants to short periods of detachment from their mothers during which a stranger entered the situation. The 'stranger situation' is a sequence of episodes involving the mother and someone who is a stranger to the child. Ainsworth believed that she could recognize three different patterns of response to separation. Some infants avoided the mother on reunion. Some infants actively sought contact with the mother on reunion and were neither avoidant nor resistant. The third group both resisted contact with the mother and actively sought it.

The Bowlby-Ainsworth theory uses the concepts of human ethology to define the normal patterns of human life from infancy onward. It gives a sense to abnormal kinds of human behavior as the result of disruption of what should have been the normal phases of development of stable personalities and orderly social behavior.

Evolutionary Psychology and Human Development

Evolutionary psychology purports to explain why there are certain widespread patterns of human behavior that seem to be independent of the immediate contemporary conditions under which children grow to adulthood. It depends on a subsidiary hypothesis, that Darwinian processes of gene selection are very much slower than the comings and goings of culture and its constituent fashions (Barkow, Cosmides, & Tooby, 1992).

An evolutionary explanation of a contemporary pattern of behavior needs three theoretical components. The first is a hypothetical picture of Paleolithic life among early humans, and the demands that survival placed on the behavior of the people of that time. The second is the identification of a behavioral pattern among modern people that is supposed to be in all essentials the same as the hypothetical pattern among our ancestors. Linking these two is a third hypothesis – that the genetic endowment that was established in Paleolithic times has persisted and offers the basis of an ethological explanation of the contemporary behavior in question. Many of the best-known examples of the applications of the theory purport to explain alleged differences in the life patterns of men and women. The basis of this way of using the theory is a presumed division of labor along gender lines said to be typical of hunter-gatherer societies. Men hunt and women gather. The male genome will be subject to selection pressures from the needs of hunters, while the female genome will be subject to selection pressure from the needs of gatherers. Thus, the claim that women are genetically programmed to talk more than men is put down to the need for hunters not to alarm the prey by needless chatter and for groups of women wandering in the woods to stay in touch.

How does it work as a theory of human development? Cosmides and Tooby in their summary article (Cosmides & Tooby, 1995) point out correctly that as a human being matures, new gene-driven functions appear at times appropriate to the stage of life the infant, child or adolescent has reached. They compare bodily stages of development, such as gene-driven changes that lead to sexual maturity at a certain age, with cognitive stages which will make their appearances at the right time. Which cognitive stage appears when it depends on which culture you grow up in and which school you go to. Evolutionary psychologists have answers to this reservation. 'In fact', they declare, 'an aspect of our evolved architecture can, in principle, mature at any point in the life-cycle, and this applies to cognitive programs of our brain just as much as it does to other aspects of our phenotype' (Tooby, 1995).

The link with the conditions of Paleolithic life comes about through the theoretical claim that the human brain is the site of information-processing devices that are highly specialized, evolved to deal with specific kinds of situations. The theory requires that the cognitive schemata revealed by studies of thinking, such as those of Jerome Bruner (1983), are actually favored processes in a neural net, for example. There is no doubt that cognitive skills and the schemata that express them are domain specific – but it is a large step to claim that these are specific brain processes that are the result of the activity of inherited neural structures, established in the genome by the minute exigencies of Stone Age living. It seems entirely plausible to suppose that generic higher level cognitive and motor skills depend on the working of neural mechanisms that are inherited, but quite implausible to offer a theoretical explanation of the apparent preference for landscape paintings to be a taste that developed on the edge of the African savannah.

Unlike the theory of an ethological basis of responses to the disruption of attachment bonds, evolutionary psychology has been subjected to a great deal of criticism, including political. It seems to support a very conservative conception of the possibilities for human beings to live different kinds of lives if so many important ways of thinking and acting are genetically driven. Some have argued that it is morally dubious because it seems to foster the alibi 'It wasn't me, it was my genes!'

Furthermore, the whole scheme depends on two radical conceptual errors. First of all, the general claim that cognition and other higher order psychological functions are brain processes in dedicated structures, commits the fallacy of deducing tasks from tools. The tools of cognition are no doubt brain modules and structures, but the tasks they are used to perform are not definable in terms of the properties of neural systems. This is true whether the brain structures are inherited via the genome and epigenetic rules, whether they are acquired by study and practice, or by psychological symbiosis (as the instrumental/cognitive/historical theory would have it). Football cannot be exhaustively defined in terms of the properties of footballs.

The second fallacy is more subtle. It concerns the grammar of psychological discourse and its incommensurability with the grammar of neurological discourse. The properties of brains are defined in the sciences of physics, chemistry and so on, and are attributable to an organ of the body. However, the properties of patterns of reasoning, thinking, experiencing emotions etc. are attributable to persons of which brains are a component, part of the tool kit that includes devices such as Blackberries. This point has been made repeatedly, starting with the writings of Descartes, though he drew a dangerously mistaken conclusion, that distinct groups of properties required distinct substances to which they could be attributed. The latest and most powerful version of this grammatical reminder can be found in Bennett and Hacker (2003).

The Child as Scientist

Piaget took science to be the end-goal and norm of knowledge. The idea of children as small scientists has had a profound influence on contemporary psychology, resulting in what is known as the 'theory theory' and the 'theory of mind' approaches.

In *Words, thoughts and theories* (1997) Gopnik and Meltzoff go beyond Piaget's claim that the child is actively and intelligently exploring its world, to the claim that the child is thinking and acting just like a scientist. Like the scientist, the child creates, tests and revises theories. In fact, the child in this respect surpasses the normal adult who is portrayed as a much duller creature. Infants as young as nine months are portrayed as creating, testing and sometimes changing theories about the world and about other people. Children have and use theories of objects, of actions, and of how other people think and feel. The authors call their theory the 'theory theory' because it is a theory about children's theories. Infants and young children do not start with the knowledge or theories that adults or scientists have, but neither do they start with reflexes as Piaget claimed. Instead they are born equipped with some innate responses and a propensity to make false recognitions. As the authors put it, children have theories which are both specific and false, as well as an ability to test, reject and form new theories.

The idea of 'theory of mind' was first introduced by Premack (see Premack & Woodruff, 1978) in his research on the intentionality of primates. Developmental psychologists studying children's social cognition then adopted this theoretical framework, partly as a response to Piaget. In the 1970s, a growing body of research showed that children were more competent cognitively and socially than Piaget had claimed (e.g. Donaldson, 1978; for a critical discussion see Costall & Leudar, 2004). This led to a revision of observational data and to certain re-interpretations, but no major or serious theoretical alternative to Piaget, and mainstream psychology emerged. Instead it led to a reinforcement of some Cartesian assumptions, by focusing on social cognition as 'mind reading' and its failure as 'mind blindness'.

The proponents of the 'theory of mind' paradigm claim that children as well as ordinary adults are like scientists forming and testing hypotheses, making inferences, constructing theories and the like from observable (behavior) to something which cannot be observed (mental processes).

Gopnik and Meltzoff's 'theory theory' postulates theory change as typical of childhood cognitive development. But this idea makes it necessary to ascribe to children all the properties that we associate with reasonable thinking and rationality. Although the specific contents of the theories change, the basic mechanisms for change remain unchanged, and are presupposed in the explanatory model the authors propose. If children are born with the ability to test, reject and create theories, there is not really any developmental difference in basic cognitive ability or rationality. In other words, there is no fundamental development and no change over time in the cognitive ability which is shared by all humans.

Also, by transferring the objective conception both of theory and theory change from science to the subjective or psychological sphere of the child they have not given us a psychological mechanism, but only a re-description of how any reasonable person would argue in similar cases. It is just a reconstruction of a rational argument in the objective sense. And by transferring rationality from the public sphere to the private and subjective level, they do not explain the observed level, because the unobserved process is as much in need of explanation as the observed.

Development as Training

Behaviorism's starting-point was that description, classification, methods of investigation, as well as theory construction in animal learning, should be applied to human psychology. This is very much restricting psychology to O-grammars, even if Albert Bandura slightly modified this. In its heyday it was widely believed that complex psychological functions could be broken down into elementary stimulus-response units. There were supposed to be some natural, rudimentary responses to simple stimuli. Development consisted of training an organism to perform more complex operations, making use of the natural responses as a platform for higher levels of performance.

The conception of development as training is based on two simple but powerful Principles:

1   **Classical conditioning: An organism can be so trained that natural responses to certain stimuli can be conditioned to appear as responses to different stimuli. The basic natural response is the reflex arc, a purely neurological process.**

2   Operant conditioning: An organism can be so trained that only one of a range of possible natural responses is elicited by a certain stimulus. At the root of this theory is the idea that organisms learn to respond to stimuli to maximize rewards.

The simple idea of development as training, originally worked out in the context of studies of the behavior of animals and birds, has opened up into three successively more people-centered theories. Classical conditioning proposed a basic mechanism by which prior stimuli were more or less permanently associated with non-natural or conditioned responses. Operant conditioning proposed a similar mechanism, but the quality of the responses was instrumental in maintaining the behavior. Responses that elicited rewards were favored by the organism. Finally, in 'social learning theory', the operant version was made more psychologically sophisticated by introducing hypothetical cognitive processes by which more subtle consequents of behavior were effective in establishing behavioral habits.

Classical Conditioning

In speculating how human character traits could be understood in the general context of the 'training' theory, Ivan Pavlov (1849–1936) added three hypothetical processes to the basic machinery of development. Each began with a 'natural' reaction to some situation that by informal conditioning developed into a character trait (Pavlov, 1927).

There was the grasping reflex, a natural response to dealing with a desired object. This is transformed into reaching for something one does not yet hold in one's hand. Further conditioning can transform this motor reaction into the character traits of miserliness and greed.

There was the reflex for liberty. All animals are naturally disposed to struggle against imposed bonds, but some more than others. Further conditioning in the social world of human affairs could lead to responses which give rise to revolutionary uprisings against tyranny and oppression.

The third natural reflex was the reflex for servility. A show of deference by a dog that has been attacked by another defuses the aggression. Conditioned by the exigencies of daily life this natural reflex is transformed into social deference between people of various ranks, roles and positions.

Pavlov believed that simple responses both natural and conditioned cluster into complex but stable patterns. He called these patterns 'stereotypes'. This, it should be noted, is an observation concept, and was not sustained by a corresponding theory of the underlying processes which would wield diverse responses into a stereotypical pattern of behavior.

Though later studies have shown the important role played by natural reflexes, simple responses to situations, so much interpretation of environmental conditions is required that the reflexes created by classical conditioning are too simple. Conditioning cannot be the whole story. Indeed, this is evident in the loose link that Pavlov and other 'reflexologists' proposed between basic response patterns and adult characteristics like revolutionary ardor and miserliness.

Operant Conditioning

The developmental theory that grew out of the techniques of operant conditioning did not involve hypotheses about hidden generative mechanisms and their sustaining models.

Rather, it appeared as a conceptual proposal – a way of redescribing and collecting many everyday behavioral phenomena under a very few concepts, concepts that drew their sense from the practices of operant conditioning. If one were to accept the redescriptions one bought a generalized operant account of the whole of human psychology.

To understand the vocabulary one needs a nodding acquaintance with this technique of conditioning. In classical conditioning, a new type of stimulus was presented along with the stimulus that activated the natural reflex. After a while, the presentation of the new stimulus alone brought forth the response. In operant conditioning, only one of a group of random actions or operants was rewarded. Soon the animal or bird produced the favored action rather than any other response to a situation. This is the familiar technique used by animal trainers – an apple for the horse which raises its hoof on command. The new twist on this technique that propelled it to the center of psychology for a while was the discovery by B. F. Skinner in the 1940s of the most successful patterns of reward and cessation of punishment (a kind of backhanded reward) to maintain the favored action (1948).

The promotion of operant conditioning as a form of developmental psychology was based on the idea that people could be trained not only to perform tasks of many kinds, but also to acquire worthwhile moral characters. By rewarding 'good' behavior, it could be established as the social norm.

This became a ubiquitous *theory* of human psychology by the generalization of the vocabulary for the original simple experiments with rats and pigeons. The key terms were 'operant', that is, a spontaneous action an organism (including a person) makes in a certain situation. 'Shaping' was the regime of rewards that led to the establishment of the 'correct' response. The overall relation between experimenter (mentor) and subject was 'control'. By redescribing all human activity, from the correct use of knife and fork to the uses of language, in terms of this simple vocabulary, the explanation of the existence of these patterns of action as the result of operant conditioning came to be the default.

Ironically, some of the most vociferous objections to accepting operant conditioning as a theory of development depended on believing that the technique would really work. If this were so it opened up the possibility of a sinister cabal of psychologists shaping the social world into a form that reflected their prejudices. George Orwell famously made use of this fear in describing how the citizens of the world of 1984 came to love Big Brother.

The most telling blow against the theory was based on the implausibility of operant conditioning as a possible explanation of how language was learned. To acquire linguistic skills by a sequence of rewards for correct uses of words would have required an exorbitant amount of time. In addition, the actual language overheard was so poor that children would be unable to learn grammar (Chomsky, 1959).

Social Learning Theory

The basic principle of social learning theory is 'self-regulation' (Bandura, 1977, p. 13). 'Self-influence partly determines the actions one performs'. This is a cognitive process. 'Through verbal and imagined symbols people process and preserve experiences in representational form that serve as guides for future behavior' (Bandura, 1977, p. 13). Furthermore, the consequences of behavior that affect future choice of actions need not necessarily be one's own. Sometimes people learn what it is advisable to do by observing the consequences of other people's behavior.

The theory proposes two kinds of inferences. Outcome expectancies concern hypotheses about the likely outcome of certain kinds of actions. Efficacy expectations reflect 'the conviction that one can successfully execute the behavior required to produce the outcome' (Bandura, 1977, p. 79). 'At the highest level of development, individuals regulate their own behavior by self-evaluation and other self-produced consequences' (Bandura, 1977, p. 103).

Apart from the neglect of the social dimension, the theory presupposes that there are native reasoning powers, such as the ability to make inferences on the basis of hypotheses linking actions to consequences. The theory is not truly developmental in the sense that there is no attempt to track the growing logical competence of individuals, nor to link ideas of logical competence to local cultural ideals. It is focused exclusively on the individual as the locus of psychological processes.

Development as a Social Process of Cultural Assimilation

Theories of development purport to provide an explanation of the observable phenomena of the maturing of an individual by offering hypothetical mechanisms which are imagined to underlie observable changes in cognitive competence, moral sophistication, maturity of personality and scope of application of human skills. Staging theories, as well as ethological and evolutionary theories, locate the hypothetical mechanism in individuals. Extra-individual influences, new experiences, drive the subsidiary mechanism of stage transition, though whether the new experience is merely assimilated or initiates a change in existing schemata is not determined by that experience. Cultural theories, notably the theory proposed by Lev Vygotsky (1896–1934), locate the main mechanism of development in the social environment in which the young human being is growing up. The hypothetical cognitive processes sited in individuals depend on the existence of social relations between the child as 'apprentice' and an older child or adult as 'master'. The members of the group, usually a dyad, work together in tackling problems. This entails that the developmental mechanisms must consist largely of symbolic exchanges or demonstrations. Where cognitive development is concerned these exchanges are likely to be linguistic. The archetype of development is apprenticeship, a relation between someone less skilled and someone with greater competence, in the course of which the skills of the 'master' are passed on to the 'apprentice'.

This theory has been summed up in the famous quotation from Vygotsky:

> Every function in the child's cultural development appears twice: first, on the social level, and later, on the individual level, first between people (interpsychological) and then inside the child (intrapsychological). This applies equally to voluntary attention, to logical memory, and to the formation of concepts. All the higher functions originate as actual relationships between individuals. (1978b, p. 57)

Higher psychological functions are acquired in the course of development, but lower psychological functions are the result of the maturation of the brain and nervous system. Generally, lower cognitive functions are involuntary. Some aspects of remembering are learned, but the underlying process is a natural function of the developing human nervous system. Higher functions are utilized and managed by individual actors in the course of carrying forward some project. Patterns of reasoning in problem-solving are acquired in the course of social interactions. Expressed another way, we can say that thought is a product of the nervous system, but it is shaped into higher forms by the acquisition of language. Higher functions are mediated by sign systems, lower by material processes in the nervous system.

So far we have only an outline of how lower psychological functions are transformed into higher functions by the transition from a public-social domain to the private-individual sphere. In proposing a theory to account for how this happens, Vygotsky introduced another powerful concept, the 'zone of proximal development', the ZPD, complementary to his conception of psychology as a repertoire of cultural/historical/instrumental practices. When a child has a preliminary and rudimentary grasp of a skill, that ability is in the zone of proximal development, on the way to becoming a mature competence.

The basic mechanism of development, the process by which a skill moves from the ZPD to the zone of actual development, is, as we now say, psychological symbiosis. The role of the senior partner in the symbiotic process is not only to supplement the efforts of the junior partner towards the achievement of some goal, but to provide a psychological interpretation of those efforts. In this the senior partner interprets the child's efforts according to a local commonsense psychological typology. A child seems to point to something in reaching for it. This is interpreted in psychological terms as the child showing that it is *wanting* something. Now there is the first moment of development – a change of function of the gesture from reaching to indicating, drawing the attention of another person to something. Once this function is secure the second moment of development occurs when the child comes to attend to his or her own thoughts, feelings, wants and so on. A lower order psychological function, indicating a want, becomes a higher order psychological function, self-attention and mental reflexivity. At some point the gesture is replaced by a verbal act, requesting or demanding or asking.

Though at all times and in every place development of higher order functions from lower passes through the ZPD, the skills acquired will not necessarily always be the same nor will they follow any particular developmental schedule. We would expect there to be marked differences in the higher functions that are characteristic of different social formations and at different historical epochs. Vygotskian theory suggests an anthropological and historical dimension to psychological research and the need to be wary of the temptations of ethnocentrism.

Conclusion

With the developmental psychology proposed by Lev Vygotsky, we already have a hybrid scheme with a place for biological aspects of maturation driven by genetic imperatives modulated by epigenetic factors, and cultural influences that impact the development of every individual as he or she acquires the local repertoire of symbolic and practical skills.

The cultural/historical/instrumental account of human development comprehends and completes both the Piagetian staging account and the Freudian stories. The Vygotskian idea of the role of language as conversation in the acquisition of cognitive and material practices in the close circle of the family allows the developmental psychologist to look for features of the ZPD which tie in with Piaget's and Kohlberg's patterns of thinking without making any presumptions about stages and temporal order of the acquisition of skills.

Similarly, the parallel between the two Vygotskian sources of personal development in the intrinsic activity of the nervous system and the shaping of that activity by the imposition of structure in the embedment of the child in a language environment, allows us to take a very much broader view of what goes into personality development than the predominantly sensual sources of the Freudians.

There is no doubt that the idea of a hybrid psychology of development is clearly anticipated by both Freud and Vygotsky. This is hardly surprising if we reflect on the very obvious fact that children grow in 'body and mind' over the years. We also know that not everyone of them will reach the same standards of competence that their culture demands.

7 Learning and Memory

Brady Wagoner

Where once Mnemosyne was a venerated Goddess, we have turned over responsibility for remembering to the cult of computers, which serve our modern mnemonic idols ... Human memory has become self-externalised: projected outside the rememberer himself or herself and into non-human machines. These machines, however, *cannot remember*; what they can do is record, store and retrieve information – which is only part of what human beings do when they enter into a memorious state. (E. S. Casey, 2000, p. 2)

Introduction

Hermann Ebbinghaus and Frederic Bartlett are generally considered the founding fathers of the psychological study of memory. Yet, they developed radically different approaches to the topic, corresponding roughly to the 'two psychologies' discussed in Chapter 1 of this volume. Ebbinghaus (1962[1885]) focused on identifying *cause-effect relations* between a stimulus and how much of it persisted in memory, that is, a regularity between events. The guiding metaphor for his research program was memory as a *storehouse* for sense impressions – that is, a *space* upon which experiences are passively imprinted, stored and later read off. This metaphor goes all the way back to Plato who described 'memory' as a wax-tablet in the mind, like those used for writing notes to oneself in the ancient world. By contrast, Bartlett (1932) approached remembering as an everyday social activity. His interest was in exploring remembering as 'effort after meaning' – that is, an active struggle to connect some material (e.g. a story or image) with something already familiar, as part of one's personal history and group conventions. He developed the novel temporal metaphor of remembering as an active process of 'construction'. Here we have a very fine example of 'agent-causality'.

This chapter does not declare the triumph of one approach over the other; instead, it aims to integrate the two for the development of a 'hybrid' psychology of learning and remembering. To do this, I first consider Ebbinghaus's research into memory-storage capacity and more recent research into the neurology of memory. Second, Bartlett's study of remembering as an effort after meaning and related developments are explored. The respective contributions of both approaches are then brought together using Vygotsky's heuristic distinction between 'natural' and 'cultural' development. The advantage of this distinction is that it allows us to explore the relationship between the two – for example, their dialectic in child development. Lastly, this chapter considers pathological cases in which 'natural' memory is enhanced or damaged, and how 'culture' is used to organize a mass of unconnected details or overcome memory losses.

Ebbinghaus and the Experimental Psychology of Memory

In 1878, Ebbinghaus began the formal experiments on himself that would inaugurate the psychological study of learning and memory, and revolutionize experimental psychology. His celebrated monograph *Memory: A contribution to experimental psychology* (1913 [1885]), created a platform on which to experimentally explore learning and memory, and is full of findings still recognized as valid and of central importance today. The book also became the model of research practice in the new discipline, instead of alternatives, like Wundt's approach. Its focus on empirical results (over theoretical speculation), rigorous application of method and statistics, and writing a research report with introduction, methods, results and discussion sections, are all now standard practice in traditional psychology.

At the time Ebbinghaus was conducting his experiments, Wilhelm Wundt's model of experimental investigation was dominant. According to Wundt, experimental psychology's object of study is immediate conscious experience. In Wundt's Leipzig laboratory, his students varied some external stimuli and recorded changes in an observer's (i.e. an experimental participant's) experience. For example, to explore different sensory thresholds they varied the distance between two pinpricks on the skin and asked 'observers' to report if they felt one or two points. It should also be noted that Wundt thought the term 'memory' was too imprecise (it meant too many things at once) and too close to everyday language to warrant its inclusion in the science of psychology; phenomena that might be called memory were investigated in Wundt's laboratory but they were given different names.

Hans Ebbinghaus (1850–1909) was born in Barmen, Germany. At 17, he entered the University of Bonn where he studied classics, languages and philosophy. His first and foremost interest was psychology, then a branch of philosophy. He was also a great lover of poetry. In 1873 he completed his doctoral dissertation on Eduard von Hartmann's *Philosophy of the unconscious* and thereafter worked as a school tutor for a number of years. During this time he happened upon Fechner's *Elements of psychophysics* in a second-hand bookstore. By Ebbinghaus's own account, it was this book that gave him the idea of applying quantitative experimental methods to the study of memory. He conducted his famous experiments at home on himself, some say so that others would not be subjected to their tedium! At this time, Ebbinghaus lived a regimented life of teaching and experimentation, but the payoff was immense: his monograph *Memory: a contribution to experimental psychology*, published in 1885, would be highly celebrated and exert an enormous influence

(Continued)

on the new discipline. Within a year of its publication, he was recommended for a salaried position at the University of Berlin. In the years that followed, Ebbinghaus worked tirelessly to promote the new discipline of psychology as an experimental science, starting a journal and securing funds for laboratories. He defended the view that it was a natural science and could be studied in the laboratory, against attacks by Dilthey to the contrary.

Ebbinghaus' study transgressed Wundt's model of investigative practice in several respects, though when Ebbinghaus began his studies in 1878 he was unaware of Wundtian restrictions. First, Ebbinghaus explicitly set out to study 'memory' (an unscientific term for Wundt) and saw its potential implication outside the laboratory; for example, in the school classroom, a context he knew well from his experience as a teacher. In contrast, Wundt thought a pure science should focus on answering basic philosophical questions removed from everyday discourse and life. Second, Ebbinghaus aimed to extend experimental methods to 'higher psychological processes' – the book's subtitle very explicitly tells us this will be 'a contribution to experimental psychology'. Wundt's laboratory focused on lower psychological processes, such as sensation and perception, which were believed to be invariable across cultures; in contrast, higher psychological processes, such as recollection, were mediated by a group's cultural products (e.g. their language, myth and customs) and thus variable between cultures; Wundt thought their study required a method that compared various group's cultural products to make inferences about the social variability of mind. Third, in order to apply experimental methods to memory, Ebbinghaus focused on quantitative memory performance rather than qualitative conscious experience, as was the focus of Wundt's experimental model. To do this, Ebbinghaus dropped the study of memory as a *recollection* of some experience and reduced the meaning of memory to *reproduction* – memory as reproduction could be counted, whereas recollection could not. What Ebbinghaus studied in his monograph might even more precisely be described as *memorization* and *retention*, a familiar practice in the school classroom where he worked as a tutor.

Ebbinghaus found that memorizing poetry and prose occurred too quickly and that there was a multiplicity of influences that changed without regularity (e.g. word associations, rhythm, interest and a sense of beauty). This would not do if he was to discover the quantitative 'laws' of memory, in the spirit of Fechner's psychophysical laws. Stimuli were needed that were simple and homogenous, that could be treated as constant and interchangeable units. This was found in his well known 'non-sense syllables' or perhaps better translated from the German original as 'meaningless syllables'. Non-sense syllables are composed of consonant-vowel-consonant combinations, such as HAL or RUR. Ebbinghaus prepared all possible syllables. The 2,300 syllables that he arrived at were mixed together and then some were drawn out by chance to construct series of non-syllables of varying lengths. Ebbinghaus presented himself with each syllable in the series for a fraction of a second, keeping the order of syllables constant, and pausing for 15 seconds before going through the series again. This was repeated until he had learned the list by heart – that is, until he could recite each syllable in the series without error. Even though Ebbinghaus's experiments were conducted solely on himself, his findings have stood the test of time and are still discussed today in psychology books dealing with memory.

Ebbinghaus conducted 19 experiments for his monograph. Let us now consider some of his most important findings.

In the first empirical chapter of his book, Ebbinghaus investigates the 'rapidity of learning series of syllables as a function of their length'. For example, does it take three times as much time to remember six verses of a poem than it does two? One of his first findings is that he can consistently reproduce a list of seven syllables (plus or minus one) on his first repetition of the list. This discovery he made long before George Miller published his celebrated paper on 'The magical number seven, plus or minus two' (1956), arguing that adults can hold approximately seven items of information in their short-term memory. After reporting this effect, he finds a near linear relationship between the number of syllables in a list and the number of repetitions required to remember it. For example, it takes 13 repetitions to memorize a series of 10 syllables, 23 repetitions for a series of 13 syllables and 32 repetitions for a series of 16 syllables. It is also in this chapter that Ebbinghaus tells us he was able to memorize poetry (Byron's *Don Juan*) 10 times faster than the equivalent number of syllables in a series of non-sense syllables.

Ebbinghaus is perhaps most famous for his *curve of forgetting*; however, there is a general misconception about what precisely he measured. His procedure was to memorize series of syllables and then see how long it took to *re-learn* them (rather than count how many syllables he remembered) after intervals ranging from 21 minutes to 31 days. By subtracting the time it took to re-learn the list from the time it originally took to learn it, he could calculate how much work was 'saved' in re-learning. He found that the greatest amount of forgetting (just under 50 percent) happens after only 21 minutes. The rate of forgetting then continues to even out, such that little more is forgotten, for example, from two days to

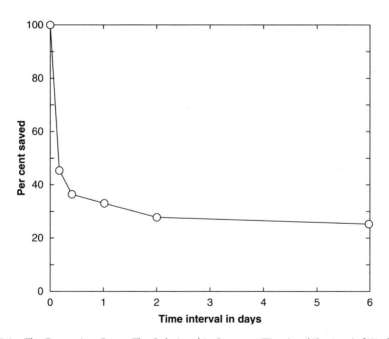

Figure 7.1   The Forgetting Curve: The Relationship Between 'Time' and 'Savings' of Work

six days (see Figure 7.1). Thus, unlike the relationship between the length of the series and number of repetitions required to memorize it, the relationship between time and forgetting is non-linear. However, it should be noted that in a later study he found a much more gradual curve of forgetting for the memory of Byron's *Don Juan*.

Many other important findings are also reported in his monograph. To briefly name just a few:

1   **It takes longer to forget material after each subsequent re-learning – thus, distributed learning rather than cramming is better strategy for exam preparation.**
2   **Fatigue decreases retention, while sleep after memorization actually increases it.**
3   **We tend to remember items at the beginning and end of a list at a higher frequency than those in the middle – this is called the *serial position effect* referring to a 'primacy' and 'recency' effect.**
4   **Changing the order of just a single syllable in a series dramatically hinders memory for the series – this was meant to test Herbart's theory of association.**

Ebbinghaus was operating with the assumption that success in recall meant matching inputs with outputs, which of course could be quantitatively measured. Ideal recall was the retention of all items in a list. When performance fell below the ideal, the question was how much 'work' was required to bring it back. Ways of optimizing the amount of work put in and the memory performance one got out were searched for. So, for example, it is a *better* strategy to distribute learning across time than to cram it all into a single session. Ebbinghaus clearly had formal schooling in mind as the context in which memory manifested itself, and it is little surprise that the biggest consumers of this research were psychologists interested in applying psychology to the field of education. This is why the Ebbinghaus version of psychology, using commonsense terms (e.g. memory) that could be easily applied to social institutions outside the laboratory (e.g. education), won out over Wundt's more philosophical approach (Danziger, 2002a).

The Storage Metaphor, Neurology and Behaviorism

Ebbinghaus very explicitly draws on the ancient metaphor of storage in general and inscription in particular to discuss his findings. According to the inscription metaphor, experiences are inscribed on the mind/brain, where they are stored as 'traces' until later 'read off' at the time of remembering. Consider Ebbinghaus's own words:

> These [experimental results] can be described figuratively by speaking of the series as being more or less deeply engraved in some mental substratum. To carry out this figure: as the number of repetitions increases, the series are engraved more and more deeply and indelibly; if the number of repetitions is small, the inscription is but surface deep and only fleeting glimpses of the tracery can be caught; with a somewhat greater number the inscription can, for a time at least, be read at will; as the number of repetitions is still further increased, the deeply cut picture of the series fades out only after ever longer intervals. (Ebbinghaus, 1913 [1885], pp. 52–53)

The root metaphor of inscription on the mind goes all the way back to Plato:

> I would have you imagine that there exists in the mind of man a block of wax...
> When we wish to remember anything we have seen, or heard, or thought in our
> own minds, we hold the wax to the perceptions or thoughts, and in that material
> receive the impression of them as from the seal of a ring. Whatever is so imprinted
> we remember and know so long as the image remains. (Plato, *Theatetus*, 191D-E)

Plato was using the new technology of wax tablets used for writing in the ancient world to
conceptualize memory. He goes on to elaborate this metaphor by saying that a person with
'good memory' has wax that is neither too hard nor too soft. Later medieval thinkers would
take the metaphor quite literally and recommend heating the back of one's head or rubbing
ointment on it to soften one's wax and therefore improve retention!

The metaphor of memory as storage of inscriptions has been pervasive throughout the
Western tradition. In addition to Ebbinghaus, Freud speaks of the mind as a 'mystic writing
pad' (similar to an Etch A Sketch) in which experiences are inscribed on two planes – the
first 'perceptual consciousness' is easily erased, while the deeper 'mnemic system' retains
enduring traces. Today memory is said to operate like a computer that 'encodes' information
onto a hard disk where it is 'stored' until later needed, at which time it is 'decoded' and
'retrieved'. The hardware is said to represent the physical (i.e. neural) level of processing
information, while software represents information processing on a psychological level.

The idea that memory is a place of storage was new at the time Plato was writing. Before
Plato, in the age of Homer, memory was understood as a divine being that imparted memory
to one from outside – both the *Iliad* and *Odyssey* begin by evoking Mnemosyne (the goddess
of memory) or her daughters (the muses) to impart memory to the storyteller. Thus, Plato
was aware that he was using a novel metaphor and with it radically re-conceptualizing
memory. In time, however, the storage metaphor, and the inscription metaphor in particular,
have become so taken-for-granted that today we have difficulty thinking about memory differently. This is dangerous in science because we forget about the assumptions that the metaphor brings with it and take them instead to be a part of reality rather than figurative
constructions. For example, memory as inscription assumes: (1) remembering is separated
into three distinct phases, now called encoding, storage and retrieval; (2) memories are stored
as individuated 'traces'; and (3) memories retain their meaning irrespective of context
(Danziger, 2002b). All three problematic assumptions never come into question if studies are
guided by this metaphor: most memory experiments (1) strictly separate learning and
retrieval; (2) use lists of isolated words or non-sense-syllables; and (3) the context of recall is
rarely considered as more than a potentially confounding variable.

At a biological level, the inscription metaphor has lead psychologists in search of the
place in the brain upon which experiences are inscribed as 'traces' or 'engrams' (literally
meaning 'something converted into writing'). This biological interpretation of the
metaphor was already in currency when Descartes was writing at the beginning of the
modern era:

> When the mind wills to recall something, this volition causes the little [pineal] gland,
> by inclining successively to different sides, to impel the animal spirits toward different
> parts of the brain, until they come upon that part where the traces are left of the thing
> which it wishes to remember; for these traces are nothing else than the circumstance
> that the pores of the brain, through which the spirits have already taken their course

on presentation of the object, have thereby acquired a greater facility than the rest to be opened again the same way by the spirits which come to them; so that these spirits coming upon the pores enter therein more readily than into the others. (cited in Lashley, 1950, p. 434)

Ignoring the role given to the pineal gland and changing 'nerves impulse' for 'animals spirits' and 'synapses' for 'pores', the theory is not so different from 20th century conceptions of memory neurology. At the end of the 19th century, the Spanish anatomist and Nobel laureate Santiago Ramón y Cajal laid the basic conceptual framework for neurology. His 'neuron doctrine' states that the brain is made up of discrete nerve cells (i.e. neurons), which function as elementary signaling units. In all animals the three basic types of neurons (i.e. sensory, motor and inter neurons) can be found; thus, complexity in the brain has to be explained in terms of the quantity of neurons and their interconnections – for example, snails have about 20,000 neurons, compared with the 100 billion found in a human being. Each neuron in turn makes about 1,000 connections with other cells, leading to a staggering degree of complexity. The functional metaphor of the brain becomes a kind of switchboard for electrical signals.

The idea that learning and memory involved the modification of processes taking place at the junction between neurons dates back at least to Sir Charles Scott Sherrington, who coined the expression 'synapse', meaning 'to clasp' in Greek. Sherrington did research on reflexes, such as cat's stretching by cutting connections between body and brain (so as to focus on the spinal cord in isolation), and then applying electrical shocks to the animal's skin to observe its response; synapses were the links in the reflex-arc function. Today, synaptic plasticity is one of the most heavily researched topics in neurology. One particularly important kind goes by the name of 'long-term potentiation' (LTP). When LTP was first discovered in the 1950s it was considered more of an experimental oddity and methodologically useful tool, than a neural explanation for memory (Carver, 2003). Working on neurons in the hippocampus, a brain region now believed to play an important role in memory, researchers noted that repeated stimulation of a neuron to fire, such that there is communication across a synapse, would result in an increased potential for synaptic communication. It was not until the 1970s that researchers would describe it as a mechanism of memory. Strong interpretations would go as far to say that memories were stored in these synaptic potentials, sometimes referred to as Hebbian synapses. Others would argue a weaker version, saying that LTP was just one component in the neurology of memory. The stronger version is particularly problematic in that changes in the synapse do not typically last more than an hour.

Learning then occurs by setting up particular pathways between neurons and modifying their strength at the physiological level and between stimulus and response at the behavioral level. Physiologists would pick up on this metaphor to describe 'learning'. At around the same time that Ramón y Cajal and Sherrington were developing their ideas, the Russian physiologist and Nobel laureate Ivan Petrovich Pavlov was studying classical conditioning, an automatic form of learning. Pavlov taught dogs to salivate (conditioned response) at the ring of a bell (conditioned stimulus) by pairing the sound with the presentation of meat powder (unconditioned stimulus). He thought these associations were made through a physical change in the neural pathway created between input and output: repeated simultaneous excitation of two neural pathways (i.e. for unconditioned and conditioned stimuli) would strengthen the pathway between conditioned stimuli (e.g. the bell ringing) and conditioned response (e.g. salivation). Later, American psychologist John B. Watson would extend Pavlov's work to study fear association and to advance his behaviorist crusade in psychology. In a famous experiment, Watson and Rayner (1920) conditioned an 11-month-old, 'little Albert', to fear (conditioned response) white rats by giving him one to play with and making a loud noise (unconditioned stimulus) whenever he touched the rat (conditioned stimulus). Little Albert began to fear not only white rats but also a non-white rabbit, a furry dog, seal-skin and even Santa Claus.

The important difference between the two thinkers was that for Pavlov 'conditioning' was the thing to be explained through a physiological investigation, whereas for Watson it was the explanation itself. American behaviorism did not see a need to make reference to physiological underpinnings of behavior (and even less talk about the 'mind', which became a kind of taboo); instead, psychology should confine itself to discovering the laws of stimuli-response (S-R) pairs. The 'classical conditioning' of Pavlov and Watson was soon supplemented with B. F. Skinner's 'operant conditioning', which explored how the frequency of behavior could be increased or extinguished through reinforcement and punishment. The catchall word in American behaviorism was 'learning', which had, of course, been used earlier by psychologists, but had never been given the role of unifying the discipline, as it did for the behaviorists. To do this, the behaviorists turned 'learning' into a highly abstract concept that would apply equally to rats, cats, pigeons, monkeys and human beings. Laws of learning found at one level were applied without modification to another; for example, Skinner (1948) uses pigeons to explain 'superstition' in humans. It should be noted that contemporary psychologists now use 'cognition' in a way that is as equally abstract and vague as the behaviorist's 'learning'.

Since the time of the behaviorists, neurologists have used animal models to look for the neurological correlates to behavioral learning. Early in this pursuit it was believed that learning and memory could be found in specific neural circuits. However, Karl Lashley, a former student of Watson, who had worked with him to replicate some of Pavlov's experiments, put this assumption into question. In search of the engram (or more specifically 'habits of conditioned reflex type' in the brain), Lashley created lesions in different parts of the rat brain and tested their effect on maze learning. To his astonishment, he found that which particular cortical area was destroyed mattered little – different regions could substitute for each other in learning. What counted was the amount of tissue destroyed, which he found to be proportional to the reduction in learning. Lashley (1950, pp. 477–478) notoriously concluded that: 'This series of experiments has yielded a good bit of information about what and where the engram is not'. The study was criticized for: (1) using a rather open learning task that allowed different abilities to compensate for one another; and (2) making lesions that were not refined enough to reflect different functional divisions in the brain. We now know that different brain regions do serve specific functions, though as Lashley's work suggests, we also know that the brain needs to be understood in terms of its plasticity and dynamism.

Evidence for the important role played by the hippocampus in memory came from brain-damaged patients, such as H. M., who was referred to in his obituary as the 'unforgettable amnesiac'. H. M. suffered epileptic seizures following a bicycle accident at the age of nine, which became worse as he got older. By the age of 27 he was totally incapacitated. In hope of alleviating his epilepsy, he agreed to take part in an experimental procedure that would remove two-thirds of his hippocampus, his amygdala and other portions of his temporal lobe. The procedure did significantly improve his epilepsy but at an enormous price: he almost entirely lost the ability to form new memories, from which he never recovered. If you entered H. M.'s room, had a conversation with him, left and returned a few minutes later, you could have the very same conversation with him without his recollection that the conversation had occurred before or that he had ever met you. H. M. could hold information as long as his attention was focused on it, but as soon as he was distracted it vanished forever. From the time of his surgery in 1953 until his death in 2008, H. M. was the subject of hundreds of research studies, more than any other patient in the history of neuroscience. In an early study, Milner (1962) made the striking discovery that H. M. had not lost all forms of memory. She gave him the task of tracing a star with a pencil while watching his hand in a mirror. Though he had no recollection of having done the task before, his performance improved significantly over three days, at a rate similar to others without brain damage. Thus, Milner had shown that some forms of memory (e.g. motor skills) rely on brain regions outside the temporal lobe.

Philosophers had made the distinction between two kinds of memory long before. In 1890, William James distinguished between *habit* (memory at the level of bodily action) and *memory* (conscious recollection of the past). Similarly, Bergson distinguished between *memoire-habitat* and *memoire-sourvenir*, and Ryle between 'knowing how' and 'knowing that'. Today, psychologists and neurologists alike use the distinction between *procedural* and *declarative* memory. Declarative memory is explicit and accessible to consciousness, whereas procedural memory is implicit and accessed through performance. H. M. and similar cases provided neurological evidence for the distinction and the possibility of more precisely exploring the reliance of different abilities on each type. Cases like H. M. not only retain motor skills but are also influenced by priming. For example, when asked to free associate to the word 'furniture' both normals and amnesiacs are much more likely to say 'chair' if they have recently been given the word. Amnesiacs will not, however, experience feelings of recognition, nor will the effect last longer than a couple of hours, whereas for normals it can last weeks. Neurologists hypothesize that procedural memory is evolutionarily older, relying on more primitive regions of the brain; declarative memory, by contrast, relies on evolutionarily newer regions of the temporal lobe.

Cases like H. M. can be revealing, but we need to be careful reading function from dysfunction – this is called the meterological fallacy. The hippocampus may be essential for memory but it is one part in a larger dynamic system. Similarly, spark plugs may be necessary for an engine to function but they only become functional when integrated into the motor. In the case of H. M. these problems are compounded in that it was not only his hippocampus that was removed but also his amygdala and large portions of his temporal lobe. Plus, he had suffered several years of seizures before his operation. And still, he was *not* entirely unable to develop memories. For example, he could, with some struggle, remember that JFK was assassinated. The metaphor of the hippocampus as a 'printer' of memories thus misleads us to think of it as operating in relative independence of other neural processes. The same criticism can be made of characterizing cerebral regions as 'libraries' for storing memories.

Memories are not simply 'printed' and then 'stored' in a location of the neo-cortex; rather they remain active, only becoming relatively stable after their acquisition. The progressive post-acquisition stabilization of memory is called 'consolidation', which has been described at both the level of the synapse and brain system (Dudai, 2004). Synapse consolidation occurs in all species and results in a relatively stable synapse after an hour or two. It involves cross talk between two neurons through a number of complex chemical processes. This process can be disrupted by chemical, hormonal or electro intervention post-acquisition thereby blocking consolidation. By contrast, system consolidation takes over a month for a memory trace to become relatively stable. In this process the trace comes to rely less on the hippocampus for its activation. Thus, in retrograde amnesia, recent memories are more likely to be lost than remote ones – this is known as 'Ribot's law'. There is a parallel with Ebbinghaus's forgetting curve: the reader will recall that most forgetting happens after the first 20 minutes. With more time, memory becomes relatively stable; however, consolidation research also suggests that each time a memory is activated a process of reconsolidation ensues, thus modifying the memory.

Thus, the notion that a memory is inscribed on the brain as a static register of 'something that happened to me' needs to be thrown out. What we find instead is fluctuating patterns of neural activity in a system that never returns to the same state twice. Even more, there is no neurological correlate to encoding, storage and retrieval. All new experiences combine with these previously acquired neural patterns, which in turn develop as a result of the encounter. Things become markedly more complicated when human experience is part of what needs to be explained: At a neurological level the similar brain regions light up when I remember my last birthday party and imagine a future birthday party. Similarly, there are no sharp brain distinctions between perception of an event and memory of it (Addis, Wong & Schacter, 2007; Schacter, Addis & Buckner, 2007). Thus, no clear neurological mechanism has yet been found that distinguishes past, present and future, recollection from perception and imagination. As a corollary, this brain research has nothing to say about whether a memory is true or false. Finally, the behavioral study of memory (e.g. running mazes) ignores the fact that for humans, memories have meaning and as such are related to our life in social groups, a point to be elaborated on in the next section.

In sum, neurological research suggests that if the storage metaphor fits at all it will have to consider storage in distributed and developing networks rather than as isolated and unchanging inscriptions in neural circuitry. We might even push this notion beyond neurology to consider how memories are distributed in the body, the social and physical context, and among members of a social group. Cognitive psychology has discussed 'state-dependent recall' and 'cued recall' but these theories still consider memory to be something entirely internal and as such continue to vastly under-emphasize the participation of processes taking place outside the head. In the next section, we will consider Bartlett's research and theory of remembering as a radical alternative to the storage metaphor of memory. In spite of the fact that most neurological research still takes the inscription metaphor as its starting point, Bartlett's theory actually fits neurological findings (of the brain as an active developing system) better than this conception.

Bartlett and Socially Constructive Remembering

Frederic Bartlett conducted his most famous experiments in the 1910s, at a time when psychology was moving towards a more holistic perspective, which did not separate an action, perception, imagination or memory from the person making it or the context in which it is done. His first set of experiments explored the influence of interests and values on perception and imagination (Bartlett, 1916), leading him to believe that these factors would also be of central importance for remembering, though they had been previously neglected in the Ebbinghausian style of experiment then dominant. Bartlett was also highly influenced by anthropology. In his 1917 St Johns College fellowship dissertation, entitled *Transformations arising from repeated representation: A contribution towards an experimental study of the process of conventionalization*, he uses psychological methods to explore the anthropological process by which unfamiliar pieces of culture (i.e. stories and images) are changed in the direction of a recipient group's conventions. It is these experiments – together with experiments on 'perceiving and imaging' – that would make up the material in Bartlett's most well-known and important book.

The title of Bartlett's book *Remembering: A study in experimental and social psychology* (1932) is noteworthy in two respects. First, replacing 'memory' (in Ebbinghaus's title) with 'remembering' signals that Bartlett intended to study an *activity* rather than a *thing*. For him, mind is an active *process,* not a passive *substance.* This idea can also be seen in his consistent use of the gerund of the verb when discussing 'perceiving', 'imaging' and 'thinking'. Second, the activity studied belongs, at least in part, to 'social psychology', and here again we see the influence of anthropology. Remembering is characterized as an 'effort after meaning', the active struggle to connect material to something already familiar, implying that remembering is regulated by social conventions. In the first chapter of *Remembering* Bartlett argues that attempts to sterilize the laboratory of meaning are never entirely successful and even worse, doing so results in wholly artificial conditions with little resemblance to remembering in everyday life. The more successful one is in removing meaning from an experiment, the more artificial the experiment becomes; thus, the smoother Ebbinghaus's curves and ratios are, the more irrelevant they are to remembering as an everyday social practice!

Frederic Bartlett (1886–1969) was born in the small English town, Stow-on-the-Wold. As a result of his poor health, he was largely home-schooled, which meant much time for independent reading. He claims to have travelled 18 miles to the nearest library once a week to read Cambridge philosopher James Ward's (1886) celebrated article 'Psychology' in the *Encyclopaedia Britannica*. In 1909, he obtained a BA in philosophy with First Class Honours and in 1911 an MA in sociology and ethics. Bartlett then decided to start another undergraduate degree in moral sciences at the University of Cambridge, where he would live for the rest of his life. Cambridge University was especially attractive to him because the psychiatrist later turned anthropologist W. H. R. Rivers was there. Bartlett's ambition was to go into anthropology but Rivers advised him that the best preparation for that career would be methodological training in psychology. Bartlett remained a psychologist throughout his life but anthropology continued to be a major influence on his work. When the First World War came Bartlett remained in Cambridge, due to his health, where he was put in charge of the psychological laboratory and worked on his experiments on remembering as well as on detecting sounds of weak intensity, which were used to design devices to monitor German submarines. His collaborator in this latter research was Mary Smith, who would later become his wife. Bartlett became director of the Cambridge laboratory at the age of 36, which he held until his retirement in 1952. Being in the most senior position in Cambridge for 30 years gave him considerable power to shape the course of psychology in Britain. Strangely, he promoted a practically minded, anti-intellectual, asocial and applied psychology, which was at odds with much of his own work; in the end, his success in this endeavor caused private misgivings (see Costall, 1992). He died in 1969 at a time when his most important work *Remembering* was taking on a second life as a key text for the 'cognitive revolution'.

In the place of non-sense-syllables and word lists, Bartlett uses complex narratives and images as material in his experiments. Word lists and purely quantitative analysis of inputs and outputs perpetuate the idea that memories are isolated impressions storied in the mind/brain. In contradistinction, Bartlett wanted to study remembering as a holistic, meaningful and everyday process. Rarely is it useful for us to accurately remember all the details of an experience; in fact, to do so is a kind of pathology of memory (see the section 'Luria and S., the Mnemonist' below). Instead, we generalize from experiences in the direction of other experiences of like kind. For example, the reader will not remember every word written in this chapter but will, we hope, remember some general ideas, which will be related to his or her previous knowledge about the subject and future orientation. Bartlett foregrounded this tendency to integrate present and past experience (what he called 'an effort after meaning') by using unfamiliar stories and images in his experiments and demonstrating their qualitative change in the direction of the familiar when remembered. Most famously he used a Native American folk story, taken from the anthropologist Franz Boas, called *War of the ghosts*:

One night two young men from Egulac went down to the river to hunt seals and while they were there it became foggy and calm. Then they heard war-cries, and they thought: 'May be this is a war-party'. They escaped to the shore, and hid behind a log. Now canoes came up, and they heard the noise of paddles, and saw one canoe coming up to them. There were five men in the canoe, and they said:

'What do you think? We wish to take you along. We are going up the river to make war on the people.'

One of the young men said, 'I have no arrows.'

'Arrows are in the canoe,' they said.

'I will not go along. I might be killed. My relatives do not know where I have gone. But you,' he said, turning to the other, 'may go with them.'

So one of the young men went, but the other returned home.

And the warriors went on up the river to a town on the other side of Kalama. The people came down to the water and they began to fight, and many were killed. But presently the young man heard one of the warriors say, 'Quick, let us go home: that Indian has been hit.' Now he thought: 'Oh, they are ghosts.' He did not feel sick, but they said he had been shot.

So the canoes went back to Egulac and the young man went ashore to his house and made a fire. And he told everybody and said: 'Behold I accompanied the ghosts, and we went to fight. Many of our fellows were killed, and many of those who attacked us were killed. They said I was hit, and I did not feel sick.'

He told it all, and then he became quiet. When the sun rose he fell down. Something black came out of his mouth. His face became contorted. The people jumped up and cried.

He was dead. (Bartlett, 1932)

Bartlett's participants read the story and were then asked to reproduce it, first after 15 to 20 minutes had elapsed, again typically after a week, and then again after several months or even years later. In his analysis of the data Bartlett attends to qualitative changes made to the story between the original to first reproduction and from one reproduction to the next – that is, what is added, omitted and transformed. He finds increasingly that 'hunting seals' becomes 'fishing', 'canoes' become 'boats', the proper names change or are dropped, rational causal links are added to the story, and all reference to ghosts and the supernatural vanishes or is rationalized. In sum, the unfamiliar is given a setting and explanation within English cultural conventions and in so doing the story is transformed in that direction.

Transformations toward cultural conventions also included changes related to the particular historical context of the First World War at which time Bartlett's experiments were conducted: One of the excuses given by participants for the young man not going to war was that his elderly relatives would be terribly grieved if he did not return. Furthermore, in an experiment I recently conducted using *War of the Ghosts* I found several participants adding the idea that the young man, who goes up the river to fight, was himself a ghost. There is nothing to directly suggest this in the original story, nor does it show up in Bartlett's data. My interpretation of the persistent inclusion of this idea is that participants were drawing on a narrative pattern familiar to them through recent Hollywood movies (e.g. *The Sixth Sense* and *The Others*), where the surprise ending is that the story's protagonist turns out to be a ghost. Applying this idea to *War of the Ghosts* helps to rationalize some of its puzzling elements, such as why the young man does not feel sick when he is hit with an arrow or his sudden death at the end of the story (see Wagoner, 2011). Clearly, the social-cultural milieu plays no small part in an individual's remembering.

It is important at this point to note some differences between Bartlett's analytic strategy and most 'replications' of his experiment: First, changes from one reproduction to the next were just as important in Bartlett's analysis as from the original to a reproduction. Remembering always involves an active reconstruction, though he observes that most of the changes in the story occur after only 20 minutes. Replications, by contrast, have focused exclusively on accuracy and distortions between reproductions and the original. Second, the focus of Bartlett's analysis is qualitative changes in single cases, not aggregate statistics, which he refers to as 'scientific makeshifts'. Single cases are used to concretely demonstrate the processes of transformation under consideration. Contemporary researchers have criticized this methodology for its lack of fit with the contemporary norms of independent and dependent variables, large sample sizes and statistical analyses of aggregated data (e.g. Kintsch, 1995; Roediger, 1997). In actuality Bartlett's methodology of working with the complexity of organization found in single cases is closer to the practice of the natural sciences than psychology's current standard methodology of aggregate analysis (Lewin, 1935). Third, Bartlett conversed with his participants during and after the experiment. *Remembering* is full of spontaneous comments offered by his participants on their own experience performing the experimental task. Many of his insights about the process of remembering come from this data source as well as more general observations of participants as they do the task. By contrast, contemporary experimentalists typically only attend to what can be easily quantified.

David Middleton, Derek Edwards and others at Loughborough University have developed this social and conversational aspect of Bartlett's research in their 'discursive psychology' approach. Whereas cognitive approaches have tended to criticize Bartlett for keeping the conditions of remembering too open, discursive psychologists have argued that Bartlett's research was not social enough. Very rarely are we individually tested on our ability to remember the details of some material in everyday life – except, of course, in formal schooling. Most often we remember in conversation with others for the purpose of relating with them. In the discursive approach, the focus of the analysis is on the variability in conversational remembering between different social contexts. Cognitive psychology and Ebbinghaus's focus on comparing quantities of inputs and outputs in remembering is replaced with a qualitative comparison of two outputs at different times. In one study, for example, Middleton and Edwards (1990) show the differences in remembering between the context of a psychology experiment and post-experiment discussion of the same material (i.e. the film *E. T.*) by leaving the tape recorder running after the formal experiment had ended; they find that in the experimental context participants focus on sequentially ordering and connecting events, whereas post-experiment their focus shifts to evaluations of and emotional reactions to the film.

Much earlier, the French Sociologist Maurice Halbwachs, a contemporary of Bartlett, had criticized psychologists' claim that they were studying an individual's mental faculty when they did experiments in a laboratory. In his book, *The social frameworks of memory* (abbreviated and translated as *On collective memory*, 1992), Halbwachs points out that even in a laboratory participants use language to help them remember and in so doing take on the perspective of a social community – language is a collective product of group life, irreducible to individual contributions. Bartlett's experiments themselves show this group influence on individual recall. Halbwachs is more radical though, arguing that: 'It is in society that people normally acquire their memories. It is also in society that they recall, recognize, and localize their memories' (1992, p. 38). When we remember we position ourselves within different social frameworks, for example, of the family, religious group, a social class, a nation, etc. In this way, social groups with different interests can construct vastly different memories for the 'same' events, by attaching particular meanings, emphasizing certain aspects here and de-emphasizing other aspects there. Wertsch (2002) shows how Russians construct a collective memory for the events of the Second World War using narrative patterns he calls *triumph-over-alien-forces*. According to the Russian account, propagated in school and media, it was only through the heroism of the Russian people that Germany was defeated. Of course, Americans tell a very different story for the 'same' happenings.

Bartlett struggled for two decades to develop a theory that might account for his findings and integrate both personal and social aspects of remembering. The Cambridge neurologist Henry Head provided him with the vital inspiration. Head attended to brain-damaged patients who had lost the ability to connect serial movements. These patients bring to the fore abilities intact in normal functioning, mainly our capacity to temporally synthesize sensations into a seamless stream in our engagement with the world. Any new action or experience encounters an organized and active mass of previous actions and experience (i.e. schema), and in turn develops them. For example, in making a stroke in tennis I do not remember all the previous individual past strokes I have made but rather sum them up in a new stroke that at the same time appropriately responds to the particular demands of the present situation. This concept of schema as an embodied action was meant to provide the foundation for a radical alternative to the storage metaphor of memory. He famously says:

> Remembering is not the re-excitation of innumerable fixed, lifeless and fragmentary traces. It is an imaginative reconstruction, built out of the relation of our attitude towards a whole active mass of organized past reactions or experience, and to a little outstanding detail which commonly appears in image or language form. (Bartlett, 1932, p. 213)

One recognizes Ebbinghaus's theory and other storage theories of memory as the targets of criticism in the first line of the quotation. The concept of schema or 'a whole active mass of organized past reactions or experience' on its own, however, did not yet provide a complete alternative theory of remembering. 'Schema' by itself only explained how activities, such as moving and perceiving, were temporally organized in a seamless flow, like a motor skill. By contrast, remembering, imagining and thinking implied that this flow is ruptured, so that the person becomes the object of their own reaction – in other words, they become self-reflective. Bartlett calls this 'turning around on one's schema and constructing them afresh'.

This process begins with an 'attitude', by which he does *not* mean a simple internal evaluation of an object (as in contemporary psychology) but rather a dynamic and holistic orientation or impression occurring largely at the level of feeling – for example, the story was 'exciting', 'familiar', 'adventurous', 'like I read when I was a boy'. The attitude is turned towards a past schema and whatever images emerge from it. Reconstruction proceeds largely as a process of justifying this initial impression or attitude. In this process, people do not normally effortlessly reproduce material like a habit, as one finds in Ebbinghaus's memorization of lists (Bartlett calls this 'low-level remembering'); instead, it is a bumpy process in which people come to ambiguities and have to say to themselves, 'this must have gone there'. This is a process of actively manipulating schema, breaking up its chronological order, and bringing other schemata into play. Bartlett gives the example of a journalist recalling a cricket match: 'To describe the batting of one man he finds it necessary to refer to a sonata of Beethoven; the bowling of another reminds him of a piece of beautifully wrought rhythmic prose written by Cardinal Newman' (Bartlett, 1935, p. 224). This interplay of different tendencies is why Bartlett says remembering is an 'imaginative reconstruction'. Furthermore, remembering is said to differ only in *degree* from imagining and thinking, not *kind*; the difference is that remembering focuses more on a single schema of the past to bring to bear on the present, while imagination and thinking more freely use multiple schemata.

One problematic feature of Bartlett's theory is that he does not *explain* how it is possible to 'turn around on one's schema' (which is what makes memory constructive); rather he claimed he was simply *describing* the process. There is certainly a difference between our embodied selves engaged with the world in a seamless flow, and our self-conscious selves (or what James and Mead would call our 'MEs'). In Harré and Moghaddam's (Chapter 1, this volume) language, the distinction between O-grammar and P-grammar is not sufficiently clear in Bartlett's account. Cognitive psychologists have avoided this theoretical difficulty by transforming the meaning of 'schema' (or now just as fashionable 'scripts' and 'frames') into a generic knowledge structure that somehow files away experiences. This, of course, ignores that whole question of 'turning around on one's schema' and simultaneously undoes Bartlett's attempt to provide an alternative to storage theories of memory. How can we rescue schema theory from becoming another storage theory of memory and at the same time explain how it is possible to 'turn around on our schema'? In the next section, I will argue that Vygotsky's theory of mediation provides the missing link.

Vygotsky and Culturally Mediated Memory

At the foundation of Vygotsky's approach is the idea that all higher psychological functions (e.g. attention, imagination, memory) begin as actual relations between people (intermentally) and only later are to be used by the individual alone (intramentally) (cf. Halbwach's 'social frameworks'). The motor driving this process of internalization is tension. Tension first appears on the social plane and then again on the individual plane. Zeigarnik (1967) has shown that unfinished tasks (where tension remains) are better remembered than unfinished tasks (where there is no longer tension). One often has the experience of being in heated debate with someone and later individually continuing the debate with an internalized other. Vygotsky's most well-known example is that of pointing, which begins as a child's failed attempt to reach an object. Their parent sees this and fetches the object for them. The child then learns that they can stimulate their parent's behavior through the gesture and resolve the tension. Thus, the child begins to orient the gesture to others rather than the object. At this point the gesture has become a *sign*, in that the child takes the perspective of the other in performing the gesture. To complete the story, the child directs the gesture at itself, using it to control its own attention. In the same way, language begins as a means of coordinating social activities with the child and is only later used by the child to guide their own thinking and action when tensions or ruptures arise in their world (compare Bartlett's notion of 'turning around on one's schema'). Thus, all higher psychological functions are inherently social in origin. Their mechanism, the *sign*, can be thought of as an internalized social relationship.

This is not to say that higher psychological functions, such as memory, are purely social. Vygotsky makes an important heuristic distinction between the natural and the cultural, which parallels O-grammar and P-grammar respectively (see Harré & Moghaddam, this volume). These two become increasingly integrated into a functioning system in child development. Putting this distinction into the research described above, 'natural' memory can be thought of in Ebbinghaus's terms as biological limits on memory capacity. This will not vary between societies. By contrast, 'cultural' memory fits with Bartlett's interest in the qualitative process of remembering and its relationship to a particular socio-cultural milieu.

In a study conducted by Leontiev under Vygotsky's guidance, they set out to explore the relationship between the natural and the cultural in children's development. As many standard memory experiments have done, children were shown a list of 15 words to remember – too many words for them to remember with their natural memory alone, thus creating a tension. In one condition of this experiment, children were given picture cards to aid them in remembering – and here is the methodological innovation: for the pictures to be useful the child would have to transform them into *signs* that would later stimulate memory for the target word. For example, one child used a picture of a sled to help them remember 'horse'.

Figure 7.2 compares the 'with picture' condition (approximating the cultural line of development) and the 'without picture' condition (approximating the natural line of development). For four- to five-year-olds there is very little difference between natural and cultural memory; children do not yet understand that the pictures can be used as signs to guide their memory. However, from five–12 years of age the cultural line of development improves dramatically over the natural line, though it should be noted that the natural line is also developing. It is during this age that children are beginning to learn how to master cultural tools to control their own activity. In later years, the lines begin to converge or at least develop in parallel. Vygotsky thought that at this stage in development children used mental images instead of the physical images. With the internalization of signs their external counterpart became redundant. Thus, the no-picture condition ceases to be an approximation of the natural line. Although this is a brilliant explanation that fits Vygotsky's overall framework, it does not perfectly match the trend of Figure 7.2 and also ignores the possibility of a 'ceiling effect' – that is, at age 12,

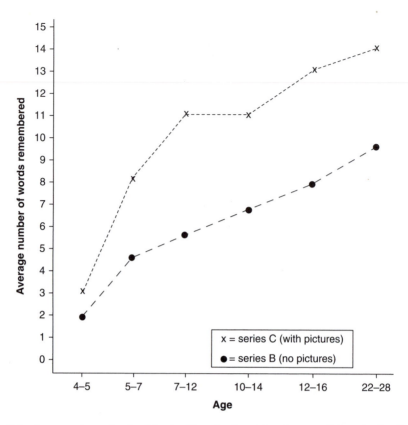

Figure 7.2 A comparison of natural (series B) and cultural developmental lines (series C)

children with the help of pictures are already remembering most of the words in the list leaving little room for improvement.

This quantitative comparison is helpful in beginning to explore how signs transform remembering, but it does not yet tell us much about how children actually use signs to solve the memory task. To investigate this question, Vygotsky would have to look more closely at the *qualitative process* by which individual children use signs to remember. In doing this, he found that children would often make non-obvious links between picture card and target word. For example, one child used a picture of a crab at the beach to help them remember the word 'theatre', explaining that: 'The crab is looking at the stones on the bottom, it is beautiful, it is a theatre.' This imaginative link resembles a narrative more than an associative bond. The child had spontaneously created a new expressive structure inside the experiment to aid them in remembering.

To further explore this more nuanced theory of mediation (i.e. sign use) Vygotsky (1987) identified qualitatively different types of children's errors, each revealing a different component of mediation not yet integrated with others in child development. First, children would often create absurd structures, such as 'I remember this like a *fish* at a *funeral*', when trying to remember 'funeral' from a picture of a fish. These children knew that they can use the picture to help them remember but had not yet integrated this discovery with their ability to imagine, think and abstract. Second, children would often create structures that clearly linked the picture with the target word but did not realize that they could use this to help them remember later on. These children had the exact opposite difficulty to those of the first type. Third, some children were unable to control their own attention so as to effectively navigate the structure they had created. One child used a picture of a lion to remember 'to shoot', saying 'they *shot* the *lion*'; however, later the child recalled 'gun' instead of 'to shoot'. In child development these three factors – instrumental control, imagination and attention – gradually become integrated into a functional system, which is highly adept at using signs to remember.

Let us now use Vygotsky's theory of mediation to answer the hanging question from the last section of how it is possible to 'turn around on one's own schemata and construct them afresh'. For both Bartlett and Vygotsky, remembering (in the self-reflective sense of the word) began with a rupture in our seamless flow of action in the world. We then reflectively use schemata (á la Bartlett) and signs (á la Vygotsky) to help overcome the tension that results from this rupture. Signs are by definition a social relation; they have at least two perspectives built into them and can be used to carry us experientially outside our embodied first-person perspective to an external social perspective. In one experiment, Vygotsky describes how when a child is put into a difficult problem-solving task they begin to talk to themselves to restructure the situation, almost as if it was their parent's voice guiding them through the task. Thus, what Bartlett missed was that the process of becoming self-reflective in remembering had a social mechanism. This insight could also help to explain the phenomena by which we move between two perspectives (the first-person and third-person or 'field' and 'observer' perspectives – see Nigro & Neisser, 1983) in remembering a particular event, as well as our knowledge and control of our own memory (what has been called 'meta-memory' – Nelsen & Narens, 1990).

In the last two sections, I will use Vygotsky's distinction to explore cases in which a person's natural memory is highly abnormal and the new role cultural memory takes in the organization of their functioning. In the first case, natural memory is greatly enhanced, while in the second it has been significantly damaged.

Luria and S., the Mnemonist

Luria worked closely with Vygotsky and continued to develop his ideas in continuity with Vygotsky's integrative cultural and biological approach throughout his career. After Vygotsky's death, Luria decided to take up medical studies, partly because his interests were moving in that direction and partly to avoid Soviet purges. When the Second World War began he was put in charge of rehabilitating brain-damaged soldiers. In the following section we will explore how this was done. Before moving onto this topic, however, we will first look at a book published at the end of his life, entitled *The mind of a mnemonist: a little book about a vast memory* (1987), which presents 30 years of research with the mnemonist Sherashvesky (or S.) on his exceptional memory and its effect on his thinking, behavior and personality.

Sherashvesky's memory was highly unusual. Ebbinghaus's laws of memory – for example, the 'forgetting curve' and 'serial position effect' – did not apply to him, nor did Bartlett's insight that we generalize experience into normalized patterns (i.e. schemata) and remember by constructively filling in gaps with their help. Similarly, S.'s memory expertise was not domain specific, as is the case for the remarkable memories of chess masters and waiters (see Ericsson, Patel, & Kintsch, 2000 for a review). By contrast, S. could remember lines from Dante's *Inferno* (in Italian, which he didn't speak), numbers, non-sense-syllables or other material 15 years after they were presented to him, without any intermittent rehearsal or prompting. Luria concluded from his investigation that S.'s memory was limitless and went on to ask the question of how this was possible.

To explain these remarkable abilities we have to understand two 'natural' capacities that set S.'s mind apart from others – his vivid mental imagery and synthesia. S.'s mental imagery was so powerful that he would often confuse it with reality. For example, he would look at a clock and see the 'same' time as when he had previously looked at it. He could also control his involuntary body processes through his imagery. When he imagined running for a train his pulse dramatically increased. Similarly, he could decrease the temperature of one hand by five degrees and simultaneously increase the other by simply imagining that one was in ice water and the other in hot water. Unlike most of us, his mental imagery did not seem to change over time, such that it did not matter whether he was tested 15 minutes or 15 years after exposure to some stimulus. His mental imagery, however, did not operate on its own; it was supported and formed with the help of his extreme synesthesia.

Synesthesia is the condition in which the stimulation of one sense modality (e.g. hearing) simultaneously and involuntarily leads to the activation of another sense modality (e.g. taste). Neurologically, this condition is believed to be caused by cross-activation of neural pathways that normally are pruned during the brain's development. Scientists think that we all have this ability to a minor degree, which allows us to make and understand cross-modal metaphors, such as 'the cheese is sharp'. Similarly, Werner (1934) describes how our perception in one sense modality is influenced by what is simultaneously presented in another: the pitch of a sound can shift the perception of a color in different directions (e.g. red shifts toward violet when accompanied by a low-pitch sound, and toward orange and yellow with a high pitch). But for real synesthetes, the experience is quite different: they vividly taste, touch or see sounds they encounter in their environment, or they experience tastes, colors or personalities from the perception of letters and numbers. The famous synesthete painter Kandinsky, for example, said that he saw images, like those in his paintings, come alive in front of him when at the symphony.

In contrast to most synesthetes, for whom there is an automatic pathway between one modality and another (e.g. voice→taste or word→color), S. had multiple pathways between modalities. Every sound he heard immediately produced an experience of light and color, as well as a sense of touch and taste. On one occasion, S. told Vygotsky that he had 'a yellow and crumply voice'. Letters and numbers also produced complex synesthetic experiences. S. said that '1 is a pointed number – which has nothing to do with the way it is written. It is because it is somehow firm and complete. 2 is flatter, rectangular, whitish in color, sometimes almost grey. 3 is a pointed segment which rotates' (Luria, 1987, p. 26).

His synesthesia was indispensable to his incredible memory for details. Above, we saw how Bartlett described the process of remembering beginning with an 'attitude' (i.e. holistic feeling towards the material), proceeding as a process of justifying that attitude and ending when this had been sufficiently accomplished by momentarily constructing a stable memory. For S., his feeling for the material immediately articulated it in so much detail that the 'constructive' process described by Bartlett never ensued, and thus blocked the possibility of generalizing experience into a typical pattern. Any variation from the original experience would be instantly noticed by S.; his synesthetic reactions checked any deviation. Consider his own description of remembering as he experiences it:

> I recognize a word not only by the images it evokes but by a whole complex of feelings that the image arouses. It's hard to express… it's not a matter of vision or hearing, but some overall sense I get. Usually I experience a word's taste and weight, and I don't have to make an effort to remember it – the word seems to recall itself. But it is difficult to describe. What I sense is something oily slipping through my hand… or I'm aware of a slight tickling in my left hand caused by a mass of tiny, lightweight points. When that happens, I simply remember, without having to make the attempt. (Luria, 1987, p. 28)

S. clearly had 'natural' abilities quite distinct from most people (viz. his vivid imagery and synesthesia) but he also developed 'cultural' strategies to help him remember more effectively. He came to independently reinvent the ancient 'the art of memory', used by the Greeks to remember speeches from memory and later by medieval monks to help them remember the contents of books, which before the invention of the printing press were in low circulation (Yates, 1966). There were two major components to the art of memory: one should imagine a familiar *place* (e.g. a house or street). Into the discrete *loci* of the place one should then insert symbolic images of the items one wants to remember. When one is to remember the material, one simply 'walks' through the place in imagination and 'reads off' the images. S. did the same. To remember a long list of words he would simply 'distribute' them along a street in his hometown or in Moscow – he frequently used Gorky Street. In the beginning, however, this technique created some problems: Firstly, he might not notice an image because it was placed in a dark spot or it blended with the background; in these cases, he would not 'remember' the word, though this was a defect of perception not memory. Secondly, when he was given words that differed dramatically in meaning, the method of 'distributing' them on a street would break down. S comments:

> I had just started out from Mayakovsky Square when they gave me the word *Kremlin*, so I had to get myself off to the Kremlin. Okay, I can throw a rope across it … But right after that they gave me the word *poetry* and once again I found myself in Puskin Square. If I'd been given *American Indian*, I'd have had to get to America. I could, of course, throw a rope across the ocean, but it's so exhausting traveling. (Luria, 1987, p. 40)

To overcome these problems, in order to better perform his memory feats for audiences, he refined his cultural strategies of remembering. First, he made sure images were clearly perceivable where they were placed. This involved enlarging them (e.g. making an *egg* gigantic, so as not to be missed), placing them in good light and at good intervals from one another. Second, he developed a system of abbreviated and symbolic mental images. For instance, the word 'horseman' would at this stage be converted into an image of a foot in a spur. This enabled him to focus on using the image simply to recall the word without being distracted by its other details. The art of memory tradition itself developed similar principles for improving memory: places should be quiet and well lit, while images should be symbolic and even strange. Third, S. created a system for converting senseless words into intelligible images. For example, non-sense-syllables were translated into meaningful images by 'semanticizing' their sounds. Thus, we see that S.'s 'natural' abilities worked hand-in-hand with 'cultural' strategies of remembering.

Trauma and Treatment

Luria's study of S. was not only revolutionary in its treatment of memory, but also demonstrates how insightful the extensive analysis of a single case can be for science. The second and only other book Luria devoted to the complex psychological organization of a single individual, dealt not with an outstanding capacity, but rather a man with devastating injury. The man's left parental lobe had been destroyed by a bombshell during the Second World War, leaving him unable to remember his name, address, all words, and how to read, among other debilitating impairments. The patient described the experience later:

> I had a huge amount of amnesia and for a long time didn't even have any traces of memories … I'm in a fog all the time, like a heavy half-sleep. My memory's a blank. I can't think of a single word. All that flashes through my mind are images, hazy visions that suddenly appear and just as suddenly disappear, giving way to fresh images. But I simply can't understand or remember what these mean. (Luria, 1979, p. 184)

Rehabilitation of injured persons such as this is a long, painstaking process but is often possible, at least partially. This patient, for example, did regain the ability to speak, read and write, as his own memory of the initial post-injury period testifies. To repair functions, Luria again utilized the theory of interrelation between natural and cultural psychological processes. He found that many cases of neurological damage could be compensated for and even restored through the use of cultural techniques. This is analogous to the way an amputated limb can be supplemented for with a prosthetic replacement.

To conceptualize the brain, Luria developed an intermediate position between the idea that its functions are evenly disturbed throughout (e.g. Lashley's theory) and the idea that functions are localized (e.g. hippocampus as memory printer). Instead, he focused on identifying and modifying a 'functional system', composed of a working constellation of activities with the corresponding working zones of the brain that support those activities. In treatment, a damaged component of the system can often be circumvented to develop a new functional system. For example, patients with damage to their frontal cortex often reported that their thoughts did not flow and had difficulty doing anything actively. If asked to recall a familiar story or an episode from his or her life, the patient would quickly stumble. Luria found that merely providing these patients with simple cues, such as 'what then?' and 'what happened next', was sufficient to keep their narration moving. Later, he would have them internally imagine that someone was asking them these questions so that they would self-regulate their remembering.

This process of rehabilitation is similar to the developmental path, identified by Vygotsky, from social interaction to self reflection, taken by children when they first learn to remember: a child remembers with the support of their parent in dialogue, and only becomes capable of remembering individually when he or she has internalized the adult's questions and their sequencing in dialogue (Nelsen & Fivush, 2004). Similarly, as in Leontiev and Vygotsky's experiment, in which they gave children picture cards to aid them in remembering, Luria also used cards with the transition words written on them – for example, 'however', 'although', 'after' and 'since' – to aid patients through their narration. With repeated use of the external cards, patients internalize them so that the external cards become unnecessary for performing the activity. At this point a new functional system has been successfully developed that circumvents the brain impairment.

Psychologists have recently adopted methods similar to Luria's for working with patients with memory impairments. At a fairly basic level, signs are put on doors and drawers in a house to remind patients where various activities can be done and different objects can be found: Similarly, planners and diaries are used to help patients remember what they have just done and what they have planned to do next. These are versions of external memory practices, giving structure to space and time, that we all engage in to some degree, when, for example, using a filing cabinet or keeping a daily planner; they have been around since human beings have been making marks on surfaces (Donald, 1991). In the case of brain-damaged patients, however, these strategies are used to enable very basic memory functions. Recently, these ancient strategies have been combined with cutting edge technology: 'smart houses' have even been created with programmable reminders and feedback systems. Others are developing verbal support technologies (e.g. GUIDE) that allow users to be 'talked through' the different component steps of a given task, such as making tea. This technology allows for user feedback in the form of 'yes', 'no', 'what', 'done', etc. to regulate the speed and progression of commands, thus emulating features of natural interaction. In this technology, we again see Vygotsky and Luria's insight about the verbal scaffolding of activity being put to productive use.

Conclusion

The words 'learning' and 'memory' have meant many different things. In Ebbinghaus's experiments, behaviorism and much of neuroscience, they are used more or less interchangeably. Ebbinghaus restricted the meaning of 'memory' to learning in formal schooling, where children memorize material and are tested on how much of it is retained. The behaviorists abstracted 'learning' to unify the discipline of psychology in a study of the laws of behavior. For them, mentalistic concepts such as 'memory' should be exorcized from the science of psychology. Neuroscientists often used behaviorist methods – such as running rats in mazes – to search for the neural correlates of behavioral learning/memory. By contrast to these approaches, Bartlett, Halbwachs and discursive psychology focused on 'memory' (or 'remembering') as an everyday human activity, emphasizing its embeddedness in social life. They tended not to discuss 'memory' alongside 'learning'; but rather explored it in its distinctly human and meaningful dimensions. Vygotsky's distinction between the 'natural' and the 'cultural' helped to integrate these two approaches: natural memory, the biological constraints on storage capacity, could be vastly expanded with the construction and use of cultural tools and strategies. This synthesis was exemplified with case studies from Luria.

Psychology has as its object the study of people. Every person has a unique biography and belongs to a social cultural context. This seems like an obvious point but too often the person is absent from texts with a focus on mechanical models and complex statistics. Somehow the discipline seems to lose sight of psychological phenomena in the pursuit of ever more abstract theories and precision of quantitative measures. Focus on the complexity of whole persons, situated in a social and physical world, has been replaced by a study of isolated responses. Recent theories in the psychology of memory are no exception to this. We are told that our memories operate like computers that encode, store and retrieve information. In this metaphor we have de-animized the mind, turned it into a kind of machine. But what a poor processor of information it is when compared to the capacity of a computer! How badly this image fares with our own experience of remembering! More adequate descriptions need to be developed that reveal the active and meaningful properties of remembering.

In contrast, the account I have presented here is a more 'peopled' description of learning and memory than is common, highlighting a number of classic studies that have focused on the systemic organization of single cases. Brains do not have memories, nor do they learn, *people* do, though of course people use their brains to do this, and as such neurological research remains an integral part of the complete psychology of memory. Analysis must start with a study of whole persons involved in learning and remembering as part of their everyday activity in the social and physical world; only then can we begin to identify what we mean when we use the terms learning and memory, and thus avoid poor theoretical descriptions of them. Once this has been done we can start to explore the biological constraints on this process, through Ebbinghausian and neurobiological research. Following the model of Vygotsky and Luria, we can even begin to investigate the relationship between biological and cultural levels of analysis. But this is still only a rough sketch of a synthesis. A full theoretical integration of these two levels, without reduction of one to the other, awaits future innovators.

8

Social Psychology

Rom Harré, Fathali M. Moghaddam and Gordon Sammut

Culture became the major factor in giving form to the minds of those living under its sway. A product of history rather than nature, culture now became the world to which we had to adapt and the tool kit for doing so. Jerome Bruner (1986, pp. 11–12)

What do we mean when we talk about a social *psychological* approach to the identification and explanation of interpersonal relationships? The project of social psychology is psychological in so far as it concerns such matters as thinking; deciding what to do and say; the emotions it is proper to express; remembering the correct way to address the president; deciding who will captain the team; and so on, all of which involve the utilization of bodies of knowledge, the staple topics of a hybrid scientific psychology.

However, *social* psychology is social in two rather different ways. On the one hand, it is concerned with how interpersonal relations are created, managed and transformed, primarily by discursive means, that is, verbally, or by means of some other shared symbolic system. On the other hand, social psychologists have recently opened up a new domain of research because it has been realized that some processes traditionally considered only as individual phenomena, occur in the course of group activities. For example, decision making is often achieved by a committee or a family conclave, while remembering often involves constructions of versions of the past by the members of a social group. This is usually accomplished in a conversation about what happened with a focus on some present or future implications of what is being said.

From our point of view, anthropology is at the core of social psychology. It opens the boundaries of research into the practices of other cultures with their distinctive languages, histories and ways of maintaining life.

Early Attempts at a 'Universal' Social Psychology

From antiquity, social psychological themes, the forms of interpersonal relations, were investigated mostly by poets such as Homer in the *Iliad*, playwrights such as William Shakespeare in *Macbeth* and *Love's Labours Lost*, and novelists such as Leo Tolstoy in *Anna Karenina*. Of course there was a great stock of folk wisdom on these matters, particularly among policemen, lawyers and priests.

From the 1950s to the 1970s of the last century there was a flurry of studies aimed at uncovering the roots of interpersonal relationships. Quickly these acquired a collective designation as 'social psychology', as a distinctive branch of psychology. Unfortunately, much of what was done in that period has to be discarded because it failed to meet the standards of good scientific work. From the beginning, this 'new wave' of research was subject to mounting criticism on various fronts, particularly with regard to its ethnocentrism and its failure to break out of a positivistic version of research methodology. Sadly, criticisms were largely ignored and for two or more generations those who worked under the banner of 'social psychology' produced work of very little scientific value.

Two main flaws became incorporated into social psychology of the 'classical' era. Many studies failed to adhere to Vygotsky's rule that one must not analyze social phenomena for research purposes to a level where their original meaning is lost. Many failed to fulfill the canons of experimental method as a source of reliable knowledge, relying on a very simple positivistic program of correlational studies, largely misusing numerical methods and making misleading statistical analyses of their results. We do not intend to rehearse the barrage of criticism which descended on these programs but was brushed aside. Many earnest researchers pursued flawed projects. Examples of such criticism can be found in Harré and Secord (1972), Shotter (1975) and Danziger (1990).

Programs that Can Be Recovered

This was not true of all the publications of the period – some of which can be recovered as contributions to the corpus of psychological knowledge when given a cultural/discursive interpretation. This can be achieved provided we can see the work not as a failed attempt to discover universal principles of social interactions, psychological laws, but as the psychology of a distinct cultural group. This is the group of English-speaking Westerners, living in democratic societies based on liberal capitalist ideals. Some, regrettably, cannot be reinterpreted by reason of deep underlying flaws.

Solomon Asch (1987[1952]) set up a situation in which a group of conspirators took part in a conversation with an innocent victim in which they insisted that three lines were of equal length though they were not. Despite being personally convinced that the lines were not of equal length, the victim tended to agree with the assertion of the conspirators. Repeating the drama with different people as victims, Asch concluded that when a false claim was proclaimed unanimously and with conviction people would tend to agree with it. No doubt! But what did Asch find out?

Solomon Elliot Asch (1907–1996) was born in Warsaw in Poland one of a large family. At that time, Poland was a province of the Russian Empire. Asch's family were Jewish and were no doubt well aware of the sporadic outbreaks of anti-Semitism in Eastern Europe. In addition to these occasional threats to the Jews, there were the long-running practices of social and professional exclusion that prevented them entering most of the professions. The Russian Revolution of 1917 took Russia out of the First World War, and made Polish independence possible. It also made emigration much easier. The Asch family left Poland almost immediately after the end of the war in

Western Europe. Young Asch arrived in America at the age of 13, ready to start high school in his new land. Like many immigrants at that time, after the ordeal of Ellis Island, the Asch's found a home in New York.

Solomon attended the College of the City of New York, taking his BS in 1928. He then joined Columbia University where he began advanced studies in psychology, taking his MA in 1930, followed by a PhD in 1932. He worked under Max Wertheimer, one of the pioneers of gestalt psychology, who had arrived from Europe in 1933, driven out by the anti-Semitism of the Nazis.

After a short period at Brooklyn College, he found a permanent post at Swarthmore College in Philadelphia. Swarthmore is one of a group of outstanding undergraduate institutions in the area. In the mid-20th century it had attracted a first-rate faculty as indeed it still does. Among the psychologists faculty was Wolfgang Köhler, the best known of the gestalt school who had come from Berlin in the 1930s. From 1966 to 1972, Asch was director of the Center for Cognitive Studies at Rutgers University in New Jersey. He moved to the University of Pennsylvania in 1972. He remained there, apart from a year at the Center for the Advanced Study of the Behavioral Sciences in Stanford, for the rest of his career.

After retirement he seems to have settled into a comfortable old age. He died on 20 September 1996, survived by his wife, Florence.

In the fashion of the times Asch described the results of his various simulated dramas in causal terms, though they are manifestly nothing of the sort. We can redescribe them realistically as the activities of agents acting in accordance with various social conventions – the student group following the convention to obey one's professor, while the victims followed a basic conversational convention of politeness.

In the various other versions of this conversation that Asch staged, different conventions came into play – particularly when responsibility for disagreeing was shared with someone else. Asch's studies are a contribution to ethnography. They do not reveal anything resembling universal psychological laws.

In the latter part of his career Michael Argyle became interested in the social psychology of happiness (Argyle, 1984). He set out to try to find out 'what made people happy'. If we examine his research methods closely, we find that he engaged people in conversations, via such devices as questionnaires, that in effect explored in what circumstances people used the word 'happy'. In accordance with the principles of emotionology (see Chapter 10), these studies throw light on the emotion or mood to which the word refers. Argyle's work opens up a corner of cultural semantics.

Each of these studies can be interpreted as the analysis of conversations aimed at revealing some of the conventions according to which such conversations unfold. Methodologically they represent agent-causal processes – because the people who are taking part with the psychologists in these events are engaged in fulfilling a task that defines the context of the interaction.

Musafar Sherif (1956) set up a model world as a summer camp for a quite large group of middle-class, Anglophone American boys. They were divided into two groups, and provided with culture-specific symbols of identity, such as a club house and a totem, and they took part in team games as members of these groups. Hostility mounted between the members of each group and pejorative opinions were expressed about each other. However,

Sherif devised a common task – rescuing the broken-down truck that fetched food to the camp – for which the boys combined in a successful cooperative task.

This is an anthropological study, drawing on the culturally specific conventions of a certain social group. It goes nowhere towards establishing a generic species-wide disposition to amplify group identities into hostility and mutual denigration.

Henri Tajfel (1978, p. 77 ff.) is credited with claiming to have shown that there is a tendency for people to form antithetical, even hostile groups, on the basis of formal, context-free criteria of difference. Recruiting a group of British school boys as participants in his experiment, he divided them arbitrarily into two groups and followed the subsequent development of intergroup attitudes. British boys are accustomed to 'picking sides' on no more grounds than the recitation of a ritual formula, while selecting their players. After that, 'team spirit' kicks in as each team tries for victory.

This too is an ethnographic study, drawing on the conventions of social life among a quite specific social group. Are people Manchester United fans because there is a generic tendency to support some club or other? Or are we brought up in a social atmosphere of competitive games so that there is a cultural convention that we take sides?

The authors of these studies presented them as if they were revealing a generic disposition to acquire specific dispositions that would explain how these generic tendencies were actualized. But there are no such generic dispositions, or at least the researches could not reveal them. The tasks set by the experimenters only made sense within the re-existing cultural framework of knowledge. Each group of participants brought to the study a powerful if tacit tradition of 'taking sides', 'forming teams ad hoc' and so on.

We can recover the results of these studies and others like them for cultural/discursive psychology. They are contributions to our knowledge of how people from our own tribe behave. They reveal certain cultural conventions.

Social Psychology as a Hybrid Project

We have emphasized in other chapters how psychological research is aimed at revealing the dispositions that are realized in actual behavior. The pattern of dispositions is complex because of the interplay between tendencies and propensities that are grounded in our biology and those that are grounded in our culture. There are first-order or basic dispositions which each one of us has as a member of the species. These have their origin in our biology – and for the most part they conform to the Paleolithic principle as enunciated by Robin Dunbar (Dunbar, Barret, & Lycett, 2007) (see Chapter 3). They have evolved as genetically sustained dispositions apt for the needs of a hunter-gatherer society. For the most part, first-order dispositions dispose people to think or behave only in rather general ways, for example, to show respect to their seniors, to resent being denigrated or humiliated, threatened, to care for infants and so on.

However, the form that behavior takes as a cultural practice depends on our having acquired some version of a huge variety of second-order dispositions. We might be required to bow deeply in the presence of an elder, to issue a formal challenge when insulted, to take turns in changing the baby's diapers, and so on. We might say that our biological heritage provides us with dispositions to acquire dispositions for culturally specific ways of behaving.

Biological groundings of permanent propensities to act in certain very general ways are taken to be states and functions of the brain. These exist as the result of the inheritance of genes and gene complexes that are expressed in proteins. These, in turn, are the building blocks of bodily organs including the brain, its neural structure and biological mechanisms that produce the molecules that mediate its activities. Ephemeral dispositions are grounded in short-term brain states and processes that are often quite idiosyncratic and personal, reflecting the unique life patterns of individuals. These provide the mechanisms by means of which people perform culturally defined and mandated tasks. Their analysis conforms to the Task-Tool metaphor.

The cultural groundings of permanent propensities to act in certain ways towards other people and in the relevant situations in which such actions are appropriate, are learned in the course of the acquisition of cultural norms and the skills required to engage in collective practices. Long-standing and ephemeral cultural dispositions are grounded in knowledge systems and patterns of belief, that is, in long-term cognitive states. General tendencies are the result of learning cultural rules, while ephemeral tendencies are grounded in interpretations of local situations. Analysis of this level of social phenomena conforms to the Taxonomic Priority Principle – culture determines meanings and what the phenomena are.

To create a hybrid social psychology we must show how cultural studies can be integrated with two very different branches of biology – ethology, the study of genetically based interactions among members of the same species, and neuroscience, the study of correlations between psychological phenomena and activity in distinctive regions of the brains of the persons involved in the episode in which the phenomenon of interest occurs. At the same time we must keep in mind the way the performance of cultural tasks feeds back into reshaping the organs of the brain with which they are performed.

There are many examples of successful hybridization of cultural and biological research projects. The way that the Taxonomic Priority Principle works in these cases depends on the kind of relation that is seen by the investigator to mediate between the behavior of animals and the conduct of human beings as people. Is it homology? Is the relevant kind of human conduct identical in character and origin with some feature of the behavior of animals and birds? Or is it analogy? Can we identify only a certain likeness between what people do and what animals do? The difference between homology and analogy is filled by cultural practices. Is the wish to have a place in the suburbs with a fine lawn around it analogous to the urge to create and defend a territory by hippopotami or howler monkeys? Or is it homologous to the animal propensity, that is, the very same psychological process grounded in the very same neural structures? If the relation is analogy there are similarities and differences and the differences can be put down to culture and history. If it is homology there is nothing more to be said. We must be content with a biological explanation.

Social Psychology as a Cultural/Discursive Study Program

Cultural psychology, as outlined by Shweder (1991b), tries to take account of the huge variety of forms in which the social life of human beings is carried on. It is also sensitive to the possibility that even the more general forms of social life that we identify in our locality and notice in our travels to foreign parts or in reading of the lives of our ancestors, may not be found in all the tribes of human kind. Of course, at a very high level of generality, certain features of social life are sure to recur everywhere – for example, there must be some arrangement for managing the relation between the sexes, for ensuring a food supply and so on. These are likely to involve social interactions, that is, interactions between a number of people, mediated by a code of shared meanings.

Reporting a survey of the concepts covered by the verbal label 'culture' which have appeared in social psychology, Carl Ratner (1997) offers three distinct but related concepts:

1 **Cultures exist as packets of *shared symbols*, the significance of which has been determined by collective meaning-making activities by 'people acting in concert'. It is the meanings of the symbols that influence social behavior, since they define the very behavior in question.**
2 **Cultures exist as socially organized *practical activities*.**
3 **Cultures exist in the bodies of knowledge and customary practices accomplished by *individuals*, drawing from various versions of the common cultural stock. Everyone has his or her own version of the culture. If we are thinking of the role of culture in explanations of social behavior this is the level to which we should attend.**

A body of knowledge is usually distributed among a group of people, no one person knowing everything germane to the carrying out of a complex social project fully and successfully. Access to a common body of knowledge is often socially structured, particularly in relation to role. Whether it is proper to discipline a child will depend on one's social relationship to that child – mother, brother, teacher or visitor.

Serge Moscovici (1925–) was born in Romania. His father was a grain dealer, who it seems changed wives as readily as he changed cities. The family were Jewish. When Romania entered the Second World War on the side of the Germans, young Serge was forced to leave school. Somehow he managed to avoid the dire fate of many of his co-religionists, and spent the war in a forced labor camp. He learned the trade of welder, and after the fall of the German Reich in 1944, he was able to use his skills in Germany and elsewhere. As the Cold War 'hotted up' he made his way to Paris. In 1948, he entered the Sorbonne to study psychology, supporting himself by factory work as a welder. In his autobiography (Moscovici, 1997) he writes of the typically Parisian way in which he combined his formal studies with time spent with the literary intelligentsia of the era. He did graduate work at Stanford and Princeton Universities in the United States. Returning to France, he took up a post in the École des Haute Études en Sciences Sociales, from which he has recently retired.

His studies, inspired by his reworking of Durkheim's concept of 'social representations', covered many aspects of social life, including the role of lay versions of psychoanalysis and the behavior of crowds.

Farr and Moscovici (1984) proposed an explanation of similarities and coordinations in the behavior of individual people in terms of common bodies of knowledge, each person having a version of the general store of social knowledge similar to every other. They suggested that the concept of 'social representation', ultimately drawn from the writings of Emile Durkheim, represents a way of bringing together attitudes and opinions, the basis of earlier efforts to identify the key cognitive factors in social behavior.

The Primacy of Practice

In cultural psychology we move from thinking exclusively in terms of causal mechanisms (biological psychology), or wholly in terms of dispositions and activating conditions (classical social psychology), to thinking of social life in terms of episodes and practices as we follow people as active agents trying to carry out the tasks in which they engaged. This is the key theoretical move in building a hybrid social psychology.

A practice is a procedure carried out by one or more people to accomplish a task. A social practice accomplishes a social task. Cultures also include practices for the management of the material world – and anthropologists have shown us how often these two components of culture are closely interwoven. Social practices involve the management of meanings and conformity to local norms of propriety. A culture is then a repertoire of material, cognitive and social practices by means of which the life of a community is maintained during several generations.

Core practices are those which if abandoned we would say that a culture has disappeared to be replaced by another. There are no clear criteria for the identity of cultures, but the abandonment of one and the adoption of a different culture is evident in such social transformations as the Islamic conquest of Arabia, the Reformation, the Industrial Revolution and other socially cataclysmic transformations of the forms of daily life.

Peripheral practices are those which can be abandoned and others taken up without our being inclined to say that the culture has disappeared and been replaced by another.

Rules, customs and conventions represent the normative context of cultural practices.

Cultural Explanations

Cultural explanations involve four main steps:

(a) What meanings do the people engaged in a social practice seem to give to what they are doing? Does the outsider interpretation ever override that of the insider?
(b) What rules and conventions seem to be guiding the actors in carrying out these practices? Again, what is the status of the outsider's hypotheses about local norms in providing explanations?
(c) How are the norms of a practice acquired by the actors? By reading a manual, by asking an expert what to do, at their mother's knee, and so on.
(d) Once these basic aspects have been made clear and explicit, research can be undertaken into the history of practices and their distribution in various parts of the world. For example, it may be important to know when and where they have practiced mortuary cannibalism, exorcism, universal suffrage, equal rights for men and women, and so on.

The level of a cultural explanation and the breadth of possible applications reflect the structure of the hierarchy of cultural forms current in a community. Compare giving an explanation of the assassination of Indira Gandhi in terms of the politics of the Congress Party, with an explanation that drew on the ideology of Hindu radicalism. The question of whether, when embedded in these different levels of explanatory detail, we are confronting the same event in each context need not concern us, since in the domain of cultural explanations the material identity of these events is at most a formal thread in the story. There is often no plausible way of settling for one cultural explanation rather than another.

Dynamics of Social Life

Unlike classical social psychology, which focused on events without attending to their long-term antecedents and consequents, in which might lie the very point of the event in question, cultural psychologists consider the social world to be a flux of continuous activity, which can be divided into sequences in many ways by attending to the short-, medium- and long-term goals of the actors. Effectively this means that we must see social life in terms of hierarchies of nested episodes, each having a means-end structure. An episode is a sequence of meaningful actions ordered as a normatively constrained structure. Since a huge number of things are happening all the time, *an* episode is a working abstraction.

However, more is required. The concept of 'meaningful action' needs careful analyzing. Thinking of real life, we are usually capable of identifying those personal behaviors which are intended as *actions*. However, there is still the question of what an action means – what is its social significance? For this we could say that *acts* are the social meanings of actions.

In Chapter 2 we introduced J. L. Austin's categorization of the consequences of the performance of various verbal formulas in social life (Austin, 1975). Recalling Austin's insights, we need to attend to two main features or forces of the successful performance of social acts:

(a) **The illocutionary force – the social act the words are used to perform in the given context as spoken by the formally or informally authorized people.**
(b) **The perlocutionary effect – what changes or other consequences the saying or writing of these words with this illocutionary force bring about in the social, and even the material world.**

In the course of a trial the foreman of the jury reads out a verdict: 'Guilty as charged'. In the context of the courtroom the illocutionary force is 'verdict', that the defendant was the responsible agent in the commission of an offence. The perlocutionary effect is that the defendant is punished, though much discursive activity intervenes before the prison door clangs shut. There is no room for causal mechanisms in the social psychology of the work of jurors or of the courts in which they serve. There are agents carrying out the tasks assigned to them according to the norms of the local system of justice. In making use of Austin's analytical categories we are implicitly drawing an analogy with ceremonials, where the forces and effects of speech-acts are most clearly seen. We could call this the 'ritual model' of social action.

In Chapter 2 we also introduced the basic principles of narratology as a research method. Among the various techniques that narratologists have used to extract the meaning system that are realized in many social phenomena was the dramaturgical model as a device to represent the processes by which social episodes are brought about by the people who take part in them.

Other models have been used for analytical purposes. The 'ludic model' bids us to draw analogies between strips of life and games. This model offers such concepts as teams, competition, winning and losing, referees and umpires and so on. The ritual model draws on real ceremonial activity to build models of strips of life as if they were ceremonies. A family dinner has its distinctive ritual acts, and so for the cultural psychologist it is convenient to analyze it as if it were a ceremony. At the same time, we bear in mind that it could also be usefully analyzed according to the dramaturgical model or the ludic model.

All three models have contributions to make to a full-scale analysis of cultural phenomenon according to the methodology of cultural psychology.

The Content of a Cultural Theory

The methods of research described above allow the social psychologist to propose hypotheses about the shared meaning system and the tacit rules and conventions that are involved in the management of social actions by actors competent in their local cultures. These theories can be looked at as 'bodies of knowledge' that make the creation and management of social worlds possible. Briefly, such bodies of knowledge include lexicons of the social meanings of actions, the aspect we called 'acts' realized by the performance of the relevant actions. There must also be clusters of norms, which can be represented explicitly as rules, conventions and customs. In recent times, it has come to be realized that in many cases the dominant norms in an unfolding strip of social life are more like narratives than cause-effect sequences.

Examples of Cultural Explanations

A Cultural Analysis of Hooliganism

Here the research made use of the dramaturgical model as an overall analytical tool, revealing one level of structure in the events to be presented within the framework of cultural psychology. Following Goffman's general plan of research, the complex phenomena of a football ground 'disturbance' were analyzed in terms of 'scene' (the ground and its seating arrangements etc), the 'actors' (the members of rival factions) and the 'action' (ritual displays to establish social mastery). The 'fights', presented as bloodthirsty and dangerous encounters, were analyzed as social ceremonies, constrained by tacit scripts, violations of which were punished (Marsh, Rosser, & Harré, 1977). The outcomes of these events were the source of the establishment and patterning of social status in the group. Status and changes in status were marked by the right to wear certain items of the group's uniform and to find a seat at socially defined levels in the grandstands.

Erving Goffman (1922–1982) was born in Manville, Alberta, Canada, the son of Max and Anne Goffman. His first wife, by whom he had a son, died in 1979. He married for the second time in 1981. He took a BA at the University of Toronto in 1945, and went on to graduate work at the University of

(Continued)

Chicago. His PhD researches, the basis of his most famous book, *The presentation of self in everyday life*, first published in 1969, were carried out in Scotland, though he presented his dissertation at the University of Chicago in 1953.

His career followed the usual pattern of short-term appointments of the budding academic, with one notable exception – his time at the National Institute of Mental Health, Bethesda, MD, where he was a visiting scientist from 1954 to 1957. In 1962, he joined the University of Pennsylvania as a sociology professor, occupying the Benjamin Franklin Chair of Anthropology and Sociology from 1968–1982. The brilliance of his observations of the unfolding of strips of life and the role of the various players in them made his books, such as *Stigma*, attractive to a very wide readership. His later work shifted towards a more explicit attention to the role of language in the creation and management of everyday life, as evidenced in his two well-known books, *Frame analysis* (1975) and *Forms of talk* (1981).

He was President of the American Sociological Association for 1981–1982. But Goffman's fame and the source of his influence lie in his writings. He was a reluctant presenter at conferences, much preferring discussions with a group of friends in the bar. He died in Philadelphia, PA.

The ritualistic character of the seemingly violent encounters was revealed in a comparison between what had been observed at these events and how they were reported. They needed to be talked up to have sufficient plausibility as evidence of bravery and daring to support claims to a consequential advancement in status. This rhetorical transformation of the nature of the events was abetted by the media. Descriptions of the 'football riots' amplified the violence, and exaggerated the amount of physical damage inflicted on either side. However, the study showed that there were limits to the reinterpretation of the events that had occurred in the 'fights'. Certain claims, particularly those that purported to describe weapons, were ridiculed by the senior members of the group.

From the point of view of cultural psychology, this study revealed the form of a cultural phenomenon and the structure and dynamics of a small-scale and isolated micro-culture. The upshot of the research was a formulation of the tacit knowledge that was realized in the various practices that created and maintained the group. This included a catalogue of socially meaningful acts and objects and the part they played in the culture; for example, items of the uniform, the significance of confrontations, the location of the fans in the stands, and the rhetoric of media reports. The second aspect, the normative constraints on action, consisted of a catalogue of the habits, conventions, customs and rules that were revealed in intercutting knowledge of the actions and their social consequences as observed by the participant observers and the body of explicit formations of these conventions brought forth to deal with an infraction of the smooth running of act/action sequences.

Social Representations of the Body in Social Life

When the idea of explaining social behavior by reference to social representations first appeared, it seemed as if this movement would fit in neatly with the methodology of psychology as the study of cultural practices. Unfortunately, the majority of those who took up the idea persisted in attempting to find 'underlying' cognitive processes with which people manipulated social representations, using old-fashioned experiments. Fortunately there were some, Denise Jodelet in particular, who stayed with the insight that there are no such mysterious processes – there are just all sorts of social practices for which social representations provide the content and the discursive style. Shweder (1991b) saw this very clearly as he explains in his account of the foundations of cultural psychology. Both approaches can be found in the classic collection of studies edited by Robert Farr and Serge Moscovici (1984).

Though the theory and method of social representations is clearly part of the general movement towards cultural psychology, it has proved very difficult to find a clear presentation of the position. Serge Moscovici's 'position paper' (Farr & Moscovici, 1984, pp. 3–69) includes a loose cluster of very diverse principles and research methods. Sometimes social representations are more or less the same as interpretative repertoires, bodies of knowledge for managing various practices. Sometimes these repertoires include folk versions of theories, for example, folk versions of Newtonian mechanics or of Freudian psychodynamics. Sometimes their content is expressed in actual images or models as concrete analogue representations. These are the kind of models used in the natural sciences. For a recent attempt to formulate a working account of the nature and use of social representations one should see Sammut and Gaskell (2010).

Creating a social representation involves two processes: anchoring, 'reducing strange ideas to ordinary categories and images'; and objectifying, 'the materialisation of an abstraction' (Farr & Moscovici, 1984, pp. 30–43).

We will use Denise Jodelet's analysis of the role of the body in thought and practice as an example of one way of thinking in terms of social representations. For the purposes of this exposition, the core of the method of social representations is the general principle of cultural psychology: that we live our lives in accordance with the meanings we give to things, events, discourses and people. Many people give the same or similar meanings to their cognitive, emotional, personal and political environments. So, some of our representations are social in the sense of being distributed among the members of a group. How do we know what these meanings are? Directly from what people say and indirectly from what they do – subject to the use of an interpretative repertoire in each case.

Denise Jodelet's study of the social representations of the body reflects this eclectic stance. She says that her project is 'to identify the mental categories, the cognitive and normative models which control lived experience and our knowledge of, and uses for, the body' (Jodelet, 1991, p. 214). In one way of reading this program, 'mental categories' *are* 'cognitive and normative models'. The nub of her analysis is the observation that 'cultural diffusion, by making prominent the viewpoint developed by the psychological and social sciences, provides new conceptual tools, new normative frameworks for thinking about the body, and changes the meaning of traditional hierarchies and values' (Jodelet, 1991, p. 236). In short, the diffusion of these viewpoints provides people with alternative interpretational repertoires. Two matters turn out to be of importance in the discourses of the people she interviewed, 'bodily experience' and 'the relationship of the individual to the environment'. One of the most brilliant pieces of research in this tradition is Claudine Herzlich's *Health and illness* (1973) in which she traces the social representations of the nature of the urban and rural environment on the practices of 'being ill' (Herzlich, 1973).

One example among many involves the transformation of the salience of emotional states, particularly negative ones such as grief, as a consequence of the spread of a generally hedonistic attitude. Morbidity is not absent from people's thoughts, but 'it is less vital … and goes along with a reduction in the attention paid to all those internal messages which were earlier of undoubted importance' (Jodelet, 1991, p. 225). Thus, having access to bodily pleasure and well being has transformed a feature of the social representation of the body, namely the degree of attention paid to certain aspects of living, bodily feelings.

A Complex Pattern of Discursive Practices

Jan Valsiner (2007) cites a number of studies which lead to cultural theories of various kinds of social and cognitive practices. One of the most insightful was carried out by Hermans (2001, pp. 323–365) by analyzing the first-person linguistic practices by which an Algerian man married to a Dutch woman created his personal social world. Herman's theory is based on the principle that the sense of self emerges from two 'intertwined' dialogues, one with him or herself and the other with others. However, according to Hermans, the former dialogue is not the locus of a core-self interacting with other core selves socially. Rather, there are patterns of I-positions in the intertwining dialogues which can be occupied by others as 'voices', or more prosaically as characters in a story. I-positions have links to narrative. The notion of 'position' in this theory is somewhat different from its sense in 'positioning theory' where it is given a distinctly moral inter-pretation, not incompatible with but narrower than Hermans' sense of position which is essentially narratological. As with other methodologies of this ilk, Hermans represents the body of knowledge that his Algerian actor uses as a repertoire, in this case of I-positions. Ali's repertoire of I-positions, such as 'I am an Algerian' through to 'I am part of a Dutch family' (altogether nearly 100 internal and external I-positions) showed the discursive resources by which he managed his family life in both ethnic and local contexts. Hermans' method of research is interesting in that he asks his informant to comment on the proper location in a kind of repertoire map of the 'I-report' he has made. This research program has links with the development of a social psychology of 'point of view' as devel-oped in a later section of this chapter.

Social Psychology in Relation to Time: Diachronic Studies

Individual lives display trajectories and patterns that are unique, but at the same time display features of the cultures in which they have been and are being and even will be lived.

The biological, psychological and social life courses of human beings are not identically mapped isomorphically onto time as a sequence of days, weeks, months and years, springs, summers, autumns and winters. Developmental psychologists have studied the changes in the cognitive skills, emotional maturity and practical aptitudes in the course of a person's life – rising and falling with the passage of the years. From a cultural psychology point of view we can also study the social trajectory of a person's life as status, social position and social relations change in the course of time. Moral careers[1] can begin before a person is born – for example, a royal infant already has status even in the womb. Moral careers do not usually end with the mortal termination of a life. A person lives on as a being with a standing in the community, at least for a while in obituaries and funeral eulogies. The ups and downs of one's status come about as one passes through various institutional settings. For example, one gains in status as one succeeds in dealing with socially significant 'hazards' such as public performances, managing difficult situations and so on. Usually, success means a small gain in status, failure means a big loss. There are interesting cultural differences in the conception of a life of honor, which could be a fascinating research program for social psychologists. Finally, many people have several moral careers because of the many institutional and semi-institutional settings of a person's life.

Social Psychology of Social Change

Setting aside the idea that social changes are nothing but the result of mutations in sociogenes that would leave us in the cave world of our hunter-gatherer forebears, we can look at theories of social change that are located in the cognitive/discursive realm of practices. The truth of the Paleolithic principle would mean that biologically based first-order dispositions for kinds of social behavior have not changed over the millennia since they were selected for their advantage to human beings. However, it could hardly be more obvious that the second-order social behavioral dispositions have changed hugely and continue to do so. These changes must be explicable, if they are explicable at all, in terms of cultural psychology. Religions have come and gone and with each transition a vast array of distinctive social practices have come and gone with them.

The explanation of social change is located firmly in the domain of cultural psychology. It has been suggested by Robin Dunbar et al. (2007) and many others that it should be possible to devise an explanatory format for cultural change that is analogous to that which we have seen at the basis of biological explanations of the establishing of the 'social brain'. This format would involve variation and selection, but now selection of the sources of social practices would depend on how advantageous it was to the flourishing of a society. Advantageous social practices would spread from family to family, from tribe to tribe and from generation to generation.

New rules, customs and so on come into existence by human ingenuity, innovation and even accident. They are 'tried out' as norms for social life. The feminist movement of the 20th century is a very clear example of this process. The rules, both explicit and implicit in the educational systems of most Western nations, are changed by the spread of equitable innovations. Some linguistic proposals caught on but others did not. Most social innovations fail to spread, and so are not picked up by the next generation. The selection environment is complex: existing social life practices, the material environment and so on. In biology, which is the source of selectionist models, the Darwinian schema requires that the causes of mutations and the selection environment are independent of one another. In social selection it is quite possible that an innovation may be proposed in the light of what someone believes about the selection environment. It may even be that efforts might be made to change the selection environment to favor a new practice or product. The former is market research and the latter is advertising.

The Individual in Society

There is no doubt that even within the most regulated social order individual people have their own 'take' on various social concerns, at many different levels of organization. To complete the account of cultural psychobiology we need a way of acknowledging individuality in the midst of conformity. We find this in the concept of 'point of view'.

The study of points of view was proposed by Asch (1987[1952]) as a way to examine the manner individuals orientate themselves in social reality. Harré and Secord (1972) similarly advocated the study of points of view in providing an explanation of individual positioning in social behavior. Subjects position themselves in relation to others in their social environment, adopting a particular outlook towards an object or issue in their social life that is meaningful in view of a social representation that renders it legitimate. Through their point of view, individuals relate to others and to the object in question. A point of *view* is necessarily relational, being oriented towards other subjects and objects in the social environment. Furthermore, a *point* of view is necessarily relative, being one point of view amongst others, that an individual could adopt or that are adopted at that time and place by others.

Social reality, like physical reality, is contingent on the perceiver's point of view. Social reality is phenomenal rather than objective, that is, it appears to the observer depending on a background of intelligibility that serves the function of interpretation (i.e. a social representation). This interpretative nature of social reality is the great paradigm shift precipitated by social constructionism (Berger & Luckmann, 1966). In addition to collective processes of social construction, whether an alternative description of social reality is admitted or influences a given public depends not so much on the characterization of that view and whether it has, effectively, some point to make. Rather, admitting an alternative discursive construction of social reality depends on the characteristic features of the appraiser's own point of view.

Point of view is fundamentally rooted in the public sphere and is itself implicated in the very nature of that sphere. Public spheres can be more or less conducive to open dialogue and the negotiation of alternative views, and through the exercise of power can legitimate some and censor others. Which views are accepted, rejected, or treated with indifference transpires at the personal level in the social-psychological features of points of view. 'Point of view' is a social phenomenon in as much as it is a view that incorporates other human beings, and it is psychological in as much as it is an individual's point, or position, that relates to others. Differences between different types of point of view (see Sammut & Gaskell, 2010) are based on intrapersonal socio-cognitive resources inherent to points of view that serve to structure interpersonal relations.

The utility of the concept of 'attitude' as the source of social behavior has proven problematic. How are attitudes linked to behavior? Attitudes are held to be predispositions towards picking out and reacting to certain 'stimuli' in the individual's environment rather than others. This presumption has been queried ever since LaPiere's (1934) study on the behavior of hotel keepers to Chinese visitors. Though the hoteliers expressed racist attitudes, they did not behave in the straightforwardly racist ways that would have been expected if their 'attitudes' had been the root of the whole spectrum of their social behaviors.

The study of social representations, alongside social constructionism (Berger & Luckmann, 1966; Gergen, 1985) and discourse analysis (Potter & Wetherell, 1987), has sought to counterbalance the focus on individualized social cognition in favor of explicating the cultural backgrounds of intelligibility (Daanen, 2009) in which a given action may elicit, amongst other alternatives, a context-rational response which reflects the way the action was interpreted (Wagner, 1993).

The divide between the social and the individual is ontological as much as it is epistemological and involves different levels of explanation (Wagner & Hayes, 2005). The social pertains to the collective life of human beings and applies to processes that take shape at this collective level, particularly discursive interchanges from person to person conversations to the output of the media and the propaganda 'machines' of authoritarian regimes. The individual pertains to the human being as a single specimen and applies to processes that take place at this level such as cognition and perception.

The gap between the two can be expressed in the distinction of aggregates from collectives. Whilst aggregates bring together individual specimens without order or structure, such as the passengers on a bus or a seaside crowd, collectives exist independently of individual cognition, so long as the members share certain discursive practices and core beliefs that ensure that looked at as a whole, the behavior of the members of a collective display an enduring structure. The hierearchy of the Catholic Church is a collective, each member of the clergy knowing his place in the system, and sharing certain core beliefs and practices with the other members. Everyday social behavior, however, retains elements of both. Insofar as it involves an element of positioning as rights and duties to act in certain ways are distributed among the members of a group relative to other, equally agentic, beings, then such behavior can be deemed social. And insofar as such interpersonal relations involve an element of perception and interpretation, then such behavior can be deemed personal and cognitive.

This characteristic duality of social behavior has confounded explanations on either side of the dichotomy. The concept of 'attitude' has been suggested as just what is needed to understand an individual's inclination towards some social object on the basis of that actor's personal characteristics including emotions and feelings, behavioral tendencies, cognitive practices, and external influences. It does not, however, provide an explanation for why individuals resort to certain courses of action given a certain situation. For instance, two individuals may be equally appalled by some event, but their individual responses may vary as a function of different cultural conditions in which they are embedded. A member of *Médicine sans Frontières* will react in one way to a massacre and an EU diplomat in another. Social representations, on the other hand, describe context-rational behavior that is deemed reasonable in certain circumstances. They describe how for a certain social group, a particular course of action is reasonable given certain conditions. Social representations, as psychologists' distillations of what is common to the members of a group, do not, however, explain why such context-rational behavior may be adopted by some individuals but not by similar others facing the same circumstances. Not all individuals react in the same way to similar events. In other words, neither the postulation of attitudes nor the reference to social representations are useful for a situational explanation of social behavior, that is, for an explanation of why a certain individual acts in a certain way at a certain point in time. This explanation requires a focus on the personal repertoire of possible actions and the personal interpretations likely to be adopted by an individual. The level of meaning that this explanation requires is idiographic. It is not the shared beliefs and practices of a collective in which the individual is systemically embedded and that legitimate individual actions in the eyes of others. Nor is it intrinsic to that individual, particularly not simply the neurological processes that take place in the brain through which an individual performs the tasks required in the here and now.

Cultural psychology requires a human being to be both an individual and a member of one or more collectives.

Psychobiology

Biology has become relevant to studies of the psychology of social processes through two major innovations. The development of ethology, the study of genetically based life relevant behavioral routines among animals and birds by Konrad Lorentz and Nikko Tinbergen, suggested the possibility of extending this idea to human life (see Chapter 3). But how do we hybridize human ethology and psychoneurology with the 'mother lode', cultural psychology?

We have already given a detailed account of the origins and doctrines of ethology in Chapter 3. Here we put these ideas into action. To account for the selection of certain genes and gene complexes as the groundings of certain behavioral dispositions we need to identify the kinds of interindividual competition that favors some over others. Genetic change occurs as individuals compete with individuals for scarce resources, since there are usually more new individuals than the environment can support. In addition, as Darwin emphasized, they also compete for reproductive partners. These principles apply to both animals and plants. The basic theory distinguishes between 'replicators', genes and gene complexes, and 'interactors', adult organisms that interact with the environment and each other. Genes which give advantages in this interactional process and in the 'mating' game, tend to be more prevalent in each subsequent generation. We note that the fate of genes depends on the fate of the interactors that realize them. Genes do not interact with the environment.

As a first stage in the search for biological explanations of some forms of human social behaviour, we need to establish that at least some first-order dispositions are genetically grounded. We need to show that there are inherited neuroanatomical structures that are the grounding of certain dispositions to behave in some very general ways in social contexts. For example, when confronted with a social superior we tend to show deference, though how this is achieved will be in accordance with local conventions. In the next section we will examine possible neurological groundings for second-order dispositions, and thus the source of explanations for some quite specific human social actions, such as taking up a religious way of life.

The reasoning from biological knowledge to explanations for some of the phenomena of human social psychology involves two moves.

1 Choosing animal models as sources for empirical data to support a biological theory of some aspect or type of human social behavior, such as forming fairly stable pair-bonded nuclear families.
2 Developing a double analogy first between the genomes of some animals, say voles, and human beings, and then between the relevant behavior, cognition, emotion etc. of the chosen animals and humans, such as being prone to depression.

We have already argued that the homology/analogy distinction for the application of the Taxonomic Priority Principle in a non-reductive way in case we settle for analogy.

Evolutionary Psychology

To make use of the seeming parallels in social practices between people and animals we need the distinction between homology and analogy. Are the animal and human dispositions the same as those of the animal, homology; or are merely similar, analogy? In order to be able to apply explanation schemata and content from animal studies to human social psychology the difference between animals and human beings must be shown to be a series of differences along a continuous spectrum, a gradual transition from analogy to homology. We will look at some research programs that have shown that there is no sharp psychological break between species in certain kinds of social behavior.

In his well-known book, *On aggression*, Lorenz (1961) claimed that Man is no different from other primates in an inherited tendency to undertake aggressive rituals in defence of territory and in seeking to dominate other members of the species. However, human beings, like other animals but to a much greater extent, ritualize these propensities. Competitive games involve aggressive acts against members of one's own species, but they are events governed by strict rules and very often with a referee or umpire to ensure that the rules are adhered to. There is no sharp line dividing human and animal tendencies to aggression, though there is a growing preponderance of cultural patterns and rules over genetically driven tendencies to engage in patterns of attack and defense.

Darwin emphasized the functional identity of emotion displays in the lives of people and animals on the basis of close and extensive comparative observations. His conclusion was that the *same principles* apply to explaining the display of emotions by animals and by people. For example, actions useful for carrying out a desire reappear when that state of mind recurs, even though the action is of no practical use. Important too are visible consequences of nervous system activity, blushing with shame, or reddening with anger.

Emotion expression is a central feature of social interactions at all levels in the great chain of being, from crouching voles to smiling election victors making high fives!

All this tended to show that there were some analogies and some homologies in the social psychology of many animals and human beings. There is a highest order disposition, for which a Darwinian biological explanation seems appropriate. It is not hard to see how in each case there would be a selective advantage for the animal in which the relevant gene variant first appears. This ensures that all else being equal, the variant will spread throughout the population of subsequent generations. However, historical-cultural factors which seem to be learned, also give advantages to their possessor and so to the members of the group in which a certain culture is predominant. Thus, lower order dispositions are shaped by cultural learning. This provides a powerful support for the use of ethology as an explanatory system for human social behavior. As Lorenz realized, the development of a theory of human aggression shows it also opens up a space for the insertion of a cultural component into the explanation format.

The Paleolithic Psychology Principle

The work of Dunbar and others tends to show that our modern genome is the result of selection pressures on our Paleolithic forebears. However, history has filled the intervening millennia with all sorts of cultural innovations. Theories of social behavior ought, in consequence, to be fusions of references to Paleolithic genomes, selected for the conditions of life at that time, the 'social brain hypothesis', and historical conditions such as climate changes, together with endless cultural overlays, thanks to the ever-active imaginations of human beings (Dunbar, Barrett, & Lycett, 2007).

How do we know what sort of social factors acted as selection pressures on human development? There is evidence from archaeology particularly in Western Europe. And there is a strong analogy between our knowledge of the ways of life of contemporary hunter-gatherer tribes, such as the Australian Aboriginal people and the Bushmen and our speculations about those of our Paleolithic ancestors. For example, among hunter-gatherers there is a favored tribal size of about 150 members, the society is organized around the nuclear family units, and while there is only a simple technology there are sophisticated concepts and thought patterns. Why should these social features have become dominant? Perhaps they evolved to protect the tribe against predators and the aggression of other tribes.

The Paleolithic psychology hypothesis is simply that there has been no substantial change in the genome of human beings since that era.

Examples of Theories in Evolutionary Psychology
Inherited Structures for the Recognition of Con-Specifics

While Lorenz's imprinting studies show that 'mother-recognition' is not inherited in many species, there are studies which suggest that recognition of members of one's own species, a necessary condition for the formation of coherent and permanent social groups, is genetically based as the result of Darwinian selection. There are two structures in the brain of higher animals that are involved in perception. The magno-cellular structure runs across the upper surface of the brain mass to the frontal lobes. It seems to be active in the detection of movement. The parvo-cellular structure runs under the brain mass to the frontal lobes and is also connected to the amygdala. It is found only in primates. It has been shown by Robert Barton (1998, pp. 1933–1937) that the number of cells in the parvo-cellular structure is proportional to the normal size of the group to which the animal belongs. Dunbar argues that this finding suggests that in the course of primate evolution a structure emerged that was closely linked to the life of the primate community. The genetic variation that is expressed in the parvo-cellular structure would be adaptive for hominids living in middle-sized social groups. However, we need an explanation of why groups of that size were likely to survive the conditions of life in that era.

It might be argued that the need for protection against predators and rival tribes required a more substantial and better organized collective than has been observed amongst chimpanzees and gorillas. The hierarchies that primate groups display are more elaborated and more powerful in human groups. Managing hunting and defensive activities is surely a desideratum when it comes to group survival. Of course, it is not the group that evolves, but the genome. However, if the group is compromised by some weakness in promoting the survival of its members, a kind of group selection will certainly occur.

Dunbar et al. (2007, p. 114) claim that neocortical volume in primates is proportional to the average complexity of the social group, arguing for a 'stone age' selection of this brain feature (Dunbar et al., pp. 116, 123) linked to the ability to recognize about 150 individuals. The Amish of Pennsylvania and the Hutterites of Western Canada live in isolated, self-sufficient communities. When a community reaches about 150 members some leave to set up another self-sufficient group, which in turn expands to about the same size, and splits again. But what do we know of preferred sizes in urban society far from the conditions of the hunter-gatherers who are supposedly our Paleolithic forebears? Dunbar reports an ingenious study based on a count of the family's Christmas cards. This should give a measure of the size of the group that people consider friends, relatives and acquaintances, close enough to warrant some sort of special attention. The average number of people linked by a family's Christmas card sendings and receivings is also about 150.

Later, bio-features such as joint attention, an infant looking where the adult looks, detecting the line of sight of another being; and shared point attention, checking back and forth by an infant to verify that it is attending to the same object as the parent, appear to be innate, that is, genetically based. These perceptual activities seem to develop without training from older members. They make possible sophisticated organization of social groups with the possibility of common targets of attention and consequently of action. We could call this the moment of the origin of *intentionality* in hominid affairs, the ability to discern at least some aspects of the mental states of others.

According to Dunbar et al. (2007, p. 117) 'These ... constraints on group size exist as a consequence of ... [reflecting] the demands made on our species sociality during the long hunter-gatherer phase of our existence'.

Biological Basis of Human Mating Patterns

It has been suggested that contemporary criteria of mate selection among human beings are based on fixed-action patterns that evolved in pre-Paleolithic or Paleolithic eras. There is a set of human first-order dispositions that are adaptations to ensure basic reproductive patterns. Here we have a powerful theory that purports to offer explanations for a variety of rather fine-grained social behavior patterns. However, as most biologists are quick to point out, this theory supports what we have been calling mostly first-order dispositions, actual observable social practices displaying second-order dispositions. Here explanations need to include a cultural or historical component. Nevertheless, some of this theorizing is quite specific, in that some of the characteristics of men that make them more or less attractive to women seem to be fairly easily discernible and those of women for men more or less the same, and perhaps independent of cultural influences.

Humans are born prematurely because our upright posture requires narrowing of the pelvis, which counts against large-brained babies. We have already noted that the size of the brain is related to quality of a social group to its members. The biological 'solution' is to select for genes that promote 'premature' birth with respect to the gestation patterns of other primates. Clearly, this development would tend to make the mother-infant pair vulnerable to all sorts of dangers. There is an observable human modification in the rise of pair-bonding as an adaptation to prolonged infancy and childhood. Is this a variation in mating practices that could be selectively established in the human genome?

We know that actual sexual relations among mammals increase the quantities of oxytocin and vasopressin in the body. This increase is experienced as a sense of well-being, apparently via an increase in the neurotransmitter, dopamine. It is easy to see that selection pressure would favor genetic versions that were expressed as biochemical processes that led to the manufacture of these neurochemicals. Is there a similar chemical background to explain the prevalence of pair-bonding in human societies, despite the instability of gender relations?

We have already noted the importance of animal models in socio-biology. Most of what we know about the bonding effect of vasopressin comes from comparative studies of two species of vole, the prairie vole and the mountain vole.

Among humanity, research (Singh, 1994) has shown that there are definite qualities that seem to mark out males sought by females. The signs of genetic quality include symmetry, height and scent. Women preferred the smell of T-shirts worn for two nights by symmetrical men over those worn by asymmetrical men! Then there are signs of a capacity for support and protection that compensate for the vulnerability of the mother-infant pair due to the premature birth of human beings. These include visible displays of resources, of course appropriate to the era, and parenting skills. How much of this is biological in origin? We simply do not know.

Corresponding female qualities sought by males are attributes relevant to fertility. These include relative youth and appearance. Men value women whose height is about 80 percent of their's. They prefer women with a waist to hip ratio of 0.7 and a body-mass index of about 20. One's BMI is calculated by dividing one's weight in kilos by one's height in metres squared. Child-like and symmetrical female faces are favored.

· Here we are presented with a variety of biological theories to explain an important social process, reproduction and child rearing, as well as male/female relationships in general. Singh (1994) argues that seeming historical variations in ideal female and male forms are within the boundaries of bio-desirability.

That these considerations cannot be the whole story is clear enough. Polygamy, particularly polygyny, seems to be an exceptional human practice which calls for a non-biological explanation. For example, it has been suggested that the Mormon settlers in Utah adopted polygyny so that widows would have a safe haven in an existing nuclear family. In many societies, mate choice has not been left to young people exercising choices according to criteria of biological origin. It has been often decided by the elders of the family and dictated by such considerations as the economic possibilities in the bringing together of two families. Even now, in many places in the East, astrology plays a part in the use of horoscopes to identify a good mate choice.

In summary, it seems there are two biological influences that can be used to explain the prevalence of the nuclear family in human societies. Mate selection seems to be based on women selecting taller, symmetrical men who look powerful, hinting at good fatherhood propensities, while men select shorter, hour-glass shaped women with round faces, hinting at good motherhood propensities. The similarity between prairie vole biology and that of human beings suggests that the production of oxytocyn and vasopressin in mating relationships induces a strong bonding between partners, be they human or rodent. As the generations pass there will be more tall, symmetrical, powerful people to pass on these desirable characteristics.

Genetic Psychology

In the previous section, we saw how a good case can be made out for an evolutionary explanation of certain very general features of human social life, tribal size and the propensity to live in nuclear families. Genetic psychology looks for biological explanations of certain first-order dispositions to perform various kinds of social acts regardless of origin. This is a distinct scientific speciality. Genetic explanations need not be grounded in selectionist theory for the social propensity in question, such as homosexuality, be explained biologically. For example, the presence of a variant of a gene or gene complex in certain people may be due not to selection processes but to an immediately past mutation. This is commonly a variant of a gene complex the role of which in the explanation of some behavioral propensity is already well known. The psychological problem to which genetic psychology is addressed is to explain the existence of propensities for certain kinds of behavior by looking for a genetic basis for some specific social psychological disposition.

It would be desirable if socially significant research into the origin of social and antisocial tendencies in human beings could be studied by research which made use of human genetics. Sometimes this is possible. The most common method for this kind of research has been twin studies. However, it is now giving place to direct studies of relations between identifiable gene complexes, their promoters and specific variants of common styles of social behavior and cognition. Twin studies are based on the principle that if a pair of monozygotic twins who have been raised separately, display similar social propensities, then this is likely to be because of their common genetic endowment. (The role of nurturance in the origins of the behavior in question being eliminated by the fact of different upbringings.) In a variant on this method, the social propensities of pairs of monozygotic twins are compared with those of dizygotic twins, who share only half their genetic endowment. Here are some examples of theories based on twin studies.

Loneliness and Depression

In a twin study comparing 4,000 monozygotic and dizygotic twins, it was found that those from monozygotic pairs were more likely than dizygotic twins to both report loneliness. Since monozygotic twins have identical genetic profiles, a causal link between some gene complex and a propensity to feel lonely seems highly likely, all else being equal.

It has been suggested that on the basis of these studies we should expect there to be a 'gene for loneliness'. Being miserable alone would be a survival mechanism in Paleolithic times, since it would prompt people to seek the company of their fellow hominids. However, research by Linda Wood (Wood & Kroger, 1986) suggests a strong cultural element in the onset of loneliness which undermines too ready a conclusion from the results of the twin studies. She found that people reported themselves to be lonely not on the basis of the proportion of their time they spent alone, but on the amount of time they thought they should spend alone. Not surprisingly, this differed a great deal from person to person depending on their life situations, and from countryside to town.

Religiosity

Hamer (2004) has called the way certain people think about the world as 'self-transcendence'. People differ in the extent to which they report 'spiritual feelings that are independent of traditional religiousness … Self transcendent people tend to see everything, including themselves, as part of one great totality …'. Non-self transcendent people 'focus on differences and discrepancies between people, places and things' (Hamer, 2004, p. 18). How are we to explain this socially psychologically highly important difference? One possibility is that the difference is the final outcome of the distribution in the population of a variant of a neurologically important gene. This suggestion is strongly supported by the fact that the distribution of self-transcendent people matches that of the distribution of the gene variant in the population Hamer studied. Even more striking is that siblings who differ in the relevant gene variant also differ in their degrees of 'self-transcendence' (Hamer, 2004, p. 76).

The gene in question, found in chromosome 10, comes in two variants differing in one base unit. The VMAT2 gene is expressed as a transporter molecule that effectively binds neurotransmitters into vesicles at the presynaptic terminals of neurons, storing them for later use and preventing their degradation by chemical agents that maintain the best concentrations of these molecules. The relevant transmitters are the monamines, such as dopamine and serotonin, involved in the way people experience moods; upbeat with dopamine and generally either depressive or aggressive with serotonin.

Hamer's population of self-transcendent people was both small and culturally fairly uniform, indeed even members of one family. As well as expressions of 'cosmic attitudes', these neurotransmitters are also associated with transcendental states. Further evidence for the role of VMAT2 in the origins of propensities to think outside the bounds of the mundane, comes from the fact that this gene is found in people such as Buddhist monks, though absent in those who have not been drawn to a religious vocation. Do they become monks because they have this gene, and monastic life fulfills the consequential propensity? That may be, but it seems more likely that among those who are attracted to the life for all sorts of reasons, some remain monks because they have this gene expressed in a superfluity of these neurotransmitters.

The reader must surely have been struck by the speculative character of much that has been described in the foregoing. Only in the case of the animal models do we find a fully articulated explanatory story with the causal format filled in at each stage and level. More convincing in general, evolutionary psychology requires the introduction of cultural factors to arrive at theories that tie the Paleolithic principle to the fine details of contemporary social life.

Psychoneurology

In order to develop a research program aimed at identifying regions of the brain active when a person is involved in some well-specified social activity, we need to invoke the Taxonomic Priority Principle in a strong or homologue form. Only if we are able to identify a person's thoughts, feelings, perceptions and actions which are socially relevant by the use of local folk categories as applied to the interpretation of the local and current discursive practices, can we then use scanning technology to identify the brain regions active when these psychological events are occurring.

However, the point of the research is to try to find the neural mechanisms and processes that subserve the social psychological activities of people. At this point it would seem obvious that the Task Tool metaphor would be the appropriate device to take the next step and to try to create a hybrid social psychoneurology. This move is problematic since, unlike such activities as remembering or reasoning, the persons involved are not *overtly* using their neural equipment as tools for the accomplishment of social tasks. Nevertheless, the socially relevant activity requires the activation of these 'mechanisms' – defects or lesions in the neural system are correlated with defective performances.

Hybridization requires a different but related linkage. To see this we must return to the fundamental structure of psychological science, the hierarchy of dispositions. Evolutionary and genetic psychology provide explanations of the existence of generic dispositions, while cultural and developmental psychology provide explanations for tribal or restricted dispositions. Third-order or ephemeral dispositions are explained by reference to the ambient situation in actual social episodes. However, the logic of dispositional attributions requires that a disposition should be attributable to a person even when that person is not actually displaying the activity in question; thinking, acting, feeling, or perceiving. This feature of dispositional analysis involves the attribution of permanent states to the people in question, that is, it requires that the disposition be 'grounded'.

In the natural sciences grounding of dispositions usually invokes hypotheses about the molecular states of the material substance to which a disposition is attributed. Sugar is sweet all the time but displays this sensory disposition only when on the tongue of a person or animal. The grounding is described in the chemical formula of sugar, with the implicit hypothesis that the gustatory system of sentient beings is adapted to detect the presence of a molecule of the relevant structure. A similar pattern is required for the hybridization of social psychology and neurology. In this case the grounding must be in the structures and processes that are established in the brain of the social actor, either genetically via the Paleological principle, or by experience and training in the use of the local symbol systems in the manner described by Vygotsky, that is, by social processes revealed by the methods of cultural psychology.

Examples of Research in Psychoneurology

We have selected the examples that follow both because they illustrate the two main techniques of social neuroscience, lesion/deficit correlation and fMRI scanning, but also because they are prominent in a widely used reader, Cacioppo and Bernston (2005). The merits of adding neuroscience studies to the repertoire of social psychological research methods and the cautions that have to be observed when conclusions are drawn from the results are evident in the examples to follow. In each case the research establishes that there are certain neural tools in use and how they work. In neither example could it be claimed that neurology has displaced cultural psychology in the planning and interpreting of the research program.

Solving Emotional Problems

The first study is aimed at testing the idea that 'emotional' and 'social intelligence' are distinct from 'cognitive intelligence'. Instead of studying how people solve emotional and social problems and comparing their methods and their successes and failures with the local standards of achievement with those by which they solve intellectual problems, (Bar-On, Tranel, Denburg, & Behcara, 2005) set about showing that people with damage to the amydala lack 'emotional intelligence' and are liable to make 'poor judgments in decision making' and show disturbances in social functioning, while they display no defects in cognitive intelligence.

The method followed the lines we have already sketched. The investigators found people with brain lesions, due to a stroke for example, and provided them with the same tasks as they gave to people without the lesions and compared the results of the activities of each group. Over the whole project about 20 people took part, 10 with brain injury and 10 with none. The tasks were discursive, and framed within unexamined and taken-for-granted cultural settings, including a hospital.

The first task was to provide a self-report of emotionally and socially intelligent behavior, which provides an estimate of one's underlying emotional and social intelligence (Bar-On et al., 2005). The questionnaire included 133 items and the participants rated their performances on a five-point scale.

The second task was to respond to an interview leading to a 'comprehensive assessment by a clinical neuropsychologist ... of each participant's post-morbid [after the stroke] employment status, social functioning, interpersonal relationships and social standing' (Bar-On et al., 2005, p. 229). Using a three-point scale, the interviewer assessed the change in the social location of the interviewee before and after the damage to the brain. No record of pre-morbid social characteristics was made use of.

The investigators concluded that 'in spite of normal intellectual capacity ... these patients ... reveal a compromised ability to experience, understand, express and effectively use emotions ... [and are bad at] decisions of a personal and interpersonal nature' (Bar-On et al. 2005, p. 224).

The people who were known to have suffered brain lesions in the amygdala region were those whose discursive capacities differed from the local norms in talking about how they had or would behave in emotional and socially significant episodes. Since they showed no deficits in logical reasoning, the differences between their storylines and those of the people who had not suffered brain lesions must be put down to the failure of the damaged regions to support emotional and social judgments.

Emotional Expression and Brain Activation

As a second exemplar, we turn to an fMRI study to try to identify the regions of the brain that are active when a certain kind of socially relevant task is being performed (Moll, Oliviera-Souza, Bramati, & Grafman, 2005). The task is discursive, to comment on 'emotionally unpleasant statements without moral considerations, emotionally unpleasant statements with moral considerations' and emotionally neutral statements. According to the investigators, 'we intended to explore the differential effect of emotional valence and moral judgment on brain activation.' It is most important to realize that this work is not about emotions in morally distinct social situations but about discursive acts. The psychological content of the study is entirely within the realm of discourse. The experiment was conducted by asking the participants to read a sentence and then to say whether it was right or wrong, by using the words 'certo' and 'errado', the Portuguese equivalents of the English 'right' and 'wrong'. The experiment was conducted in Portuguese but described in English.

The interpretation of the discursive-cultural analysis of the 'experimental' episodes depended on assuming that restricting replies to only two words the participants would 'make standard decisions regardless of the specific content of each sentence' (Moll et al., 2005, p. 65). The distinction between non-moral social violations and moral social violations is a conceptual distinction for which empirical evidence is irrelevant. It corresponds to the distinction between embarrassment and shame. The project illustrates the structure of a hybrid research program very well, though the details could be greatly refined.

The investigators created three different conditions, each identified by the content of the statement presented to the participants. In the NTR condition, the presented sentence was emotionally and morally neutral, for example, 'The elderly sleep more at night.' In the NM condition, the content of the sentence was unpleasant but there were no moral connotations, for example, 'Judges often eat rotten food,' while in M condition, the content was unpleasant and there were moral connotations, for example, 'The judge condemned an innocent man' (Moll et al., 2005, p. 66).

The fMRI scans revealed a consistent pattern of activation for the three conditions. The scans revealed that reading moral and non-moral descriptions of unpleasant social events activated different regions of the brain. However, though there is plenty of evidence that the amygdala is activated when a person is involved in an emotionally demanding situation, 'contrary to our expectations' say the authors, 'the amygdala was not activated in the moral judgment condition, even though those statements were rated as most emotionally evocative' (Moll et al., 2005, p. 70).

The discussion section of this paper is instructive. The authors found that 'different sectors of the OFC were activated when moral or non-moral social judgements were being contemplated' (Moll et al., 2005, p. 71). In particular, the amygdala was not activated by *statements* of moral judgments even if the situation described was unpleasant. The experiments showed that the neural nets activated in each of the conditions were different. Does it follow that their activity is integrated in the case of social interactions that combine moral, social and emotional demands? It does not. The participants were required to comment on *descriptions* of morally and emotionally diverse situations, not on situations in which they were involved. Even if fMRI scanning were to be possible when someone was actually engaged in some social activity, the experiments reported here depended on independent understanding of the statements presented to the participants as embedded in cultural patterns and discursively presented. This experiment was only made possible by prioritizing cultural and discourse analysis in order to have material for the participants to view.

The most interesting finding of the study came from a discourse analysis of the material presented to the participants. They found that there was a significant relationship between moral content and emotionality of the statements the participants read. Judgments in the M condition (morally relevant situations) were described with moral terms such as 'pity' and 'indignation'. But for non-moral content emotion words like 'disgust' were used more frequently.

Thus, as with almost all attempts to link brain activity patterns to social behavior, this style of research is only possible if it is developed within a hybrid social psychology.

Across the whole range of examples we have discussed, the hybridizing move has been accomplished by adopting the Taxonomic Priority Principle to identify and classify social activities, collective and individual. We have seen this as a necessary component of correlating the results of any studies in neuroscience with social behavior. However, the analysis would be incomplete if we left it at that. Each of these projects implicitly or explicitly draws on the Task-Tool metaphor.

Conclusions

We have now examined two very different ways of trying to understand the way people behave socially, neither of which are compatible with the theory and practice of classical social psychology, though they must both conform to the double disposition format that any psychological study demands:

1   **Social behavior is the realization of genetically determined propensities, selected by Darwinian processes to favor certain genes and gene groups.**
2   **Social behavior is the result of active human agents using their knowledge of the rules and conventions of their cultures to bring about various social projects, by performing meaningful actions.**

Both approaches seem to capture some of the scientifically acceptable principles social psychology would need to advance beyond the unsatisfactory program of classical social psychology. Can a synthesis be achieved to bind these approaches into a single coherent branch of psychology? We have illustrated the viability of the hybrid project in the studies described above. The Taxonomic Priority Principle is necessary for there even to be a project in psychobiology or psychoneurology. When the phenomenon under study is social process, where people are living out episodes of social acts with a project in hand, the research must be framed with the Task-Tool metaphor shaping the explanatory phase of the work. What is the social task being accomplished or failing to be accomplished and what are the instruments by which the people are trying to perform it? Issues of social cognition are, of course, already accounted for with the application of the dramaturgical or ludic models, assigning parts to players. Not all social actions are accomplished with forethought – for example, laughing is a biological response to a cultural phenomenon and a fit study for a hybrid project (Shami & Stuss, 1999).

Classical social psychology cannot be incorporated in a hybrid system since it does not meet the historically grounded requirements of scientific rigor and method. It lacks a refined and coherent taxonomy of social phenomena, making use only of ad hoc categories tied into particular research projects. These are often quite vague. What does 'helping behavior' include? What does 'aggression' mean? Even when sequential regularities are identified there is no coherent account of the generative mechanisms that underlie them. Classical social psychology lacks a systematic method of generating hypotheses about the unobservable processes which produce the observable phenomena. This is perhaps the most serious drawback of the classical style, reflecting as it does the way that social psychologists have clung to the positivism that has departed from most other fields of scientific research.

Psychobiology has the powerful taxonomy of ethology to base its categories on and has not hesitated to integrate this with the categorical systems of vernaculars. It has a highly systematic way of generating explanatory hypotheses about unobservable generative mechanisms having the whole of neuroscience to draw on, grounding all of that in the processes of organic evolution. Cultural psychology too has a well-grounded taxonomical resource in the vernaculars which define psychological phenomena culture by culture. It also deploys a powerful explanatory system in the literal and metaphorical developments of the concepts of meanings and the rules for managing them.

Ethnographic Taxonomy Is Conceptually Prior to Biology

To identify a certain gene as 'the gene for X', where X is the final behavioral outcome of the relevant gene expression, we need to have an independent criterion for X. Wittgenstein argues that we could not identify a case of X from our knowledge of biochemistry and physiology of that gene, its form of expression and complicated chain of biochemical processes that eventuate in some kind of behavior. People could identify cases of X long before they could undertake biological research. For example, we could not identify a gene for loneliness unless we could already identify a person's condition as 'lonely'. We could not identify a gene which is expressed as a protein involved in the uptake of serotonin as grounding a propensity to recklessness unless we could identify cases of reckless behavior. 'Reckless' is culturally relative!

People Use Biological Tools to Carry Out Culturally Defined Tasks

Tasks are performed by people using certain relevant tools. How are these tasks set? Certain biological necessities must be met – nourishment, reproduction and so on involve practices in which biology is heavily overlaid with culture. Certain social necessities must be met, such as establishing status and respect hierarchies. Even if these are ultimately grounded as the end product of gene expressions, the role of cultural norms is paramount.

With what tools are tasks performed? Compare 'digging a ditch by using a spade' with 'remembering who is the person to be honored by using one's brain'. The tasks are socially defined, even ditch digging in the last analysis, but the way the tools work is to be discovered from physics and physiology. Tennis is another example of the Task-Tool explanation format. The tools are a complex kit including the players' bodies, their racquets, the court and so on; the game is a cultural device by which the sociobiological propensity to engage in competitive rituals to establish or maintain status is reworked into a social practice. These tools are material beings drawn into the game under the aegis of constitutive rules. Some tools have no material role. Their efficacy is wholly determined by their cultural definitions. The temporal food offerings in Buddhist ceremonials were not intended to provide material nourishment, nor were the flaming crosses of the Klu Klux Klan intended to immolate their enemies. They were meant to threaten and alarm them.

An important consequence of adopting the Task-Tool metaphor is the opportunity it provides to preserve the concept of 'person' in social psychology. In using the double dispositional method in the old social psychology, interpreted according to the Humean causal format, the concept of 'Person' was effectively deleted from the classical paradigm. Human beings were not considered to be active agents, that is, persons, but sites for regular sequences of like pairs of events, causal processes in the Humean sense. If we were to reduce all task concepts to their biological roots there would be no place for the concept of a person, and the basic explanatory concept would revert at best to generative mechanisms, at worst to correlations. But if we preserve the social aspect of task concepts, that is, projects that people undertake, the tool aspect of some material object is defined only relative to the culturally defined task. A spade is only a digging tool where there is the social practice of digging, something people do, cheerfully or reluctantly, carefully or carelessly and so on. This move preserves the concept of 'person' as active agent, using tools.

Thus, most of our current culture would be preserved even as we incorporate sociobiology and neuropsychology into culturally sensitive social psychology.

A full explanation of social phenomena requires a contribution from both fields. Psychobiology provides explanations of how there come to be historically persistent and species-wide first-order social dispositions, while cultural-historical psychology provides explanations of the form that second-order dispositions take, the dispositions the activation of which will explain the social behavioral phenomena of everyday life.

Note

1   This term was coined by Erving Goffman (1968).

9 Motivation and Social Representations

Sandra Jovchelovitch and Vlad P. Glăveanu

As over against the inferential conception of motives as subjective 'springs' of action, motives may be considered as typical vocabularies having ascertainable functions in delimited societal situations. (C. Wright Mills, 1940, p. 904)

'Unless there is com-pression nothing is ex-pressed' said John Dewey in his book on *Art as Experience* (1934, p. 69). Indeed, it is pressure and turmoil that create, sustain and guide human action. This 'inner' pressure, always developed in relation to an external environment peopled by objects, persons and social institutions, is conceptualized in psychology as motivation. Etymologically, the Latin root of the word takes us back to the verb *movere*, to move. Motivations move persons, and, as we argue in this chapter, also move human groups, communities and societies. As a matter of fact, whenever questions are raised as to why a certain action is taken and not another, why at a certain moment and not another, and why directed towards a certain 'object' and not another, it is the underlying motivations that are sought after. It comes as no surprise then that motivation is said to lie 'at the heart, the very center of psychology' (Weiner, 1992, p. 1).

But where is the locus, or the source, of human motivation? What makes us move? Understanding where motives come from has been of great importance for traditional psychology in search for explanations based on a simplistic idea of what a 'causal' discipline could be (see Chapter 1) because motives were supposed to be fundamental pieces in the puzzle of how the concepts of 'causes' and 'effects' related to human behavior. If all human behavior is *motivated behavior*, then by knowing the underlying motivation one can presume what kind of action is taken and how it will be performed. But knowing *underlying* phenomena has never been simple in psychology. Motivation theories in the 20th century (see Hollyforde & Whiddett, 2002; Weiner, 1992) express well the tensions between biological, humanist and cognitive accounts of human behavior as they struggled to identify the sources and mechanisms of human motives. From early theories of drives and arousal, to theories based on human needs and self-actualization, to the more recent cognitively inspired and neurological theories of motivation, we also find the schisms and difficulties that marked the conceptual development of psychology as a whole. Traversing this journey is the long-standing problem of anchoring human behavior and motives in the individual alone, something further accentuated by the strong tendency of early 21st-century psychology to return to brain processes in order to explain the stuff of human consciousness and what makes our will and motivation. How this tendency can be melded with the project of cultural psychology without mutual reduction is the aim of this book.

In this chapter we approach motivation as a social psychological phenomenon related to theories of self and representation, experience and human action. We propose that the complexity of our motivated actions cannot be located solely in the brain, or in the isolated self, but in the interrelations between body, mind and environment that constitute human experience. We shall locate human motivations in the 'in between': between subject and world, between self and other. This vision has deep roots in psychological science, from psychoanalytical, developmental and social psychological writings about early ontogeny (Marková, 2003; Tomasello, 1999; Vygotsky, 1978a; Winnicott, 1971), to ideas developed by pragmatists and symbolic interactionists about self, action and human experience (Dewey, 1934; Mead, 1934), to socio-cultural traditions in psychology (Piaget, 1962; Vygotsky, 1978a) and the theory of social representations (Jovchelovitch, 2007; Marková, 2003; Moscovici, 2000, 2008; Von Cranach, Doise, & Mugny, 1992; Wagner & Hayes, 2005).

In developing this approach we seek to contribute to Harré and Moghaddam's timely proposal for a hybrid psychology, that is, capable of considering persons as totalities in psychological science. Substituting mind for brain and considering only 'north of the neck' as Fodor once put it, cannot do for organisms that are at once embodied and situated as well as individually, socially and culturally aware. A brain without a subject, a subject without a body and a body without a socio-cultural grounding simply do not exist. Any comprehensive psychology must embrace the complexity of human consciousness and explore human reality beyond the confines of the brain, the individual or environments alone. This approach, we argue, is part of a comprehensive account of why and how we 'move' as agents in the social world.

Motivation: A Brief Survey

The term motivation is as old as psychology (Forgas, Williams, & Laham, 2005). Its immediate philosophical ancestor was the notion of 'will', which continues to inspire debate and controversy across many disciplines today (see, for instance, Baer, Kaufman, & Baumeister, 2008; Habermas, 2008; Libet, Freeman, & Sutherland, 2000). Both in their philosophical and psychological coats, motivation and will are notions that relate to the 'origin' of action. In psychology, definitions of motivation generally refer to a process with three distinct functions: initiating, directing and energizing individual behavior (Green, 1994). Most are written in the language of event-causation presuming the Humean positivistic meaning of that concept, locating these 'causes' in individuals, implying a rather direct and unmediated relation between motivations on the one hand, thought and action on the other (see Hogg & Abrams, 1993). Motivation explains *'why human and subhuman organisms think and behave as they do'* (Weiner, 1992, p. 1; italics in original). As such, the general motivational question is 'why?' and the verb associated with motivation is 'to want' (Higgins & Kruglanski, 2000). In over a century of studying motivation, psychologists have worked to expand their vocabulary so that today we talk about needs, drives, motives, goals, expectations, valences, desires, interests, impulses, aspirations, etc. Many of these terms represent different theoretical orientations which we will briefly review.

The first set of motivation theories centered on the notions of drive, instinct and activation. They linked motivations with arousal and discharge and generally conceived of them as forces that put considerable pressure on the organism, directing it towards fulfillment. This original conception, fundamental for later models of motivation, took inspiration from biology and the natural sciences. Many would place here the writings of Sigmund Freud and his theory of instincts. Freud took the notion of instinct or drive and made it the cornerstone of a psychological system meant to explain all forms of behavior, 'normal' and pathological alike. A few decades later, theories such as activation theory, associated with the work of D. E. Berlyne and W. E. Scott, found a solid ground in physiology alone, describing motivation in terms of a 'heightened and depressed level of activation and arousal on the brains and bodies of organisms' (Hollyforde & Whiddett, 2002, p. 21).

By the middle of the 20th century, several well-known theories of motivation emerged based on the classification and hierarchization of human needs. This approach is perhaps best illustrated by the famous 'pyramid of human needs' created by Abraham Maslow (1970). Potentially one of the most familiar theories of motivation of all time, Maslow provided a hierarchical classification of human needs including basic physiological needs (like hunger or thirst), safety needs, the need to belong, needs related to self-esteem and, finally, at the top of the pyramid, the need for self-actualization. Maslow, as a leading figure of humanistic psychology, emphasized the fact that people can and should reach higher motivational levels, especially self-actualization. In his words: 'What humans *can* be, they *must* be' (Maslow, 1970, p. 22). Although general reviews of research show only partial support for Maslow's original formulation (see Wahba & Bridwell, 1976), his work continues to be influential, in psychology and beyond.

Cognitive theories of motivation focus on the role of cognition in motivation and have flourished in a psychological environment where the cognitive predominates, betraying the unending fascination of Western psychology with the model of the person as a rational decision-maker. Generally grouped under the umbrella of expectancy theories (Weiner, 1992), these theories have their origins in Gestalt psychology, particularly Lewin's field theory and Heider's balance theory. Modern expectancy theories assume that people expect actions to achieve results – thus expectancy – and that results can be desired or avoided – have a valence (see Hollyforde & Whiddett, 2002, p. 77). Thus, Weiner's (1992) suggestion that cognitive perspectives on motivation are constructed around a God-like metaphor: the sovereign individual in full control of his actions and capable of knowing it all. This clearly implies the adoption of agent-causality in contrast to simplistic event-causality, moving away from the idea that people are mere puppets pushed and pulled by the power of motives, be they needs or desires.

Recent advances in neuroscience and physiology, triggered to a large extent by technological progress around fMRI (functional magnetic resonance imaging), generated a rediscovered interest in the neurological correlates of motivational and affective states, taking us to a conceptual territory that is not too far away from early activation theories. Most of these studies seek to establish correlations between affective and motivational states and activation in areas of the brain. This research has located motivation at the diencephalic and telencephalic levels (respectively the posterior and anterior portions of the forebrain) and discussed motivational states in terms of the interrelated subcortical neurobiological systems of 'liking' and 'wanting' (Bernston & Cacioppo, 2008), appetitive motivation and subsequent experiences of pleasure (Berridge & Robinson, 1998) and 'irrational wantings', which have been linked to mesolimbic activation, especially dopamine-related activation (Berridge & Aldridge, 2008).

Clearly animated by a 'localization project' (see Vul, Harris, Winkielman, & Pashler 2009), neuropsychologists seek in the brain the line of causation that can explain subjective experience, motivation and consciousness. They hope, as Gazzaniga (2010, p. 292) put it, 'that by understanding the parts, they will understand the whole' and are constantly looking for the parts of the brain that 'correspond' to certain psychological phenomena, leaving us with the old assumption that mind is an ephiphenomenon of brain activity. Not surprisingly, this research has renewed the debate about human agency, motivation, free will and determinism, because it rekindles the question of who is making decisions and what moves human action. Is the brain making decisions about how and why to act before the person does (Baer, Kaufman, & Baumeister, 2008; Wegner, 2002)? Current research on the neuroscience of motivation throws volitional processes and agency into dispute, something Libet (1999) tried to address in his experimental studies on the physiology and psychology of volitional processes with limited success. His studies identified brain activity *before* a voluntary act (called readiness potential), but showed that a person consciously vetoes and controls these acts. The problem, as we discuss next, is the assumption that it is in the brain and in the brain alone that we can locate and understand motivation and the will to act.

Beyond the Individual Brain as the Center of Motivation

This brief survey of theories of motivation takes us back to the roots of our views about mind-body relations and how we conceive the position of the individual person in the world. Research on motivation left us with a variety of theoretical perspectives that reflect the key and most fundamental questions philosophers and psychologists continue to ask about the causes of human behavior: where is the locus of our agency? Are we over-determined by our biology, our own unknown and unconscious desires, or the social forces of our environment? Or is the person in full control of itself, owner of its actions and holder of transparent knowledge that guides the will and motivated action? These are thorny questions that partially explain why it is difficult to theorize motivation and escape from the unresolved dualisms that have haunted psychology since its inception.

Most motivational theories assume that motivation 'comes' from the individual, is acted upon by the individual and serves specific functions at the individual level. By and large, the individual remains unquestioned as the *true locus* of motivation. Current neuroscience research exacerbates this trend by locating in the brain and its activity the 'underlying' mechanisms that would ultimately cause behavior. While cognitive theories rebelled against biological determinism and excessive behaviorism, new neurological approaches have put this proposal firmly back in the agenda of psychology (Miller, 2010). What is common to both is the focus on the individual organism as the sole center of analysis for understanding human beings. Despite repeated calls for integration of languages and appreciation of diversity, the tendency to reduce psychology to biology and to the individual has not abated.

However, neither the brain nor the individual self alone are the locus of motivation. Mental events are not solely in the brain nor are they brain events, in the same way that mind is not only in the self or inside the individual. The brain is one of the conditions of possibility of psychological phenomena, but so is a socio-cultural environment. The immaturity of the human child at birth makes the environment and a context of care necessary conditions, without which she will not become a person, indeed she will not survive. To locate the mind only in the brain is partial at best and misleading at worst; there is mind in a gesture, there is mind between minds and there is mind in the world. Dancing as a ritual of community and cultural expression cannot be reduced to the brain, desire for social change and a new political organization cannot be reduced to the brain and the normative utopias that guide the motivation and projects of human groups towards a moral and ethical life cannot be reduced to the brain. What the brain does while we exist as persons in the world is not the whole story and cannot be equated to mind. We exist out of our heads (Noë, 2009) and recent theories of the 'embodied' and 'extended' mind are gradually trying to envision 'brain, body, and environment as dynamically coupled' (Marshall, 2009, p. 120).

While understanding neural events is a worthwhile project, it should not colonize psychology and substitute the study of psychological categories in their own right. Mental events are not the same thing as neural events, human experience cannot be described or fully explained in terms of synapses, ion flows and so forth. Mental events and brain events belong to different logical categories and one cannot replace the other. As such, it is not possible to reduce the language of psychology to the one of neurobiology, a Cartesian error eloquently discussed by Bennett and Hacker (2002) who point to the fact that, although certain processes take place in the brain while the person thinks, feels and wills to act, it is not the brain who thinks, who feels or who wills to act. The same logic applies for motivation. The brain doesn't want, desire or need anything, the situated person does, and it would be both reductionist and misleading to conceive otherwise.

Individualism, as Farr (1996) argued, is part and parcel of a Cartesian heritage in psychology. Be it by locating mind in the individual self, or by locating it in the brain, the confusion between biological, psychological and social dimensions runs deeply associated with the dualism Decartes introduced. Paradoxically, it is this dualism that is being rejected when the brain is conceived as the 'physical' substratum of mind, a brain that 'thinks', 'perceives' and 'does' things in general. But escaping from the ghost of Descartes requires more than finding somewhere physical to locate the mind because the duality here is not just a question of kinds of substance. Bennett and Hacker (2002) call this error the 'mereological fallacy' in neuroscience: 'the mistake of ascribing to part of a creature attributes which can logically be ascribed only to the creature as a whole'. Brains and individual selves do not think or do anything, only persons do. And persons cannot be reduced or equated to one single part of their overall makeup.

This becomes apparent when we ask ourselves who is the subject of the brain and what makes the human self possible? Everything in the life of a person, from thinking to feeling to motivated action, relies on relationships between body, self and the wider socio-cultural and natural environment. We are located totalities in a world of objects and of others. Drives and needs exist only because we inhabit a greater social environment that comforts, nurtures, and oftentimes challenges and endangers our existence. By being in the world and with the world, we aim at the world – including objects, others, ourselves – and are, in turn, aimed at by the world. It is this space of interaction and communication, peopled by the relational complexities of human life, that frames motivation and shapes what we want, why we want it and how we want it. The self has deep and meaningful connections to the 'outside' and hence motivation most of all is a strictly relational phenomenon. What defines my motives as an individual self cannot be reduced to my being alone and cannot be reduced to my being an organism, as there is always around me a field of action, interaction and communication that constitutes my experience as a totality. As Mills pointed out long ago, 'the motivational structures of individuals and the patterns of their purposes are relative to societal frames' (Mills, 1940, p. 911). That is why motivation is not a phenomenon that can be solely understood from the self-enclosed perspective of the brain or the individual alone. It requires an understanding of the field of relations that in communication and joint action moves people individually and collectively. That is what we propose in the following pages.

Motivation in the Context of Human Experience

In *Art as Experience*, a book based on his lectures on aesthetics delivered at Harvard University in 1934, Dewey provided a model to understand how action of a certain kind is at the basis of human experience. Acting is mediation between life and environment and it is only possible in the context of this relationship:

> The first consideration is that life goes on in an environment; not merely *in* it but because of it, through interaction with it. No creature lives merely under its skin; its subcutaneous organs are means of connection with what lies beyond its bodily frame, and to which, in order to live, it must adjust itself, by accommodation and defence but also by conquest. At every moment, the living creature is exposed to dangers from its surroundings, and at every moment, it must draw upon something in its surroundings to satisfy its needs. The career and destiny of a living being are bound up with its interchanges with its environment, not externally but in the most intimate way. (Dewey, 1934, p. 12)

Against this background of constant interaction between living creature and world Dewey offered the means to conceptualize motivation. He used the term 'impulsion' to designate the origin of every expressive form of action distinguishing it from the related notion of 'impulse'. Impulsion, according to Dewey (1934, p. 60), is 'a movement outward and forward of the whole organism to which special impulses are auxiliary'. This distinction is paramount. Traditional motivation theory has often dealt with impulses, compartmentalizing and specifying motivations more and more until one would speak of the impulse to perform certain behaviors (lift a cup, move the tongue and lips, etc.) and lose sight of the impulsion that incorporates them. Impulsions engage the being in its integrity, motivate complex forms of action and initiate multi-faceted interactions with the environment. As such, impulsions stand as the natural unit of motivation and can be considered the building blocks of every experience.

But what is an experience? Dewey shows that an experience is above all motivated action and it is not accidentally that he places it paradigmatically in the work of art. Experiences can never be separated from the context of interdependence between self and its surrounding environment. In fact, 'experience is the result, the sign, and the reward of the interaction of organism and environment' (Dewey, 1934, p. 22). Dewey's theory of experience is fundamentally based on a theory of motivation, since not only experience is said to begin with an impulsion, but also to run its course towards fulfillment. This dynamic is crucial and the journey from impulsion to fulfillment in any experience is being shaped by the relation between doing and undergoing. The self acts on the world (doing) and experiences the results of its action (undergoing) in a permanent cycle that constitutes the texture of our existence as living creatures.

In order to talk about an experience, and not just a state of continuous and undifferentiated living, our impulsions have to meet obstacles, something that deflects them or opposes them. Obstacles create tension and emotion, indispensable ingredients for every experience. Doing and undergoing, our connections to the world of objects and of others, are never dispassionate and mechanical, otherwise we would not talk about experiences but routines, monotonous and unconscious movement. This is precisely why motivation cannot be fully understood in terms of what the brain does or the individual alone does. Motivation as experience involves full engagement with body and world, a psychological state that is made of the complex transactions between body, self and world and phenomenologically experienced as a totality. Obstacles, which are outside ourselves in the world of objects and others, play a key role in making us reflect on our actions, in making us become aware of the intent behind our impulsions, in giving meaning to our experiences in and of the world (see also Mills, 1940). This whole succession is captured in Figure 9.1.

Figure 9.1 depicts the relationship between action, motivation and representation, which we expand upon in this chapter. Actions (doing) start with impulsions, and the 'resistance' of the world towards the intentions of the self (undergoing) generates emotions, and, most importantly, prompts the representational work of meaning-elaboration and sense-making, of trying to understand oneself and the surrounding environment:

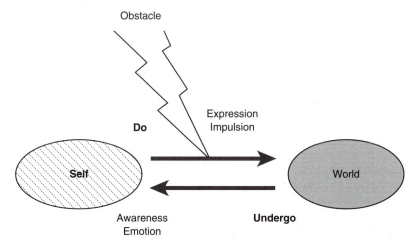

Figure 9.1 Human Experience

'Not without resistance from surroundings would the self become aware of itself' (Dewey, 1934, p. 62). Representations guide motivated actions on their path towards fulfillment, towards *full* experiences. But equally important, representations are also formed by this motivated action; without the desire to engage with others and the world there is no representation.

This line of thought was in fact not unique in psychology at the beginning of the last century, and it is certainly in dialogue with many other foundational theories such as Freud's (the pleasure and reality principles), James's (consciousness) and Mead's (self as a social structure). It also informs current research on the relation between emotion and motivation, conceptualized as dependent 'on the relationship between the organism and its environment' (Parkinson & Colman, 1994, p. xi). In fact, if there is any limitation to Dewey's solid theoretical construction, it lies in the fact that he left the notion of 'world' or 'environment' insufficiently theorized, especially in what the social world is concerned. Often Dewey's examples refer to the material environment and tell us little about the types of self-other relations that build up our experience. In this regard, the theory of social representations can be instrumental in furthering Dewey's valuable insights.

Motivation and Representation

To represent is a fundamental process of all human life and the emergence and circulation of representations establishes the ways in which we understand the world and the contexts in which persons, communities and societies interact with each other. Social representing (both as a process and its product), and any process of knowledge formation for this matter, is never 'disinterested' or 'unmotivated'. There is investment from both individuals and groups in the construction of representations about self, others and the world, and only by integrating the motivational aspect into this phenomenon can we come to realize what 'drives' us to build, promote, actively support or contest certain representations in the public sphere. As such, motivation and representation can never do without each other.

What Is in Representation?

Representation is an action of mind in society (Vygotsky, 1978a). It is a mediating construct between subject, other and object that develops both ontogenetically (in individual minds) and sociogenetically (in public spheres). It is both a practice and an outcome: as a practice, it is an act of substitution that engages arbitrary tokens (symbols) to make present what is actually absent, as when the child evokes the caretaker through a toy or when we use the word 'dog' to evoke the actual animal who barks, plays or bites. As outcome, representation is a socio-cognitive system with power to *signify*, to invest and render meaningful persons, things, relations and worlds, as when we see a picture (think of *Las Meninas* by Velasquez), construct beliefs about ethnic groups, madness and climate change (think about the asylum, segregation and pollution), or dream about social change (think of Martin Luther King's 'I have a dream' speech). Because of their symbolic and social character, representations are open games that entail at once conventional and uncharted territories, allowing persons and societies to reproduce and at the same time reinvent themselves. In all representation there is thus a motivational game, a game of why we represent in specific ways and even why we represent at all, which is related to meaning and what makes or does not make sense for persons and forms of life.

The 'Why' of Social Representations

Why representation? First and foremost, because the desire to know and make sense of the world emerges out of the complexity of self-other relations, is intrinsic to our human life and to the very constitution of mind (Tomasello, 1999). Human beings cannot exist in a world that remains completely strange and alien to them. In order to function and act as humans we need to understand the world and to appropriate it, which is precisely what the symbolic function enables. It is because we are able to represent, to build representations and communicate them, that we can invest the world with meaning and share a reality in which we cooperate with others for the achievement of common goals. It is a basic form of motivation, the epistemic drive, that 'moves' us towards making sense of the world, together with other people, through the elaboration of representations. This process is 'hot' from the start, relying as it does on human interaction: 'the road from object to child and child to object lies through another person' (Vygotsky & Luria, 1994, p. 116). With others we are able to reduce the uncertainty of the world and are motivated to deal with what Hogg and Abrams (1993, p. 177) referred to as 'the ultimate human need … to construct meaning and order from the "booming, buzzing confusion" of raw sensory experience'. And in the quest for uncertainty reduction is the 'what for' of all representation: to make the world familiar, to tame and domesticate the unknown, to find ourselves 'at home' in the world.

Why do we represent the way we do? A central feature of human representational systems is diversity: there are not one, but many different modalities of representation. Processes of knowledge construction take many forms, all articulated to the motives we invest in our representational systems. Think about science, religion and common sense for example. Each involves a different modality of representing the world and a different type of engagement between the representing actor and the world. Science's general motivation – at least ideally – is mainly related to knowledge-seeking, and less so to the identity of its creators, while religion builds representations that are deeply expressive of the identity of groups or nations; they care less about the objects they refer to and more about the cultural traditions and identities they seek to represent. Common sense is wise about the pragmatics of everyday life and enables human communities to respond to the experience of life on a daily basis. The diversity of situations and cultural experiences we encounter require special adaptation efforts, an increased plasticity of our knowledge and flexibility of motivations. The ways in which we represent the world are varied, expressing the polyphasic nature of our cognitive systems and motives, something which in itself is highly adaptive and functional for human life.

Finally, why do we represent specific objects the way we do? Consider for instance representations of madness, or representations of AIDS. Both reveal underlying motivations that relate to our fear of otherness and our attempts to keep the threat coming from different others at bay (Jodelet, 1991; Joffe, 1999). They mingle with powerful signifiers of sexuality, humanity and difference and respond to the intensity of human affects related to these themes. Representing AIDS or madness is different from representing a chair or a city, thus revealing the importance of the extended world of objects for our motivations. The 'object' of representation (e.g. a chair) by its very nature and set of affordances can satisfy certain needs but not others (e.g. sitting) and direct representational work to certain outcomes (e.g. the chair as a sitting object). The complexity is even greater if we consider that people, groups and communities are also objects we represent because the construction of representations about self and others is always driven by very concrete motives such as power, status, self-esteem, etc. The complexity of objects that frame our experiences introduces the power of the extended material world to motivate representational processes and puts forward the importance of empirical contingency in studying the why of representations. Lewin's classical study on how things themselves motivate action has long ago offered evidence to the role played by objects in motivated actions, something Vygotsky (1978a, p. 96) noted and took up: '"things" dictate to the child what he must do … things have such an inherent motivating force with respect to a very young child's actions and so extensively to determine the child's behavior'.

The 'How' of Human Motivation

In the 'how' of motivation, social representations stand as important milestones, providing meaning and the parameters against which and within which actors act and 'move'. Culture and larger social representations mould motivation by intervening in action, shaping its course and the expression of impulses. Motivated action is constituted by a succession of doings and undergoings, of acting based on the original impulse and of taking in the 'resistance' of the environment. Our capacity to represent, to construct meaning around this 'resistance' will lead us further towards attaining our goal by pointing to the means and methods we should use.

The types of activities we engage in, the career choices we make, the people we choose to be surrounded with, all depend on the representations we hold. These representations impact on the expression of our needs – for social stimulation, status, affiliation; indeed even our most basic needs are traversed by the mediation of representational structures. Take for example the cultural differences that exist around the world in ceremonials that have to do with eating, physical and sexual activity. We all experience hunger, but the way we satisfy this impulse depends on what we know can be eaten, on how and when we know it is appropriate to eat, etc. The same logic applies when we think about courtship in different cultures and the profound impact larger systems of normative representations such as religion and the law have on who we decide to meet, who we choose or are allowed to marry, if and how we can separate from our partner and so on. Generally, what our cultures (in families, in communities, in society as a whole) praise and blame, what they value and what they condemn, leave a strong mark on the composition and expression of our drives and motives. Mills (1940) refers to these as 'vocabularies of motive', or societal discourses about what should and should not be 'wanted' in a particular cultural and historical context. The link between culture and motivation becomes even more transparent when we think about expectancy theories since our 'expectations' and the 'valences' we attribute to objects or persons in our environment are certainly the work of representation, of everyday interaction with our environment and communication with others.

We never come to be 'carried' by our impulses without representation of our past actions. Motivated action is meaningful action, that is, it is an 'act' and it is often organized in 'episodes', to use distinctions proposed earlier by Harré (1993). Acts are the meaning of actions and human action has the quality of being *meaning-full*. Furthermore, it also has the quality of being poly-motivated, something that points to the phenomenon of cognitive polyphasia.

The Complexity of Human Motives: Dialogicality and Polyphasia in Motivation

Traditional motivation theories have very often worked within monological frameworks that separate the body from the brain and mind, the 'inside' from the 'outside', the self from the world. In this context, motivation has been depicted as a 'force' from 'inside' that 'moves' individuals. This movement is also considered as organized and consistent. Individuals are said to be motivated by one motivation at a time (the one that becomes 'activated') and to pass to another type of motivation once the first has been satisfied. In a hierarchy of needs model, it could even be 'predicted' what kind of motivation would follow, considering its strength and place in the hierarchy. Human action, as a reflection of this succession of activated motivations, obtains a certain regularity, a certain organization in time.

However, it is rarely the case that human motivations are organized and consistent. We exist as dialogical beings: relational, dynamic, compound, and never fully complete, co-constituted by relations with other persons in the social world (see Marková, 2003). The interdependence between ego and alter introduces simultaneously relevant groups, identities and social representations in our motivational structures, establishing multiplicity and polyphasia in motivation. These characteristics are captured by research on social representations and language, where concepts such as cognitive polyphasia and heteroglossia describe the diversity of ways of knowing and talking about self and the world. Cognitive polyphasia was first formulated by Moscovici in his study on the reception of psychoanalysis in France and it refers to the co-existence of different rationalities and different modalities of knowledge in the same individual or collective (Jovchelovitch, 2008; Moscovici, 2008). The term polyphasia comes from physics, where it denotes 'the existence of alternative and simultaneous currents which, however, can be out of phase with one another' (Marková, 2003, p. 111). In psychology, the notion captures the flexibility and plasticity of human psychological structures. Individuals and groups, finding themselves in different situations, will often be able to simultaneously draw on different bodies of knowledge, sometimes from different and even 'opposing' sources. Our actions reflect this polyphasia in the form of polypraxia. In the words of Moscovici (2000), cognitive polyphasia is intrinsic to mental life just as polysemy is to the life of language. The polyphasic state of human motivation becomes clearer in the analysis of the social as motivation.

The Social as Motivation

In the foregoing we have suggested that motivation theory needs to move from the individual to the relational level of inquiry, taking the space in-between the living self and the social world as its privileged domain of investigation. We propose that the 'social', in the form of interactions and representations, plays a threefold role in developing motivations, not unlike the three roles that motivation is said to have for human behavior: initiation, orientation and dynamization. We will speak of the social as nurturing the ontogenetic development of motivation through the development of imagination and anticipation, the social as integrating motivations in the form of projects, and finally, the social as nurturing motivation, in the expression of creative flow. Let us elaborate on each of these aspects.

Nurturing Motivation: Anticipation and Imagination

It is the fate of a living creature, however, that it cannot secure what belongs to it without an adventure in a world that as a whole it does not own and to which it has no native title. Whenever the organic impulse exceeds the limit of the body, it finds itself in a strange world and commits in some measure the fortune of the self to external circumstances. It cannot pick just what it wants and automatically leave the indifferent and adverse out of account. (Dewey, 1934, p. 61)

The ontogenetic history of motivation begins with the relationship between self and environment, between a subjective sphere and the 'objectivity' of the outside world. The dialectics between subjectivity, through intersubjectivity, to the constitution of objectivity is paramount for the development of the symbolic function and for the development of motivation, for the emergence of the child as an agent, a desiring social actor. Coming out of this relation, and being expressive of it, are the first forms of the imagination found in symbolic representation, in pretend-play and later in adult artistic and cultural experience. One of its most important achievements is that of allowing individuals to 'free' themselves from the immediacy of objects and the boundaries of the present. Once the object is represented, it no longer requires being within a perceptual field that is the concrete 'here and now'; it can become an object for play, for anticipation, for imagination, a more malleable form that is adaptable to the needs and desires of the actor.

The primacy of inter-subjectivity in the ontogeny shows how the social is central for nurturing motivation. It allows the self to imagine a future time-space not yet realized, where desires, endurance and persistence in the face of obstacles materialize in the construction of projects and possible futures. What defines human motivation is exactly its orientation towards the future and the possible, a relative autonomy from what exists here and now and capacity to be guided by the 'not-here' or the 'not-yet-here'. Our ongoing research on how children represent public spheres shows clearly how young children engage the imagination to represent their social world (Jovchelovitch, Priego-Hernandez, & Glăveanu, 2010). Aversive public spheres, institutionalization and poverty motivate young children to imagine and produce representations that are mainly based on their hope for a different world. Children living in institutional settings depict not only 'the world that is', but the world they aspire to, the 'world that is not there' and 'the world that could be'. Drawing the family home the child has never known, or friends from school joining for an unlikely birthday party, or the world of the future, where there is a big family in a big house, 'where everyone has a room of his own', illustrate the motivational and anticipatory function of representations as part of broader strategies of coping and survival.

Young dispossessed children experience an acute need to live in a secure and hospitable world, which they seek even if the 'insult' of reality deprives them of this experience. Thus the need to 'change' the world using the resource of the imagination; seeing the world not only as it is, but also as it could or should be. Here are the origins of our ability to build projects for the future, to turn the anticipatory or 'future making' function of representations into an active motivational 'engine', capable of moving individuals, groups and entire communities.

Integrating Motivation: The Social Construction of Projects

Motivations are articulated in the course of interaction between subjects, groups and larger communities, and they are directed towards future goals. They are organized in a temporal succession that can be referred to as a project. The notion of project, as it relates to social representations, has been outlined by Bauer and Gaskell (1999; 2008). They define project as a 'future-for-us'; an ongoing movement, an anticipation of 'not-yet' that defines both the object as well as the experience of actors (Bauer & Gaskell, 2008). They argue that all subject-object relations are relative to a project, something that is already clearly articulated in Moscovici's seminal study on the reception of psychoanalysis in France (Moscovici, 2008). Studying how psychoanalysis was appropriated and represented by three different French social milieus in the 1950s – Communists, Catholics and Liberals – Moscovici found that for each group, psychoanalysis represented far more than just a body of knowledge. In representations of psychoanalysis there were projects, indeed very large projects, linked to the future of the world revolution and spiritual salvation (Bauer & Gaskell, 2008). Through representational work, these groups accommodated a system of thought that proposed an unsettling vision of the human mind and at the same time put forward their own. The story of Moscovici's study is a story of cultural struggles, of projects and visions of the world clashing as different communities fight to appropriate an idea, to align it to their trajectories and transform it in ways that suit their purposes.

The representational work of different communities is thus organized around different projects. Based on the anticipatory function of representations, these projects are at once motivational and representational. They serve to build a common vision of the future and are defined only in the relation between in-group members on the one hand,

and in-group and out-group members on the other. It is this social dynamics, especially in moments of tension, conflict or rupture, that shapes motivational projects and activates the generation of representations. Such projects steer and energize the attitudes and practices of social groups, sustaining not only their own action but also their relations to other groups and other representations. Motivations are therefore fundamentally embedded in the dynamic of public spheres, as different groups will be motivated to create different representations and to challenge the representations of other groups about the same object.

The construction of representations and knowledges about the future by different groups and communities is simultaneously a cognitive, social and emotional process with deep motivational roots. Cognitively we construct projects, visions about the future and the world to come. Socially, we build utopias, common ideals of how the world should be in times to come. Emotionally, we are nurtured by a feeling of hope, perhaps the strongest motivator for the production of projects and utopias, the emotional bond that holds groups and communities together and 'moves' them towards collective forms of action (Jovchelovitch, 2007, p. 114).

Fostering Motivation: Flow, Creativity and Sociality

Experience involves a totality of self-world relations that are never direct and unmediated. Environments are never completely open to the needs and desires of persons and that is why, when engaging with the outside, we have to go through a process of doings and undergoings, of facing obstacles and suffering ruptures. Environments are neither fully congenial to the straightforward execution of our impulses, nor fully hostile and destructive: they demand action and, in doing so, facilitate development and maturation. Growth, psychologically, biologically and physically, involves a degree of pain and a degree of pleasure. Overcoming the rupture between self and world and finding a direct route for the expression of our impulses through total immersion in an activity comprises the optimal motivational state. Sociality and our connections with persons and objects is what allows us to achieve this state, which has been captured through Csikszentmihalyi's (1990) concept of flow (particularly as described by young people today as 'being on the zone') and Winnicott's (1971) concept of the potential space.

The potential space is a 'third-area of living' that merges child and world, subjective experience and the objectivity of the outside environment. It is a central concept in the psychology of transitional spaces, which uses representation to connect arbitrary objects such as a blanket or a toy to the loved caregiver. In dealing with moments of painful separation from the caregiver, the child employs the first symbolic means for rebuilding the lost feeling of union, for representing in immediate objects the other who cares and loves. These representations, at once cognitive, emotional and social, are invested with the desire of the child for closeness, for social contact, for safety and for knowing and mastering the outside world. The potential space provides the ontogenetic basis for flow, a motivational state that we reach when we are capable of dedicating ourselves completely to one activity, being absorbed by it and delighted by its intrinsic rewards. When we are in flow we seem to lose contact with the outside world because we are in total fusion with it: our action is in full synergy with both ourselves and the external object with which we are engaging. Winnicott described this potential space of flow as the area where self and world are one, creating the psychological basis for play, art and cultural experience. This, as Glăveanu

(2010) argues, is the essence of creative work, one of the most common outcomes associated with being in flow.

The social world creates the context for the development of representation and motivation in early ontogeny by grounding the human self in the dialogical cycle of self-other relations. The emotional and cognitive outcomes of the space in-between allow anticipation and the imagination to steer further the actions of self towards the world, which in its turn responds, creating the cycle of doing and undergoing that produces the totality of our motivated experience. In playing the violin, as Boesch (1997) beautifully demonstrated, we can find this totality of self-other relations that constructs the violin, the player and the promise/project of a beautiful sound, the anticipation of a not yet realized potential of action. As he notes:

> Mastery is not independent of goals and goals are polyvalent and anchored on networks of coordinated action, of thought, beliefs, rules and values … Action and object thus concur to form combined structures; mastering the violin will ultimately unite men and object in that intimate symbiosis resulting in a beautiful sound, and we are likely to find comparable interactions in men's use of other objects. (Boesch, 1997, pp. 182–183)

This potential space of action, constructed through the synergy between the embodied mind and its context of living, is central to the distinctiveness of human action in the world: it reminds us that human behavior carries the potential for meaning, for becoming motivated action.

Conclusions

In this chapter we have proposed motivation as a social and relational phenomenon, highlighting its connections to representation and action, to the construction of self and to everyday human experience. Departing from etymological roots, we focused on the links between motivation and action, and especially on how motivated action is both shaped by and shapes systems of knowledge and representation. We reviewed theories of motivation and criticized the long-established view of motivation as located 'inside' the individual, be it the brain or the individual mind. We recuperated Dewey's work on experience, theories of dialogicality and social representations to approach motivation as a relational phenomenon, grounded in the space of self-other relations and social interactions.

We argued that motivation must be understood beyond the individual level of analysis and showed that the social is also a locus for motivation. This is evident from early ontogeny, when the gradual process of decentration and the development of the symbolic function open a world of possibilities for our motivations, beyond the immediacy of 'here and now'. Imagination and the anticipatory function of representations propel motivations into the space of the future and of the possible, and extend their realm from the world that is to the world that could be and the world that will be. These processes are fundamental for the collective construction of projects and utopias, moving groups and communities towards a common future, coordinating their actions and representations according to a projected ideal. Finally, we have suggested that motivations are intrinsic to our sociality, to the manner in which we direct our action to others and objects, enabling us to enter states of flow that overcome the ruptures and disjunctions of our experience and immerse us in the world of others and of culture.

Dewey's model of experience deserves to be expanded not only by researchers of motivation, but also by researchers engaged with the theory of social representations. The notion of experience is highly difficult to define and to study. And yet experience is the actual substance of our existence as human beings and a building block of our daily life. Capturing, describing and explaining human experience is a conceptual and methodological challenge that requires sustained efforts to overcome. Its phenomenological totality makes it well suited for the project of a hybrid psychology that does not displace, substitute or colonize its internal variety but rather the opposite, can live up to its promise of understanding the diversity of the human person as a biological animal, a psychological subject and a social and cultural being.

10 Emotions

Rom Harré

We had the experience but missed the meaning. (Attributed to T. S. Eliot)

Academic psychology in the 20th century was inhibited in its program for the development of a truly scientific psychology by methodological shortcomings such as the reliance on simplistic experiments, and by mistaken theoretical presuppositions, such as the presumption of the Humean version of cause-effect framing for explanations of psychological phenomena. The pervasive physicalism meant that the phenomena themselves tended to be shorn of the intentionality or meaningfulness that gave them their psychological character. We have drawn attention to these points in earlier chapters, but there are deeper presuppositions that are particularly important in the search for a psychology of the emotions. These are highlighted in an important essay by Catherine Lutz (2007, pp. 19–29).

Lutz draws our attention to the main features of the dominant EuroAmerican ethnotheory of emotions, which, she says, 'continues to serve as a template against which emotion concepts and practices of other cultural systems are understood and assessed' (Lutz, 2007, p. 21).

What are these features? The most fundamental is the assumption that thought and feeling are attributes of individuals, and that emotions are physical events. Here is a quote from Tomkins (1980, p. 182): 'Affects are sets of muscular and glandular responses located in the face and also widely distributed throughout the body which generate sensory feedback that is either inherently "acceptable" or "unacceptable".'

Coupled with this, Lutz finds the idea that public responses, particularly facial expressions and gestures, are taken to be authentic while speaking and acting are in general untrustworthy as guides to the personal attributes as defined by Tomkins. This is also a mistaken assumption.

Catherine Lutz (1952–) was born in Jersey City, New Jersey, one of six children. Her father was a food chemist and her mother became a lawyer after raising the family. Her early environment was a homogeneous suburban and middle class one, later punctuated by the social upheavals of the 1960s. She went on to be curious about cultural differences and the possibilities they suggest for social change, eventually leading her to anthropology and her well-known investigations of the emotional lives of the people of a small Pacific atoll. After schooling in New Jersey and Connecticut, she took her BA at Swarthmore College and went on to Harvard for her PhD. First conducting research on Ifaluk

A much broader canvas on which to lay out the main themes of a psychology of the emotions is provided by Anthony Manstead's (2008) *Psychology of emotions*, a collection of papers arranged into five sections. Each section is independent of the others, and though the scope is rich enough, a hybrid synthesis is still lacking. We hope that it will be found in this chapter. An equally rich but more manageable book is the excellent one-volume study by Keith Oatley and Jennifer Jenkins (1996) *Understanding emotions*.

We cannot ignore the simply staggeringly vast literature on the topic of 'emotion' in our attempt to show how a viable cultural/discursive/neuroscience hybrid can be constructed. In this chapter only a few works will be selected as sources or for commentary, typifying extensive literatures in each aspect of the field. It would be easy to select a different bundle of source materials to illustrate much the same points.

The evident bodily perturbations that are a feature of emotional episodes and the equally evident social role that emotion displays achieve, offers a tempting spectrum of possibilities for essentialist claims. The claim that an emotion is an expression of a physiological state or organic process produced by the activation of a mechanism of genetic origin is set against the claim that an emotion is an embodied form of a judgment about some environmental situation with a personally relevant meaning and is the performance of a relevant social act. The creation of a hybrid psychology of emotions must enable this polarity to be integrated into a coherent whole.

From a philosophical and a psychological point of view, emotions are not theoretical states; they involve practical concerns, associated with a readiness to act. Since emotions are evaluative attitudes, involving a positive or a negative stance towards the object, they also entail either taking action or being disposed to act in a manner compatible with the evaluation (Ben-Ze'ev, 2002, p. 84).

Anthropological Research

As a result of anthropological research, there seems to be good grounds for the view that there are cultural differences in emotion repertoires, some minor, some major. However, care must be taken in how language differences are interpreted. British people sometimes congratulate themselves on the absence of a neat translation for the German word *schadenfreude*, as if the British never took delight in the troubles of another. Of course, they do. The emotion has not been blessed with a single term in English. Sometimes the lack of a neat verbal equivalent is significant. The Spanish phrase *verguenza ajena*, referring to the shame that overcomes someone who is witnessing the foolish behavior of a total stranger, has no equivalent in English. This is an emotion indigenous to Spain.

The work of Catherine Lutz (Lutz, 1988) is based on a lexical comparison with respect to word-for-word translations between English and Ifaluk with a context-sensitive account of the occasions in which the words of the Ifaluk vocabulary are used. For example, the word for one of the many kinds of 'fear' (*metagu*), is not used in situations of physical danger, but only for social anxieties. For physical threats, say from a shark in the fishing grounds, the Ifaluk word has contexts of use that suggest links with shame and despair. How does Catherine Lutz know this? By tying word use to social and personal situations. A comparative linguistic study needs an ethnography to give a rounded picture of the emotion repertoires and their uses in cultures other than ours. Even in analyses confined to emotions indigenous to an author's own world there is an implicit ethnography, evident in the choice of examples to illustrate analytical points.

From Abstract Noun to Concrete Adjectives and Adverbs

In order to take the first steps to establishing a fruitful synthesis between the three main aspects of the domain of the psychology of emotions, biological, cognitive and ethnographic, the discussion in this chapter will focus on emotions as attributes of people rather than abstractions. Instead of focusing on abstract entities like 'love', 'fear', 'anger' and so on, we will take our start from life episodes, unfolding sequences of actions, thoughts and feelings that typically involve more than one person. In life episodes we find concrete entities like 'fearful children', 'angry housewives', 'loving couples', 'proud winners', 'chagrined boasters' and so on, linked through mutual understandings (or misunderstandings) of public emotional displays.

This shift of stance will enable us to draw on such important determiners of emotional states and expressions as storylines and the moral presuppositions of social contexts. The main research object will be the emotional *episode*. For example, anticipating, being awarded and receiving a prize and dealing with the actions of other people relevant to this event make up an episode. Watching over the last moments of a mother or father, managing the funeral arrangements, the funeral and the disposition of the possessions of the deceased make up an episode. Discovering that a partner is 'seeing someone else', bringing the matter into the open and resolving or failing to resolve the issue is an episode. We believe that the scientific study of emotions as feelings and displays cannot be properly carried out without attention to the features of the episodes in which they occur. Should we not say 'in which they typically occur'? Sometimes an incident can be used as an exemplar of a type, but sometimes not.

In the light of this reorientation, the 'emotion' vocabulary will be used to describe topics that arise in the discussion of such phenomena as 'being angry', 'being jealous', 'being joyful' and so on, but not with such phenomena as 'feeling nauseous', 'being in pain' and so on. We will avoid as much as possible using the word 'emotion' as a noun, since it encourages the use of the noun forms of the words of emotion vocabularies. The practice of making use of abstract nouns is replete with misleading implications just from the grammatical role alone. In choosing to write of 'anger', 'love', 'envy' etc., abstract nouns for abstract entities, we will prefer to use process and activity forms of these expressions as above. Such forms are used to express loose clusters of dispositions, propensities to speak, think, act and feel in certain distinctive ways. 'Being angry', 'being jealous', 'being ashamed' are indicative of the *sort* of thing a person is doing and likely to do rather than ascribing a certain definite attribute or state to a person, or implying a specific response to a situation.

Gilbert Ryle (1949, p. 98ff) made a similar point about moods. He argued that a mood like 'sadness' (abstract noun creeping in again, where we mean the condition of a 'sad person') is a complex of long-lasting dispositions to feel, do and say certain sorts of things. Each component disposition is an indispensable part of what it is to be sad. So sadness is not just a shading of one's life in tones of grey, but also a matter of what one is disposed to say and do. Gabriella Taylor (1996) argues in similar vein in her analysis of how we use the words 'grief' and 'grieving'.

The shift to a focus on episodes also allows us to make the study of emotion expressions and their meanings in the episodes in which they occur the center of research programs. We will treat an emotional display as in many ways equivalent to a verbal expression of a judgment of a situation, particularly one in which the actions of other people are germane to how the episode unfolds. Here we will encounter the ethology of emotions, the study of how emotions are expressed in gesture, posture and so on. This will lead us from the work of Charles Darwin in the 19th century to that of Paul Ekman in the 20th.

Outline of a Hybrid Theory

There will be four aspects of the hybrid theory we are aiming at. One will be the nature and dynamics of emotional episodes with sensitivity to cultural diversity. Another will be the repertoire of gestures, expressions, and discourse genres and so on with which emotional expression is presented in emotional episodes, the ethology of the emotions. Another will be a comparative study of the verbal repertoires with which people identify and discuss emotional episodes, the local 'emotionology'. Finally, we turn to the neurological mechanisms through which the flux of feeling and cognition is brought about as emotional episodes unfold. Thus, we have a ladder of features of our emotional lives. It is very important to keep in mind the order of dependence one has upon the other. The dominant feature is the character of emotional episodes, as they are lived in everyday life. Both the ethology and the lexicon of emotional episodes are shaped by the cultural meanings realized in such episodes. The identification of the processes and organs of the limbic system and its links to the cortex is conceptually dependent on the other three features of emotional episodes.

The first three features comprise the discursive/cultural account of human emotional phenomena, while the fourth is the methodologically dispensable but fascinating neurobiological account. We will complete the chapter by applying the two hybridizing paradigms from Chapter 1 to the material we have outlined. Our point of view has been anticipated by others, for example, a forward-looking proposal by R. R. and A. M. Kleinginna published in 1981:

Emotion is a complex set of interactions among subjective and objective factors, mediated by neural/hormonal systems, which can (a) give rise to affective experiences such as feelings of arousal, pleasure/displeasure; (b) generate cognitive processes such as emotionally relevant perceptual effects, appraisals, labeling processes; (c) activate widespread physiological adjustments to the arousing conditions; and (d) lead to behavior that is often, but not always, expressive, goal-directed, and adaptive. (Kleinginna & Kleinginna, 1981, p. 371)

However, though the authors of this passage identify the four aspects of emotional episodes, they fail to distinguish those phenomena which have their place in Humean causal processes and those which are made sense of in discursive frames, requiring us to think in terms of agent causation. The crucial importance of attending to discursive frames is evident in the unsurpassed and detailed studies of 'other' emotion vocabularies by Anna Wierzbicka (1999), to which we will return at various points in the chapter.

Antecedents of the Discursive Account of Human Emotions

In philosophical terms, the first strand, the emphasis on meaning, grew out of Kenny's (1963) argument that emotions have, as it were, proper objects. Emotions are intentional, not merely felt bodily reactions to stimuli. This links to the discussion of motivation in the previous chapter. In other words, the very notion of, say, 'being angry' or 'grieving' involves the presupposition of an appropriate object to which the emotion is directed. This insight was one of the points from which the development of a strongly cognitive account of emotions took its start. Not only were emotion displays and feelings intentional, but they expressed judgments as to the propriety, offensiveness, life-enhancing quality, and so on of the emotion-provoking actions of other people and of life situations. The situation must be interpreted as dangerous, joyous, one of loss, humiliation and so on, for the person encountering it to be afraid, happy, grief-stricken, chagrined etc. William Lyons (1980) anticipated future writing with his argument that which emotion is supposedly experienced is determined by the evaluations of the situation that has provoked a somatic reaction, the ratio being dependent on the evaluation. Opening up a related dimension, it has been argued that there is a close connection between the emotions appropriate to situations and the moral standards of a particular social order. The tie between morality and emotion has been explored by Gabrielle Taylor (1996) and more recently by Martha Nussbaum (2001).

Developing the cognitivist account further led to the idea of the 'social construction of emotions' (Averill, 1982). Not denying the affective, sensory quality of an emotional experience, the social constructionists argued that displays of emotion had something of the character of speech-acts, that is, they had illocutionary force. *Saying* 'You stupid fool' is a verbal way of responding to something offensive someone else has done. It is an act of protest, but expressed in speech. An angry display, such as shaking a fist, turning pale and so on, can also serve as a protest, that is, as a social act, but now expressed non-verbally. Studies of displays of embarrassment as acts of contrition for improper behavior strengthened this interpretation (Parrott & Harré, 1996). A more general 'communicative' account of the role of emotions in everyday life has been proposed by Oatley (1992), based on a more formal cognitive basis.

The flux of opinion in the philosophical literature of the last few decades sketched above has been a refinement of essentially cognitive approaches to the nature of emotions. This story can be followed in detail in an admirable review article by de Sousa (2007).

The Emotionology Principle

This principle asserts that we can discover what a particular emotional phenomenon is by charting the conditions for the use of the relevant words in the culture which we are studying. The rules for the use of an emotion word will show us how the local people identify an act, a gesture, or a saying as the expression of this or that emotion. The absence of a word may not necessarily show that an emotion recognized in one locale does not exist in another culture. But the lack of any form for its expression would rule it out as part of the repertoire of a certain people in a certain place and time.

The result of the cataloguing of the uses of an emotion word will very likely be a broad field of uses linked by similarities and differences in the way the word is used. The many ways an emotion word has been used show up vividly in systematic studies of the emotion vocabularies of past times. Peter Stearns has shown the diversity of uses of the words around 'grief' and 'grieving' in the last three centuries in English-speaking cultures (Stearns & Knapp, 1996). It is important to resist the temptation to take one of the uses of a key word as a model for all the other ways the word is used, the essential or real meaning, so to speak. Carol and Peter Stearns (Stearns & Stearns, 1988) showed how the uses of the *word* 'anger' and its cognate forms changed from describing how people behaved to referring to private feelings. Other cultures may have different emotion repertoires from ours. How would *we* be able to tell? Lutz (1988) used the analysis of the meanings of local words in relation to the situations in which they were used, to work out the unique emotionology of the Ifaluk people. I believe that just as Carol and Peter Stearns revealed a subtly different emotion repertoire among our ancestors, so Catherine Lutz has revealed a markedly different range of emotions among the Ifaluk.[1]

Taking each of the major emotion words as a focus, Lutz explored the ranges of situations where the local people would use the word in commenting on, amplifying or criticizing the actions and displays and presumed feelings of actors and onlookers. The word is left untranslated in the analytical excerpts. Its meaning emerges as it is embedded in various contexts, described in translation. There is a presumption – that words for events like 'death', 'leaving the island', 'boasting about fishing successes' and so on are intelligible across the translation divide without serious loss of content. Against this presumed stability the indigenous meanings of the key emotion words emerge.

We will follow Lutz's analytical study of the uses of *fago*. A similar excerpt of her studies of *metagu* (which cuts across the meanings of some of our fear and anxiety vocabulary) and *sort* (which overlaps with some of our uses of 'anger') are quoted in detail in Oatley and Jenkins (1996).

The uses of *fago* encompass some of the semantic spaces of 'compassion', 'love' and 'sadness' – without the sense of condescension that often goes with the use of 'pity'. In the excerpts Lutz presents us with, the word appears as a transitive verb – 'I *fago* such and such a person'.

The first context is where the person of concern is in need or is suffering. When someone is sick he or she is not only miserable and in need of company, but also in need of health and of medicine. *Fago* seems to reach across quite heterogeneous needs.

The second main context is *fago* for the dead (Lutz, 1988, p. 126). Not only do the dead lack life but also the essential companionship of the living. In embedding this use of *fago* in a determinate but extended episodic context, Lutz describes the long drawn out dying of a child from the time of falling ill to the deathbed scene and after.

These two contexts seem connected and also fit with another context, in which someone says 'I *fago* such and such a person' because he or she is going away, and will suffer the deprivation of the life of the home. (Lutz, 1988, pp. 128–129). In a very detailed account of the form of such an episode Lutz describes how 'people who are leaving may comment on their own immanent homesickness (*pak*) or speak about their *fago* for those who will be left behind in some neediness, without recourse to the traveler's help'. So far so coherent a range of uses.

However, the word is also used for a seemingly very different range of situations where the person of whom one would say 'I *fago* him or her' is drunk, the center of attention, and one who is then and there suffering social embarrassment.

Yet another context for the use of the word is to express an emotional stance to someone who has the supreme Ifaluk virtue of *maluwela*. 'You *fago* someone because they are calm and socially intelligent' (Lutz, 1988, p. 137). Looked at another way the Ifaluk insist that 'the ability to experience "*fago*"' is seen as one of the central characteristics of the mature person' (Lutz, 1988, p. 140).

Assembling a cluster of English words to encompass a similar semantic field we would need to add 'pity' and 'admiration' to 'compassion', 'love' and 'sadness'. We do not *fago* anyone, but after reading Lutz's analysis we can imagine how it might be to do so. The situations are meaningful, though not in the same way when embedded in European or American folkways. We understand them because there are universals – death, departure, success and failure. But how episodes in which these aspects are salient unfold in terms of human relations and local moral orders, vary widely.

Anticipating the discussion of the possibilities of hybridization of aspects of the psychology of emotion, it is quite clear that taking records of vital signs and subjecting the people talking about various situations in Lutz's account to fMRI scans would not advance our understanding of *fago* in the slightest. Recounting more episodes and linking *fago* talk with the uses of other emotion words would.

A recent study of the degree of match in the meanings of 'sympathy', 'compassion' and 'empathy' with the Russian best equivalents, *sočuvstvie*, *sostradanie* and *sopereživanie* shows some interesting differences. Among them are the following: *sočuvstvie* reflects a closer personal relation than the English 'sympathy'. *Sostradanie* is called for in more severe troubles than 'compassion', while *sopereživanie* suggests that there is a shared emotional experience which is not implied by the English 'empathy'. The overall picture is of the expression of a more intense interpersonal emotional life among Russians than among English speakers (Gladkova, 2010).

The 'Expression/Description' Distinction

Wittgenstein pointed out that words for subjective feelings, for example, 'joy' or 'pain', could not have been learned by pointing to exemplars, because subjective feelings always remain essentially private. How we learn them must involve a different procedure from the way we learn words like 'cup' and 'elephant'. We learn these by attending to a public exemplar when the word is used by someone else. He suggested that the words for private feelings are learned as substitutes for behavioral expressions, such as smiling for joy and groaning in pain. We learn to say 'I'm happy' and 'I'm in pain' as substitutes for the characteristic behavior. The behavior is characteristic of a feeling because to have a tendency to smile or groan is part of what it is to be joyful or in pain (Wittgenstein, 1953, § 244).

In the examples sketched above, the words 'fearing', 'angry', 'jealous' and so on appeared in *my* analysis. The physiological-experiential, cognitive and social act conditions described in these analyses were constituents of experiencing that emotion, and, according to the emotionology principle, necessary and sufficient conditions (almost) for the use of the word – but by whom? People rarely express fear, anger, jealousy, chagrin, joy and so on by using the corresponding words in a self-description. However, this does not seem to be so for words that are used for feelings that are not generally included among the emotions, such as 'pain', 'needing to go the bathroom' and 'nausea'.

'Angry' is rarely used expressively. In most cases when one says 'I'm angry with you [about that]', rather than shouting, turning red in the face and waving one's fists about, one isn't really angry. However, emotion words in the third person are used descriptively, 'she's very annoyed', while the characteristic displays are expressive but make no use of the word 'annoyed'. An angry person might verbally display anger by shouting 'F*** you!!' but not 'I am angry with you'. 'I am angry with you' is a reprimand, neither an expression nor a description of being angry. This leads to questions about what are the primary language games in which the emotion words are used. It seems that there is no simple answer to this question as there is to the question about the expressive substitutions of all displays by words for simple bodily feelings such as nausea or pain. In the case of an emotion it makes perfect sense to ask 'How much of an occasion that calls for the use of the word "grief" is a matter of feeling and how much a matter of appropriate displays?' (Stearns & Knapp, 1996, pp. 132–150). An exception to this principle might be the displays used by 'injured' footballers to get the referee to award a penalty.

Fields of Use

The study of the uses of emotion words, be they from the emotionology lexicon or from the working vocabulary by which emotions are expressed, reveals a domain of diverse uses of almost every one of the relevant items from a culturally established vocabulary. There are no essential meanings, rather a variety of context-sensitive uses which are linked by similarities and differences in the conditions that require their use. This is not to say that some uses are not more important or more frequent than others.

Close study of the uses of 'envious' discloses a distinction between 'benign envy' and 'malign envy' (Sabini & Silver, 1998). The former might be expressed as 'I wish I had one of those too' while the latter comes through such remarks as B declaring 'I don't think A has any right to X, and anyway I am the person who really deserves it'. Malign envy is rather like jealousy without perhaps the strong implications of the injury to B that comes from A's possession of X. Suffering malign envy, B, feeling slighted, might set about trying to destroy X, letting A have a taste of the feeling of loss. The sufferer from jealousy might try to injure A as punishment for the injury B believes he or she has suffered at the hands of A.

Here we have a nice example of a fragment from an extensive field of uses that are linked by similarities and differences, and cannot be understood by reference to some underlying or core meaning. If this is a correct report of the grammar of part of that field it precludes the question 'What is envy *really*?' We might be tempted to suggest that there is a core meaning by claiming that at least two people and a valued item are required for the word to have any application – granting that there are various patterns of relationship between the three entities in question. What if it is B's good luck to have a splendid physique? Or a shapely bosom? Moreover, even if it is a necessary condition for the use of the word 'envy' which of the above considerations throw into doubt; it is a condition (perhaps necessary) for several other emotions.

It seems to me that such a three-fold interpersonal relation occurs in the grammar of 'being jealous'. By way of contrast, acts of sexual betrayal notoriously lead to displays and feelings of anger rather than those of jealousy. The grammar of 'chagrin' involves a protagonist, a project and the people round about who heard the protagonist make the claim for competence that is later found to be spurious. The good in question is the highly abstract one of succeeding at some task one has claimed to be able to perform, and maintaining face in the course of doing so.

Drawing on social psychology and socio-linguistics, we can appropriate the notion of a 'frame'. Deborah Tannen (1993) and Erving Goffman (1975) have pointed out that all human activities take place within loose systems of presuppositions that give local meaning to those activities. Emotion displays are always framed by such sets of presuppositions. A laugh in Japan expresses embarrassment, while in Europe it (usually) expresses amusement and sometimes triumph. So laughing as a human activity is *framed differently* in Japan and Europe.

Emotions often seem to overcome one, to be out of one's control. Is it plausible to take the display of an emotion, be it privately as a significant feeling, or publicly as an action, as something somebody *does* rather than something that happens to somebody? Is it more like walking than it is like indigestion? Two constituents of the emotional situation seem to be more like doings in that a person may take control and manage them. One is the interpretation of the situation and its implications as to the source of the bodily disturbance. The other is the kind of response that is appropriate to the situation, when it is read in a particular way. This may involve managing bodily movements or considering the performative force of this or that legitimate response. Here are some examples of each kind of management.

The soft answer sometimes turns away wrath. Instead of angrily rejecting a criticism of a treasured piece of reasoning, a reaction that is likely to rile the critic too, one can say, 'Oh, I see what you mean – you may well be right. Thanks'. Or on seeing a friend stepping into a new silver Maserati Biturbo, one thinks better of expressing a pang of envy and says 'Lucky you'. Both owner, perhaps a bit embarrassed by the ostentation of his transport, and you, emerge from this encounter feeling good.

The use of words in establishing a primary language game entails that in similar situations it cannot be wrong to use that word in just the way it has been established in the primary language game. Spiraling out from primary language games there are all sorts of secondary language games which depend on tacit knowledge of the primary. There are primary language games for emotion words – in particular because certain fields of use with family resemblances to one another depend on such a primary situation in which the meaning is first established. 'Fear' looks a good candidate for a word the uses of which cover a wide field of family resemblances. Is there a primary language game for 'fear'? Consider 'I feared for my life when the rope broke'; 'I feared for my reputation when the story got out'; 'I fear I may have left out the salt' etc. Is there a case for taking situations of physical danger and threat of injury as those occasions on which a core meaning is established? How could one argue for such a claim? Whatever is germane must be compatible with a rejection of any essentialist claim as to what 'fear' really means.

The following entry appears in the *Compact Oxford English Dictionary*:

Fear

Noun:

1   An unpleasant emotion caused by the threat of danger, pain or harm.

2   The likelihood of something unwelcome happening.

Verb:

1   be afraid of.

2   (fear for) be anxious about.

3   regard God with reverence and awe (archaic).

The compilers of the OED offer two uses of the word 'fear' in distinct contexts or frames. The emotional situation is closely bound up with physical danger in one case but with the merely unwelcome in another. This seems to suggest that we should so structure the semantics of 'fear' that we recognize two semantic fields. They resemble one another in the respect that the situations are aversive, but differ in whether the body has an essential role in the situation.

Biological Accounts

To develop an adequate psychology of the emotions, attention must be paid to several disparate strands that unite in the emotional experience, its sources and its role in a strip of life. Biological, cognitive and cultural historical elements feed into the totality of an emotion as experience and its display as a meaningful social act. We begin by looking at the most famous neuro-biological theory, that proposed by William James. We will note both the omission of essential steps in the process by which an emotion is generated, as well as inconsistent admissions of the role of assessment and judgment in the psychological account of this process.

The Simple Response

William James and Carl Lange offered an early and somewhat schematic biological account of the psychology of emotions. Here is James's oft quoted presentation of the theory:

> My theory … is that the bodily changes follow directly the perception of the exciting fact, and that our feeling of the same changes as they occur is the emotion. Common sense says, we lose our fortune, are sorry and weep; we meet a bear, are frightened and run; we are insulted by a rival, are angry and strike. The hypothesis here to be defended says that this order of sequence is incorrect … and that the more rational statement is that we feel sorry because we cry, angry because we strike, afraid because

we tremble … Without the bodily states following on the perception, the latter would be purely cognitive in form, pale, colorless, destitute of emotional warmth. We might then see the bear, and judge it best to run, receive the insult and deem it right to strike, but we should not actually feel afraid or angry. (James, 1884, p. 189)

This theory depends on the existence of automatic stimulus – response patterns that are simply neurological. It is the activation of these patterns that is experienced as the feeling that we identify as the emotion.

The theory has been widely criticized largely on the grounds that it omits the necessary cognitive steps that seem to be needed to set the process that generates an emotion going. As Damasio (2000, p. 130) puts it '… he [James] gave little or no weight to the processes of evaluating mentally the situation which causes the emotion [construed as a bodily feeling]'. However, James's theory is really more of a muddle than a simply biological explanation of the existence of emotions. In the above passage he says, 'judge it best to run' and 'deem it right to strike'. Judging and deeming are surely cognitive activities, and might indeed be matters of rapid reflection on the part of the person so threatened rather than automatic responses of the nervous system to environmental stimuli.

The point can be illustrated with a personal anecdote. Once, walking, through a pine wood in rural Spain with two children I came out beside a farmhouse. A dog appeared snarling in a threatening way. I felt my arms tensing to push the children in front of me – but exercising conscious control of the musculature, I thrust them back behind me, and we retreated into the safety of the woods. The contrast between the Jamesian reaction and the responsible adult behavior illustrates the power of conscious thought and the moral frame in which the episode was embedded in such situations. Neither the perception of the stimulus as a threat nor the actual response were simple biological phenomena.

If, as James thought, the reaction would occur without an evaluation of the stimulus, his account is seriously defective. The actual reaction, pushing the children behind me, was a conscious cognitive override of the inbuilt Darwinian-Jamesian reaction to shelter behind them.

Biology and Expression

How should we insert the bio-neural component into the study of emotions?

If there are organs of the brain of a person that are activated when that person is taking part in the course of an emotional episode there are two questions that arise:

1 **What is the genetic basis of the presence of that organ and its links with other organs of the brain and what are the selective advantages of such a system having been evolved?**
2 **How does the system as it exists in a modern person function on some particular occasion of the unfolding of an emotional episode within a common local frame?**

The attempts to answer the first question take us to the important work of Paul Ekman on emotional expression. He has correlated facial and other body displays with the 'emotion' which the investigator thinks they are used to express. Is there a set of distinct facial expressions with sufficiently determinate meanings that they can serve as a lexicon for the expression of emotions? Paul Ekman undertook a massive research program to try to show that such a lexicon existed (Ekman, 2003). His work has suffered from two major flaws. He assumed that the facial expression or gesture was related to a specific subjective emotional state, particularly a bodily feeling. His research method involved presenting expressive faces to the participants in the majority of his experiments divorced from concrete social frameworks, such as episodes of everyday life. Bearing in mind that the correlative feeling is consciousness of a body state in need of interpretation in some local frame and the expression is a social act with illocutionary force, Ekman has proposed that '… the most distinctive feature of emotion is that the events that trigger emotions [taken to be physiological states] are influenced not just by our individual experience, but also by our ancestral past'. Our ancestral past is sedimented in each human being in an 'auto-appraiser'. These devices 'are powerful, scanning continuously, out of our consciousness, watching out for themes and variations of the events that have been relevant for our survival' (Ekman, 2003, p. 29).

In a massive study of the way people interpret facial displays in emotionally loaded situations, Ekman aimed to show that a certain basic and universal repertoire of such expressions is the survival of that 'ancestral past'. In order to incorporate the striking fact that patterns of emotional response differ across cultures, even if the repertoire of expressions are a common feature of humanity, he introduced the idea of 'display rules'. They are:

socially learned, often culturally different rules about the management of expression, about who can show which emotions to whom and when they can do so … These rules may dictate that we diminish, exaggerate, hide completely, or mask the expression of the emotion we are feeling. (Ekman, 2003)

Except for the very last phrase, we have here a powerful formula for the hybridization of two of the three sides of psychology of the emotions, as if what 'we are feeling' is the real or authentic emotion.

Ekman's researches have revealed a repertoire of signs available for use in emotionally charged episodes, but this falls short of a lexicon. The meanings of the 'native' signs depend on the display rules, which in turn, depend on the moral orders of the local cultural practices. This point is easily tested for oneself by trying to interpret the emotions displayed in Ekman's own portrait gallery. For example, the portraits of an angry person and a disgusted person (Ekman, 2003, p. 12) strike me as pictures of someone concentrating and of someone skeptical about something.

Biology and Process

We turn now to investigate the second question raised by the evident involvement of biology in the psychology of the emotions, the emotionally relevant structures in the brain and their modes of working. A valuable resource for a survey of the most recent work in this genre is the fifth volume of Manstead (2008).

For many years, work on the way that brain processes and organs subserve or are structurally isomorphic to patterns of experience and display was dominated by the principle that cognition and emotion were subserved by different parts of the brain. Roughly, cognition was subserved by processes in the cerebral cortex, particularly the frontal lobes, while emotion was subserved by processes in the limbic system, a ring of interconnected organs particularly linked by the amygdala, the hippocampi and so on. This finding was based on an extensive program of research using the deficit-lesion methodology. The most prominent of these animal studies (Douglas & Pribram, 1969) involved sucking out the amygdalas through holes cut in the base of the skull. Once the monkeys had recovered, their social and emotional behavior was compared with the way it had been before the operation. There seemed to be a marked change in these aspects of monkey life.

The role of the amygdala, an important component of the limbic system, seemed to have been established beyond doubt. However, though this organ has been shown to be actively involved in the neurological processes coordinate with emotional experiences, the idea of the primacy of the processes in the paired amygdala turned out to be mistaken. The fault lay in how the monkey brains were lesioned. The aspiration procedure removed not only the amygdala itself but part of the cortex to which it was connected. More refined techniques dissected out the amygdala, leaving the cerebral connections intact. In these cases, the deficits in expressive and social behavior were far less marked. Some researchers have thrown the very idea of a limbic system into doubt (Kotter & Meyer, 1992, pp. 105–127).

In all such studies the basic method as described in Chapter 3 is the use of animals in models that stand outside the moral constraints that are imposed on experimenting with people. These models can be either homologues of human episodes, that is, they are deemed to be in all essentials the same, or they can be analogues, in which we judge the worth of the model by comparing similarities and differences between animal and person.

We have now covered two of the main features of emotional episodes as sketched above. There is the episodic situation or storyline with the meanings of the sorts of situations that people encounter. Identifying and analyzing this feature is an indispensable research tool, since it leads to hypotheses about the social meaning of emotional expressions. There remains the question of bodily feeling that some psychologists, for example, William James (1884), thought comprised the core of an emotional experience.

Damasio, though far from being a bio-reductionist, offers an interesting attempt at characterizing the 'feeling' component in the emotional experience. '... the essence of feeling an emotion is the experience of such changes [in body state, neuro-electrical and neuro-chemical processes] in juxtaposition to the mental images that initiate the [body change] cycle' (Damasio, 2000, p. 145). Somehow 'mental images' have made a gratuitous appearance in the story! We think what he means is that a feeling is the experience of certain goings on in the body that are the result of how certain events are perceived, that is, on the meanings that are given to them by that person in that situation. 'In juxtaposition to' is not the kind of intimate relationship between a meaning and its bearer that is significant as a component of an emotional episode. Furthermore, we do not see representations of snarling dogs, smiling shop assistants, severe traffic policemen and indulgent wives – We see dogs, shop assistants, traffic policemen and wives. A main point in the emphasis on emotional episodes as the target of research is to reject the idealism of a view of cognition that leaves the actor trapped in his or her subjectivity in a world of representations.

It has long been realized that any differentiations that we make among feelings are not the result of a close attention to the phenomenology of feelings but to the meanings that this or that body sensation has in the situation in which it is embedded. The classical study by Schachter and Singer (1962) has been shown to need qualification in various ways, but the basic result is robust. One group of participants were given injections of epinephrine. Some spent time with a confederate of the experimenters who behaved in a cheerful way, while others found themselves with a grumpy and angry person. The bodily feeling induced by the epinephrine (adrenaline) was interpreted by the first group as happiness and excitement and by the second group as anxiety and irritation. Another group were given injections of sterile water and were only mildly affected by the behavior of the confederates. In many, probably most circumstances, bodily sensations are systematically ambiguous, that is, gain specificity only in concrete situations and in relation to the meanings that the situations have for the participants.

Here is an example of the interplay of research in neuroscience and cultural studies, work that was reported in the popular press. The relation between neural activity and women's attitude to ideal body shape – fat or thin, was studied by Seligman. Women from several cultures were shown artificially 'fattened' mages of themselves while their brains were being scanned. Brain regions associated with unhappiness became highly active. However, when the same experiment was performed with men there was no excessive activation in the corresponding centers. What should we conclude from these studies? We cannot conclude that this propensity is 'hardwired' into women's brains as a result of genetic sedimentation of aeons of mate choice. Since we know that ideal female body forms have changed greatly even in recent times, these results only confirm that individual people can learn to like or dislike something, not that a pro or con response to an experience is inherited and so unchangeable. If the brain is the organ of thought then the results are just what we would expect.

Hybrid Accounts

Recent treatments of 'the emotions', such as those of Damasio (2000), Oatley and Jenkins (1996) and Manstead (2008), suggest that after the lingering reductionist pitch of such authors as Plutchik (2003), psychologists have more or less settled on a four-fold account of emotions, with cultural and neurological components, the expressive aspect appearing in the discursive features of emotional episodes and in the ethological gestures, postures and so on that become integrated with them in a sophisticated emotional culture.

Distilling the research patterns and conceptual analyses of the recent past, there is a kind of loose consensus that a person is properly said to experience an emotion when three conditions obtain. Applying the principle of emotionology, these conditions will be reflected in the rules for the use of the relevant vocabulary:

1   A person undergoes a perceptible disturbance of his or her normal bodily states, due to some event, which may be extrinsic (encountering a snarling animal) or may be intrinsic (the recollection of a past act). By itself this event is neither here nor there. It becomes a trigger for emotional phenomena just in so far as it is given a certain meaning within the local cultural frame. Darwin and Lorentz have shown us there are 'natural' reactions to situations that anticipate emotional responses – having significance for the other creatures in the neighborhood.

2   The judgment one has made, explicit or implicit, as to the significance of the situation in which abnormal bodily states are experienced or other people are seen or heard to make certain kinds of responses ('That dog is dangerous'; 'That remark was a gaffe'; 'That sunset is romantic' and so on) initiates a complex process with discursive and neurological components.

3   The tendency to act in response to such a situation is shaped not only by the implicit judgment a person makes of the character of what is going on but also by local moral conventions, counsels of prudence or cultural archetypes as to the proper response to the triggering condition so interpreted. So when faced with a political dogmatist one calmly backs off because political debate is frowned upon at the club. Becoming angry is unacceptable in certain circles though enjoined in others. A display of embarrassment is functionally an apology.

Not only are one's own reactions germane to how an episode unfolds, so are those of other people on the scene. When one has spilled coffee on a priceless oriental rug, displays of shame and contrition, perhaps embarrassment, are called for, even perhaps a touch of chagrin at one's clumsiness. When one apologizes to the host (at the very least) one does so not just as an expression of shame, but also because one recognizes the importance this possession has in the life of its owner. There may be a nasty little whiff of *schadenfreude* in one's own soul, stemming from envy of the host's possessions. The graciousness of the host may serve to heap coals of fire on the head of the transgressor.

However, when moved by the setting sun on a solitary evening stroll, one sighs, perhaps overcome by romantic longings and nostalgia for a time gone for ever, displaying a rare sensibility, even if it is only to oneself.

Each condition in the hybrid account needs to be qualified:

1 **A situation may become emotionally significant when it is given a new interpretation. For example, I may not be aware for a moment that a remark directed at me was intended to be offensive. The realization that it was may lead me to change my good humored response into a protest. My bodily calm is then shattered by a rush of adrenaline.**

2 **An interpretation may involve beliefs about patterns of rights and duties and other features of a local moral order. These beliefs tend to become premises in the cognitive processes by which interpretations of impinging events are made. Cognitive conditions, such as longstanding beliefs and conventional judgments are complex, since rights and duties are contestable. Positioning theory has shown the intricate relation between local moral orders and the narrative structure of an episode, particularly an emotional one (Harré & van Langenhove, 1999). The interpretation of a perturbation as a component of a particular emotion complex may depend on the storyline one takes to be unfolding.**

3 **The action that someone performs, or the words that are used in an emotionally charged situation, may need to be interpreted in terms of their social force as acts. For example, a shout might be a protest or a demand for an explanation. An angry display may have the force of a protest against injustice, or it may be a response to what one takes to be deliberate humiliation. This is what we called the illocutionary force of a display as a social act.**

The scheme presented above is clearly a hybrid theory – there is a physiological component, a cognitive-discursive component and a cultural-social component. The last might be more prudential than moral in some contexts. According to the emotionology principle, the three components are also the three sets of conditions for the correct local use of an emotion word. Thus, I would call myself 'angry' if I felt a certain kind of agitation; if I thought that I had been unjustly treated or injured without good cause in some way; and if I had a tendency to respond to the situation in some rather strong manner. Other people might judge me to be angry more on my public display than their guesses as to my private feelings, but the three components would play a part in the judgments of any bystander.

Each of these conditions is nearly necessary and together they are almost sufficient to establish a person's joint state of mind and body as the core of the experience of an emotion. The emotionology principle makes this hybrid pattern of events, meanings and dispositions the grounds for the use of a certain word to describe the whole situation, personal and environmental. The qualification 'nearly' is needed because sometimes there is no bodily disturbance discernible either by the person producing an emotional display or by the bystanders. Pride, in the sense of quiet satisfaction in a job well done, might be an example. The qualification 'almost sufficient' is needed, because one can sometimes be persuaded to reinterpret an emotional situation: 'They were only trying to say they were sorry.' The complexity of the conditions leaves room for change in assigned meanings.

A treatment that at first sight seems to be an anticipation of the hybridization advocated in this chapter can be found in Antonio Damasio's *Descartes' error* (2000). Starting with the biology, he suggests that there are responses to certain features of the environment that depend on an inherited neurology. Then there is an awareness of the feeling of the response in connection with the object that excited it. This ties in with 'conscious, deliberate consideration you entertain about a person or situation' (Damasio, 2000, p. 136). So it looks as if a discursive procedure interacts with a bio-neurological process to complete the genesis of the pattern of feelings, interpretations and meaningful responses that constitute an emotional episode.

These considerations are 'maintained as images' so that non-conscious 'networks in the prefrontal cortex automatically and involuntarily respond to signals arising from the processing of the above images' (Damasio, 2000, p. 136). From thence this response is signaled to the amygdale affecting a great many systems in the body, including skeletal muscles, neurotransmitters and the endocrine system. Of course, this prepares the organism for action.

Antonio Damasio (1944–) was born in Lisbon, Portugal. After attending Liceu Passos Manuel, he entered the University of Lisbon Medical School. He did his neurological residency there and completed his doctorate in 1974. The topic of his doctoral dissertation was the neural basis of higher brain functions. Later, he moved to the United States as a research fellow at the Aphasia Research Center in Boston. His work there on behavioral neurology was done under the supervision of the late Norman Geschwind. From 1976 to 2005, Damasio was M. W. Van Allen professor and head of neurology at the University of Iowa Hospitals and Clinics. In 2005, he moved to the University of Southern California where he is Dornsife professor of neuroscience, and director of the Brain and Creativity Institute.

Damasio has proposed that emotions play a critical role in high-level cognition. He showed that emotions and their biological underpinnings are involved in both positive and negative decision making. He has also suggested that they provide a kind of scaffolding for social cognition.

Damasio has made a number of studies aimed at revealing those regions of the brain that are active in relation to emotional experience. For example, he demonstrated experimentally that the insular cortex is a critical platform for feelings, a finding that has been widely replicated. He has also shown the role of ventromedial prefrontal cortex and amygdale as induction sites for human emotions. In 1994, he published a widely read book *Descartes' error: emotion, reason, and the human brain*, (reissued in a Penguin edition, 2005), where he discusses his ideas on emotion and decision making.

His current work involves the social emotions, consciousness and the creative interface between neuroscience and the arts, especially music and film. He is married to Hanna Damasio, his colleague and frequent co-author. His most recent book is *Self comes to mind: constructing the conscious brain*, published by Pantheon in 2010.

Unfortunately, this way of creating hybrid psychology of the emotions falls very far short because the 'conscious and deliberate considerations' disappear. What would it be to be 'maintained as images'? The word 'image' does all the work – an image is relevant to life in so far as it has a meaning, and it is realized as a material structure in some system, for example, a canvas by van Gogh. But as a collection of colored pigments it has no artistic meaning. In a brief analysis of the notion of 'feeling' in this context, Damasio (2000, p. 145) begs the crucial question more overtly. 'The essence of feeling an emotion' he says 'is the experience of such changes [in neuro-electrical and chemical body states] in juxtaposition to the mental images that initiated the [body changes] cycle.' What can the relation of 'juxtaposition' possibly be? It cannot be neurological, since one of its components is a meaning. It cannot be a semantic relation since one of its components is the perception of physical states of the body.

Though Damasio's account is a huge advance on that of James, it fails at a crucial point – the very point where a Janus-faced imagist theory of visual arts or music fails.

Fear of a dangerous dog is a simple emotion – rightful pride in an accomplishment is a good deal more complex. Each of the three components of the 'total emotional situation' would need to be elaborated in particular cases.

Given that emotions are specific to certain features of everyday episodes and that they are shaped by the presuppositions of a culture, are there higher order groupings of emotions that would be germane to the discursive research project? What do the uses of the words 'anger' and 'jealousy' have in common? Is there a higher order pattern of use that informs both? What about 'pride' and 'chagrin'? And 'joy' and 'being pleased'?

There are obvious superficial answers. 'Angry' and 'jealous' are used when the bodily component of the emotional occasion is unpleasant, and there is a marked implication that the one who has such an experience condemns the actions and perhaps also the character of another person, but invoking different aspects of the local moral order. 'Being proud' stands at the opposite pole from 'being humiliated'. The latter is a prime ingredient in the grounds for describing one's emotional experience as 'chagrin'. 'Joyful' and 'pleased' are used when an experience is agreeable, and which one might like to repeat.

These categorizations are also often linked to moral judgments about the people involved. In everyday life there is a strong tendency to believe that an unpleasant experience is someone's fault, hence displays of emotion such as 'being angry' in certain situations. There could be an emotive aspect of the fundamental attribution error. There does seem to be a tendency to explain the behavior of other people in terms of their traits and beliefs and so on, and to excuse one's own behavior in terms of situational factors. He tripped over the step because he was clumsy – I tripped over the step because it was badly made. This distinction seems to be a prime part of the background to the range of uses of 'anger', 'jealousy' etc. as third-person descriptions of first-person practices constituent of our way of life. Our lived practices take this form – but only occasionally do people actually say that they believe whatever it is that makes up the content of such a presupposition. 'Envy is the appropriate response to someone else's good fortune' might be true as a description of the emotionology of the Western way of life. But we believe it rarely passes anybody's lips. Instead we train children how to display pleasure in the successes of others without the other aspect of such situations appearing in public, namely the chagrin at having come second. This illustrates how the expression of emotions dominates the public scene.

Understanding the Emotions of Another Person

Wittgenstein's many remarks pointing to the importance of the natural tendencies on which the human form of life rests, emphasizes the ethological or Darwinian roots of the knowledge we seem to have of other people, in particular their feelings and emotions. We do not ascribe feelings to stones since they are inert, neither writhing nor jumping up and down! However, some sense of an emotional life could begin with the wriggling legs of a fly. The point is an important and subtle one. We do not *infer* an animate being's feelings from their behavior, but we *experience* them in their expressions. In the terminology of philosophy we can say that an expression is *internally* related to that which is expressed. That is, it would not be pain if one had no tendency to groan, complain, and writhe and so on. It would not be joy if one did not have a tendency to smile. Wittgenstein suggests that we don't need to be taught basic empathies and sympathies. They come with the whole package that includes the human repertoire of basic emotional responses:

It is a primitive reaction to tend, to treat, the part that hurts when someone else is in pain, and not merely when oneself is – and so to pay attention to other people's pain behaviour, as one does not pay attention to one's own pain behaviour … But what does the word 'primitive' meant to say here? Presumably that this sort of behaviour is pre-linguistic: that a language game is based on it, that it is the prototype of a way of thinking and not the result of thought. (Wittgenstein, 1972, §§ 540–541)

In short, these practices are to be seen in the light of the biological aspect of emotions. They are among the topics of ethology.

Is there deeper knowledge of others to be found in reflecting on the repertoire of displays through which one comes to know of their emotional life than their mastery of the relevant repertoire of words and actions? There is no doubt that we make characterological and personality attributions in the light of how people react emotionally to situations. We may see them as cold and unfeeling, as they calmly pull the injured from the wreckage. We may see them as flighty and foolish if they react extravagantly to every passing social situation. Cold by what standards? Flighty by what conception of the dignity required of a person like that?

Emotion displays are always up for assessment as to their propriety in the presumed situation, and of course, as to what sort of persons are there. In this respect too the emotional life presupposes certain unspoken hinges.

The topic of tendencies to act as an ineliminable part of the total package that is an emotion has already been broached. The question of character and personality calls for the use of dispositional concepts. How are emotions and personal dispositions related?

Misleading Grammatical Models

The familiar pairing of noun forms with adjectival and adverbial forms in the grammar of emotion words can be a convenient starting point for exploring temptations to misunderstandings.

We have 'anger, angry, angrily'; 'happiness, happy, happily'; 'fear, fearful, fearfully'; 'pride, proud, proudly' and so on.

The adjectival and adverbial forms seem to be more uncontroversial than the nouns, since displays of characteristic and specialized ways of performing routine actions directed to some normal end do not offer much in the way of temptation to invent abstract nouns. 'She was angry'; 'She slammed the door angrily' are not forms likely to encourage ontological proliferations.

However 'anger', 'pride', 'fear', 'joy' and so on do. One of the editors of this volume once attended a Synanon Group meeting in the US, in the guise of an anthropologist we hasten to add. The procedure involved picking on one member of the group, insulting and abusing the victim until he or she became angry. Afterwards the target was calmed down by being rolled around by the members of the group. The leader accounted for this activity as a way of releasing all the anger that had been accumulated during the week between Synanon meetings – rather like releasing the air from an over-inflated tyre.

How could it be shown that the Synanon members who bought this nonsense were making a *grammatical* mistake? So far as I can see, lacking any formal guidance from Wittgenstein at this point, the best strategy might be to recover the primary language games in which each triad of forms was established and demonstrate how it could not have been grounded in a referential act from the noun form to a mysterious substance. The same style of argument that disposes of bodily sensations and feelings as inner things while not denying their privacy and reality, could perhaps dispose of 'anger' as the name of a quasi-substance. The disparity between the criteria for 'same feeling' and 'same thing' (say 'coconut') shows that feelings are not mental things. Let us compare the grammar of the noun 'anger' with the grammar of a genuine bodily fluid, say 'blood'. We do not know of the presence of blood in the body by bloody expressive acts, as we discern anger in angry exchanges and doors slammed angrily. We learn the word 'blood' by direct acquaintance with some of the stuff that has unfortunately leaked out.

The primary language game for the anger triad must also involve the priority of expressive acts, since for the same reason that 'pain' cannot be learned as the name of a feeling, 'angry displays' must be the ground of the relevant language games. The semantics of 'anger' must rest on the language games of displaying or expressing the complex state of feeling and cognitive judgments that angry people are doing.

Moreover, the grammatical subject of most emotion words is the person. People are angry, sad, proud, chagrined, and joyful and so on. There is no such thing as embarrassment, but there are plenty of embarrassed people. This points back to an earlier point – the ineliminable involvement of local moral orders in the grammar of certain words. The unit of analysis is something like 'people in situations'. The more morally sensitive a person is, the more readily are emotion displays triggered by the relevant type of situation.

Modern people in the West have learned the art of 'bottling up emotions'. It is also common practice in many oriental cultures. This points to another important aspect of the expression of emotions. The expression may be entirely private subjective, without a flicker visible to others. In the general store in the village near the former house of one of the editors in Spain, the manager was a certain Señor Benavent. When provoked by a difficult customer, he would bend down below the counter where he had secreted a bundle of sticks. Snapping a few relieved the tension and up he came smiling.

Here we come back to the original problem with emotions – the problem that has led people to slip into an unsustainable physiological reduction of emotion states to neurochemical goings on. If 'being angry' must have a referent, then perhaps some bodily state or process would have to do. But we saw above that the primary language game for this family of words is adjectival or adverbial, not nominal. 'Being angry' does not need a referent since its meaning comes from 'angry man', 'stamped angrily' and the like. There is no primary language game for 'anger' as a noun. In particular, we do not need to take a blood sample to know whether someone is angry or depressed or joyful. There is no place in our lives for emotion breathalyzers! 'Is he angry? – let's do a blood test!' is absurd.

How do we reconcile the reactive and even automatic response by a person to an emotion-provoking situation with the powerful role that cognitive schemata evidently play in interpreting both situational and bodily feelings as this or that emotion (or mood) from the vast repertoire available to us? The argument of this chapter is that here, as in other cases in psychology, no reconciliation is possible. The ontology of molecules and the ontology of meanings neither overlay one another in perfect synchrony, nor do they reduce one to the other in either direction. Emotions partake of the molecular ontology in that we become aware of bodily disturbances. Emotions partake of the cultural, cognitive and discursive aspects of life, in that we give meanings to these disturbances – some of which are personal and embedded in local moral orders.

Some disturbances are very like those that get affective interpretations but draw on cognitive interpretations other than the emotional. For example, there is indigestion, sunburn, influenza, fatigue, need to 'visit the bathroom' and so on. Similarly, the complex event of an environmental disturbance and a bodily perturbation requires the use of a cognitive schema to determine whether it is part of an emotional experience and which emotional experience that is.

Conclusion

From whichever direction we approach the topic of the emotions, whether via the study of the grammars for the use of the words in emotion vocabularies, the cultural contexts in which emotion displays occur, or from observation of the natural responses that appear in episodes we would regard as emotional, or from the monitoring of bodily states, the four-fold character of the emotion concepts such as 'love', 'despair', 'anger', 'jealousy', 'chagrin', and their adjectival and adverbial forms appears very clearly. Sometimes the situation is as James (1884) describes it – a bodily state brought about as a purely physical response to a situation that is so primitive that it does not need to be interpreted as an emotional experience. We are equipped to respond in this way as the result of the selection of the genetic basis for certain neural mechanisms over aeons. Sometimes the situation is reversed, particularly in the case of the emotions of personal interactions. What someone does, interpreted in a certain way, brings about a bodily state, felt as a deviation from the usual way we feel. In either case there is both a physiological and a cognitive aspect to the full experience. However, emotional states are expressed to oneself and to others. They have a meaning appropriate to the situation in which they occur. We should follow Wittgenstein in thinking that the form of expression and the categorization of the emotional state are internally related. It wouldn't be joy if one had no tendency to smile or laugh. These displays have illocutionary force – as protests, apologies, pleas, and so on.

The upshot of these analyses is the idea of 'emotion' as a four-way hybrid, though we must be wary of taking the noun form as displaying the true nature of emotional experiences that occur in the unfolding of episodes of human and animal life. The scientific study of emotions needs physiology, ethology, grammar and social anthropology to do a 'proper job'. Looking back over the last 40 years, we can see a steady movement towards this eclectic but critical point of view both in the writings of philosophers and in the work of many psychologists.

Finally, this survey of the main themes of contemporary psychology of the emotions suggests that there are well-established bridges that link the cultural and the biological aspects of emotion in a coherent and non-reductive way.

The project of a psychology of emotions could not even begin unless the Taxonomic Priority Principle, TPP, were in use, overtly or tacitly, in identifying which aspects of our biology, ancestral or contemporary, were relevant to understanding the way emotionally charged episodes of human life unfold. We cannot begin to ask whether adrenalin has anything to do with anger unless we have a prior understanding of what sort of behavior, expressions and so on the word 'angry' refers to. It is a word the meaning of which has a history long before the advent of biochemistry.

The Task-Tool metaphor, the other bridge established in Chapter 1, has much less importance in the hybridization of the psychology of the emotions than, for example, in the psychology of remembering or deciding. However, there is some biological research that is relevant. There is no doubt that the findings of ethology explain how certain responses have become deeply embedded in the genetically established core of human nature. To a very large extent the biologically grounded responses are not tools which a person can use, unlike the memorial devices such as the hippocampus. However, locally valid display rules are used to override the ethological imperatives. Ethology identifies repertoires of actions that could be the bearers of displays, but it offers only the crudest interpretation of the meanings of such displays. For that we need ethnography, discourse analysis and the panoply of research methods available in cultural psychology.

When we turn to the other major contribution that biology makes to psychology, the discovery of the brain processes and structures that people can use as tools for the performance of some of the tasks demanded of them by their life situations, a survey of the current literature, very well laid out in Manstead (2008), there is little positive to be learned.

The thrust of this chapter can be summed up in the words of Richard Shweder: '… "emotion" terms are names for particular interpretative systems (e.g. "remorse", "guilt", "anger", "shame") of a particular story-like, script-like, or narrative kind that any people in the world might make use of'(1994, p. 52).

Note

1   The research program both as an exemplar of the ideal form for psychological research and in the detail and depth of the results is an exemplar of the very best work in psychology.

11 Intelligence

Fathali M. Moghaddam

… at 9 years of age, variation in brain structure is associated with individual differences in intelligence measures. This relation is entirely explained by genetic factors common to both sets of traits. The genes that influence brain volume, probably influence intelligence…(van Leeuwen, Peper, van den Berg et al., 2009, p. 189)

It is now clear that intelligence is highly modifiable by the environment. Without formal education a person is simply not going to be very bright – whether we measure intelligence by IQ tests or any other matrix. (Richard Nisbett, 2009, p. 2)

The above quotations reflect what on the surface seem to be two very different perspectives on intelligence, which for now we can define as problem-solving ability. Problem solving is something humans do routinely in everyday life, and so at one level it would seem a straightforward and uncontroversial task to develop measures of intelligence. We would want such measures to be *reliable*, achieve consistent results in retests, and also *valid*, measure what the test is actually supposed to be measuring; that is, problem-solving ability independent of experience, including educational and cultural experiences. But this seemingly straightforward challenge has proved to be both complex and highly controversial from the start of modern attempts to develop scientific measures of intelligence, which began in the latter part of the 19th century.

There are currently two very different approaches to measuring intelligence. On the one hand, intelligence is being measured by examining brain structure, genetics, and inherited characteristics (as reflected by the above quotation from van Leeuwen et al., 2009). On the other hand, the traditional paper and pencil tests are being used, but in the interpretation of test results the role of the environment in shaping intelligence is being emphasized (as reflected by the above quotation from Nisbett, 2009).

In line with this dichotomy, this chapter focuses on both (1) neuroscience and (2) cultural approaches to intelligence. The neuroscience approach is relatively new and, on the surface, implies that intelligence is part of our inherited biological makeup and 'fixed'. The cultural approach, on the other hand, implies that intelligence is a social construction, and something that can only be understood in cultural context. A person is not 'intelligent' independent of culture, because the same action can indicate different degrees of intelligence in different cultural contexts. The neuroscience and cultural approaches to intelligence seem to be very different. As we shall see in this chapter, however, there are also important commonalities between the two perspectives on intelligence. These commonalities tend to become obscured by the complexity of research on intelligence, as well as the political controversy associated with this research.

Complexities and Controversies Surrounding Intelligence Testing

A major reason for the complexity and controversy involved in measuring intelligence is the question of the relationship between biological and psychological processes. One line of thinking goes like this: some people are more intelligent because of their biological characteristics, particularly their 'special' brains. The use of terms such as 'egghead' and 'brainy' reflects this assumption as shared in the wider culture. Presumably, a person who is referred to as an 'egghead' or 'brainy' has a different kind of brain. In line with this, Albert Einstein's brain was examined by researchers after his death, and it was found that his parietal lobe was markedly different from that of a comparison group who had normal intelligence (Witelson, Kigar, & Harvey, 1999). You can see the complexity of this approach to intelligence when it is pointed out that out of about seven billion human beings, at least several million have parietal lobes very similar to Einstein's, but these 'similar' individuals did not produce the theory of relativity – or anything like it! The idea that people with different levels of intelligence have different biological characteristics was first systematically investigated by Francis Galton (1822–1911) and, after a long decline, interest in this line of thinking has surged again, a topic we discuss later in this chapter.

The challenge of measuring intelligence has proved to be highly controversial because of the political significance test results can acquire. For example, ethnic group differences on intelligence tests were used in the 1920s to restrict the immigration of the members of certain ethnic groups (e.g. immigrants from China) to the United States, on the basis of the idea that they would lower the intelligence of the American population. This was completely unjustified, in part because lower scores for immigrant groups often simply mean they need more time to learn English, the language used for testing. There are now a number of tests that attempt to overcome this problem by measuring intelligence with less reliance on verbal ability; the most notable example being the Raven's Progressive Matrices Test, which we discuss later in this chapter.

More recently, the idea that intelligence is determined by inherited biological characteristics has been used to attack certain educational programs. Why should scarce resources be invested in educational 'enrichment' programs such as Head Start, if intelligence is inherited and such programs can do little to change individual intelligence? Surely it would be best to take a 'realist' approach and just accept that environmental enrichment programs do little for those born less intelligent?

These are the kinds of questions some critics have raised, basing their attacks on programs such as Head Start on research by Arthur Jensen (1998, 2006) and others, who in three main ways follow the tradition established by Galton in the 19th century. First, there is an emphasis on the (assumed) hereditary roots of intelligence. Second, physical measures, such as reaction time, are used as indicators of intelligence. Third, the wider policy implications of the research are explored, sometimes explicitly. In the case of Galton, one of the policies proposed was eugenics, the selective breeding of humans to achieve a more intelligent human stock – a policy the Nazis took up seriously. Although such horrendous policies are not explicitly raised by researchers in the 21st century, the implications of some current research are just as controversial.

Francis Galton (1822–1911) was born near Birmingham, England, into a fairly affluent family in England, and was a cousin of Charles Darwin. After a hybrid education involving home schooling and some university studies (focusing on mathematics), he embarked on life as a gentleman-scholar, making important contributions to a wide range of areas, including exploration of cultures and languages in Africa, meteorology, and research methodology. His pioneering work on the statistical procedure now known as correlation proved to be particularly influential for all research domains, including psychology.

In his quest to demonstrate the hereditary basis of intelligence, Galton made a number of contributions that proved to be highly influential, but only some of these contributions were constructive and correct. Among his least useful contributions was the idea of eugenics, the selective breeding of human beings to achieve a better stock of people. Another flawed contribution was his book *Hereditary genius* (1869), which assumed that because eminent people in England were related to one another at a rate above chance, this must mean that intelligence is inherited. Obviously such an assumption neglects the role of environmental factors: wealthy people use their superior resources to support their own relatives, and this could explain why so many eminent people are related to one another.

But in at least three ways Galton's research continues to influence modern psychology in highly constructive ways. First, Galton was the first to develop procedures to assess intelligence under standard conditions using standard measures. Second, Galton's idea that intelligence is associated with physiological differences is being pursued again by 21st-century researchers, now using fMRI and other recently developed techniques. Third and most importantly, Galton was the first researcher to recognize the important role that twins can play in research designed to identify the relative contributions of heredity and environment to intelligence and other psychological characteristics.

Galton's broader influence on psychology has been the development of methodology that precisely measures individual differences. The concern with individual differences continues to dominate mainstream psychology, although critics have pointed out the serious shortcomings of this approach (Lamiell, 2003). By focusing on differences between individuals, psychology could well neglect understanding the person.

This chapter is organized around three main questions. First, is intelligence unitary or multiple? The traditional approach assumes that intelligence is unitary, but more recently some researchers have argued that there are multiple types of intelligences. The challenge has been to demonstrate that these 'multiple intelligences' can be measured independently, and that they really are different from 'general intelligence'. The second question is: how should intelligence be measured? The traditional measures of intelligence are paper-and-pencil type tests, very similar to the standard tests in schools and universities. More recently, neuroscience researchers have developed measures of brain characteristics and activities that they claim directly measure intelligence and are more accurate than traditional measures.

In addressing questions about the unitary/multiple nature of intelligence and how intelligence should be measured, we also inevitably address the issue of the sources of intelligence. On the surface, it would seem that neuroscience research will point to biological characteristics that are inherited and 'fixed'. However, we shall see that the characteristics of the brain are influenced by experience and environmental conditions. A cultural approach to understanding intelligence can also incorporate neuroscience research.

Is Intelligence Unitary or Multiple?

In the movie *Rain Man*, Dustin Hoffman played the role of Raymond Babbit, a savant based on the true case of Laurence Peek (1951–2009), who had a photographic memory and by the end of his life could recall the exact contents of thousands of books. In other respects, Peek was unimpressive in his mental abilities. There are a small number of other savants like Peek, individuals who demonstrate remarkable memory in a deep but very narrow area. You might not know savants such as Peek, but no doubt you know of some people who are very good at one type of problem solving (such as mathematics), but very poor in other areas. Such cases seem to suggest that the 'case is closed' and intelligence is multiple rather than unitary; that a person can be very high on one type of intelligence, but low or normal on other types.

Alfred Binet (1857–1911) was born in Nice, France, and gained a law degree in Paris in 1878. His interest in the science of mental life led him to study hypnotism and suggestion, taking advantage of the presence of J. M. Charcot at the Salpétriére teaching hospital. In 1894, he completed a doctorate in natural science with a thesis on the nervous system of insects. Throughout this period he also carried out studies of thinking and problem solving, using his two daughters as participants in his studies. Binet was struck by how the two girls differed in their thinking styles and personalities. In 1895, Binet helped to launch *L'Anee psychologique*, which became a pioneering and leading journal for the publication of psychological research in Europe.

Binet became a pioneer in applied psychology after accepting the invitation of a committee set up in 1904 by the French Minister of Public Instruction, to help make decisions about 'subnormal children' in French public schools. Binet was very critical of the traditional medical diagnosis of 'subnormal children'. He recognized that a variety of different markers were being used to identify 'subnormal children' by medical doctors, and that what was needed was an objective measure of mental abilities. Through his studies of his own children as well as children in Paris schools, Binet had already developed ideas about how to measure intelligence. His approach was going to be very different from that of Galton in England.

In collaboration with Victor Henri (1872–1940), Binet published a series of papers on individual differences, and criticized what they saw as an overly narrow focus in attempts to measure intelligence. They moved to a broader conception of intelligence, as involving higher mental abilities such as problem solving, and particularly different types of memory. Working with a new collaborator, Theodore Simon (1873–1961), Binet published the first modern test of intelligence in 1905. This test was developed through use with large numbers of children in schools, and it involved a series of tasks of increasing difficulty. Importantly, Binet-Simon provided instructions as to how the tests should be administered: under standard conditions and without prior coaching of the children using the test. This was the start of the modern intelligence-testing movement, which has grown to become an enormous industry employing thousands of applied psychologists in different countries around the world.

But throughout the history of modern intelligence testing, there has been a continuous debate about the unitary or multiple nature of intelligence. The first intelligence tests to focus on higher mental abilities of comprehension, attention, and other cognitive aspects of problem-solving were designed by the Frenchman Alfred Binet (1857–1911) and his collaborator Theodore Simon (1873–1961) in 1905, and expanded in 1908. The main objective of the Binet test was to help identify children with learning disabilities, who needed to be placed in special education classes in the newly expanded French education system which required all children to attend school. Innovations in the Binet test included the distinction between mental age and chronological age, and performance norms for each chronological age group.

Such 'standardization' meant that the score of a 'normal' child could be established for each (chronological) age group on the Binet test. Test results could also establish if a child with a given chronological age had scored below, at, or above his or her mental age. For example, the score achieved by eight-year-old Jane puts her at the same level as most nine-year-olds; so mentally she is nine. William Stern introduced an innovation which has become synonymous with intelligence testing: the Intelligence Quotient, or IQ, which was computed by dividing mental age by chronological age and multiplying by 100. For example, in the example above, Jane's IQ is 112.5, which means she is 12.5 IQ points above the mean (IQ scores are standardized to have a mean of 100).

The concept of 'IQ' has helped to reinforce the idea that intelligence is unitary and can be measured using just one index. This view of intelligence being 'unitary' received support from the research of Charles Spearman (1863–1945), who explored the associations between the scores of people on many different tasks, such as following directions, making arithmetic calculations, writing, matching objects. Spearman found that there was a positive correlation between performances on many different tasks. Think about this from your own school experiences: children who are in honors class in English tend to be in honors class in social studies and in honors class in science, and so on. Spearman concluded that these correlations reflect a general intelligence factor, which by tradition is termed 'g'. Spearman recognized that there are many specialized intelligences (s's) that partly overlap with g, such as musical, spatial, and logical abilities.

The most commonly used intelligence tests continue to produce a single IQ score, but also have sub-tests that indicate intelligence in more specific areas. In 1917, the Binet test was standardized for the American population and became the Stanford-Binet intelligence test, and this test has had many subsequent revisions. Another set of widely used intelligence tests are the Wechsler tests, designed for people of all ages, from very young children to adults. These standard tests follow along with Spearman, in assuming a g and multiple associated s's. A different line of thinking that views intelligence as multiple has its roots in the distinction made by Ramond Cattell between fluid intelligence, the ability to reason and use information, and crystallized intelligence, information, skills, and knowledge acquired through life experiences and formal education. For example, consider your experiences when you start a new course at university: fluid intelligence is your ability to problem-solve in the new course with new materials, crystallized intelligence is the knowledge and skills you bring to the new course.

Measures of Multiple Intelligences

The 21st century is an age of diversity and of celebrating cultural differences. This general focus on diversity and 'every child being a star' has no doubt influenced researchers to conceptualize intelligence as not one thing ('g'), but multiple different abilities. The idea of 'multiple intelligences' suggests that people can be intelligent in many different ways, and that the standard IQ tests are not appropriate for assessing the many different types of intelligence for which some researchers argue.

Attempts to further develop the idea that there are different types of intelligence, and that these can be measured independently, have all faced the challenge of demonstrating that they are 'going beyond g'. The triarchic theory put forward by Robert Sternberg focuses on three different features of intelligence: analytic, creative, and practical intelligence (see Sternberg & the Rainbow Project Collaborators, 2006, and discussions in Sternberg & Grigorenko, 2002). Analytic intelligence is basically what the standard IQ tests measure. Creative intelligence is thought processes that bring about novel solutions, it is 'outside the box' type thinking. Creative thinking is closer to divergent thinking, problem solving that can lead to explorations of new territory, as opposed to convergent thinking, which is homing in on 'the one' already known correct solution (as assessed in the standard multiple IQ tests). Practical intelligence is problem solving in everyday life situations; for example, a homemaker balancing the family budget in the face of competing demands for money from different family members. Sternberg has attempted to measure analytic, creative, and practical intelligences independent of one another.

On the one hand, there is considerable value to highlighting the importance of creative and practice intelligences, both of which are neglected in the standard tests of intelligence, such as the Stanford-Binet and Wechsler tests. The value of creativity is often emphasized in the arts and music, but creativity has no less a vital role in industry and commerce (Markman & Wood, 2009). Think of the enormous boost that innovations in computer technologies continue to provide to the economies of the world, by increasing worker productivity (nano-technologies may well be the new drivers of economies in the next few decades). Practical intelligence is also of great value: for example, having the practical sense to organize one's personal finances and affairs efficiently. Every year there are unfortunate examples of individuals who are brilliantly creative, but never manage to get their finances straight and end up in the bankruptcy court. But to what extend is 'practical intelligence' reflected in the standard tests that measure 'g'? We return to this question later.

The search for 'multiple intelligences' has been pushed even further by Howard Gardner (1999, 2004), who includes in the list of 'intelligences' not only analytic (logical) and mathematical reasoning and language, but also musical abilities, bodily movements, self-understanding and self-control, sensitivity to and understanding of other people, and object recognition. The discussion of intelligence has also extended to emotional intelligence, the ability to effectively regulate one's own emotions and interpret the emotions of others; Machiavellian intelligence, strategies for manipulating others for personal gain, even at times against the other's self-interest; social intelligence, comprehension of social situations and contexts and behaving appropriately; and even mating intelligence, the ability to attract and retain a mate and reproduce successfully.

All these different types of intelligences seem to match the 'every child is a star' value system pervading public education, because there are so many different ways in which a person could be found to be intelligent. If Joe does not score high on analytical reasoning, then 'bodily movements' or 'emotional sensitivity', among many others, are also ways of looking at intelligence. But critics have argued that even the main 'types' of intelligence, such as Sternberg's trio of analytical, creative, and practical intelligences, actually measure the same underlying 'g' or general intelligence (Brody, 2003). Other critics contend that historically intelligence has been considered as purely cognitive, and it is not clear what is gained by expanding the notion of 'intelligence' to include all these different 'skills, competencies, and abilities' (Kanazawa, 2010, p. 282). Is bodily-kinesthetic ability or sensitivity to the emotions of others really intelligence?

The re-interpretation of intelligence as 'multiple' and the move to go beyond the standard paper-and-pencil type tests has added weight to arguments that both the concept of intelligence and tests of intelligence are cultural constructions, and as such reflect particular cultural biases.

How Should Intelligence Be Measured?

Francis Galton in England was the first Western researcher to attempt to measure intelligence under standardized conditions. In his Anthropometric Laboratory (established in 1880), Galton measured the sensory capacities of thousands of participants: he tested audition, perception, sensitivity to touch, reaction time (to sight and to sound), and various other physical characteristics of individuals (such as 'strength of squeeze'), all of which he took to be indicators of intelligence. Galton's assumption was that we acquire our knowledge through the senses and, therefore, those with better sensory capacities would gain better knowledge from the world and prove to be more intelligent. Now, we might assume from this that Galton was taking a 'Lockian' view of human nature and giving priority to the environment, since John Locke (1632–1704) famously imagined the mind of the newborn as a *tabula rasa* (blank slate) onto which experience writes. On the contrary, Galton gave priority to the view that intelligence is inherited, and he interpreted the theory of evolution put forward by his cousin Charles Darwin (1809–1882) as supporting this view.

By the early 20th century, Galton's ideas about intelligence testing had been pushed aside by the Binet tests, which were paper-and-pencil tests focusing on comprehension and 'higher' mental abilities. From this period on, the standard tests of intelligence became immediately recognizable to students, because they are paper-and-pencil tests that look similar to those students routinely take in schools, including tests to gain entrance to university undergraduate and graduate programs (the Scholastic Aptitude Test, SAT, and the Graduate Record Examination, GRE). The correlation between IQ scores and school performance is around 0.5 (Flynn, 2007); a 0.0 correlation means there is no association between two variables, and a 1.0 correlation means there is perfect association. Thus, although standard IQ tests were developed specifically to predict performance in school, and IQ is a fairly good predictor of academic achievement, it is far from a perfect predictor (a perfect indicator would be 1.0 rather than 0.5).

The association between tests of intelligence and tests of academic performance points to one of two major challenges that continue to confront researchers: how to measure intelligence independent of experiences, including academic training and language skills. In other words, intelligence tests should ideally measure fluid intelligence, rather than crystallized intelligence. But in practice, intelligence tests not only look like the kinds of tests used in Western schools and universities, they tend to measure the same things. For example, consider the Binet intelligence test that was adapted for the United States and became the Stanford-Binet. Test questions increased in difficulty with the age of the child, with the following being typical questions: copy a square (age four), name the colors red, yellow, blue and green (age five), count 13 pennies (age six), repeat five digits (age seven), and count backwards from 20 to one (age eight). Clearly, drawing geometric shapes, counting, and the like are activities that are practiced in schools, and children with no experience of schooling would be at a huge disadvantage.

The needs of the French education system led to the development of the Binet tests, and the next innovation in intelligence testing arose out of the needs of the military during the First World War (1914–1918). Approximately 1.7 million military recruits were tested in the United States alone, as a way of better placing them into jobs that best suited their abilities. The Army Alpha was a test for literate recruits, but the real innovation came with the Army Beta, a test for illiterate recruits that relied a lot on identification of patterns and recognition of differences in images. These 'performance' type questions became highly influential in the work of David Wechsler (1896–1981), who developed the Wechsler Adult Intelligence Scale (WAIS) in 1939. The WAIS moved away from Spearman's notion of 'general intelligence', and had two broad categories of items: verbal and performance, with sub-categories under each of these two broad categories. The items in the category 'verbal' still remind us a lot of school tests, which are focused more on crystallized intelligence. For example, there are items testing vocabulary (e.g. questions on word definitions), arithmetic (includes arithmetical problems), and general information (such as questions about world geography). The performance section relies more on fluid intelligence, through items such as block design, pattern recognition, and picture arrangement. However, even these items are not 'pure' measures of intelligence independent of experience, because cultural experience with geometric patterns and social life undoubtedly gives some test-takers an advantage. For example, the 'picture arrangement' items ask test-takers to re-arrange a series of pictures to portray the correct sequence of events – such as a person going fishing. If a person has experience of going fishing, they are at an advantage; for example, children who live in a desert region or in an urban center might never have an opportunity to go fishing or even see anyone fishing.

The Wechsler intelligence tests have been revised many times and are now the most commonly used tests around the world. Their popularity is in part because from early in their development these tests offered a profile of an individual on 10 or so sub-tests, and not just one IQ score (the Binet tests only provided a single IQ score until 1986, when sub-test scores were introduced). Wechsler was trained as a clinician and developed sub-tests because he viewed intelligence as related to the whole person, with intelligence and personality as integral to one another.

One of the other limitations of the Wechsler tests, as well as the Stanford-Binet, is the high reliance on language skills (e.g. English in the United States and in the UK). Recall that one of the early controversies about intelligence testing arose because immigrants with little knowledge of English did poorly on intelligence tests administered in the early 20th century, and these results were used to try to justify restrictions on immigration from certain countries. The performance sub-tests on the Wechsler intelligence test, and later the Stanford-Binet and other intelligence tests, attempt to overcome the high reliance on verbal skills, for example, by having test-takers complete pattern recognition tasks. However, well before this development came the Raven's Progressive Matrices Test (1938) which attempted to have minimal reliance on verbal skills and served as a model for the later 'performance' sub-tests in intelligence tests generally.

The Raven's Progressive Matrices Test builds on the tradition set by the Army Beta test, in that it relies as much as possible on non-verbal items. For example, test-takers are presented with a series of geometric shapes that differ from one another in a systematic manner, and asked to identify the next shape in the series. This kind of non-verbal test is seen as a more direct measure of fluid intelligence, because it is assumed that performance on these tests relies less on educational background and training. However, research evidence shows that the cultural context in which individuals are socialized can influence how they 'see' the world. This evidence includes studies on animals: kittens raised in an environment in which they could only see 'horizontal lines' were unable to see vertical lines when placed in normal environments (Blakemore & Cooper, 1970). Studies on people raised in highly 'carpentered' environments, with angles characterizing most of the spaces and objects around us, and with less experience of open landscapes, demonstrate differences in perception compared to people raised in less carpentered environments and more experience of open landscapes. One way this difference is manifested is that people from more carpentered environments tend to be more susceptible to the 'perceptual illusions' discussed in most introductory psychology texts, including the horizontal-vertical, the Müller-Lyer, and the Ponzo illusions (for a more extensive discussion of cross-cultural research on this and related topics, see Berry, Poortinga, Breugelmans, Chasiotis, and Sam, 2011).

Richard Nisbett has developed a broad conception of cultural differences in perception, arguing that Asians are socialized to develop a more holistic view of the world, compared to Americans who are more analytic. Because the Asian system focuses more on collectives, whereas individuals receive greater attention in American culture, Asians tend to pay more attention to context (Nisbett & Miyamoto, 2005). There are a myriad of other cultural factors that could influence how people attend to objects: for example, Arabic, Farsi, and Hebrew are examples of scripts that are read from right to left, unlike English, French, Spanish and other scripts that are read from left to right. Training in these different scripts will influence how a person draws patterns and, very probably, attends to geometric shapes (Amenomouri, Kono, Fournier, & Winer, 1997). Consequently, the role of culture is not negligible in performance on the Raven's Progressive Matrices Test and other measures of intelligence that involve differentiating between, and in other ways cognitively engaging with, geometric shapes, and relying less on verbal skills.

Twins Research

In order to better differentiate the relative contributions of heredity and environment to intelligence, Galton pioneered two methods that are still among the very best available to researchers. The first is the adoptive family method, which involves studying children who have been adopted and grow up in environments different from that of their own parents. For example, Galton studied boys adopted and brought up in the households of Catholic Bishops as their nephews. If intelligence is shaped by the environment, such adopted children should become eminent to a degree similar to that of natural-born children of eminent families. But Galton found that this was not the case, although his methods of study were far from rigorous.

A second, more promising research strategy pioneered by Galton was the twins method, which is probably the best strategy available to us for differentiating between the contributions of heredity and environment to intelligence. Galton gathered evidence about twins, and discovered two different patterns. He concluded there are two different types of twins. The first type, 'identical twins', tend to be far more similar to one another in both physical and mental characteristics, even when they end up living in what seems like different circumstances, and this, he reasoned, must be because they are genetically more similar. The second types of twins tend to be less similar, and Galton assumed they must be genetically less similar. Of course, Gregor Mendel's (1822–1884) discoveries about genetics did not become well known until the early 20th century, and Galton did not know the details of the role genes play in heredity among monozygotic (genetically identical) and dizygotic (fraternal or genetically different) twins. But Galton's instinct told him that some twins are more similar because of their genetic similarity, although he had no direct evidence of this.

Galton argued that identical twins who have been separated in childhood and brought up in different environments are very similar to each other in terms of intelligence, and this demonstrates that intelligence is shaped by inherited rather than environmental characteristics. The same line of research was followed by Sir Cyril Burt (1883–1971) in England, who purportedly amassed evidence from large numbers of twins who had been separated early in life. But Burt's case shows the complexity and controversy surrounding research on intelligence. Driven by a strong motivation to demonstrate the hereditary basis of intelligence, Burt is shown to have falsified his data (see the definitive biography of Burt by Hearnshaw, 1974). Of course, false data presented by intelligence researcher(s) does not demonstrate that an entire research approach is wrong; it simply points to the direct intrusion of politics into research on intelligence.

Does research on twins demonstrate that intelligence is inherited? While the influence of inherited factors is undeniable, more care needs to be taken in interpreting evidence from twins research. Just because monozygotic twins reared apart show high similarity does not demonstrate the source of such similarity to be purely inherited. Flynn (2007) shows this in his discussion of 'multiplier effects'. Consider the case of twins Joe and David, who as ten-year-olds are taller and faster than most other children in their schools. Although Joe and David were separated soon after birth and now live in different American cities, they both get identified as promising basketball players and play in local basketball teams during their early teens. They both get picked to play on their high-school basketball teams, where they receive first-rate coaching, and by the time they are high-school seniors they are far, far better than average in their basketball abilities.

Now, consider Jane and Mary, who are also twins separated soon after birth. By the time they are ten years old, they are identified as 'talented in mathematics'. Although they live in different cities, the fact that they both have inherited a slight 'math advantage' begins to put them in a special situation. In both of their cases, teachers label them as 'girls with math talent' and they receive special attention. They are placed in honors math classes and special summer math camps. By the time they become high school seniors, the difference between Jane and Mary and other girls in their schools has been 'exaggerated'. Describing such cases, Flynn argues that genes can 'profit' from multiplier effects that are environmental and ultimately result in twins becoming more like one another, and different from other people.

Neuro-Intelligence and Neuro-Metrics

Galton (1883) argued that intelligence is an inherited part of the central nervous system. A logical next step to Galton's theoretical viewpoint was to measure the physiological characteristics of the brain as a way of assessing intelligence. Thus, Galton can be considered to be an early explorer in research fields now known as neuro-intelligence, which seeks to identify the neural basis of intelligence, and neuro-metrics, measuring intelligence by assessing brain characteristics, such as cortical thickness.

The other aspect of Galton's thinking that was ahead of his time, and to which we seem to have come back in a circular manner, is that physiological differences between individuals correlate with differences in intelligence. He believed that physiological differences account for differences in reaction time and that speed of response on simple cognitive tasks can be used as a measure of intelligence. Remarkably, research in neuro-intelligence and neuro-metrics has brought us back to these ideas.

Galton was the first to try to systematically measure the speed at which individuals carry out different elementary perceptual and discrimination tasks. His focus on reaction time would seem, at first glance, to be an unlikely indicator of intelligence. After all, professional boxers are known to have fast reaction time, but they are not renowned for having high intelligence. But when Sheppard and Vernon (2008) reviewed the results of 172 studies they found a positive correlation between 'mental speed' and intelligence, the measures of mental speed including reaction time, general speed of processing, speed of short-term memory processing, speed of long-term memory retrieval, and inspection time. Typically, the studies reviewed measured speed of reacting to a light or lights appearing on a panel. Although the correlations reported between mental speed and intelligence have been in the low to medium range, the tendency has been for this correlation to climb higher as task complexity increases: the difference between low intelligent and high intelligent individuals increases as the complexity of the task increases.

Although contemporary research supports the idea of a positive association between 'mental speed' and intelligence, using a variety of measures (Leite, 2009), we must keep in mind a few critical points. First, speed is only one aspect of problem solving; some of the 'great thinkers' in history have been renowned for their focus, stamina, and resilience in thinking, rather than speedy reactions. Taking time to think, and being able to come up with new solutions to problems, seems to characterize the likes of Albert Einstein and Ludwig Wittgenstein in the world. A second issue concerns the use of reaction time as a measure of mental speed. Because reaction time is relatively easy to measure and can serve as an objective gage of thought-processing speed, it has been commonly used in psychological research, and in research on intelligence in particular.

But the use of reaction time in research must take place with the awareness of the particular characteristics of reaction time scores. Most importantly, reaction time distributions are 'decidedly nonnormal' (Wagenmakers & Brown, 2007, p. 830). When the distribution of scores for individual participants in a study are skewed, special care must be taken not to obscure the particular pattern of results for individual participants by using aggregates of data. In other words, group means could well obliterate the pattern of reaction-time results for individual participants. This brings us back to the larger debate between supporters of nomothetic research, which emphasizes general trends and aggregates in groups (e.g. changes in IQ scores in a population over time), and idiographic research, which focuses more on case studies of individual cases (e.g. changes in Jane's IQ score as she goes through the lifespan and into senior years).

Brain Characteristics and Intelligence

The second aspect of Galton's thinking that was ahead of its time was the proposition that physiological differences between individuals correlate with differences in intelligence. Until the late 20th century, the techniques were not available for researchers to attempt to study the characteristics of the brains of people with different levels of intelligence. Almost a century after Galton first put forward his ideas, Richard Haier and his associates brought the research almost full circle by presenting physiological data showing that individuals who score higher on the Raven's Progressive Matrices Test have more efficient brains (Haier, Siegel, Nuechterlein, Hazlett, Wu, Paek, et al., 1988). This research represents the launching of the modern fields of 'neuro-intelligence' and 'neuro-metrics', only made possible by rapid advances in electronic measurement devices and neuro-imaging technology. For example, in the study by Haier et al. (1988) positron emission tomography (PET) was used to show that glucose metabolism in regions around the cortex was lower in individuals with higher scores on the Raven's Progressive Matrices Test. This result was interpreted to mean that more intelligent individuals have more efficient brains, because smarter people were using less energy when they solved problems on this standard 'non-verbal' intelligence test. (PET scans provide images of brain metabolism by detecting amounts of low-level radioactive glucose used by neurons in the process of firing and communicating with other neurons.)

The neural efficiency hypothesis proposes that the brains of more intelligent people use fewer resources to solve problems, through the more focused use of specific task-related brain areas. Since the initial Haier et al. (1988) study, there have been numerous other studies examining the neural efficiency hypothesis, using various techniques, including PET, the electroencephalogram (EEG) and functional magnetic resonance imaging (fMRI) (these methods were described in Chapter 2). The general trend in findings from about 80 percent of these studies supports the neural efficiency hypothesis, although some studies suggest that there are important differences between some groups (e.g. males vs females) and even across individuals (Neubauer & Fink, 2009).

Evidence of differences in neural efficiency in males and females has been found specifically on some tasks of spatial ability (males showing greater efficiency) and verbal ability (females showing greater efficiency), corresponding with results on some paper-and-pencil tests showing males to be higher in spatial ability and females to be higher on verbal ability. However, this conclusion is tentative, because a lot depends on other aspects, such as the level of practice and other environmental factors. At this point, an important link becomes evident between the biological characteristics of the brain and the characteristics of the environment in which an individual lives and takes shape.

Contrary to the stereotype of brain characteristics being 'fixed', evidence suggests that the brain structure is malleable, highly so in some respects (Kelly & Garavan, 2005). For example, practice has been shown to markedly improve an individual's level of fluid intelligence, as measures by the Raven's Progressive Matrices Test (Jaeggi, Buschkuehl, Jonides, & Perrig, 2008). A great deal of what we regard as 'expert skills', such as playing chess for example, depends to a large degree on deliberate practice and not just on intelligence (Ericsson & Ward, 2007). In line with this, there is evidence to suggest that as London taxi drivers navigate the streets and develop richer cognitive maps of the city, the size of their posterior hippocampi increases (Maguire, Gadian, Johnsrude, Good, Ashburner, Frackowiak, et al., 2000). Thus, brain plasticity is not just a feature of childhood, but in adulthood, also, experiences in the world change our brains. More specifically, deliberate, repeated practice of a skill such as navigation in a city, or playing chess or a musical instrument, has been shown to markedly change brain structure.

The research evidence regarding brain plasticity also leads us to re-think the traditional view of the heritability of brain structure. On the one hand, there is no doubt that at least some parts of the brain have genetically inherited limitations. On the other hand, 'The heritability of brain structure, although certain, is neither final nor static' (Toga & Thompson, 2005, p. 16). For further clarification, consider the characteristic of body weight and height. The heritability of weight and height is also certain, but factors such as nutrition, exercise, and so on, can play a vitally important role in determining a person's weight and height. Similarly, although the heritability of brain characteristic such as cortical thickness, found to be positively correlated with intelligence (Karama, Ad-Dab'bagh, Haier, Deary, Lyttelton, Lepage et al., 2009), is certain, these characteristics can be influenced to a considerable degree by environmental conditions.

In conclusion, neuro-metrics has resulted in an alternative way of conceptualizing the measurement of intelligence. Rather than the standard paper-and-pencil tests, such as the Wechsler and the Stanford-Binet, the focus is on a number of brain characteristics, such as cortical thickness and neural efficiency. However, although brain characteristics are influenced by heredity, they are not static and fixed. Repeated practice in tasks both improves performance and changes brain structure.

Conclusions

An underlying assumption in both the standard paper-and-pencil tests of intelligence and the new 'neuro' approach to intelligence is that speed is of fundamental importance. Basically, the assumption is that 'faster is better'. A second assumption has been that more memory is better. But these assumptions could be leading us down the wrong path, because intelligence testing has failed to focus enough on teaching rational thinking. In an insightful analysis of *What intelligence tests miss*, Stanovich (2009) discusses a thought experiment in which people take a pill that increases their memory capacity and processing speed. The outcome, according to Stanovich, is that people would continue to think in the same irrational way, but only faster. For example, people would '... carry on using the same ineffective medical treatments because of failure to think of alternative causes ... keep making the same poor financial decisions because of overconfidence...keep misjudging environmental risks...' (p. 196). According to Stanovich, instead of investing so much time debating the hereditary and environmental roots of intelligence, we should place greater emphasis on rational thinking, because it clearly can be taught. Perhaps this idea of improving rational thinking ability is of greatest value in the domain of intergroup relations and collective conflict (the topic in Chapter 15). Despite our assumed 'superior intelligence' relative to other organisms, we humans continue to routinely engage in destructive wars to kill our own kind, as well as wipe out other species, in very large numbers.

12 *Personality*

Rom Harré

> There is no such thing as anyone's real personality. Personalities are the product of the initial feelings or attitudes someone takes upto the needs of the situation they find themselves in ... and, for that matter, the initial feelings themselves are the products of earlier conflicts of that sort. There is a dialectic of personality, just as there is a dialectic of history (and it's just as unpredictable). (Michael Parson, quoted in S. Faulks, 1997, p. 322)

The topic of 'personality' and related personal characteristics is one of the most problematic in contemporary psychology. In order to examine theories of personality we must start with some idea of what these theories are supposed to explain. Unfortunately there is an essential ambiguity in what is meant by the concept of 'personality'. Sometimes these concepts are used to refer to a 'something', a supposed inner and enduring state that is responsible for a person behaving in certain characteristic ways. For example, Ryckman (1999, p. 5) proposes the following: 'a dynamic and organized set of characteristics possessed by a person that uniquely influences his or her cognitions, motivations and behaviors in various situations' – in short, it is something that influences or causes a person's thoughts and actions to take the form they do. Here we have an example of a supposed generative mechanism type of explanation. What these supposed hidden states are is left mysterious.

Sometimes the concept has a linked behavioral reference, as in the Friedman and Rosenman (1974) distinction between what characterizes type A and type B personalities. These personality types are both descriptors of distinctive ways of living and of the underlying permanent states that are supposed to explain why people do as they do. The theory has become more complex as these 'underlying states' have been identified with certain neurophysiological conditions, doubling up the causal substrate of the explanation. Here we have the first signs of the need to manage a hybrid personality theory. Neurophysiology is a discipline that seeks to identify hypothetical neural mechanisms. However, displays of personality, character and temperament are interpretable only if endowed with meanings. They are not identifiable either by neurophysiological or by neurochemical criteria, though there may be reliable correlations between neurological states and tendencies to display certain personality traits. They belong in the discourse of the P- or Person grammar.

Logical Features of 'Personality' Concepts

The concept of a disposition, tendency or trait is crucial to both the description of personality displays and their explanation. Looking closely into the logic of dispositional concepts and their place in a scientific discourse, be it psychology or physics, requires one to attend to the complex forms that underlie the uses of dispositional assertions and ascriptions. An ascription of personality tendencies or traits expresses a hypothesis as to how that person will behave in personality-displaying ways in certain circumstances at some other time, usually future but occasionally past.

We outlined the structure of dispositional concepts in Chapter 2. It is important to bear in mind the distinction between occurrent and dispositional properties, those that are permanently displayed from those displayed only from time to time. Dispositional ascriptions are expressed as conditional propositions, that is, in the form 'If certain conditions prevail then such and such a display will be observed'. They are usually held to be true because on similar occasions in the past the relevant display has been observed in those or similar conditions.

We want to say that a person has a certain disposition even when he or she is not displaying the relevant behavior. How can that make sense? Only if we also believe that the individual possesses some relevant permanent attribute or property independent of the various occasions when a certain associated performance is displayed. What that condition is may be very difficult to ascertain. Whatever it is, its description will include none of the properties that are referred to in the conditional statement with which a disposition is ascribed. The molecular structure that explains the solubility of common salt does not invoke the concept of solubility! Nor are the adrenal glands themselves irascible when they secrete adrenalin! The link is created by the Taxonomic Priority Principle.

The Idiographic/Nomothetic Debate

Before we can tackle the task of setting out the various theories that have been proposed to account for the differences in the way people behave, that we sum up in their personalities, characters and temperaments, a fundamental question must be addressed. How unique are the psychological propensities of each individual person? How much do someone's behavioral propensities resemble those of others? More precisely, should a theory of personality, character and temperament be based on the principle that each person occupies a single location on each of a number of universal scales representing universal human attributes? Or should we consider the possibility that there are personal characteristics that are unique to each individual person? We know for sure that each person has a unique autobiography – but does each person have a unique personality? If so, in what way?

These questions have been raised from time to time, notably by Gordon Allport (1961) and by James Lamiell (2008), developing ideas originally put forward by William Stern (1938). The debate has turned on the distinction between an idiographic science concerned with a systematic study of individuals, and a nomothetic science, which aims to discover universal laws applicable to each and every individual in the relevant domain.

This distinction was first made by Windelband in 1894. In the natural sciences, astronomers treat each planet as a unique object, planetary science is largely idiographic. However, they also treat each planet as subject to Newton's universal laws of motion. In studying the unique individual attributes of the planets, astronomers make use of chemical concepts that are universally applicable wherever they may be, but come in distinctive combinations in each planetary object. Astronomy has both idiographic and nomothetic aspects. Is this true of the psychology of human beings, particularly the attributes we are concerned with in this chapter, such as personality, character and temperament?

'Personality' and Related Concepts

Whether we think in idiographic or nomothetic terms, there is a rich vernacular vocabulary in most languages for the kind of personal performances and displays that are subsumed under the general idea of 'personality'. Which ones are we going to pick out as the components of *personality*?

Roughly speaking, 'personality' refers to how a human being appears to other people in predominantly non-moral matters, for example, 'easy going', 'pernickety', 'excitable', summed up in clusters as the content of such neologisms as 'extravert' and 'introvert', and so on. As we have seen, the word 'personality' may also be used to refer to what it is that is responsible for these observable differences. 'Character' refers to the attributes of a person in relation to conduct in which other people are involved, particularly moral conduct. For example, 'honesty' is a character trait rather than an aspect of someone's personality. 'Temperament' refers to what seem to be the natural or inborn sources of those attributes of a person's conduct over which that person has little control. For instance, someone might have a sunny temperament.

Some psychologists have given a prominent place to character as a major component of 'personality'. For example, Roback (1927, p. 4), remarks that while 'character is not an introspective datum, nor even a subconscious fact, it nevertheless constitutes an integral part of personality'. He notes that 'character' is sometimes used to mean more or less the same thing as 'personality'. Sometimes it is used to mean the moral make-up of a person; 'honesty', 'fair dealing' and so on. In these uses, aspects of character are dispositions or traits. Sometimes it refers to the strength a person has to inhibit or give in to individual tendencies and temptations. In the third sense, character comes in degrees from strong to weak. It is not a disposition or tendency but a personal power.

Discussions of temperament have faded out in recent years in the psychological literature. However, 'temperament' played a major role in the work of Ernst Kretschmer (1925). Though the impetus for his studies came from psychiatric observations, he presented a general theory of the relation between body types and temperaments in which he argued that both were products of the state of the endocrine system. The major influence on both is chemical. If this is so, then each body type should go along with a distinct temperament. If we include temperament as a large component of personality, Kretschmer's proposals to link body type to temperament, and ground both in biochemical explanations ultimately derived from the inheritance of different genetic packages, it would make biological phenomena the ultimate core of a theoretical understanding of personality.

The three vocabularies appropriate to the three associated person characteristics slip and slide into one another. Some central cases of terms typical of each group of attributes can be picked out, but there are many words that cross the boundaries between personality, character and temperament. However, all are used characteristically in ways that are implicitly conditional. Almost all are used to ascribe not only behavior and conduct to people but also traits or dispositions. One might say of a friend that he is easily led, even when no one is tempting him into some folly at that moment. The implication being that if he were to meet an emissary of the devil he would very likely carry out the friend's reprehensible suggestions.

The concept of 'personality' also plays a major part in clinical psychology, in the phrases like 'personality disorders' or 'disordered personalities'. Introducing such a concept presupposes the possibility of discerning personalities that are *not* disordered. The cultural relativity of the classification of at least some personality types as 'disordered' is very obvious in the definitions used in DSM IV TR. A disordered personality is:

> an enduring pattern of inner experience and behavior that deviates markedly from the expectations of the individual's culture, is pervasive and inflexible, has an onset in adolescence or early adulthood, is stable over time, and leads to disturbance or impairment [relative to local standards of 'good' functioning] (2004, p. 1230).

The traits someone displays may be discordant with the expectations of one culture but might be just what is expected and approved in some other. Should one flee from danger or stand up to it? Should one take offence at the slightest infringement of one's dignity or let insults pass?

Personality Types

Personality theorists generally assume, as did their Renaissance predecessors, that while each person has his or her idiosyncratic way of being, nevertheless there are personality types – that is, that certain features of personality displays generally go together and are found to some degree in a great many people. Explanatory theories would try to account for these clusters whether the theorist was primarily concerned with how people learned a certain performance style, say in ascending the throne, or with the alleged neurological basis for tendencies to present oneself in certain consistent ways. There have been proposals to link the distinction between introvert and extravert behavior with certain formations in the brain. Some theorists, while conceding that there are personality types, would link these types to individuals in a many-one schema. Any one person might have the ability to display a situation appropriate-personality type drawn from a repertoire of personality types recognized in a cultural locale. For example, Walter Mischel (1986) has promoted this idea as a response to those who dismiss personalities as long-standing person attributes on the grounds of their situational variability. If someone appears introverted with some people and extraverted with others, then, so Mischel argues, that individual must have two dispositional systems, two sets of traits.

Does the level of generality of personality types permit useful inferences about how this or that particular person will behave and how he or she will think in specific circumstances? In other words, does the use of a measure of where a person is located on three or five or more dimensions as a representation of a person's character, temperament and personality, have of any practical use? It may be that though the nature of each person can be represented by a unique location on each of the favored universal dimensions, the differences between people are sufficiently great that each person has to be treated as an individual. If no two people are alike in their personality attributes, personality psychology must, despite making use of universal dimensions, be confined to an idiographic level of knowledge.

The same considerations emerge if we adopt a dramaturgical theory of personality, rather than a trait or dispositional theory. Though each person is acting out the demands of a limited repertoire of action scripts, the performances of individuals may be idiosyncratic. That someone is living out the 'martyrdom' script or the 'playboy' script, may yet make predictions of moment-by-moment behavior vague and even pointless. Every actor creates his own Hamlet and every actress her own Ophelia.

There has also been a tendency for personality psychologists to aim at identifying a small number of personality relevant dispositions or traits which different people display in different degrees, rather than lumping together a small set as defining a 'personality' type. In the case of Hans Eysenck's personality psychology, the generic clusters of lower order dispositions spawn types, so 'introverted' defines an introvert, while 'extraverted' defines an extravert. Dispositions like 'tendency to display an introverted style of life' become types, 'introvert' (Eysenck, 1967). This terminology was introduced by Carl Jung (1923).

Carl Gustav Jung (1875–1961) was born in the small Swiss village of Kessewil. Carl's father, Paul Jung, was a country parson. His primary education was heavily slanted towards the classical languages, including Sanskrit. At 13, he entered boarding school at Basel. At the University of Basel he studied medicine. There he came under the influence of Krafft-Ebing, turning towards psychiatry as a career.

His first post was at the Burghoeltzli Mental Hospital in Zurich. Here he came under the influence of another distinguished psychiatrist, Eugene Bleuler, the man who had renamed Krepelin's *dementia praecox* 'schizophrenia'. In 1903, he married Emma Rauschenbach. In addition to clinical work at the mental hospital he taught at the University of Zurich and opened a private practice.

In 1907, he met Sigmund Freud in Vienna. There was an immediate rapport and Freud enthusiastically claimed him as his heir apparent. However, during their famous visit to America in 1909, with William Stern, their efforts at mutual analysis led to Freud's breaking off this 'entertainment' and eventually their once close relationship.

Though his ideas about the role of archetypes in human life, and his famous concept of the 'anima', colored the popular perception of Jung as psychologist, his importance for this chapter lies in his invention of a system of personality categories, based on the distinction between introversion and extraversion.

In the following years he travelled widely, visiting many of the people whose psychological make-ups he had studied at second hand. He retired in 1946, and on the death of his wife in 1955, more or less withdrew from public life. He died in Zurich.

Renaissance psychologists writing in English used a terminology that was derived from a general physiological theory that had survived from ancient times. It was an important ingredient in the psychology and physiology passed on to the Latin Middle Ages from Ancient Greece. According to that theory, the general state of the human organism was determined by the balance between four distinct life principles, or 'humors'. In turn, the humors were combinations of yet more fundamental aspects or principles of the universe, the hot, the cold, the wet and the dry. Each humor was a duality drawn from the principles. Thus black bile, the melancholy humor, was constituted by the wet and the dry, while choleric humor was constituted by the hot and the dry. And so on. This scheme yielded four personality or character types, the melancholic, the phlegmatic, the choleric and the sanguine.

Renaissance psychiatry, for example, as expounded by Robert Burton in his *Anatomy of melancholy* (2000[1621]) was based on this theory. Some treatments for clinical conditions were devised on the idea of restoring a balance between the humors. For example, if the person had a preponderance of the melancholy humor, too cold and wet, purgations ought to help restore the balance or equal temperament of the psychologically and bodily healthy person.

Hans Eysenck (1916–1997) was born in Berlin into a theatrical family. His parents divorced when he was only two. Thereafter he was brought up by his grandparents. The family was Jewish, and like many from that community, he left Germany at the age of 18 just as Hitler and the Nazi party took over the government. He came to England, where he remained for the rest of his life.

He entered the University of London as an undergraduate and continued there to take his PhD in 1940, under the supervision of Sir Cyril Burtt, about whose researches there has been a good deal of controversy. During the Second World War, Eysenck held the post of chief psychologist at Mill Hill Emergency Hospital. This milieu provided him with his first major research opportunity, to test the reliability of psychiatric diagnoses. The issue of the best treatment for the mentally disturbed continued to interest him, particularly as he had come to develop a hostile attitude to standard psychiatric practice, and to Freudian psychotherapy in particular. Many years later, he published an influential attack on the efficacy of the 'talking cure' (Eysenck, 1985).

After a spell at the Maudesley Hospital, the rest of his working life was spent at the Institute of Psychiatry in the University of London. He took up a post there in 1946. He founded the first course in clinical psychology in any British institution of higher learning. There, he conducted the stream of statistical studies from which he drew the material for a prolific output of books and articles. He retired from the position in 1983, but continued to work until his death.

In the 20th century, one simple scheme became very widespread, and even made its way into ordinary language. This was the concept cluster used by Hans Eysenck (1967 and 1970) in his influential studies of personal differences. The key concepts, 'introversion' and 'extraversion', were introduced into *psychology* by Eysenck. He elaborated the scheme so that individuals were distinguished by the degree to which they exemplified each of supposedly three universal 'dimensions' of personality – introversion, extraversion and neuroticism. These attribute words soon spawned nominal categories, 'introverts', 'extraverts' and 'neurotics'.

The most recent attempt at something similar, referred to earlier, has been nicknamed 'the Big Five', referring to the use of five 'dimensions' as a popular theoretical grounding of personality differences between people, rather than Eysenck's three. It is important to realize that each of these generic terms comprehends a variety of kinds of observable behavior. No one displays 'introversion' as such. A typical introvert is quiet and retiring, while a typical extravert is outgoing and socially engaging. Similarly, when we come to examine the Big Five as a category system for describing ways that people differ from one another, we will observe the same logical structure. Each of the Five Super Traits comprehends a cluster of simpler and often apparently unrelated ways of thinking and acting. How could this make sense? We will see that the Big Five are not real human attributes but artefacts of a certain kind of analytical method, factor analysis.

Various unsuccessful attempts have been made to extend the scope of these supposed traits from the personalities of the English-speaking middle-class to members of non-Western cultures (Cheung, Cheung, Leung, Ward, & Leung, 2003).

Extra-Personality Personal Attributes

There are other personal attributes that vary from person to person but have a different flavor from those lumped under personality, character and temperament. For example, 'self-efficacy' (Bandura, 1977) is a personal characteristic that varies from person to person but is not generally treated by personality psychologists as part of their domain of interest. Self-efficacy, according to Bandura (1986), 'is the belief in one's capabilities to organize and execute the sources of action required to manage prospective situations'. Bandura seems to mean something like 'means' rather than 'sources of action'. Over a lifetime of research into and reflection on this differentiating feature of the way human beings live in the world, Bandura has emphasized not only the degree to which self-confidence makes success more likely, but also how lack of it gets in the way of effective action. Though 'efficacy' suggests a personal power, in Bandura's theory it is a belief. Allied to self-efficacy is another feature of individual psychology, namely 'locus of control' (Rotter & Hochreich, 1975). Does someone generally think that he or she is more or less in control of what they do, or do they believe that their thinking and acting is more or less under the control of extra-individual influences, the environment or other people?

Another rather different though related personal characteristic that varies from one individual to another has been called 'cognitive style', sometimes called 'field dependency'. Beginning with the relation a person might have to the perceptual field, Witkin described those who tended to take the field as a whole, neglecting detail, as 'field-dependent', while those who were readily able to analyze it into its components he called 'field-independent'. With several collaborators he went on to generalize this difference in style into a typology based on a fundamental distinction between those who differentiated themselves from the environment and within their own psyches, differentiated psychological activities – the field-independent – and those who did not make such differentiations with such sharp boundaries – the field-dependent (Witkin & Goodenough, 1981).

Then there is the vexed question of the cluster of cognitive attributes summed up in the concept of 'intelligence' (see Chapter 11). People certainly differ in how successfully and swiftly they can solve problems. However, some people are good at one kind of problem while others are good at a different kind of conundrum. Should this individual difference be included in personality? Usually it is treated independently, along with its recent sibling, 'emotional intelligence'.

A merit of the recent writing of McCrae and Costa is that they have tried to take these issues into account. But the methodological slippage between classifying and explaining some domain of the phenomena has prevented them from creating a realistic *theory*. Because of the way that they have used factor analysis to create genera of personal attributes there is even some doubt as to the intelligibility of their project. More troublesome is their failure to maintain an adequate degree of plausibility with respect to the cognitive foundations of their five-factor theory.

Theories and Descriptions

Psychologists are not known for the elegance of their prose – but there are some notable exceptions. It must be said that McCrae and Costa (2003) is one of the best written books among recent psychological publications. It is all the more awkward to have to take them to task. In each of the major sections of this chapter we must bear in mind the lesson of Chapter 1 of this book to remind ourselves of the basic requirement for research to be 'scientific', in the sense that research in physics and chemistry is scientific.

According to McCrae and Costa (2003, p. 184) 'Scientific theory is a broad and abstract account of the general principles that are thought to explain a set of phenomena, like the General Theory of Relativity or the Theory of Evolution.' It may be that the General Theory of Relativity is an abstract account of gravity, that is, a (tensor) calculus, but the Theory of Evolution is not abstract at all. It is a concrete hypothesis about a possible causal mechanism that would, if it existed, generate new species. What is more, this theory stands now at the apex of a hierarchy of subordinate theories, reaching down to the bedrock of quantum mechanics. There are very few abstract theories in physics and chemistry. The content of most theories is quite concrete. McCrae and Costa have confused the positivistic reduction of theory to covering laws with the requirements for a genuine explanatory theory. The point becomes very clear in their remark that 'Trait theory pointed researchers to general styles of thinking, feeling, and acting …'. Trait theory is logically no more than a system of classification of the ways that people behave. Since it is built on the basis of factor analysis of the answers to questionnaires it could be no more than taxonomy. Lions and tigers are felines and carnivorous. But to offer 'feline' as the concept on which an explanation of their being carnivorous can be built is empty.

Personality theory comprises or should comprise both a taxonomic or classificatory dimension and an explanatory dimension. Classification systems make possible a disciplined practice for describing a class of phenomena, by distilling a descriptive vocabulary from the rich and varied resources of the vernaculars of various cultures for consistent and perhaps universal categories. The categories which have been used to identify personality types, personal attributes that cluster to describe an individual's personality, are the result not of a distillation of empirical research and observation, but of the modification of the indigenous categories of everyday life. Classifying phenomena is essential to science but is never explanatory. However, explanations of displays of personality must be coupled with explanations of the existence of personality traits, persistent dispositions, right down to supposed neurological features of the actor's body. As we saw above, the fulfillment of the requirements for an explanation can take three different paths – yielding three different kinds of explanation.

The explanatory task is to account for the existence of common patterns of individual acting and thinking, and for the origin and stability of the clusters of attributes that comprise a personality type by proposing hypotheses about the mechanisms that bring these phenomena about. Being an introvert does not make one shy and retiring. It is a classificatory category under which we comprehend beings who display these ways of living. Being a gemstone does not make a chunk of rock hard and refractive.

Broadly speaking, there are two main styles of theorizing with respect to the alleged grounding of stable personality traits, if any such exist. According to one influential point of view, typified by the proposals of Hans Eysenck, personal characteristics are the outcome of inherited brain structures and processes, which are related to the normal level of arousal in this or that particular person. These form a fixed background to displays of personality, character and temperament. Once the structure of the brain has been laid down these characteristics do not develop. At the other extreme is the theorizing of Sigmund Freud, for whom personal attributes are determined during complex processes of maturation that are social and psychological in essence. Once they have been fixed in the course of various vicissitudes of development during childhood and adolescence they remain pretty much the same throughout life. However, both types of theorizing presume that personality attributes exhibit a certain logical form, that is, they are stable dispositions, permanent possibilities of certain kinds of displays.

What Methods Are Appropriate for the Study of the Psychology of Personality?

Another major reason for the problematic character of personality research is methodological. Currently the most influential account of personality in dispositional terms, at least judging by publications in 'main stream journals, is based on the alleged ubiquity of the Big Five personality traits: 'openness to experience'; 'conscientiousness'; 'extraversion'; 'agreeableness'; and 'neuroticism', the classificatory scheme proposed by McCrae and Costa, which we have discussed already. Each trait represents a dimension along which individuals vary. 'Jim is more conscientious than John but less conscientious than Henry'. However, these 'traits' have not been arrived at by observing the way people behave but by factor analysis of how they answer questionnaires (McCrae & Costa, 1990).

Factor analysis serves a classificatory purpose. It allows us to collect up similar phenomena into species and then into genera, families and so on. Personality traits do the work that the morphological attributes used by Linnaeus did for biology, collecting up plants and animals into groups, species, genera, families and so on. They do not do the work that Darwin did! They explain nothing. However, only when the species taxonomy had been invented could the question of the origin of species be raised. No Linnaeus, no Darwin!

However, is trait theory, as presented by the trait theorists, really a taxonomy of human modes of thought, feeling and acting, collected up according to some taxonomic principle? Remember that this research is based on questionnaires, structured interviews and the like – essentially *conversations* between researchers and participants. Taken literally, the results of such studies could be an indirect presentation of grammatical and social conventions for producing a certain kind of discourse, namely questionnaire answering. Without observational research it is hard to say whether the way someone answers self-report questionnaires relates to how they behave in real-life situations. What little evidence there is suggests that there is often little correlation between the characters people display in their responses when questioned about some matter and how they can be observed to behave in the absence of the prying psychologist. It is no good, as trait theorists have tended to do, to correlate the answers given by other people to how they view the target of the research to try to show that there is a cross-situational consistency in how they come across.

Finally, there is the question of the part played by situation and culture in personality displays. Does a person always 'remain in character' so to speak? The current orthodoxy simply presumes that whatever personality is, be it an underlying 'something' or a cluster of patterns of public display, it is a stable and long-lasting personal attribute. However, there is a good deal of evidence to the effect that a display of personality for any given individual may be situation relative; for example, extravert on some occasions and introvert on others. A related issue is whether the personalities recognized in American culture, those most frequently represented in personality research, are also recognized in other cultures, such as Hispanic, Japanese, Kenyan, Polynesian and so on.

Explanatory Formats

There are three key features that have played a decisive role in the way psychological explanations of the differences in personality between individuals have been proposed. Focus on one or other of these issues leads to three major theories of personality.

The first feature of psychological explanations of individual ways of thinking and acting is the setting up of a *hierarchy* of relevant dispositions grounded in distinctive physiological characteristics of each person. Displays of the kinds of behavior that interest personality theorists are supposed to be grounded in permanent features of the person, traits or dispositions. For example, in Eysenckian theory, a person's characteristic way of behaving and thinking is explained by reference to three personality defining dispositions: introversion, extraversion and neuroticism. These in their turn are supposed to be grounded in the long-standing biological characteristics of the person as an embodied being. Finally, the distinguishing neurological and endocrinogical features underlying each major disposition are referred to personal and unique genetic constitutions. This structure is the standard format for theorizing in the natural sciences, with a phenomenal level of observables, for example, chemical reactions, which are tied into behavioral dispositions such as acidity and alkalinity, which are themselves grounded in a second level of unobservable structures and generative processes, the electronic structures of atoms and molecules. This is the 'heterogeneous' format.

The second feature is some working resolution of the familiar question of how a balance is to be struck between nature and nurture, between theories which see personality displays as predominantly learned and theories which treat them as biologically, particularly genetically driven. Of course, any combination of these features might be useful, in that there may be cultural constraints or conventions on how a biological urge is expressed or suppressed! In so far as personality is a culturally distinct cluster of dispositions it is something that is learned. Furthermore, if that is so, any psychological theorizing apropos of personalities as learned patterns of thought and action must include a development aspect.

The third feature is the role, if any, played by aspects of the immediate environment or situation in the explanation of personality displays. Is there such a thing as an individual's personality as a permanent and stable cluster of relevant attributes, be they dispositional or underlying, or is it rather that each individual has a repertoire of personality displays available to manage various kinds of situations?

In addition, psychological theories of personality have to account for the actual balance between personal factors and environmental influences, not only for each individual person but also for the interpretation by others, including personality psychologists, of what a person does in terms of *personality* characteristics. It may be that the very same display in terms of gestures, speech-acts and so on, would be seen as indicative of one kind of personality in one context but indicative of another kind in another context, or perhaps not be thought germane to personality attributions at all. From this point of view, personality is to be explained in dramaturgical terms as a form of tactical or strategic self-presentation.

Set against all three theoretical formats is the personality theory of psychodynamics, notably developed by Sigmund Freud and his followers. According to psychodynamic theory, there is a universal sequence of stages in the development of individuals. Personalities are determined by the history of the passage of an individual through them.

In short, we can discern four major theoretical stances to explaining why people have their distinctive ways of thinking and acting: biologically grounded hierarchies of dispositions; learned responses to particular situations; displays of personhood drawn from a local repertoire of acceptable ways of being; and finally, as the result of developmental processes that are in essence psycho-sexual.

Dispositional Theories of Personality

If a trait is a permanent tendency it may be presumed to be some state of the brain of the person who possesses it. Traits in this sense are scientifically speaking, theoretical entities. The existence of a trait, in whatever form it is supposed to exist as a permanent feature of a person, is a candidate for serving as part of the explanation of a display of the relevant characteristic personality attribute. Allport took a robustly 'realist line'. A psychological trait is a 'neurophysiological structure having the capacity to render many stimuli functionally equivalent and guide equivalent (meaningfully consistent) forms of adaptive and expressive behavior' (1961, p. 347). Logically, an Allport trait is not a disposition but the grounding of a variety of dispositions, clustering in some consistent manner. However, the slipperiness of the trait concept comes out in his well-known distinction between common and personal traits. The former are 'those aspects of personality to which most people in a population can be compared' (Allport, 1961, p. 347). However, this comparison does not involve the neurophysiological structures of these people, but the way they comport themselves!

Gordon Allport (1897–1967) was born in the small town of Montezuma in Indiana, the youngest of four boys. His father was a physician, with a clinic attached to the family home. Gordon was educated locally at the Glenville High School. In 1915, he entered Harvard, where his elder brother, Floyd, had studied psychology. He took his BA in 1919 in philosophy and economics.

He spent a year at Robert College in Istanbul, returning to Harvard to begin preparations for a doctoral study in psychology with Hugo Münsterberg. He took his master's degree in 1921 and his PhD in 1922, with a study of personality traits.

A scholarship took him to Germany, where he became particularly close to William Stern and Franz Koffka. He then went to Cambridge in England to work with Frederick Bartlett. He returned to an instructorship at Harvard, in 'social ethics', for the years 1924–1926. He married Ada Gould in 1925. Between 1922 and 1961, he moved away from an exclusive concentration on a psychology of traits to a much more sophisticated and eclectic view of human nature, increasingly emphasizing the contingencies of the situations in which people act, and the idiosyncracy of individuals.

His most important publication on personality psychology was his *Pattern and growth in personality* (1961), a thorough revision of his pioneering *Psychology of personality* (1937), which came out in 1965.

The pattern of concepts here is complex. Only one of these meanings is explanatory, that is, it can be used to refer to some feature of the constitution of the being to which the disposition to be explained is ascribed. It can become part of a theory when it is used together with a statement of the existence of a certain predisposing condition. Thus, we can explain why a tennis ball has a disposition to bounce when it hits the court (condition) by referring to the molecular structure of the stuff of which it is made (permanent constitution). This tennis ball may not have a disposition to bounce because the molecular constitution of its constituents has decayed.

Let us now apply this analysis to the five-factor model of personality to see if it has any claim to be a theory of personality rather than a system for classifying certain human characteristics. Each 'factor' comprises a group of bipolar dimensions, labeled in a variety of categories, some political, some temperamental, some moral and some psychological in a broad sense. For example, the dimensions grouped under the supertype 'openness to experience' comprise the following: down-to-earth – imaginative, uncreative – creative, conventional – original, prefer routine – prefer variety, uncurious (sic) – curious, conservative – liberal. Setting aside the factor analytic influence of this lay out, we can see that the first three dimensions are variants of the same polarity. The 'uncreative – creative' dimension could be mapped in either direction of the 'prefer routine – prefer variety' dimension. A very creative artist or author may be locked into an almost superstitious pattern of actions, a routine, without which nothing is accomplished. Leaving aside the fine details of the scheme, it is evident that trying to *explain* why Henry is creative but James is not, by declaring that Henry is open to experience but James is not, is an empty gesture. 'Open to experience' is to 'creativity', as 'feline' is to 'tiger'. Being creative is a species of the genus 'openness to experience'. At the same time, it is likely some creative people are not open to experience, in the lay meaning of the phrase, that is, of pursuing a lonely obsession with an extraordinarily isolated life interest. The philosophy of Ludwig Wittgenstein comes to mind. He pursued his studies of the illusions that language gives rise to without serious interest into either the people or the culture of the world he experienced.

It should be said from the start that the 'model' has one strong point in its favor – at the level of observable or reportable phenomena it makes use of predominantly American middle-class vernacular English – so those of the readers of the study who are fluent in this dialect can understand what is being said. No pseudo-technical terminology appears at the level of observable phenomena. Most educated English speakers understand the descriptive vocabulary very well. However, there are some words used to describe a personality that have a much more restricted use. For example, the vividly evocative 'flaky' is widely used in US English but not much elsewhere. 'Cool' has a wider currency.

The first question to be asked of the McCrae and Costa scheme, which can stand in for any 'trait' theory, such as that of Hans Eysenck or the 'source trait' scheme of Raymond Cattell, is whether real attributes cluster under a fabricated supertype because they are members of a family of words linked by similarities and differences into a semantic field, or because they are words used in descriptions of phenomena that are the effects of a common cause. For instance, under the supertype 'conscientiousness', we find 'aimless', 'negligent' and 'disorganized' on the socially disreputable pole of three of the dimensions. On the socially acceptable pole we find 'persevering' and 'hardworking'. The technique of 'factor analysis' lumps these under their respective poles and supertype because they are used in a highly correlated manner. Does someone work hard and persevere at a job because he or she is lucky enough to have a characteristic on another logical level, conscientiousness? Or are perseverance and hard work ways of being conscientious? Is the correlation empirical or grammatical? Try this – do you know anyone who is 'aimless' and 'highly organized'? Or who is 'hardworking' and 'ready to quit'? Of course you don't. Not because there are no such people out there, but because of the *grammar* of these words. There could be no such people out there. We are still between the covers of the dictionary.

In personality theory, the higher, or observational level, makes use of psychological concepts, drawn ultimately from the vernaculars of human cultures. The lower, or explanatory level, uses concepts from biology and physiology to account for the phenomena that are represented by the higher level concepts. These higher or lower 'levels' are not ordered in any pattern of esteem. The 'higher' and 'lower' simply represent the logical order in which the concepts occur. The higher are the means for describing the explanandum, what is to be explained, and the lower for describing the explanans, which does the explaining. On offer to take the explaining role have been body types (Kretschmer, 1925), brain structures (Eysenck, 1967) and the preservation of ancient behavioral adaptations in genetic material.

Body Types and Endocrine Secretions

Kretschmer linked the species that he included under the generic psychological attribute of temperament closely to the physical types of human bodies. He identified two normal types of temperament, cyclothymes and schizothymes (Kretschmer, 19, pp. 254–255). These are determined 'with regard to their physical correlates, by similar parallel activity on the part of the secretions … the whole chemistry of the blood…' The parallel 'brain and mind' is to be replaced by 'soma [body] and mind'. Malfunctioning of the glands accounts for deviations from temperamental normality. There are an almost infinite variety of shades of personality types, and within the whole gamut of versions of each main personality type there are unhealthy extremes around a healthy median form. Kretschmer described his two main categories as follows:

Cyclothymes: They range along a dimension that, in extremes, displays the polar states of manic excitement and depression and melancholy. Within the normal healthy range of temperaments he identified the 'gay and mobile' and the 'comfortable and slow' (Kretschmer, 1925, p. 258).

Schyzothymes: Among the mentally healthy versions of this temperament we find people of 'tender sensibility, sensitivity to art and nature, tact and taste in personal style, [and] sentimental affection for certain individuals' (Kretschmer, 1925, p. 259).

Kretschmer, as we noted above, was of no doubt that the types of people he had identified came about by virtue of the activity of the endocrine glands. At the same time, his most original idea was the tie in between the broad personality types and the three main body types – cyclothymes displayed a pyknic physique, short, round-headed and stocky; while schizothymes were asthenic, long-limbed and narrow in body, and athletic, well-built, broad-shouldered and muscular. Resisting the simple theory that explains personality by 'anatomical variations in the brain-apparatus' (Kretschmer, 1925, p. 254), Kretschmer points to the clarity with which the relation between glandular disturbances, abnormality of physique and psychic temperament is evident in extreme cases. By analogy, ought one not to take the same view of the origin of normal personalities and temperaments – '… where one has a polyglandular disturbance on the physique, on the growth of tissue, and also on the psychic functional capacity' (Kretschmer, 1925, p. 254)?

Problems with Trait or Dispositional Theories

The logic of trait ascriptions and their organizing into clusters by factor analytical methods requires that the higher order concepts, such as 'introversion' or 'openness', are similar to genera in biology. That is, their role is classificatory. They cannot be explanatory. Furthermore, the features that characterize the dimensions of these persisting traits and presumably their persisting foundations in permanent states of the individual are those of middle-class Westerners, the Big Three of Hans Eysenck – Extraversion, introversion and neuroticism, or the Big Five of McCrae and Costa, in which openness and agreeableness are added to the Eysenck genera.

Trait theory proposes a variety of permanent states, processes, structures and conditions that continue to exist in individual people whether or not a trait is displayed in behavior, thought or feeling. These hypothetical attributions are genuinely explanatory. The only problem is the great variety of seemingly incompatible kinds of explanatory hypotheses that has been proposed. There is no consensus among trait theorists as to the categories that are to be drawn on in the explanans level of dispositional theorizing. At one time, super or source traits were proposed, making trait theory of personality into a double lay-ered concoction. The source traits referred to in the explanatory domain would be of the very same type as those referred to in the domain of the displays to be explained. Unfortunately, the logic of dispositions – and source traits are as much dispositions as surface traits – requires a sustaining level with which to account for the correctness of declaring that someone is 'irritable', 'self-effacing', 'boisterous' and so on, even when they are not displaying these attributes.

Cultural Repertoires as Theories of Personality

Dramaturgical Models of Personality

Some version of the dramaturgical theory of personality and character has been about for centuries. The basic idea is simply that personality is a cluster of characteristics that are ascribed to a person by certain specific others in certain specific situations. Instead of looking for an explanation that presumes that these ascriptions are reflections of stable personal characteristics, the dramaturgical model explains current ascriptions as the product of schemata for managing actions that reflect the role that a person is then and there called upon to play in an ongoing drama. This explanatory framework derives from a certain way of analyzing social performances, Burke's Pentad. Kenneth Burke (1969[1945]) proposed the use of a scheme for analyzing the actions of people engaged in a life-episode in terms of five aspects, drawn explicitly from likening a life performance to a stage play. This view broke explicitly with the behaviorist thesis that behavior was the product of stimuli applied to an individual who had been trained and or was pre-wired to respond in a certain way to stimuli of a certain kind. Burke rejected both the atomicity of the behaviorist approach but also with its individualism. Personality was a joint product of the schemata or rules for how to act in a certain social interaction, not a permanent cluster of personal dispositions. The five important components of a life episode in which people displayed something like personality were scene, agent, agency, purpose and act. What sort of personality do you display to your doctor? The scene is the consulting room, the agent is the physician, the agency is the diagnostic interview, the purpose is to discover the nature of the patient's complaint, and the act is a diagnosis. Goffman (1990) emphasized that the personality a person is seen to display is a joint product of the interpretation of a person's actions by others and the intentions of the actor to display him or herself in a certain manner. In more sociological terms, personality is tied to role. Just as someone can take on this or that role, usually but not always successfully, so too a person can display this or that personality, that is, display a group of personal characteristics drawn, for example, from those extracted from questionnaires by McCrae and Costa, that are appropriate to that role. Dramaturgical theory of personality explains the characteristic of personal performances by reference to knowledge, implicit or explicit, of the stylistic and moral demands of role performance.

It is important to see how much this point of view in personality studies differs from the trait theories of Eysenck and McCrae and Costa. Burke's theory is dynamic. It is based on the idea of episodes or strips of life in which people engage, usually, but not always, with some end in mind. There are scripts, conventions, rule systems and the like according to which episodes evolve (Harré & Secord, 1972; Schank & Abelson, 1977). These set standards of correct performance including what have been taken to be the personality dimensions. Of course, it also follows that violation of the rules is a noticeable fault and usually calls for some kind of exculpatory account or apology (Garfinkel, 1967).

Goffman made a life-long study of the way the personality displays of individual persons changed with the social situation. 'Not men and their moments;' as he famously remarked, 'but moments and their men [sic]' (Goffman, 1967, Introduction).

The narratological theory of personality, advocated by McAdams (1990), for example, runs along similar lines. McAdams distinguishes three levels. At the first level of the hierarchy of components of 'personality' there are dispositions, long lasting enough to be called 'traits'. These are the personal attributes that are displayed in a wide variety of a person's interactions and in many situations. These are highly generic. At the second level, there are displays that reflect personal concerns, such as liking someone. The third level involves life narratives, the storylines that a person lives out as a member of a cluster of social worlds, variants within a distinctive culture. At this point McAdams's approach runs parallel to that of Burke and Goffman. Explanations of the origin and analyses of the components of personality types as well as explanations of personal displays of one's own version of one or more of these personality types all turn on cultural conventions and, in the end, on social history and even the geographical locations of the culture at the focus of research.

The theories of personality just outlined play down the role of traits or permanent dispositions in the explanation of displays of person-types by individuals. Any one individual may display a variety of clusters of thought, feeling and action, each of which would figure as a distinct person-type on any of the standard versions of trait theory.

However, does the overwhelming evidence for plasticity of performance necessarily dispose of trait theories? We might say that the correct response to observations like – 'a child is a hellion at home and an angel outside' – is to elaborate the dispositional theory. That child, familiar to most parents, is characterized by two sets of dispositions, those that come to the fore at home and those that come to the fore outside. When Argyle and Little (1972) demonstrated the flexibility and situatedness of middle-class behavioral styles what this showed, if we take this line, was that each socially competent and psychology healthy human being has a wide repertoire of behavioral dispositions. However, this approach runs counter to the well-established point that there are coherent clusters of displayed attributes, each of which is coherent and appropriate to a situation, but is not being presented while any of the other clusters are to the fore.

Abnormal Personalities, Characters and Temperaments

Psychological theorizing must be able to account for the nature and origin of abnormal personalities, both types and unique individual clusters characteristics. The typology of the Big Five has found its way into clinical psychology and psychiatry, particularly in the diagnostic manual, DSM IV. In this respect it is a rival to the once popular psychodynamic accounts of personality and deviations from what is taken to be normal for human beings.

The Origin of Deviant Personalities

The Freudian theory of how a personality is established in some human beings is based on the idea of a sequence of stages in the mastery of powerful urges to achieve various kinds of gratification. According to psychodynamics, the infant begins its development of a personality at an oral stage, a time when pleasure is derived from suckling. The mouth is the focus of satisfaction or dissatisfaction. The next stage is anal, when pleasure is derived from defecation. The anus is the focus of satisfaction or dissatisfaction. The third stage is the genital, where pleasure is derived from the sexual organs. This sequence was first briefly discussed in Chapter 6. The mature personality is achieved by a sequential transition through these stages, reaching a balanced, moderate and appropriate interest in the pleasures of life, within the framework of the social norms of the surrounding culture.

A person who fails to make the necessary transitions to maturity has a personality and character that reflects the stage from which the normal process of psychic maturation has failed to evolve. Oral-passive people are weaned later than most infants and are dependent on others in later life, favoring oral gratifications such as the pleasures of smoking. Oral-aggressive people are weaned too soon. They are given to bursts of anger, biting and chewing on pencils and the like. Anal-aggressive people have been cajoled during potty training and tend to be excessive in their social demands both friendly and aggressive. Anal-retentive people, strictly disciplined in infancy tend to be perfectionists and avaricious.

However, the Freudian theory has a second dimension – the changing relationships between the young child and the parents. This begins with the oedipal stage when the child develops a sexual attachment to the parent of the opposite gender and a corresponding hostility to the other parent, seen as a rival. These attachments are impermissible as they really are. The child develops a healthy and balanced personality as its interest shifts to the members of the opposite sex outside the immediate family circle. During this developmental process boys usually take on the attributes that they believe are responsible for the power of the father, traditional masculine traits, so to say. Girls resolve their version of the parental crisis by adopting feminine ways. Sometimes girls giving up the father as a love object nevertheless take on some aspects of masculinity, while boys following the same path take on some of the traits of femininity. Just what is responsible for these deviations for the path of normal development Freud does not explain.

A third aspect of personality, character and temperament comes about through relationships with the parents. Either pole of paired extremes of personality traits may develop from the same faulty parental relationship. Boys rejected by their mothers may become reclusive, or through some subtle influence, macho and aggressive. Girls rejected by their fathers may reject the masculine style or embrace it. Boys favored by their mothers may be either arrogant or effeminate. Girls favored by their fathers may turn out to be vain and demanding, or, tomboys and as we now say, 'butch'. The point of these observations is to account for deviations from the calm, well-organized type of person favored by the 19th-century middle-class. Adventurers and courtesans are on the margins.

Taking all Freud's observations together we arrive at a powerful theory, in which the way people turn out as persons is not determined by inherited dispositions, nor is it determined by training in the favored modes of the local society. It is determined by the interaction of pleasure seeking, parental relationships and the demands of social propriety.

Personality and Health

The concept of personality has had an important part to play in hypotheses about and conceptions of psychological and somatic disorders. There is a sense of 'theory' in which a theory is just a hypothesis concerning possible causes of some condition. For example, having a certain kind of personality is supposed to predispose a person to a certain kind of ill health. The concept of personality has also been used in defining forms of abnormal behavior, for example, a way of behaving identified as 'borderline personality disorder'.

Personality and Physical Health

It is not wholly fanciful to suppose that a person's temperament and personality could have an effect not only on their social and psychological well-being but on their physical health as well. As originally proposed, the theory made use of a broad classification of people into Type A and Type B personalities. Those of Type A were highly strung, tense and given to anger and excitement, while those of Type B were more relaxed and easy going. It seemed that there was a correlation between a Type A personality and a tendency to coronary heart disease. This simple two-fold scheme was elaborated by Hans Eysenck into four personality types (Eysenck, 1970). Type 1 people suffer great stress by their inability to succeed in reaching some valued object. They are prone to cancer. Type 2 people regard their failure to achieve a valued object as the main cause of their unhappiness. They are angry and aggressive. They are prone to coronary heart disease. Type 3 people shift between Type 1 and Type 2 attitudes to a valued object, alternatively thinking of it as the main possibility for well-being and as the main cause of their personal unhappiness. Type 4 people are able to distance themselves from these intense emotional relations to valued objects. People of Types 3 and 4 can expect a long and healthy life.

As a theory within the domain of personality psychology it appears to be of the naïve, covering law form. Empirically established generalizations are serving an explanatory role. 'Why did Joe suffer a heart attack? He had a Type 2 personality'. Scientifically, all is left to play for since the link is so far missing.

Conclusions

Throughout the 20th century a certain method of enquiry was undertaken, based upon a questionable idea of human personality. The use of questionnaires tends to beg some fundamental questions as to the very nature of personality. If personality is something like the style of a person's life as experienced primarily by other people, then the use of a body of questions addressed to the person at the focus of a personality study is perhaps the least likely to reveal how people 'see themselves as others see them'. Furthermore, the working up of questionnaire results in theories of personality that require that dispositions be inferred from the answers to the questionnaire and then reified as permanent attributes of a person, contrary to basic logical principles.

Gordon Allport (1961) raised a fundamental difficulty with the use of factor analysis to reveal genuine psychologically relevant aspects of personality. Factor analysis, however sophisticated, can do no more than lead to the creation of higher order taxonomic categories. As a method it is *logically* incapable of yielding explanations of why certain people act, speak and think in certain apparently stable and coherent ways.

Lamiell's criticism of individual differences is also germane to this research. (Lamiell, 2003). The point is very simple – individual *differences* are not and could not be the attributes of anyone. Only the actual attributes between which differences exist among different individuals could be explanatory of anything. Personality studies are necessarily idiographic, that is, they provide data that are legitimate only as ascribed to individuals.

The ontological presumptions of trait theories must be kept in mind. What are personalities? We have seen how difficult it has proved for psychologists to master the logic of dispositional properties in relation both to displays of the relevant personal attributes and to hypotheses about their permanent foundations. This comes out most clearly in attempts to tie personalities to attributes of the brain.

All we ever can observe are people acting and thinking, in so far as they are willing to share their thoughts. Each individual acts and thinks in certain characteristic ways. Some individuals seem to think and act similarly to others – but before we can leap to the conclusion that this is because they fall under the same personality, character or temperamental type, we must be satisfied that these personal attributes will be displayed in a similar way and in a reasonable proportion of the kinds of situations in which those people find themselves. It is not enough to show that they do so in the peculiar circumstances of answering personal questions asked by a psychologist. Only if the circumstances for these displays are clear, can we ascribe a disposition or trait to the person who thinks and behaves thus.

From a logical point of view, dispositions can only legitimately be ascribed to something or someone if there is some permanent feature of the being in question in which they are grounded when they are not being displayed. To say that someone behaves in an introverted way because they are an introvert is empty rhetoric.

A more realistic account of personality might go something like this: in these circumstances people tend to act in an introverted manner and in other circumstance in an extraverted manner. Then we have to decide how much of the features of these styles of life are sourced from the immediate environment, say, from seeing what others are doing when in the presence of the dictator or in the reactions of their spouse, and how much is grounded in brain states and processes. Whoever is in charge, this person will behave in a servile manner, or be discreet about boasting of their prowess in the garden.

It is important to be clear about what is *not* being implied by this criticism. It may well be true that when someone is displaying the kind of behavior taken to be indicative of the type to which they belong, that the brain then differs in its state of arousal compared with the level and location of arousal when someone is displaying a different style of thought and behavior. The display to brain process link may be strong, even when the idea of types of persons identified by their personalities is weak. This illustrates once again the fundamental role of the Taxonomic Priority Principle.

In short, personality studies are intrinsically hybrid.

13 Disorders and Treatments

Steven R. Sabat

We schizophrenics say and do a lot of stuff that is unimportant, and then we mix important things in with all this to see if the doctor cares enough to see them and feel them. (Joan, a client of R. D. Laing in Laing, 1965)

Mental illness has been part of human life for millennia. How we have understood it has been related intimately to how we have attempted to help those who have been diagnosed. In this chapter, I will explore two different, contrasting approaches to understanding and treating mental disorders.

The first approach, grounded initially in medicine and, more recently, also in neuroscience, entails the view that the root problem of mental illness is biological and is based primarily in the brain. For example, Magnetic Resonance Imagery (MRI) studies have indicated that some people, especially men, diagnosed with schizophrenia have enlarged ventricles in their brains. The cerebral ventricles are spaces in the brain in which cerebrospinal fluid is found. This may mean that there is an abnormal lack of brain tissue, either due to loss of cells during one's life, or to a lack of those cells from the beginning (Lawrie & Abukmeil, 1998; Nopoulos, Flaum, & Andreasen, 1997). In addition, when the brains of people diagnosed with schizophrenia are examined during autopsies, missing or abnormally sized neurons have been found in the frontal and temporal lobes (Black & Andreasen, 1994). Presumably, the lack of these brain cells affect brain function as a whole so that the brains of such persons work in abnormal ways. Functional magnetic resonance imaging (fMRI) studies have indicated abnormal functioning in the brains of people diagnosed with schizophrenia (Carter, Mintun, Nichols, & Cohen, 1997; Chua & McKenna, 1995).

The second approach, a 'meaning-based' approach, involves a very different way of thinking about and understanding mental disorders. Rather than focusing solely on biological aspects and possible abnormalities in the brain, this view recognizes that people are more than their brains and that understanding how their brains are built (neuroanatomy) and how their brains work (neurophysiology) is not the same as understanding what people experience in their daily lives. In other words, what we understand in the language of neuroanatomy and neurophysiology is very different from what we understand when we examine what people say and do, their discourse. The major point is that we cannot hope to understand the content and the meaning of a person's experience solely by examining the neuroanatomy and neurophysiology of that person's brain. And if we cannot understand the meaning of a person's experience (be it 'normal' or 'disordered') in terms of how his or her brain is built and how it works, we cannot hope to figure out what to do to help a person if his or her experience is 'disordered' simply by trying to alter, by using drugs, the way the person's brain works. How a person's brain works can be altered by pharmaceuticals (drugs), but drugs are not the only means by which brain physiology and a person's experience can be changed. Another, very powerful but not well understood, means of change involves a person's expectations and beliefs and is demonstrated very clearly by the placebo effect.

What we expect, what we hope, what we fear, can produce physiological changes in the brain. Thus, people who expect that the pill they've been given will make them feel better, often feel better even though the pill they were given contained no active ingredient whatsoever. Interestingly enough, the placebo effect has been found to vary in different cultures, with Brazilians showing virtually no effect, but Germans showing a very strong placebo effect. Placebo effects seem to be more powerful if the pills are expensive and taken a number of times during each day, and more powerful if one's physician believes in them (Moerman, 2002; Shapiro & Shapiro, 1997). So what people *believe* can have a very strong influence on what they experience and how their bodies work. That is why a 'meaning-based' approach to psychology is so important – we need to understand what people are experiencing and what they believe and we cannot do that unless we interact with them person-to-person in a way that goes beyond examining how their brains work. That is to say, in order to understand mental disorders and how to treat them, a meaning-based approach requires that we do more than simply describe the disorder and treat it solely as a biological phenomenon.

Among our earliest theories about mental illness was that evil spirits possessed persons by affecting their brains, thereby producing the pathological behavior displayed. If it were true, then, that evil spirits were lodged in the person's brain, it followed that in order to relieve the person of this affliction, the evil spirits needed an exit – that was then provided via a method called trephining, which was the purposeful making of holes in the afflicted person's skull. Alternatively, the person was starved or treated in another very discomforting way in hopes that such treatment would cause the occupying spirits to be uncomfortable and thereby encourage them to leave the body they inhabited.

Closer to our own time, during the Middle Ages, mental illness became understood as a type of disease that was similar to other physical illnesses that were caused by some germicidal problem (Allderidge, 1979). Accordingly, people diagnosed with mental illness were incarcerated in special hospitals that were hardly supportive of healthy psychological life. People were, in the words of Foucault (1965, p. 72), '... chained like dogs ... and separated from keepers and visitors alike by a long corridor protected by an iron grille ...'. This 'treatment' also included being forced to sleep on straw covered floors and this was thought to be logical because such people were viewed as being nothing more than 'wild beasts' and so should be treated as such. Indeed, curiosity seekers could visit such hospitals and, for a small fee, view the inmates much as a person would view animals in a zoo. It wasn't until the late 18th Century that Phillipe Pinel instituted reforms in the Paris hospital system so that the inmates were no longer chained and were allowed to go outside.

However, people who were thought to be mentally ill were still assumed to have a physical disease that produced the accompanying mental alterations such as delusions (a person claiming to be Jesus, for example). In keeping with the idea that mental illness was fundamentally like any other physical illness, its understanding became part of the domain of medicine and a medical model of mental disorders evolved. This model asserts that:

- **Mental illness is like any other illness with an organic problem at its root.**
- **The treatment consists of the administration of drugs and psychotherapy.**
- **Treatment is provided in a 'patient-physician' relationship.**

Also part of this approach to mental illness is the description, or classification, of different types of illnesses in terms of their 'signs' (how the 'patient' behaves) and 'symptoms' (the 'patient's' complaints). This is in accordance with the approach taken by physicians to understand physical illnesses. There are two different classification approaches, developed in the latter half of the 20th century, in which the signs and symptoms of each form of mental illness are detailed and each illness is thus described. These two approaches are: (1) the *International Classification of Disease System* (ICD-10), published by the World Health Organization; and (2) *The Diagnostic and Statistical Manual of Mental Disorders* (DSM), published by the American Psychiatric Association and used widely in the US. The DSM has undergone several revisions since the first edition was published in 1952 and, at present, the DSM-IV, revised in 2000, is the standard classification scheme. This manual is essentially devoid of theoretical efforts to explain why a person experiences this or that mental illness. Rather, it is focused on the signs and symptoms of each of the approximately 400 disorders identified, the prevalence in the population, and other demographic features. In what may be an unintended irony, this approach is 'depersonalized', because there is no human face, as it were, on any of the mental illnesses that are described in the DSM. There are only abstract clinical descriptions of each illness and so this approach is essentially what mental illness is like 'on the outside'. People who are diagnosed with mental illness are called 'patients' so that we frequently see references to 'schizophrenic patients' or 'dementia patients' rather than people diagnosed with this or that condition. I shall address this issue more fully later in this chapter, but for now suffice it to say that if we refer to someone as a 'patient', and if we are not physicians, we are compromising the person's social standing and social identity and thereby may be indirectly contributing to or exacerbating the person's problems.

More specifically, the DSM uses five so-called 'axes' to guide the clinician in making a diagnosis. Axes I and II refer to the person's present psychological condition in that Axis I includes clinical problems (e.g. depression), while Axis II includes problems such as developmental disorders (e.g. learning disabilities) and dependencies on drugs. Axis III includes factors that could contribute to the person's present psychological condition (e.g. chronic pain), Axis IV includes social or environmental difficulties and Axis V is the overall, or global, assessment of how well the person is coping. Let us now examine how the medical model of mental illness is revealed in our understanding of one of the most serious and widespread of mental illnesses, schizophrenia.

Schizoprenia

An example of the influence of the medical model and classification scheme can be found in the way schizophrenia is described. It was originally named *dementia praecox* by Emil Kraepelin and given its present name by Eugen Bleuler. A serious mental illness, schizophrenia interferes tremendously with a person's ability to meet the ordinary demands of everyday life. Among the reasons for this is that the person experiences hallucinations and delusions. Hallucinations are blatantly false sensory experiences. The person in question hears voices that no one else hears, sees things or people that no one else sees. Auditory hallucinations seem to be reported more frequently than visual hallucinations and auditory hallucinations of the verbal type have been found to be accompanied by increased blood flow to Broca's area, the area of the brain involved in the motor aspects of speech (McGuire, Murray, & Shah, 1993). This area of the brain also shows increased activity when people who are not diagnosed talk to themselves silently, as we all do at times. Delusions, on the other hand, are blatantly false beliefs. According to Charlish and Cutting (1995), 90 percent of all people diagnosed with schizophrenia experience delusions. Thus, a person will claim to be Jesus or someone other than who he or she happens to be. In such cases, a person may also show evidence of what are called ideas of reference, in which a rather prosaic occurrence, such as a television commercial for toothpaste, is believed to have been directed specifically at him or her and is laden with deep meaning. People who behave in this way are deemed psychotic and it is assumed that they have 'lost contact with reality'. It is further assumed that those defined as 'healthy' have the ability to decide what is real or not real for others. This point is not meant to provoke amusement, but is quite a serious matter that I shall take up later in this chapter.

Also found among the abnormalities associated with schizophrenia is what is often referred to as disorganized speech, or loose associations. It seems as if the speaker has no coherent train of thought, but behaves in a stream-of-consciousness manner in which seemingly irrelevant thoughts and sensory experiences are brought into the mix of what the person says or writes. One of Bleuler's patients exhibited this in a letter, part of which is as follows:

> I am writing on paper. The pen I am using is from a factory called 'Perry & Co.' This factory is in England. I assume this. Behind the name of Perry & Co., the city of London is inscribed; but not the city. The city of London is in England. I know this from my school-days. Then, I always liked geography. My last teacher in that subject was Professor August A. He was a man with black eyes. I also like black eyes. There are also blue and gray eyes and other sorts too. I have heard it said that snakes have green eyes. All people have eyes. There are some, too, who are blind. (Bleuler, 1911, p. 17)

Although listed as a 'sign' of schizophrenia, there is no discussion about what such loose associations, in speech for example, might accomplish for the diagnosed person. Such a discussion would logically assume that talking in this manner was not 'caused' by the illness in the same way that red spots on the skin are caused by the independently identifiable biogenic agent in what we call 'measles'. There are no regular antecedent conditions, nor any known mechanisms that link kinds of talking. That is to say, there may be, from another perspective on mental illness, some goal-directed activity that is reflected in what is called 'loose associations' or 'disorganized speech', and I shall address this matter in a subsequent section of the chapter. Someone is trying to say something!

There are different forms of schizophrenia as defined by their signs and symptoms. For example, there is 'simple schizophrenia' in which the person so diagnosed lives what seems to be a hermit-like existence, is apathetic about his or her personal appearance and hygiene, often wears tattered, soiled clothing, lives on the streets and refrains from social interaction with others beyond a superficial level. Another, more serious, form of schizophrenia is called 'catatonic schizophrenia'. People diagnosed with this form of schizophrenia may behave in one of two different ways. There is the 'inhibitory' type of catatonia in which the person does not speak or otherwise interact with people in any social way, may remain in one position for a long period of time without moving, and is therefore apparently withdrawn from the world. Seemingly opposite to the inhibitory type, there is the 'excitatory' type of catatonia in which the person speaks quite animatedly although seemingly without coherent meaning or content; this kind of speech is often described as a 'word salad'. In each of these manifestations, the person is said to be 'inaccessible' to others in that it is very difficult to know what he or she is thinking and feeling. And to complicate things further, some people diagnosed with schizophrenia may exhibit 'inappropriate affect' in that they will appear to be happy when the more appropriate reaction to a situation would be sadness, or they'll appear to be sad when healthy people in the same situation would respond with signs of happiness. The inappropriateness of the display is clearly a daunting problem for the person diagnosed as well as for healthy others to understand and it is no wonder that our attempts to unravel how it is that people come to be this way have revealed great complexity as well.

What Are the Conditions that Favor the Onset of Schizophrenia?

This question inspires a multiplicity of responses that include a person's genetic endowment, the pre-and post-natal environment in which the person grew, and the possible involvement of brain structure and function. In terms of genetics, studies of twins are suggestive: if one of a pair of identical twins is diagnosed with schizophrenia, the likelihood that the other will be so diagnosed is between 25–50 percent, whereas if the twins are fraternal, the probability is between 10–15 percent (Gottesman, 1991). Still, it is not possible to separate completely the effects of genetics and environment and the environment includes the uterus as well as aspects of the outside world after the child is born.

Researchers have identified a number of possible environmental factors including birth complications such as a lowered oxygen supply that might affect the infant's brain and its subsequent development (Cannon, Rosso, Hollister, Bearden, & Sanchez, 2000) as well as possible viruses during pregnancy (Brown, Cohen, Harkavy-Friedman, & Babulas, 2001). This points to the idea that schizophrenia is a developmental disorder that further environmental stressors may exacerbate. The idea that a combination of genetic and environmental interactions is critical is reflected in what is known as the diathesis-stress model (Zubin & Spring, 1977) wherein certain factors such as a genetic component, the diathesis, create a risk for a disorder and another set of factors in the environment, the stress component that could include a traumatic experience, triggers the onset of the disorder. Both factors are required according to this model. So if there is a combination of a diathesis and a stress, what happens to bring about the onset of the signs and symptoms?

One proposal is that there are alterations in the neurotransmitters in the person's brain, specifically in dopamine, for the neural networks that involve dopamine show exceptionally high levels of activity in people diagnosed with schizophrenia. Accordingly, drug treatments (such as Haldol) that block the activity of dopamine receptors in the brain relieve many of the symptoms (Snyder, 1976). Still, there are multiple neurotransmitters involved and so the effects of a diathesis and a stress are likely to be tremendously complex and these, along with some structural abnormalities, may give rise to problems with sensory processing as well as executive functioning (Green, Kern, Braff, & Mintz, 2000). It should be clear by now that unraveling the mystery that is schizophrenia is not a simple task and this is further complicated by the fact that there is great variation from person to person in terms of signs and symptoms, how they respond to drug treatments, and in prognosis.

Thus far, we have encountered schizophrenia in an abstract way. That is, we have been talking about the 'illness the person has'. This approach is a logical outgrowth of a 19th- and 20th-century medical approach to understanding mental illness. Notice that we have not discussed any person at all in the previous pages, only the illness and how it 'presents itself', as if it were a living being. This is what it means to understand something from the 'outside'. Clearly, this approach alone does not provide us with a rich understanding of the person who is diagnosed and what life is like for him or her on the 'inside', and so it is to this aspect of schizophrenia that we now turn our attention.

Schizophrenia from the Inside

Trying to understand the 'person the illness has' is quite different from trying to understand the 'illness the person has', for we need to have a great deal of interaction with the person in order to know, or to attempt to know, life as he or she experiences it on an ongoing basis. Among the first to provide us with an insight into the subjective experience of the person diagnosed with schizophrenia was the Scottish psychiatrist, R. D. Laing, through what he called the existential phenomenological approach. Laing proposed a number of what were considered rather radical ideas about the importance of the social world in the lives of people diagnosed with schizophrenia. Among them was the notion that it is of great import that we, those deemed healthy, accept the idea that what is real to the person diagnosed with schizophrenia, is quite real to them, even if it's not real to us. So to tell such a person that 'there's no one there' in response to him or her saying, 'I see Jesus standing in the doorway', is to deny the reality of that experience to the person speaking. We cannot deny the existence of another person's private experience; we cannot tell a person that he or she is wrong when saying things like, 'I feel cold in this room.' What might be called a hallucination, is quite real to the person who claims to see Jesus standing in the doorway and we must respect that his or her reality may be quite different from ours. So to say that a person 'has lost contact with reality' is an incoherent statement from Laing's point of view. More accurately, from Laing's point of view, one might say that the person has lost contact with 'our reality'. If we are interested in treating the person so diagnosed, it is vitally important that we engage him or her in a trusting relationship and that requires that we appreciate the world from his or her point of view. This is true of any social relationship between people. We have trusted friends because we believe, in part, that they understand and respect our point of view – how we think and feel about things. From Laing's vantage point, the same dynamics need to be applied to people diagnosed with schizophrenia.

R. D. Laing (1927–1989) was the only child of a middle-class family in Glasgow. He graduated in medicine from Glasgow University, and was immediately called up for military service. It was then he began to develop his interest in people with psychiatric problems. He became very well known as a Scottish psychiatrist who wrote extensively on mental illness, publishing the widely read book *The divided self* (1965). Laing's views on the causes and treatment of serious mental dysfunction, greatly influenced by existential philosophy, opposed the mainstream orthodoxy of contemporary psychiatry, even though he never denied the existence of mental illness. He believed that the expressed feelings of individual patients or clients were valid descriptions of their lived experience rather than simply symptoms of some separate or underlying disorder. Although Laing was associated with the anti-psychiatry movement, he rejected the label. At the same time, however, he recognized that the definition of mental illness was equivocal in many ways and questioned the use of drugs alone as a way to treat mental illness. Rather, he believed in using the person's ability for 'relatedness' to achieve therapeutic ends.

Most of his career was spent in London at various clinics and in collaboration with a number of different people. His family life was chaotic. His three marriages were difficult.

A striking illustration of this important point and of how a person's experience and behavior may be interpreted is presented in Laing's book, *The divided self* (1965), in which he presents Emil Kraepelin's account, to a lecture room of his students, of one of his patients showing the signs of catatonic excitement:

The patient I will show you today has almost to be carried into the rooms, as he walks in a straddling fashion on the outside of his feet … He is eighteen years old … with a pale complexion on which there is often a transient flush. The patient sits with his eyes shut and pays no attention to his surroundings. He does not look up even when spoken to, but he answers beginning in a low voice and gradually screaming louder and louder. When asked where he is, he says, 'You want to know that too? I tell you who is being measured and shall be measured. I know all that, and could tell you, but I do not want to.' When asked his name he screams 'What is your name? What does he shut? He shuts his eyes. What does he hear? He does not understand; he understands not. How? Who? Where? … You don't whore for me … Are you getting impudent still more?' At the end, he scolds in quite inarticulate sounds. (pp. 29–30)

Kraepelin notes the patient's *inaccessibility*: 'Although he undoubtedly understood all the questions, he has not given us a single piece of useful information. His talk was … only a series of disconnected sentences having no relation to the general situation' (Kraepelin, 1905, pp. 79–80).

Laing does not deny that the person was clearly showing the 'signs' of catatonic excitement, but he opens up the possibility that there is more than one way to interpret what the young man was saying here. Where Kraepelin asserts that the patient has given us no useful information, Laing asserts the opposite. Of course, this hinges completely on what one defines as being 'useful'. To Kraepelin, useful meant receiving answers to his questions and since the patient didn't answer his questions, but instead engaged in a diatribe of catatonic excitement, there was no useful information given. But to Laing, there is more to the patient's outburst than Kraepelin alleged.

Let us examine the situation from the beginning in order to understand what Laing is seeing here. Recall that Kraepelin is 'presenting a patient' to a lecture room filled with students and that Kraepelin noted that the boy had a pale complexion but often showed a 'transient flush'. The 'patient' is 18 years old, not very different in age from the students in the room and he is being used, as it were, as a demonstration aid. What, do you suppose is the nature of the 'transient flush' on his face? Might he be blushing out of embarrassment or humiliation? It is hardly far-fetched to admit to that possibility and if the boy does feel embarrassed at being treated akin to a circus animal, surely he is not going to be happy about being placed in that position, nor would he feel as if this situation is of any help to him. Given these possibilities, it is hardly a stretch to assume that he might be angry about being used in this manner and so his exasperation is revealed, according to Laing, in what he says to Kraepelin by mimicking the renowned psychiatrist and then saying, 'You don't whore for me?' That is, he is saying that he is not going to prostitute himself by behaving like a circus animal for the benefit of a lecture room full of students. Laing sees not only catatonic excitement in the boy's outburst, but also his objecting to the way he is being treated. He is not interested in being measured and tested, but wants to be helped, to be heard, to be engaged with as a person and not perceived as a 'visual aid' or some kind of classroom demonstration.

Emil Kraepelin (1856–1926) was born in Neustrelitz in Germany. He began medical studies in Wurzberg, then moving to Leipzig where he came under the influence of Wilhelm Wundt. Becoming disillusioned with Wundt's experimental methods, he decided to turn to psychiatry. He won a prize for an essay on the treatment of mental illness. On graduation in 1878 he moved to Munich as an assistant to Johann von Gudden. Even then he turned more to understanding the causes of mental illness than their content. Among these causes he picked out tobacco and alcohol. Later, in his own clinic, he invented a soft drink, Kraepelinsaft, which he insisted on giving to patients, staff and visitors alike. However, he realized that psychiatric medicine lacked a sound system for the classification of mental illnesses.

He completed his 'Habilitation' in 1883, and was appointed as a professor in the university.

At the age of 15, he became engaged to Ina Schwabe, and they married in 1885. After another short spell in Munich he became director of a clinic near Breslau in Silesia. At this point he began the publication of his ideas on the classification of mental illnesses that became the *Compendium of psychiatry*. He then took up a post in Leipzig but became embroiled in a 'turf war' that erupted between Wilhelm Wundt and Paul Flechsig over the use of laboratory space. He went to Estonia, and after some years in Tartu, he returned to Munich, appointing Alois Alzheimer as his assistant, becoming director of the Deutsche Forshungsanstalt fur Psychiatrie. He retired from this post in 1922.

Laing's point is that when we view this young man only through the lenses of psychiatric nomenclature, we see someone being uncooperative, aggressive, and pathological, who is not providing us with useful information. If, however, we look at him from an existential-phenomenological viewpoint, we see him as a person placed in what would be an embarrassing situation for any of us, a very different picture. Indeed, *not* objecting to being embarrassed is, itself, worrisome. From this point of view, his objection is a sign of health, even though his way of expressing his objection is complicated by his mental/emotional problems. So, at the very least, the young man is acting as a semiotic subject: a person whose actions are driven by the meaning of the situation he is experiencing (Shweder & Sullivan, 1989). So, in spite of his mental illness, the young man is still able to comprehend and experience a social situation as being threatening to his sense of self-worth. Such a person would require a different sort of treatment than would someone who was thought to be incapable of understanding at this level of thought and emotion.

So in the above situation, there is a type of logic to the actions taken by the boy diagnosed with catatonic excitement. Might there be a similar logic in other signs of mental illness? From Laing's point of view, the answer to such a question would be a clear 'yes'. The following can serve as an example from the realm of delusions.

Recall that a delusion is a blatantly false belief. Suppose a person says such things as, 'I am made of glass' and 'I am an unreal man'. Saying that one is made of glass is incorrect, for persons' bodies are made of flesh and bone and sinew. Laing, however, approaches these statements not literally, but figuratively. The person who utters these sentences is, according to Laing, experiencing a conflict similar to one that each of us experiences at one or another time in life: the desire to reveal himself and the desire to conceal himself. Most of us deal with this conflict in a more or less satisfactory way. Doing so, however, depends on our ability to experience ourselves as beings who have private thoughts and reactions that no one else knows about unless we choose to share them. He asks us to recall how there was a time in our lives when it was otherwise, when we believed that our parents could read our minds, see right through us, as it were. What was it that allowed us to stop believing that our parents could read our minds? Laing (1965) asserts, … 'what an accomplishment it was when we, in fear and trembling, could tell our first lie and make … the discovery that … within the territory of ourselves there can be only our footprints' (p. 37).

So when we were able to tell a lie without being detected as lying, we learned that we have privacy of thought. Some people do not learn this and so they never feel fully private and, as a result, they feel more exposed and more vulnerable to others than we do. It is this person who says, 'I am made of glass', meaning that he feels transparent, fragile, breakable, that people know by looking at him, what he is thinking and feeling. At the same time, however, he yearns for privacy and so he '... learnt to cry when he was amused and to smile when he was sad. He frowned his approval and applauded his displeasure' (p. 37). So these actions are not his real self and he is, therefore, unreal. Everything that he has done is somehow logical in light of the original faulty premise (that he has no privacy). What does Laing assert about other signs of schizophrenia?

Recall that Kraepelin noted the boy's inaccessibility. From Laing's point of view, the person feels tremendously vulnerable. Therefore, just as when most of us feel that way, there is a great need to be sure that others can be trusted before revealing all that one wishes to reveal. One of Laing's patients, Joan, gives us great insight into her thought process:

> We schizophrenics say and do a lot of stuff that is unimportant, and then we mix important things in with all this to see if the doctor cares enough to see them and feel them … The patients … try to please the doctor but also confuse him so he won't go into anything important. When you find people who will really help, you don't need to distract them. You can act in a normal way. I can sense if the doctor not only wants to help but also can and will help. (pp. 164–165)

So what might be termed inaccessibility is a way of behaving so as to keep others at a distance until they can be trusted. One can keep others at a distance by being totally unresponsive (inhibitory catatonia) or by uttering a diatribe that doesn't allow the other person to engage in conversation (excitatory catatonia). In both cases, the person diagnosed with schizophrenia acts in accordance with the meaning the situation has for him or her. Therefore, one can view the same behavior as being solely pathological or as being meaning-driven and propelled logically given the person's premises about trusting the physician.

Joan provides yet another insight for us when she says:

> The patient is terribly afraid of his own problems, since they have destroyed him, so he feels terribly guilty for allowing the doctor to get mixed up in the problems. The patient is convinced that the doctor will be smashed too … The doctor must fight his way in; then the patient doesn't have to feel guilty. (p. 167)

So the 'inaccessibility' of the diagnosed person may not be without strategic meaning and, therefore, is a form of goal-directed behavior. Clear also in this example is the idea that it is possible to interpret the same behavior as either pathological or as meaning-driven. Which interpretation is employed may well depend upon how the diagnosed person is positioned by others (Harré & van Langenhove, 1999). In other words, if we see the person solely as a 'patient', our expectations of that person will be such that what the person does and says will be seen in light of the diagnosis so as to confirm the storyline that emphasizes pathology in the actions of the person in question. This phenomenon was illustrated in a striking way by Rosenhan (1973) in his examination of the basic tenets of the medical model.

Is Mental Illness 'In' the Person?

Recall that from the standpoint of the medical model, mental illness is something that a person has, much in the same way that a person can have malaria. Rosenhan argued that if this were true, then mental illness should be detectable in a person who has it and normality should be likewise detectable. Rosenhan and seven other normal people presented themselves as pseudopatients at various hospitals in different states in the US. Each pseudopatient phoned the hospital in question for an appointment and arrived at admissions complaining of hearing unfamiliar voices that were of the same gender as the pseudopatient and that said things like, 'thud', 'empty', 'hollow'. Although each pseudopatient used an assumed name and falsified his or her occupation, all significant life events and histories were given accurately. Each pseudopatient was admitted to the hospital's psychiatric ward and immediately behaved normally. Each, except for one, was admitted with a diagnosis of schizophrenia. If they had any concern at all, it was that they would be exposed as frauds. Each kept a journal of his or her observations on the ward. None of the pseudopatients was detected as being normal by the staff and all who were diagnosed with schizophrenia were eventually discharged with a diagnosis of 'schizophrenia in remission'.

Although the staff did not recognize the pseudopatients as being normal, 35 of the 118 patients on the ward voiced their suspicions by saying things such as, 'You're not crazy, you're a journalist or a professor. You're checking up on the hospital.' On the other hand, the staff already positioned the pseudopatients as having a psychiatric problem and so they interpreted what they witnessed in pathological terms. For example, nursing records for three pseudopatients indicated that the note taking was viewed as pathological: 'Patient engages in compulsive writing behavior', even though this activity was never questioned directly. One of the pseudopatients was an acknowledged expert on depression and had conversations about depression with staff members. In his chart, staff notes indicated that he had a very intellectualized form of depression. The fact that expectations and positioning can have such powerful effects on the ability to distinguish mental illness from sanity calls into question the validity of the medical model and compels us to think about the social and cultural determinants of mental illness.

Culture and Mental Illness

The DSM-IV acknowledges in an appendix that mental illness has a social and cultural component. There is not a great deal of space devoted to this aspect of mental illness, but in recent years it has become clear that some disorders are found only in this or that culture at particular times in history (Shorter, 1986). Indeed, according to Shorter, it seems that culture affects the expression of mental illnesses as they have been, until recently, strikingly different from place to place. What has happened in recent years according to some researchers (Lee & Lee, 2000; Watters, 2010) is that there has been a globalization of the US notions of mental illness. By the second half of the 1990s, between 3 and 10 percent of young women in Hong Kong experienced eating disorders and reported that fat phobia was the main reason for their intentional starvation. This stood in stark contrast to the 1980s and early 1990s when women in Hong Kong did not intentionally diet or experience a phobia about fat, but complained instead of having bloated stomachs. The influx of information in the mass media about anorexia during the intervening years was dominated by the US diagnostic manuals, and within a decade there was a striking increase in women reporting that they were experiencing the Western version of anorexia. Lee and Watters suggest, on the basis of such information, that expectations and beliefs can shape the experience of the person who is suffering. Just as Rosenhan's work showed that expectations shaped how psychiatric hospital staff interpreted the actions of pseudopatients, it seems that expectations driven by mass media can shape the ways in which people interpret their own experience. Expectations, of course, can be formed by cultural traditions as well, and that is why, according to Watters (2010), mental illness cannot be understood without understanding the larger culture of which the person suffering is a part. Cultures create storylines about mental illness and thereby define the experience as well as the treatment that is considered appropriate. Agreement with this perspective is found in a recent multidisciplinary work (Jenkins & Barrett, 2010) that brings together the perspectives of anthropologists, psychiatrists, psychologists, and historians, and shows that culture plays a huge role in virtually every aspect of schizophrenia, including diagnosis, social responses, stigma, and the outcome of treatment. The authors make clear the idea that the subjective experience of schizophrenia and one's recovery from that condition are connected intimately to the local world of the person diagnosed.

Therefore, according to the contemporary Western conceptualizations at a time when brains are spoken about as if they were persons (Sabat, 2010), mental illness is understandable in terms of neurochemical and neuroanatomical problems in the brain. As noted earlier in this chapter, there are aspects of brain function and structure that have been found to be abnormal in people diagnosed with schizophrenia. What we don't know, however, is whether those abnormalities are the causes or the effects of schizophrenia, in the sense of prior and successive events or states. For a number of reasons, the adoption of the medical model was thought to be an advance over and above earlier conceptualizations of mental illness such as demonic possession. One reason offered was that with the contemporary approaches, the stigma of mental illness would be reduced, if not eliminated because, after all, a person could not be held responsible for having a brain disease. So, has the stigma of mental illness actually been reduced as a result of Western medical conceptualizations of mental illness as brain disease?

Mehta and Farina (1997) investigated this very question in an experiment by having subjects believe that they were taking part in a learning task with a partner who was, unbeknownst to the subjects, a confederate of the investigator. Before the experiment began, the pairs of people (subjects and confederates) conversed and exchanged some autobiographical information, during which time the confederate indicated that he or she suffered from a mental illness. The confederate was instructed to say either that the illness was: (1) a result of things that happened when he or she was a child, or (2) due to a brain disease that affected his or her biochemistry. In the subsequent experiment, the test subject had to teach the confederate a task and when the confederate made a mistake, the subject gave feedback by (supposedly) giving an electric shock that was either 'barely discernible' or 'somewhat painful'. The authors found that the subjects who believed that their partner had a brain disease increased the strength of the shocks at a faster rate than did those who thought their partners had a mental illness that was caused by events in their past. So it may actually be the case that when we believe that a person has a brain disease, we treat him or her more harshly than when we believe a person has a mental illness due to psychosocial problems. Rather than reducing the stigma, Mehta and Farina argue that the medical disease model actually increased the stigma. Might this circumstance have any effect on the recovery from serious mental illness?

A World Health Organization (WHO) study of schizophrenia in 10 countries revealed that:

> … at two-year follow-up, the percentage of cases with full remission after a single episode ranged between 3% in the USA and 54% in India (Jablensky, et al., 1992) … A substantial body of evidence shows a more benign course and better outcome in developing countries (León, 1989; Thara, et al., 1996). This undoubtedly means that environment plays a crucial role as an outcome determinant in schizophrenia. (World Health Organization, 1996, p. 8)

Thus, the WHO data indicate something counterintuitive in that people diagnosed with schizophrenia in developing countries seem to do better over the course of time than do their counterparts in the developed world where important resources such as research universities and pharmaceuticals abound. One possible explanation for these findings can be found in the research of McGruder (2010) who, for a period of years, studied people diagnosed with schizophrenia and their families in Zanzibar, where Swahili spirit possession beliefs are employed to explain the actions of anyone who violates social norms, including those diagnosed with schizophrenia. Those who are diagnosed reside with the family or kinship group rather than in a psychiatric hospital or similar places. Rather than performing exorcisms to cast out such spirits, people in Zanzibar 'coax' the spirits into leaving with food, song, and dance, and this treatment also includes acts of kindness such as writing Koran-based words or phrases on drinking vessels so that the mentally ill person can 'drink' the holy words with whatever liquid is being imbibed. Finally, because the illness is interpreted as something that has its origins outside of the person, it is viewed as an affliction rather than as part of the person's identity.

McGruder is careful to assert that this treatment is not a cure for schizophrenia. Rather, it is a way for maintaining a non-anxious presence, or low 'expressed emotion' in those who surround the person diagnosed. High levels of expressed emotion, in the form of criticism, hostility, and intrusiveness, have been found in 67 percent of US families with a member diagnosed with schizophrenia, but only in 23 percent of Indian families. Interestingly, this is a reflection of a basic difference in cultural attitudes: the US being an individualistic culture, India being more of a collectivist culture. In the US one is thought to be the captain of one's own ship, as it were, but in collectivist cultures, one's identity is more bound up with one's family and kinship groups and ancestors. Indeed, the Zulu concept of *Ubuntu* connotes the idea that 'a person is a person through others'. This is far from the individualistic emphasis in US culture. McGruder sees that families in Zanzibar thereby draw strength from what is a less isolating belief about selfhood in particular and human nature in general. This point of view is not far afield from some of the foundations of family systems theory as proposed by Bowen (1978), who recognized the important role of the family system in mental health. So we can see how the environment, in terms of culture and local kinship groups, can exert a profound effect on the way in which mental illness is viewed, treated, and the degree to which it is ameliorated.

Not all mental disorders are as serious as is schizophrenia, but even in cases of so-called mood disorders, we can see the effects of culture in their conceptualizations and treatment.

Mood Disorders

These are also known as 'affective disorders' as they involve the emotional life of the person. Of these, many have been named and classified, including mania, which can be difficult to distinguish from being extremely upbeat, but is far more obvious when a person stays up night after night, talking about all sorts of things that aren't necessarily connected to one another, and feels omnipotent and euphoric. Its opposite, depression, involves feelings of hopelessness, worthlessness, apathy about life, so that the person loses interest in virtually everything. Suicide can be a real risk, especially if the person seems to be coming out of the depths of depression. Data on the incidence of suicide show that women are three times as likely to attempt suicide as are men, but men are more likely to succeed in their attempts.

Other mood disorders involve, as their primary symptom, anxiety. Whereas generalized anxiety disorders involve the person feeling chronically apprehensive for no apparent reason, always fearing the worst, phobias involve an intense and irrational fear of some object (spiders, or arachnophobia), or situations (closed in places, or claustrophobia, open places, or agoraphobia). Explanations of such phobias have included classical conditioning wherein a neutral object or place is paired with/connected to some fear-producing traumatic experience. Given that, from this perspective, a person has *learned* to be fearful of what he or she knows intellectually is not frightening, one approach to treatment that has been successful is systematic desensitization, wherein the person learns, methodically, to relax in the face of the feared object or situation. The approach is similar to the desensitization approach that is used in the administration of allergy injections to make a person less and less reactive to the allergen.

Traumatic experiences can, however, have long-lasting effects that do not involve an irrational fear of some otherwise neutral object or place. For some people, traumas are long-lasting and if reactions to trauma persist for more than a month and reveal themselves in sleep disturbances, outbursts of anger, difficulties in concentration, a diagnosis of post traumatic stress disorder (PTSD) may be made. Whether or not a person will respond to a traumatic event this way is associated with many factors, including the severity of the trauma, the level of social support the person has, childhood abuse, and whether or not the person has a parent who has experienced PTSD.

As with more serious mental illnesses like schizophrenia, the causes of mood disorders are thought to be heredity, neurochemistry, and one's life experiences. In the US, however, the emphasis on the neurochemical aspects has had profound effects. In 1987, Prozac was approved by the Food and Drug Administration. Between 1988 and 2000, the adult use of anti-depressants almost tripled and by 2005, 10 percent of Americans had been given prescriptions for one or another antidepressant. Why is this happening? Greenberg (2010), a clinical psychologist, asserts that depression is not a mental illness, but, as Laing suggested, rather a sane reaction to an insane world and that part of contemporary US culture is the pathologizing of melancholy and despair and the idea that such feelings are nothing more than a neurochemical problem. Indeed, there is a host of difficulties in life that logically should provoke a response of intense sadness. To feel otherwise, would be 'inappropriate' in psychiatric terms. Yet, the DSM does not prevent such a person from being labeled as disordered. Thus, a person who used to be considered shy, now is diagnosed with 'social anxiety disorder' and will be encouraged, via advertising, to 'ask the doctor' about this or that pharmacological treatment, such as Paxil, so that his or her 'disorder' can be 'treated' with what David Healy (1997) calls 'the pharmacological scalpel'. Here, the logic involved is that if a drug can have an effect on something about a person (being shy), then being shy is, ipso facto, a disorder called social anxiety that requires pharmacological 'treatment'.

Another question that remains unanswered in this approach is fundamental in its importance: Is a condition (depression, shyness, for example) *caused* by some biochemical problem in the brain, an underlying mechanism that links antecendent and subsequent conditions, or is there a *reason* behind a person feeling this or that way? If a person is depressed because they have a brain disease, then there is little purpose in listening to them describe what they consider to be the *reasons* for their feeling as they do – their narratives. As I have noted earlier, we do not know at this point whether or not biochemical changes in the brain are the biological correlates of a psychological state of mind. There is a vast difference between a fact and an hypothesis, yet the hypothesis that states of mind are nothing but brain chemistry has been treated as if it were a fact and that, in turn, has spawned the vast increase in the use of pharmacological treatments. At this point we need to remind ourselves of the radical distinction between the S- and P- grammars for telling a human story, presupposing for many the existence of souls and for all of us the foundations of life in persons, and the O- or organism and M- or molecular grammars that are to be integrated with them in a workable hybrid scheme. The narratives that people provide have not been shown to be without significance. Long ago, Freud noted that it is not possible to discriminate melancholy from mourning simply by observing a person's behavior. One needs to have available the person's *narrative*, a person's story, wherein the differences may then become clear.

Conclusion

Abraham Maslow (1966) noted, 'If the only tool you have is a hammer, you tend to see every problem as a nail.' Human beings are complex. We are biological organisms and we are thoughtful, social, goal-directed agents. To look at persons in only one of these dimensions is to have only a partial understanding. There is nothing wrong with partial understandings as long as we recognize them as being partial. To see the whole person, we require many different methods, different levels of understanding, including biological nature and psychological narrative. This is eminently true with regard to the psychological disorders that people experience and the treatments that are employed for their amelioration. Philosopher Mary Midgely stated it best:

People sometimes say that the human brain is the most complex item in the universe. But the whole person of whom the brain is a part is necessarily a much more complex item than the brain alone. And whole people can't be understood without knowing a good deal both about their inner lives and about the other people around them. Indeed, they can't be understood without a fair grasp of the whole society that they belong to, which is presumably more complex still. (Midgely, 2001, p. 120)

14 Psychology and Justice

Fathali M. Moghaddam

This is a court of law, young man, not a court of justice. (Oliver Wendell Holmes, jr. American judge and jurist, 1841–1935)

Our focus in this chapter is on 'subjective justice', how people think and behave in the realm of 'right' and 'wrong'. This is sometimes referred to as 'commonsense justice', but since how people think and behave can often be contrary to 'common sense', the term 'subjective justice' is more accurate. Subjective justice reflects justice as it actually takes place in the messy 'real world', as opposed to justice as it is 'on the books' according to 'black letter law'. As the quotation from Judge Oliver Wendell Holmes indicates, there is often a gap between justice and what actually happens in the law courts. From this perspective, the law has priorities, such as maintaining social order and stability, which can trump justice. This suggests that the priority given to justice, and ideas about the nature of justice, can vary to some degree across time and cultures. In the medieval era, duty was given higher priority than justice.

Ideas about appropriate punishment have also changed dramatically over the centuries. Until the 20th century, the prison population in Western societies was small, because prison sentences were not seen as appropriate punishment for most crimes. Public flogging, 'trial by fire', and all kinds of other punishments were used; punishments deemed 'unjust' in contemporary Western societies. But there are still cross-cultural variations in how societies punish convicted criminals. For example, a favorite slogan of critics aiming to reform prisons in the United States is: 'Welcome to America, which has 5 percent of the world's population and 25 percent of the world's prison inmates.' The use of prison sentences as punishment and the experience of living in prisons has become far more normative in the United States than it is in the rest of the world.

Imagine Sam, an athletic 26-year-old, is captured trying to cross a national border from country 'A' to country 'B', and authorities discover that she is carrying three pounds of illegal drugs and is wanted for other crimes in both countries. The security guards of both countries help in her capture, which happens exactly on the border, and one guard from each country suffers serious injury in the ensuing violent conflict during the capture. A dispute arises as to which of the two countries should put the accused criminal on trial. In country 'A' she would most likely be sentenced to 25–30 years of jail, and in country 'B' she would probably be sentenced to having her left hand cut off. Each country tries to convince the international community that it has a better system of justice, but there is disagreement as to whether a jail sentence of 25–30 years really is fairer than losing one's left hand. Think about it: perhaps you would rather lose your left hand than to lose 25–30 years of life and end your jail sentence as a much older person? This kind of moral dilemma has led some researchers (e.g. Louis & Taylor, 2004) to argue that justice is relative and varies across cultures, that there is no 'universal justice', and that the most powerful people in each group determine what comes to be generally accepted as 'just'. Thus, a first debate about the psychology of justice concerns whether there are universals in justice, or whether justice is 'situational' and can vary across cultures (Jasso, 2005).

This debate between those who argue that justice is 'situational' and those who propose that there are universals in justice behavior, is related to another historic debate between consequentionists, who argue that justice is or ought to be about the 'greater good', and various deontologists, who propose that certain moral principles must be upheld in all circumstances. For consequentionists, such as John Stuart Mill (1806–1873), the consequences of an action should determine its morality, which makes moral judgment more situational. In contrast, deonologists, such as Emanuel Kant (1724–1804), line up more with a universalist perspective, because they give priority to principles that must be upheld in all conditions.

A second debate concerns the sources of justice, 'where justice comes from'. The traditional debate about the sources of justice has been about two very different categories of explanation. The first category, referred to as natural law theory, has longer historical roots, and assumes that 'the laws of justice' are derived from divine, natural sources and discovered by humans. For example, a religious believer might claim that 'the laws of justice come from God'. An alternative view, known as positive law theory, proposes that the laws of justice are human constructions and change (at least to some degree) over time and across cultures. These two viewpoints have very different implications. If the laws of justice come from a divine source, then they can be changed by the same divine source but not by humans. If they are constructed by humans, then humans can change them to fit changing circumstances and needs.

Positive law is the prevailing viewpoint of contemporary researchers, but within this perspective there are considerable variations. While some researchers look to societal conditions and cultural narratives to explain conceptions of justice, others look more to processes internal to individuals. In recent years there has emerged a fascinating new line of neuroscience research, exploring how and where in the brain decisions about justice work (e.g. Greene & Haidt, 2002; Young & Saxe, 2008). Are there particular 'justice centers' in the brain, and more broadly, what is the role of the brain in justice behavior?

In the first part of this chapter, we discuss a universalist-rational approach to justice. From this perspective, moral development progresses stage-wise, from the highest to the lowest. Those individuals who reach the highest form of moral judgment apply justice principles universally, meaning they are consistent across contexts. We critically assess this 'stage' approach to moral development and further explore the idea of universals in justice behavior.

In the second major section of the chapter, we will consider the idea that humans have a 'need' for justice, and that this 'need' has certain consequences. According to traditional research, this 'need for justice' results in individuals interpreting the world as just, even when on objective criteria they are not being treated in a just way. Much of the research in this domain (implicitly at least) endorses the idea that decision making on justice issues is irrational; that is, people are making decisions without necessarily being aware of why or how they reached a particular decision. Thus, for example, on objective criteria Ashraf is treated unfairly: she lives in Iran, which is a dictatorship that is particularly repressive toward women. Although Ashraf has an extremely high IQ and was top of her university class, she is unable to find work in Iran suitable for her high qualifications, because of government sponsored bias against women. According to traditional research on 'the justice motive' (following the tradition established by Lerner, 1980), Ashraf interprets the world so as to make things 'look fair'. As I will show later in this chapter, this traditional view has some serious limitations.

In the third main section of the chapter, we will review evidence showing that the human sense of justice has long evolutionary roots, and that there are some very basic 'foundational' universals in human justice. Exciting research is being done to demonstrate that chimpanzees and some other animals manifest behaviors that reflect what we typically consider to be a sense of justice (Bekoff, 2005; de Waal, 1996). Given the evolutionary roots of our sense of justice, it is not surprising that our justice decisions are also reflected in brain processes, and that 'morality and the brain' has become a focus of neuroscience research (e.g. Young & Saxe, 2008). Thus, following the discussion of the evolutionary roots of justice behavior, we will discuss the emerging neuroscience research on moral judgments.

We end by reviewing the narrative explanation of justice, interpreting justice as what is seen by people in a time and place to be the most correct way of constructing, using and judging stories about right and wrong.

The Universalist-Rationalist Approach Inspired by Kohlberg

The most influential psychologist in the domain of moral thinking and justice has been Lawrence Kohlberg (1927–1987). Kohlberg's (1963, 1976) approach was in at least two major ways influenced by the scholarship of Jean Piaget (see Chapter 6 of this book). First, following Piaget, Kohlberg focused on rational problem solving. He presented participants with moral dilemmas and assessed how well they solved the dilemmas, rather like a problem on the SAT exam might be solved. Second, like Piaget, Kohlberg adopted a stage model of development, but with a narrower focus; Piaget's stage model encompasses cognitive development broadly, Kohlberg's stage model encompasses moral development specifically.

Lawrence Kohlberg (1927–1987) was born in Bronxville, New York, and studied psychology at the University of Chicago. From early on, he focused particularly on moral development and justice. Although he is best known for his research with children, his theory of moral development has important implications for adults, and his work also extended to the applied domain.

Kohlberg first developed his stage-wise model of moral development while at the University of Chicago, and expanded the model when he joined the faculty of Harvard University. The fame of his model was only increased when it came under attack from his Harvard colleague

(Continued)

Carol Gilligan, who argued that Kohlberg had neglected the moral voice of females, which she claimed is different. Kohlberg ventured to extend his ideas into the practical arena by developing model 'just communities' within institutional contexts, such as schools and prisons. The goal of 'just communities' was to nurture moral growth by having open dialogue about differences and conflicts, and resolving disputes through the intervention of trusted others. Particularly through dialogue with others who had reached a higher moral stage, the person would be able to grow morally.

Kohlberg also explored variations in justice systems across cultures, and it is believed that during a trip to Belize in 1971 he contracted a tropical disease. Unfortunately this disease had serious detrimental health consequences, and he suffered both physical and mental health problems for the rest of his life. His death came when he took leave from the hospital where he was being treated, drove to the coast, and drowned in the Atlantic Ocean.

In terms of research methodology, whereas Piaget studied cognitive development by direct observation (mostly of his own children), Kohlberg presented participants with hypothetical scenarios about moral dilemmas, and analyzed the reasoning they used to solve the dilemmas. For example, consider the case of a man whose wife falls fatally ill. The medication she needs to recover is offered for sale by a druggist at one of the pharmacies in town, but it is too expensive for the husband to purchase. Should the husband break into the pharmacy and steal the drug so as to try to save the life of his wife?

Kohlberg adopted a stage-model to interpret the reasoning participants used to justify their solutions to the dilemma. Some participants based their solutions on punishments and rewards (e.g. 'He should not steal the drug, because he will get caught and go to jail' or 'As long as he can get away with it, he should go ahead and break into the pharmacy'); these individuals are categorized as 'pre-conventional' thinkers. A second 'more advanced' group come to a solution by reference to 'the law' (e.g. 'It is against the law to steal, so he should not do it' or 'If the law lets him get away with it, then he should steal the drug'); these are 'conventional thinkers'. A third group use principles to arrive at a solution (e.g. 'It is never right to steal, so he should not break into the pharmacy' or 'Life always has the highest value, so he is duty-bound to break in, take the drug, and save a life'); these individuals are labeled post-conventional or principled thinkers. Kohlberg assumed that post-conventional thinking is the highest form of moral reasoning, and pre-conventional (which goes according to 'punishment and reward') is the lowest.

An initial criticism against Kohlberg was that his model does not tap into the more 'communal', 'care' style of moral thinking. Some feminist researchers argued that women solve moral dilemmas in a more communal, 'inter-dependent' manner, based on an ethics of care, and Kohlberg's dilemmas are designed more for men, who make moral judgments in a different manner, based on abstract universal rules of justice (Gilligan, 1982). Another criticism has been that the moral dilemmas provide data that can be interpreted subjectively in different ways, and more objective measures of moral reasoning are needed. In response to these and other criticisms, researchers have tried to develop more objective measures of moral reasoning appropriate for both women and men (James, Narvaez, Bebeau, & Thoma, 1999). The weight of expert opinion now is that styles of moral problem solving can be 'communal' and 'care based' among both men and women, and that gender differences are less pronounced than Gilligan (1982) and others first claimed.

An example of a study that supports this line of thinking was conducted by Ryan and others in the context of the Australian National University, the top research university of Australia (Ryan, David, & Reynolds, 2004). Students were presented with a moral dilemma involving another student from a much lower status educational institution who desperately needed a book: Would the 'elite' students go against their university rules and borrow this book from their library on behalf of the student from the lower status institution? Participants were 'primed' before this task in three different ways. Group one was primed by being asked to think about gender stereotypes; group two was primed to put themselves in the shoes of students from the lower status institution; group three were primed by reminding them of their membership in the top research university in Australia. While there were gender differences in moral judgments among group one, with women adopting a 'care', 'communal' approach more often, in group three both males and females adopted such a 'care' based moral reasoning. These findings suggest that how we think of ourselves in any given situation can lead to different 'care based' and 'justice based' moral reasoning.

Related to this is research suggesting that even the traditional finding that women are more 'empathic' than men can change when men and women are primed with different expectations. In a study using the Interpersonal Perception Task (IPT), a test of social sensitivity, female and male participants were primed to either expect men to do worse than women, or men to do as well as women (Koenig & Eagly, 2005). As predicted, men showed themselves to be 'less sensitive' when they had been told that previous research results showed such a trend. It is almost as if the male participants were being told: be a man, be insensitive! In addition to contextual factors influencing empathy and other behaviors related to justice, there is the issue of personal ideology. This relates to the possibility that Kohlberg's foundational assumption is incorrect: the key issue is not about the *ability* to solve moral problems in particular ways, but the *interest* to do so.

Ideology and Moral Judgment

In assessing the narrative that people provide about justice, we need to keep in mind the possibility that everyone is able to use different narratives, but individuals show a preference for particular ones because of local cultural rules and what they see to be their personal interest (Kitwood, 1980). Perhaps the question is not so much whether a person can apply moral principles, but rather whether it is in his or her interest to do so. This is an essential distinction that I think about each time I hear that 'ethics courses' are being taught in the top business schools as a way to improve moral behavior on Wall Street. Of course the top business school students can achieve high grades in ethics courses and solve hypothetical moral dilemmas 'in the best way'; there is no question that they have the ability to do so – they are 'straight A' students. However, there are questions about motivation and interest: are financial regulations such that the smartest individuals on Wall Street are motivated and see it in their own interest to solve real-world moral dilemmas ethically?

The distinction has been clarified by an interesting set of studies that show most people are capable of applying principled moral reasoning, but only do so if and when it is in their interest. For example, individuals of left-wing, moderate and right-wing political persuasions apply principled reasoning to bolster their political positions, but drop such reasoning when it does not suit them (Emler, Renwick, & Malone, 1983). Consider a 'pro-life' supporter who argues that 'life is more important than anything and must be protected at all costs', but also supports capital punishment (and thus 'putting an end to life') on the grounds that murderers must receive the harshest punishment available. Or, consider a supporter of minority rights who argues for 'equal opportunities for all', but also votes against limitations on pornography – which harm women, children, and other minorities. Another typical example of the same phenomenon is politicians who support various rights, freedoms, and collective movement, such as labor unions, as long as they are in other countries, but are far less supportive of such movements in their own countries.

In a study I conducted with a student collaborator, we presented participants with moral dilemmas and changed the context of the behavior, and discovered that even 'principled' moral thinkers shifted positions across contexts (Moghaddam & Vuksanovic, 1990). For example, even pro-life supporters shifted in their judgments about an abortion case, specifically the rights of the fetus versus the rights of the mother, when the context changed from Canada, to India, to Russia. There is, therefore, evidence to suggest that the moral reasoning style a person adopts can shift across contexts, and is often influenced by their ideology. Thus, it is not just a question of, 'Can Sam use principled reasoning to make moral judgments?' but 'Does Sam see it in her interests to use principled reasoning in this situation?'

Rationality, Stereotyping, and Justice

Just as Kohlberg (1976) put forward a rationalist account of moral reasoning, some researchers have argued for a rationalist explanation of stereotypes (see Arkes & Tetlock, 2004), culturally based generalizations about groups. In everyday life we use 'stereotype' as a derogatory term, and assume that stereotyping behavior necessarily results in unjust outcomes: either because people ascribe negative stereotypes to a group (e.g. 'Those 'X' people are lazy and stupid; make sure one of them does not get the job') or because they give some groups undue advantages (e.g. 'Those 'Y' people are always super-smart and hard-working, so naturally we should make sure one of them gets the job').

But an alternative view is that when people engage in stereotyping, they are acting as 'amateur statisticians' (D'Souza, 1995, p. 268) and motivated to achieve accuracy rather than to show inter-group bias. For example, Jane is walking home alone late at night and three young black males are standing on the next street corner. Jane clutches her handbag and quickly crosses to the other side of the street. According to one viewpoint, she is not showing prejudice, but simply acting as an amateur statistician: a high percentage of crimes in her neighborhood are committed by young black males, so she calculates that if she is mugged then the attackers will more likely be young black males (rather than older black females, for example). Indeed, there is evidence that under certain conditions some stereotypes are fairly accurate and based on a 'kernel of truth' (Lee, Jussim, & McCauley, 1995).

A potent criticism of the rationalist view is presented by researchers who highlight motivations to continue or expand inequalities. The distinction between acting irrationally and manufacturing rationalizations for our actions was explored by Freud (1961[1930]). For example, John is a billionaire who uses his wealth and power to drive down wages and eliminate the collective rights of employees in his many companies while at the same time buying every advantage for his own family. He rationalizes that he and his family deserve to be 'on top' and his employees and their families deserve to be 'at the bottom' because everyone is competing on a 'level playing field' and 'only the best rise to the top'. John stereotypes 'people at the bottom' out of a motivation to justify inequalities, rather than as a way of gaining accurate information.

Researchers have further explored this topic by using a measure of *Bayesian racism*, 'the belief that it is rational to discriminate against individuals based on stereotypes about their racial group' (Uhlmann, Brescoll, & Machery, 2010, p. 10). Individuals who score high on Bayesian racism endorse statements such as, 'If you want to make accurate predictions, you should use information about a person's ethnic group when deciding if they will perform well' (Uhlmann et al., 2010, p. 13). Individuals who endorse such statements tend to also have negative feelings about minorities, but score lower on indices of rational thinking and accuracy. For example, those high on Bayesian racism tend to reject statements such as, 'By relying on statistical probabilities, we can make our judgments much more accurate' (Uhlmann et al., 2010, p. 11). These findings suggest that the use of negative stereotypes can arise out of racism, rather than a concern for accuracy.

The Justice Motive

When a 15-year-old girl was gang-raped after a homecoming dance at a Richmond High School, one of the consequences was 'blame the victim' reactions from various commentators (http://www.salon.com/life/broadsheet/feature/2009/10/30/richmond_rape). It was insinuated that she deserved what she got, because she had drunk alcohol illegally. In so many instances of rape, violent crime, natural disaster, and other misfortunates, there is a tendency for people to 'blame the victim' and to interpret disastrous outcomes in ways that maintain a view of the world as just (Hafer & Bègue, 2005). For example, by saying 'That girl did wrong by drinking at such a young age and hanging around after a football game … she was kinda asking for it', some people put the blame on the rape victim and excuse the rapists.

Why do people tend to blame the victim? One explanation pioneered by Lerner (1980) is that people are motivated to believe that the world is just and orderly, a place where we get what we deserve. If Joe is out of work, behind with the mortgage payments, and has lost his home, it is because he is lazy. If Jane is overweight and suffering from feeling she is 'fat', it is because she lacks self-control (Quinn & Crocker, 1999). Lerner's formulation of the justice motive rests on the idea that a personal social contract evolves between the individual and the larger society: the individual adopts the view that 'if I play by the rules, then I will be treated justly. Whatever results I end up with, I have to accept as fair.'

One way in which individuals can maintain a sense of the world as fair is to shift perspectives from short-term to long-term. For example, Mahmoud lives in a dictatorship in which all the wealth in the country is funneled into the foreign bank accounts of the local despot and his huge extended family. No matter how hard Mahmoud works, he and his family can never achieve a decent standard of living or have a chance for real progress. However, Mahmoud tells his family that all will be well 'in the next world' and they will receive their rewards 'in heaven'. Religious conviction is associated with greater tolerance for injustices in this world (Hafer, Bègue, Choma, & Dempsey, 2005).

But surely when we see innocent people suffer, there must be some cost to (mis)interpreting the situation as 'just'? Hafer (2000) demonstrated there is a cost, in a highly innovative study that used the stroop effect, which involves asking a person to identify the color of the ink in which a stimulus is printed while he or she attempts to ignore the stimulus itself (see Chapter 10 of this book). For example, a stimulus could be the word 'blue' written in green ink. Participants take more time to identify the color of the ink when it is incompatible with the stimulus (e.g. when 'blue' is written in green ink) than when it is compatible (e.g. when 'blue' is written in blue ink). Research has shown that people take longer to identify the color of words that are associated with whatever they are emotionally concerned about. For example, people anxious about their health would take longer to identify the color of the word 'surgery'. Hafer demonstrated that after viewing a news story about an innocent victim of violent crime, participants took longer to identify the colors of justice-related words (e.g. fair, unequal). The results suggest that the injustice of the innocent victim's outcome posed a threat to the participants who had 'observed the crime'.

Limits to the Justice Motive

In 2009, there were widespread demonstrations in Iran by people protesting against the blatantly fraudulent presidential elections that kept Mahmoud Ahmadinejad in power in that country. Unfortunately, rigged elections are nothing new in Iran, but it was a real change to have people openly demonstrating their opposition to the dictatorship. After the 1979 revolution against the dictator Shah, many Iranians had thought they would achieve a democracy – only to find that religious fanatics had snatched power and re-established dictatorship under a new guise. Throughout my years of research in post-revolution Iran, I came across many people who firmly believed that the world is not fair and that their nation had not ended up with a just system (Moghaddam, 2002, 2008b). They felt deprived because Iranians have made so much effort, but achieved so little progress toward establishing a real democracy. The plight of Iranian women in particular has been terrible, and many women in particular see themselves as the victims of an unjust medieval system.

The example of many people in Iran points to limits to the justice motive. It may be that victims of injustice, such as many ordinary Iranians and particularly women, want to see the world as just, but their everyday experiences enforce a view of the world as unjust. The intensity and extent of the injustices experienced by the victims of injustice in Iran, North Korea, and some other dictatorships, cannot be demonstrated in a laboratory setting with undergraduate students as participants, so this is not an easy topic to study experimentally. However, Fasel and Spini (2010) conducted a study of belief in a just world with participants from war-torn regions in the former Yugoslavia, and demonstrated that victims of war in Bosnia and victims of exclusion in Macedonia were less likely to believe in a just world than non-victims. Moreover, accumulated experiences with injustice made it more likely that victims abandoned the belief in a just world.

But there is a broader cultural limitation to Lerner's just world theory, and this relates to the role of justice in cultural systems. It may be that 'the justice motive' is central in some cultures, and that 'seeing the world as just' is important to people in these cultures. However, in other cultures more central concerns might be 'honor', 'obedience', 'duty', or 'fidelity'. 'Seeing the world as just' may be a peripheral issue. Indeed, if asked by Western-style researchers about their perceptions, people in such cultures might even respond by saying that the world is unjust, as Fasel and Spini (2010) discovered.

From 'Rational' Balance to 'Irrational' Relative Deprivation

For much of the first half of the 20th century, academic psychology was dominated by the behaviorist school of psychology. Although behaviorism was influenced in important ways by European researchers, such as Ivan Pavlov (1849–1936), it was in the United States that behaviorism really flourished, particularly after John Watson's (1878–1958) so-called 'behaviorist manifesto' (Watson, 1913). Behaviorists believed that the science of psychology must discard all references to consciousness and thinking, and focus exclusively on observable behavior. From a behaviorist perspective, justice involves the system of rewards and punishments adopted by society to shape and control behavior. Behaviorists were not concerned with how people felt or what they thought about the system of rewards and punishments, only how observable behavior came to be shaped in the arena we refer to as the 'justice system'.

In the 1950s there was a turn away from behaviorism, and with the so-called 'cognitive revolution' psychologists once again took up the study of thinking (Miller, Galanter, & Pribram, 1960). Some psychologists adopted the model that is well known in traditional economics: humans as rational and self-serving. These psychologists had a new tool through which they could simulate human cognition and test different models of how humans think: the computer. This line of research has been associated with artificial intelligence, the science of designing machines to simulate human thinking (see Chapter 10 of this book). Research on artificial intelligence has helped in the design of better machines and brought tremendous benefits to humankind (Russell & Norvig, 2009). However, one of the shortcomings of the rational model of humankind is that humans often do not seem to behave rationally or in our own best interests. That is, as individuals and groups we do not always seem to know why we behave as we do, and we certainly do not always behave in ways that best serve our (rationally defined) interests. For example, we routinely engage in unnecessary and destructive wars, such as the US-led invasion of Iraq in 2003. Indeed, casting a critical eye back over our long history of destructive wars, irrationality seems to be a hallmark of our experiences. This point is illuminated by equity theory, the next justice theory we discuss.

Similar to Lerner's (1980) 'justice motive' is the equity theory assumption that people strive for justice in their relationships and experience anxiety when they perceive injustice (Adams, 1963; Homans, 1961; Walster, Walster, & Berscheid, 1978). Equity theory proposes that in social relationships, we continually calculate the ratio of our inputs and outcomes (the ratio of what we 'put into' a relationship and what we 'get out' of it), and compare this with the ratio of inputs and outcomes of others. For example, Joe compares the ratio of his inputs and outcomes with the ratio of his employer. If the ratios are different, then he sees inequity and feels anxious. For example, if Joe sees that he puts 10 out of 10 into his work and gets only five out of his job; but his employer puts five into the workplace and his output is 10, then Joe will feel that there is inequity:

Own input = 10, own output = 5 (ratio = 0.5); employer input = 5, employer output = 10 (ratio = 2).

According to equity theory, being undercompensated will result in a feeling of inequity for Joe; but the perception that one is overcompensated will also result in a feeling of inequity. That is, equity theory predicts that receiving more than one thinks one deserves will also result in feelings of discomfort (Randall & Mueller, 1995), although there are some cultural variations in how this general trend is manifested in different cultures (Jasso, 2005). In line with the 'self-centered' model of humans, evidence suggests that being undercompensated has a more powerful effect on behavior than being overcompensated (Bloom, 1999). That is, getting less than I deserve will affect me more than getting more than I deserve. Nevertheless, the perception that I am overcompensated can negatively impact my motivation.

The counter-intuitive finding that being over-compensated can negatively impact me goes against the strictly self-centered, rational model of equity. If I am strictly motivated to maximize my profits, then I should be happy with being overcompensated. But if I am motivated to achieve equity, then this should be reflected in how I behave toward others who are relatively worse off or better off than me. I might even be willing to behave dishonestly in order to restore equity. This idea was experimentally explored by Gino and Pierce (2009), who randomly assigned participants to be 'wealthy' or 'poor' (i.e. receive high or low rewards) for acting as the grader or the problem solver on an anagram task. Graders could overstate or understate the performance of solvers. In one condition, graders could gain greater rewards themselves by misreporting the performance of the solver. In essence, this experiment pitted the self-interest of the grader with the motivation of the grader to achieve equity. The results show that participants behaved dishonestly, they over-paid or under-paid others, in order to relieve the emotional distress of inequity. The implication is that negative emotions, such as envy, can lead a person to give dishonest evaluations of the performance of others, but positive emotions, such as empathy, can result in the same outcome.

Thus, gradually there has been a move away from the universalist-rationalist perspective of Kohlberg, as well as from the perspective, inspired by Lerner, that there is a universal 'need' for justice that results in people constructing the world as just. While these views have some merit, they do not give sufficient importance to context and the continuous framing of the world through the continuously changing self. However, this is not to reject the idea that there could be universals in justice behavior. In the next section, we see that evolutionary processes could be a source of such universals.

Evolution, Justice, and the Brain

It is useful to view justice as integral to the long evolutionary path taken by humans, from the turn to bipedelism about six million years ago. Well before humans developed complex language capacities, they evolved a number of primitive social relations, basic social actions that are essential for survival (Moghaddam, 2002). For example, turn-taking is a primitive social relation that has enormously important survival functions and is found in all human groups (Moghaddam & Riley, 2005). All important forms of human communications depend on turn-taking, and later we shall discuss how turn-taking forms the basis of complex legal and political systems in advanced human societies.

Turn-taking builds on imitation, now considered an innate capacity (Meltzoff & Moore, 1994). Infants are able to imitate almost immediately after birth (Meltzoff & Moore, 1977), suggesting that they have mental representations even at this early period (this poses a challenge to the traditional Piagetian model, which proposes a shift from sensorimotor to representational functioning only at about 18 months of age, see Chapter 6 in this text). Turn-taking plays an important role in infant–caretaker communications well before the development of verbal language. Initially, the infant is only able to take one turn, such as by imitating the facial gesture of a mother. Gradually, turn-taking through imitation becomes more complex, as the infant learns to take multiple turns: mother makes facial gesture, infant imitates, mother repeats, infant takes another turn, mother takes a turn, and so on (Nadel & Butterworth, 1999).

Turn-taking forms the basis of successful communications in all human groups. Adult communications involve smooth transitions, made possible through turn-taking and the ability to maintain continuity in the subject of conversation. This process is also assisted by non-verbal cues, such as eye contact, changes in pitch and loudness of voice, bodily movements, inhalation, and pausing. These non-verbal cues are learned early in the socialization process. For example, by the second year infants use the 'terminal gaze' to signal the end of their turn in conversation (Rutter & Durkin, 1987).

My argument is that turn-taking evolved early in human evolution, and much later this 'primitive social relation' was interpreted culturally as involving rights and duties, such as 'free speech' as a normative right in democracies. This interpretation took place in both informal, everyday contexts and in formal, institutional contexts. Within the informal context, turn-taking is best understood as part of a set of rules and norms that regulate 'politeness' behavior.

Of course, polite behavior varies considerably across cultures. For example, in traditional Western contexts 'politeness' means that a host asks guests whether they would like a certain type of food on offer, and the guests respond 'yes please' or 'no thank you'. But in Persian culture, 'taroff' is practiced, which means that it is impolite for a guest to say 'yes' the first time a food is offered, and it is impolite for a host to only offer food once. The host is required by politeness rules to offer the food repeatedly, and the guest is obliged to refuse repeatedly, until after a number of repeated offerings the guest 'reluctantly' accepts what is offered. Thus, the host and guest take turns in 'offering' and 'refusing', until politeness rules obligate the guest to accept. Cultural variations also influence how turn-taking takes place in formal organizations, such as in the legal and political systems.

In democratic societies, turn-taking plays a vitally important role in political systems and institutions. For example, term limits mean that an incumbent has to step aside to give other candidates 'a turn' at serving in key political positions (e.g. the president of the United States has a term limit of eight years). In the legal system of democracies, turn-taking plays a vitally important role in court cases (e.g. turn-taking in cross-examining witnesses). But irrespective of the nature of political systems, turn-taking is central to all aspects of life in modern societies: for example, automobile traffic could not move without adhering to turn-taking at cross-roads. Every driver has a right to a turn, and a duty to give other drivers their turns. Even in the backroads of low-income countries where traffic lights are not used, turn-taking plays a vitally important role.

Interestingly, new technologies can sometimes transform traditional turn-taking. For example, traditions might indicate that 'ladies go first' (in Western societies), or 'women follow men' (in traditional Islamic cultures), but this has been transformed by the requirements of modern transportation. Irrespective of the gender of the driver, the car that arrives first at the cross-road takes the first-turn (of course, in some countries, such as Saudi Arabia, women do not have the right to drive automobiles).

'Justice' and Animals

If the evolutionary picture outlined above is valid, and our modern justice systems have their roots in primitive social relations that evolved over the course of millions of years, then there should be signs of such justice even in lower animals. Research certainly suggests this to be the case; various animals have been shown to behave in ways that can be interpreted as reflecting 'fairness' (Bekoff, 2005; de Waal, 1996).

Integral to a sense of fairness is *empathy*, the ability to understand and feel what others are experiencing. In a study in which mice witnessed pain inflicted on other mice, it was found that the suffering of cagemates, but not that of strangers, elicited 'empathic behavior' from mice (Langford, Crager, Shehzad, Smith, Sotocinal, Levenstadt, et al., 2006). Among animals who differentiate between others on the basis of collaboration skills (Melis, Hare, & Tomasello, 2006), presumably empathic individuals would be preferred because they would make more effective group members. This kind of 'justice related' behavior might be, in part at least, learned and nurtured in the young as a form of primitive culture passed on from generation to generation among groups of animals. Such 'cultural transmission' does not exclude the possibility that there are also innate 'moral grammars' that shape the rules of overt behavior among both groups of animals and humans (Hauser, 2006).

More directly relevant to 'justice', is research demonstrating that some animals behave according to a sense of fairness (de Waal, 1996). This kind of 'sense of fairness' is probably first acquired through play behavior, which (in both monkeys and humans) involves a great deal of 'tit for tat', turn-taking, and reciprocity. In an innovative study by Brosnan and de Waal (2003), appropriately entitled 'Monkeys reject unequal pay', monkeys trained to complete the same task for the same reward became less cooperative and 'acted up' when they received a less favorable reward. Brosnan (2010) reports on subsequent research showing that chimpanzees, Capuchin monkeys, and domestic dogs, are among a number of species that respond in ways that indicate they perceive 'unfairness' if they receive a reward that is less favorable compared to that received by a social partner for completing the same task. Interestingly, a number of other primate species, including orangutans, squirrel monkeys, and common marmosets, do not show the same unfavorable reaction to unequal treatment.

But in one sense 'inequality' and 'unequal treatment' is integral to much of animal and human life, in so far as hierarchies and differential treatment exists. Group members learn to think and act differently, and more deferentially, in the presence of higher ranked others, and this is reflected in neural processing (Zink, Tong, Chen, Bassett, Stein, & Meyer-Lindenberg, 2008). Such inequality encompasses not only resource allocation, with 'higher ups' getting more, but also health and welfare generally (Sapolsky, 2004). Rank in a group influences health of individual animals and humans (with socioeconomic status, SES, being the best indicator of rank in humans). In general, lower-ranked individuals suffer more from stress-related illnesses, although in unstable groups higher ranking individuals can experience greater stress.

Justice and the Brain

Given the evolutionary roots of human behavior in the domain of justice, it is not surprising that neuroscientists have searched for 'where' moral judgments take place in the brain. After all, if a sense of 'right' and 'wrong' evolved over a very long time among animals and then humans, it is logical that brain activity should reflect moral judgments. Thus, two leading neuroscientists wrote about this topic under the title of, 'How (and where) does moral judgment work?' (Greene & Haidt, 2002).

An important research method used to address the above question is to focus on modern versions of the now famous Phineas Gage case, the railway worker who because of an explosion suffered an iron bar passing through his brain in 1848, but survived his injury (Macmillan, 2000). Gage 'changed personality', and lost the ability to make sound judgments. Modern versions of Gage, patients with medial prefrontal cortex damage, have been found to have affective deficits and to make poor real-life judgments (Damasio, 1994). Studies of anti-social individuals, who are more likely to steal, cheat, and harm others without feeling remorse, similarly show a greater likelihood of damaged prefrontal cortex (Bechara, Tranel, Damasio, & Damasio, 1996). Another group of researchers have studied the behavioral outcome of frontotemporal dementia (FTD), which involves an insidious neurodegeneration of the frontal lobes, the temporal lobes, or both, and has been associated with changes in moral behavior (Mendez, 2006). An important feature of FTD is a loss of accurate judgment in moral and emotional domains, and the development of a severely 'self-centered' view of the world.

When patients with FTD are assessed in terms of their knowledge about right and wrong, evidence shows they have retained information about moral rules and norms (Mendez, 2006). In this research, participants complete the 'Moral behavior inventory', which asks them to assess 'how wrong is it' if they carry out a number of acts. Examples of the acts listed are: 'sell someone a defective car', 'cut in line when in a hurry', 'drive out the homeless from your community', 'take credit for others' work'. The responses of FTD patients on this inventory are similar to normal patients, suggesting that they do not lack knowledge of moral conventions. However, FTD patients have been shown to be low on empathy toward others, and to have deficits in the ability to understand the motives, feelings, and experiences of others – what is referred to as Theory of Mind (see Chapter 4 of this book).

But efforts to find links between specific parts of the brain and moral judgment have to proceed very cautiously, because the available evidence suggests that '... there is no specifically moral part of the brain' (Greene & Haidt, 2002, p. 522), a point underlined by various researchers ('... morality is not represented in one place in the brain ...' Schaich Borg, Hynes, Van Horn, Grafton, & Sinnott-Armstrong, 2006, p. 816). Studies of patients with brain damage reveal that there are multiple forebrain sites associated with antisocial behavior (Moll, de Oliveira-Souza, & Eslinger, 2003). Very importantly, there are many examples of patients with frontal lobe damage who never develop antisocial behavior. For example, Moll et al. (2003, p. 300) refer to the case of patient SR, '... who sustained a massive destruction of the polar and mediobasal parts of both frontal lobes, had all the "right" ingredients that supposedly give rise to sociopathy.' Yet, like many other similar patients, SR behaved in socially inadequate ways, but not in immoral ways intended to take advantage of others.

The idea that there is no specific 'moral center' in the brain matches the idea that moral judgments involve both rational and emotional processes. One group of researchers have attempted to assess this rational/emotional difference by distinguishing between 'personal' and 'impersonal' moral judgments (Greene, Nystrom, Engell, Darley, & Cohen, 2004). Personal moral judgments are reflected in terms of 'me hurt you'. That is, the action must cause serious bodily harm. Second, the target of harm must be a person or persons. Third, the cause must be intentional action (rather than accidental, for example). In order to study the personal/impersonal distinction, researchers have used moral dilemmas, such as the following (from Thomson, 1986).

Trolley dilemma: A trolley has got out of control and is about to hit and kill five people. By hitting a switch, you can divert the trolley onto an alternative track, where it will hit and kill one person. Will you hit the switch and divert the trolley? If you say yes, you are in agreement with the majority of people who answered this question.

Footbridge dilemma: As above, a trolley is out of control and about to hit and kill five people. You are standing on a footbridge overlooking the tracks, and a large person is standing in front of you. By pushing this person off the footbridge and onto the track, you could stop the trolley and save five lives. The large person you push would be killed. Will you push the large person in front of the trolley? If you say 'no', you are with the majority of people who responded to this question.

The footbridge dilemma is described as 'personal' because you are asked to consider taking direct action that results in the death of a person (the large person you push), rather than just sidetracking an out-of-control trolley. In line with this, the Doctrine of Doing and Allowing (DDA) states that it is harder for people to justify doing harm (e.g. pushing a person to his/her death) than allowing harm (not preventing a person from falling to their death). The Doctrine of Double Effect (DDE) states that it is harder to justify a harm that was intended either as ends or as means (e.g. pushing the large person onto the tracks) compared to justifying a harm that came about as an unintended side effect (deflecting the trolley onto another track). Because these two doctrines propose that factors such as intentions matter, they contradict the consequentialist idea that only overall consequences matter. In this sense, the Doctrine of Doing and Allowing and the Doctrine of Double Effect are in line with legal and religious systems that give importance to intentionality. For example, in Western law courts a verdict of intentional homicide results in a more severe punishment than a verdict of accidental homicide.

In order to try to tease apart differences in brain activity when people make judgments on moral dilemmas as opposed to non-moral dilemmas, researchers have developed scenarios that are similar in length and semantic complexity, but differ with respect to moral content. For example, Schaich Borg et al., (2006) used the following dilemmas in their research:

> You find yourself locked in a room in front of a one-way mirror. On the other side of the mirror, there is a machine holding six people, three on each side. A sign on the floor says that if you do nothing, in 10 sec, the three people on the left will be shot and killed and the three people on the right will live. If you push the button in front of you, in 10 sec, the people on the right will be shot and killed, but the people on the left will live. There is no way to prevent the deaths of both groups of people. Is it wrong to push the button so that the three people on the right will be shot? Would you push the button so that the three people on the right will be shot? (Schaich Borg et al., 2006, p. 807)

A non-moral dilemma presented by Schaich Borg et al. (2006) involved the decision to burn two acres of wildflower land in order to try to save five acres of your land threatened by brushfire.

Neuroscience research suggests that people use a combination of emotive and cognitive facilities to tackle moral dilemmas. A reason why no specific 'moral center' is found in the brain is that making moral judgments involves both 'cold' rational cognitive processes and 'hot' emotional processes. Also, making moral judgments involves the self (Robertson, Snarey, Ousley, Harenski, Bowman, Gilkey, & Kilts, 2007), and so implicated in the process of moral decision making is the question, 'What kind of person am I?' The moral decision that I make is integral to the kind of person I think I am. In line with this, the extent to which the self is directly involved in a moral dilemma is reflected in brain activity (Kédia, Berthoz, Wessa, Hilton, & Martinot, 2008).

Thus, the psychology of justice can usefully be understood in evolutionary context: the roots of human moral judgments can be found in long-term functional processes, and there is evidence that some animals have a 'sense of fairness'. Our brains have evolved as important tools in making moral judgments, and research suggests different types of moral judgments can be associated with different neural networks. However, we should take care not to exaggerate the degree of specialization in neural pathways and types of moral judgments, because both affective and cognitive processes, as well as the self more broadly, are involved in thoughts and actions on the moral domain.

Justice as Culturally Preferred Narratives

In this final section, I argue that thinking and acting in the realm of 'right' and 'wrong' boils down to deciding between various alternative narratives of justice, and selecting a narrative we accept to be 'correct' in any time and place. Consider, for example, a trial by jury taking place in a court of law. During the trial, witnesses appear and are cross-examined, various types of information are presented to the judge and jury, and different versions of events are narrated. Lawyers for the prosecution and the defense present contrasting stories: one depicting the accused as guilty and the other arguing that the accused is actually innocent. Members of the jury have to decide which narrative is more plausible: the story presenting the accused as guilty or the one depicting the accused as innocent? Which story do they find more believable? We know that in many cases the judge and jury get it wrong: DNA evidence has exonerated hundreds of individuals, some of whom spent many years in jail, because at their criminal trials the stories depicting them as innocent presented by the defense attorneys proved to be less convincing than the stories portraying them as guilty presented by the prosecution.

From this perspective, the psychology of justice is closely related to the psychology of persuasion, which means that group-based differences in resources become highly important. From certain critical perspectives, the legal system in capitalist societies is simply a means by which the rich protect their property rights. From this viewpoint, the rich also use the media, education system, organized religion, and other means to support a justice narrative that legitimizes wealth and power inequalities. This would explain how Americans accept the growing inequality, and the further amassing of wealth by the super-rich, that has characterized American society particularly in recent decades (Pierson & Kacker, 2010).

One of the most powerful justice narratives is 'the American dream', the idea that 'anyone can make it in America' independent of their group membership – as long as they work hard and have talent. This dream is particularly powerful because it is shared by hundreds of millions of people aspiring to immigrate to America, as well as those who succeed in immigrating to America. Underlying the American dream is the assumption of an open society, with individuals moving up and down the system depending on their personal characteristics; the same fluid social mobility that Plato proposed in *The Republic* as essential for the long-term survival of any society. Of course, belief in the American dream and the justice of the 'open' American system is somewhat divorced from the reality of social mobility: a child born to poor parents in America has roughly as much chance of moving up to join the affluent classes as a child born to poor parents in other

Western societies (see Moghaddam, 2002). However, the important point is that belief in the American dream is alive and well in America, and so the dominant narratives of justice continue to highlight how it is a fair system in which anyone who works hard and is talented can 'make it'.

One of the greatest influences on justice narratives in societies as different as the United States and Iran is religion. Most importantly, religion encourages believers to look at the long term: 'I am poor and powerless in this world, but in the next I will be in heaven'. A second factor is that the major monotheist religions, Christianity, Judaism and Islam, are hierarchical, with strict rules about how the faithful must obey higher authorities. Despite the occasional role of religious figures in instigating reform, for most of history major religions have endorsed narratives that depict the status-quo as just and fair.

Conclusion

Research on the psychology of justice was influenced in important ways by the universalist-rational model of Kohlberg, who argued for a universal 'stage model'. However, subsequent research showed that the question is not so much 'can' people make moral judgments at the different levels proposed by Kohlberg, but do they see it to be in their interests to do so? The criticism of Kohlberg's model raised by Gilligan based on gender differences did not prove to be valid, again because both women and men have been shown to be able to make moral judgments based on the ethics of 'care' and on the ethics of 'justice', but whether they do so can be influenced by how they view their own roles in that particular context. Women will be more caring and more empathic, and men less so, when they are reminded of their 'traditional' gender roles and how they are supposed to behave according to tradition. More recent neuroscience research has not found a 'moral center' in the brain, but this research has shown that both 'cold' cognition and 'hot' emotions are involved in moral judgments, and more broadly the self and 'the kind of person I think I am' is integrally involved in how I make moral judgments.

15

Intergroup Relations and Diversity in a Global Context

Fathali M. Moghaddam

The governments of Muslim countries are likely to continue to become less friendly to the West, and intermittent low-intensity and at times perhaps high-intensity violence will occur between Islamic groups and Western societies. Relations between the United States, on the one hand, and China, Japan, and other Asian countries will be highly conflictual, and a major war could occur if the United States challenges China's rise as the hegemonic power in Asia. (Huntington, 1996, pp. 238–239)

The 21st century began with a number of major attacks by Islamic terrorists, in the United States on 11 September 2001, in Spain on 11 March 2004, and in London on 7 July 2005. In addition, there were hundreds of terrorist attacks against Western interests around the world, such as bombs that ripped through Western hotels in Jordan on 9 November 2005. Thousands of people were killed in these terrorist attacks against Western targets in different countries. During the same period, United States military forces invaded Afghanistan and Iraq, toppling local governments and installing 'pro Western' leaders in power in both countries. Hundreds of thousands of people have been killed in the continuing Afghan and Iraq wars, millions more have been injured and displaced. Samuel Huntington (quoted above) presented one interpretation of post-cold war rifts in the 21st century, when he predicted that the next major conflicts would be along cultural differences at the global level.

The goal of this chapter is to use psychological theories and empirical research to better understand intergroup conflict in the contemporary world, and to assess different claims about the roots of intergroup conflict. In addition to assessing the role of 'culture' and 'identity', we will examine interpretations of intergroup conflict from a biological perspective, including contributions from neuroscience and evolutionary psychology (the term 'evolutionary psychology' has replaced the term 'sociobiology', because the latter has become politically tarnished). We will also weave the themes of subjective justice, material factors, and rationality into our assessments, since these are also important in psychological explanations of intergroup conflict (Moghaddam, 2008a).

Although the focus of this chapter is on groups and explanations of why group conflict arises, a basic question continues to be with us from earlier chapters discussing individuals: How malleable is human behavior? To what extent can human thought and action be changed? Also, if there are factors limiting the extent to which human behavior can be changed, what are they? At the one extreme, we will encounter theories that depict human behavior as almost completely malleable, so that characteristics such as 'selfishness' and 'individualism' can be transformed to altruism and 'giving priority to the interests of the collective'. On the other hand, we will encounter theories that view human behavior as in some important ways fixed and unchanging, because of genetic, cognitive, or some other dispositional (i.e. intra-personal) factors. The implication is that some theories view intergroup conflict as an outcome of certain conditions, and predict that intergroup conflict could end under certain other conditions. From this perspective, we can arrive at peaceful relationships and avoid wars, provided we can reform environmental conditions in the necessary ways. Another set of theories predict that intergroup conflict arises out of certain fixed human characteristics and at best it can be controlled, but not ended. We begin by examining the materialist approach to understanding intergroup conflict, which includes biological accounts.

Materialist Accounts of Intergroup Conflict

Materialist accounts of intergroup conflict encompass a wide range of theories and empirical studies, but what they all share in common is the idea that such conflict arises out of features of the material world either inside (e.g. genes, brain structure) or outside (scarce resources of various kinds, such as oil, land, water) persons. A second common theme in these materialist accounts is the idea of irrationality underlying human behavior, and the assumption that people are generally unaware of the influence of material factors in their behavior – although they can become aware under certain seldom achieved conditions.

Biological Factors

In answer to the question, 'Why is human history characterized by wars and deadly conflicts of various types?' an answer provided by some researchers is, 'Because humans are born that way'. These researchers see the root explanation of conflict to be in our biology, and they specifically rely on evolutionary theory as pioneered by Charles Darwin (1809–1882) and as re-oriented by Richard Dawkins and other researchers more recently (Dawkins, 1989; Wilson, 1975). The rapid advance of brain imaging technology (see Chapter 3 in this book) has given these biologically oriented researchers additional tools, to explore brain activity associated with aggression and violence.

Genes and Conflict

During the 19th century a number of developments resulted in both intergroup conflict and group-based inequalities as being seen to be 'natural'. A first great idea in this tradition was put forward by Robert Malthus (1766–1834) in his essay on the relationship between population growth and food production (Malthus, 1983). Malthus argued that food production increases arithmetically (1, 2, 3, 4 …), while population increase is geometric (2, 4, 8, 16 …). This disparity, Malthus proposed, results in periodic food shortages and a perpetual cycle: population increases until food supply is insufficient, with the result that famine and war rage on until population growth stagnates and food supply catches up. For a period of time there is sufficient food to feed the population, but soon population increases outstrip food supply again, and the whole 'Malthusian Cycle' begins anew. Thus, human societies are in a constant state of competition and conflict for food, water, and other such essential resources. During the 'Malthusian Cycle', some people survive the intense competition, others perish. This idea influenced the two men who first pioneered modern evolutionary theory, Charles Darwin (1809–1882) and Alfred Wallace (1823–1913).

Darwin's revolutionary work *On the origin of species by means of natural selection* (1993[1859]) influenced a group of thinkers who became known as the 'Social Darwinists'. They applied the idea of 'survival of the fittest' to the social world, to explain and justify group based inequalities: some groups are naturally superior and will rise to the top, while others necessarily are in a subservient position – they are unable to succeed in this 'survival of the fittest' competition. Thus, inequalities on the basis of 'race', social class, and the like are justified, because people with 'naturally superior' talent rise to the top (of course, this viewpoint wrongly assumes that society is meritocratic). These 19th-century researchers did not have knowledge of genetics; Gregory Mendel's (1822–1884) ground-breaking genetic research did not become known until the early 20th century, and it was not until the latter part of the 20th century that serious attempts were made to provide a genetic explanation of intergroup relations and social relationships more generally.

The new genetic approach to social relationships has involved a shift in emphasis from the individual to the gene as the unit of analysis, with the assumption that human beings are 'convenient vehicles' for carrying genes. It is proposed that humans are programmed to cooperate with genetically similar others, but to compete with and show aggression against those who are genetically dissimilar. Of course, this process is ongoing without conscious awareness among those cooperating and competing with genetically similar and different others. Illustrative of this new approach is the research of Napoleon Chagnon (2004), who for decades analyzed patterns of behavior among the Yanomamo, natives of the Amazon jungle across Brazil and Venezuela. Chagnon focused on understanding how social interactions, particularly aggression, have reproductive consequences, '... Favoring and disfavoring neighbors in social interactions had reproductive implications because it could potentially be a way to spread your own genes, a radical new twist to Darwinian theory' (2004, p. 40). According to Chagnon and other genetically oriented researchers, a clear pattern of aggression is found across different cultures: males attacking to kill males from groups carrying rival genes, and capturing and raping women in order to pass on their own genes. This pattern, it is claimed, is evident in recent wars such as in Eastern Europe, Ruanda, and the People's Republic of Congo.

Researchers have applied this genetic framework to explain ethnic and racial conflicts. For example, arguing that ethnicity and race are extensions of kinship, Van den Berghe (1987) proposed that 'There exists a general behavioral predisposition, in our species as in many others, to react favorably toward other organisms related to the actor. The closer the relationship is, the stronger the preferential behavior' (pp. 18–19). From this perspective, a whole range of intergroup behaviors, from racial discrimination to genocide, can be explained through genetic similarity and the 'whispering within' that moves people to be aggressive against genetically dissimilar others, but to cooperate with and assist those who are genetically similar.

In a detailed analysis of international homicide patterns, Martin Daly and Margo Wilson (1988) have also highlighted sex differences in aggression. International statistics show that homicide typically involves two young males: one who kills and the other the victim. Daly and Wilson interpret this as demonstrating a pattern that fits the genetic framework: males compete for access to and control over reproduction with females. Males use violence as a tactic to perpetuate their own genes, and to eliminate rival genes. Within the family, these authors argue:

> Perhaps the most obvious prediction from a Darwinian view of parental motives is this: Substitute parents will generally tend to care less profoundly for children than natural parents, with the result that children reared by people other than natural parents will be more often exploited and otherwise at risk. (Daly & Wilson, 1988, p. 83)

Their survey shows that within the family, stepchildren are more likely to be the victims in killing and violent 'accidents' of various kinds because, Daly and Wilson argue, they do not carry the genes of the step-parents. In line with this, doubt about the paternity of a child can result in a man killing his wife. There are fewer cases of wives killing husbands; according to evolutionary psychologists this is in part because wives are certain of the maternity of the child. This is in line with broader evolutionary arguments that sex differences in aggression are explained by sexual selection rather than sex roles and socialization processes (Archer, 2009).

While sociobiological accounts have gained some support (see Moghaddam, 2005, ch. 19), there are also serious objections to the sociobiological account of intergroup conflict. A first set of objections revolve around the number and distinctiveness of our genes. The results of the Human Genome Project demonstrate that there are only about 20–25,000 protein-coding genes in the human genome (International Human Genome Sequencing Consortium, 2004), far fewer than had been expected, with a tiny number being unique to humans. Indeed, we are 98.8 percent genetically similar to chimpanzees and 75 percent genetically similar to chickens (Potts & Sloan, 2010). A second point is that humans are 99.9 percent genetically similar to one another.

These facts about our genetic characteristics have a number of important implications. A first implication is that, given the small number of genes and enormous variety of human behavior, any influence of genes on human behavior must be the outcome of complex interactions between genes and environmental factors, rather than through a direct gene-behavior causal link. Second, given that humans are so highly similar genetically, variations in their behavior must be for the most part associated with cultural rather than genetic variations. For example, to explain variations in collective aggression, we should focus on the cultural differences between groups such as the Yanomamo who are high on collective aggression and those such as the traditional Tiwi of Northern Australia who are low on collective aggression.

A second implication of these new discoveries about our genetic characteristics, and this directly relates to weaknesses in the evolutionary psychology account, is that major wars are not explained through genetic explanations. For example, consider the alliances during the Second World War: Britain was allied with India and China, among others, while Germany was allied with Italy and Japan. How exactly is such a set of alliances supposed to be explained by 'genetic similarity'; even if we assume that *phenotype*, physical features, accurately indicates *genotype*, genetic makeup? The correct answer is that such alliances are far better explained by ideology than they are by genetics.

Finally, another fatal flaw in the genetic account of intergroup conflict is that it assumes phenotype can be used to accurately gage genotype. That is, it is assumed that by observing the outward physical characteristics of persons, we can accurately estimate the extent of their genetic similarity/dissimilarity with ourselves. Of course, this is an incorrect assumption, since one cannot use phenotype to accurately gage genotype.

Disregarding the over-generalizations made from an evolutionary psychology perspective, there are more promising lines of research that focus on genetic risk for aggression. For example, one line of research has established a relationship between the monoamine oxidase-A (MAOA) gene and aggression, as in the case of Dutch males who were monoamine-oxidase-A deficient and showed a high tendency toward acts of impulsive aggression, including sexual violence and arson (Brunner, Nelen, Breakefield, Ropers, & van Oost, 1993). Subsequent research suggests that this aggression arises because mono-amine-oxidase-A deficient individuals are emotionally hypersensitive to socially negative experiences, such as rejection in social contexts (Eisenberger, Way, Taylor, Welch, & Lieberman, 2007). Also, studies indicate that MAOA is implicated in impulsive/reactive, rather than instrumental and goal-directed types of aggression (Buckholtz & Meyer-Lindenberg, 2008). That is, a 'spur of the moment' inter-personal assault can be better explained by this type of research than planned collective warfare. Despite its limitations, this line of research could lead to promising findings, at least at the individual level, and there are broader evolutionary accounts of intergroup conflict that are also promising, and we turn to one such approach next.

Lorenz's Ethological Approach to Intergroup Conflict

Konrad Lorenz (1903–1989) has presented a highly innovative account of aggression from an evolutionary perspective, one that provides a compelling explanation of why intergroup conflict among humans is often so deadly (we have already discussed some aspects of Lorenz's research in Chapter 8). Like all evolutionary based explanations, Lorenz's (1966) account of aggression is functional and asks: 'What purpose does aggression serve?' In order to better understand Lorenz's account, it is useful to distinguish between different types of fighting.

One kind of fighting takes place between animals of different species, with the purpose of acquiring food. For example, consider a lion hunting a zebra. The hungry lion looks at the zebra as a hungry human might look at a juicy piece of steak; not filled with emotions such as anger and hatred, but with a simple desire to satisfy hunger pangs. This kind of between-species fighting, typically between hunter and prey, is very different from fighting within species, which invariably involves combat between young males seeking to gain access to and control over females for the purpose of reproduction. For example, consider two male wolves fighting for leadership of a wolf pack, along with control over access to females. Unlike fighting that takes place for food, this kind of fighting seldom results in the death of the combatants; as soon as one of the animals demonstrates dominance in size, strength, and so on, the dominated animal signals signs of submission. These signals of submission serve as inhibitory mechanisms, which limit aggression and allow the defeated animal to withdraw without suffering serious injury.

There are good functional reasons why intraspecies fighting should not lead to death. After all, the defeated animal is often a young male who is likely to be a 'champion' in the future. It would be dysfunctional to injure or kill future 'champions'.

Lorenz argues that humans are also influenced by inhibitory mechanisms that limit aggression. This explains why it is so difficult for humans to kill one another, particularly at close quarters. Imagine trying to kill another person with your bare hands; having to hear, feel, and smell that victim as you attempt to kill him or her. Most people experience revulsion when they kill, even in a war situation (Grossman, 1995). Any signal of defeat from the potential victim as we attempt to kill him or her at close quarters, such as crying or pleading, is likely to result in us showing compassion.

But imagine if instead of using your bare hands, you were able to use night-vision technology to fire a rifle in the dark at the victim from a long distance, so that he or she could not even see you. Or, imagine if you were able to hit the target person with an unmanned drone, the kind used by the United States military in Afghanistan in the 2010s, as you sit in the control room thousands of miles away and use satellite imagery to home in on the target. The person you have targeted will not see or hear anything threatening until it is far too late, and there will be no opportunity for inhibitory mechanisms to influence your behavior. In effect, modern weapons technology has enabled humans to sidestep the inhibitory mechanisms that limit within-species killing. Ironically, rather than strengthening peace, advances in science and technology have enabled us to kill one another with greater ease.

But there are ways in which modern technology can help revive the role of inhibitory mechanisms among humans. Images of killing shown on television, YouTube, and other mass media outlets can have a strong impact on public opinion, resulting in greater anti-war sentiment. That is why governments are generally concerned to control journalists and the images they send back from war fronts. For example, during the presidency of George W. Bush (2000–2008), journalists were not permitted to photograph the caskets that brought the bodies of dead American soldiers back from the Iraq and Afghanistan war fronts, and the US government has continued to deny the full impact of these wars on civilian populations. If the US population becomes fully aware of the hundreds of thousands of Iraqi and Afghani civilian casualties, in addition to the millions of seriously injured and displaced civilians, then opposition to the wars would probably become even stronger – as happened during the Vietnam war in the 1970s.

Lorenz provides a compelling account of why modern humans are able to kill one another in such large numbers. However, another feature of technological advances that Lorenz did not predict is the development of electronic games that simulate violence, including killing and rape. The research of Albert Bandura (1973) demonstrates that young people can be socialized to become more aggressive, for example, by viewing violence on television. Since Bandura's seminal studies in the 'social learning' tradition, numerous studies have demonstrated that violent videogames increase the likelihood of aggressive behavior (Anderson, Shibuya, Ihori, Swing, Bushman, Sakamoto, et al., 2010; Huesmann, 2010). The implication is that we have now entered a new era, in which our 'entertainment' routinely socializes the young to be aggressive. Given that it is largely young males who dedicate their time to violent video games, it may be that we are side-stepping the 'non-violent' influence of inhibitory mechanisms in a new way among the most violent prone group – young men.

Research in the social learning tradition underscores the cultural molding of violent behavior. Even if we accept that there are biological factors pushing young men to be aggressive, such aggression can be directed into all kinds of activities – from athletic competitions, to dancing, to physical work, to fighting and war. In the major societies today, war is planned and directed mainly by older men (who remain safe far away from the battlefields), but the actual fighting is carried out by young men.

Brain and Conflict

Given that our powerful human brains have enabled us to produce the atom bomb, unmanned drones, and supersonic fighter jets, is it in the brain that we should look to explain intergroup conflict? Although the issue of collective aggression has seldom been tackled directly, researchers have explored aggression at the individual level and asked questions about the possible 'special characteristics' of aggressive individuals, such as violent criminals.

Cesare Lombroso (1836–1909) was among the first researchers to systematically study the brains and bodies of criminals, including those who had committed violent crimes, to explore how they might differ from the non-criminal population. He conducted post-mortem studies of the brains of criminals, and concluded that there were certain similarities with the brains of lower animals. This supported his concept of *atavism*, that criminality (including physical aggression against others, resulting in serious injury and murder) was the result of primitive urges that in most people has become controlled or extinct, but survives in some individuals. The idea that violent offenders are physically different from ordinary people, in terms of their brain characteristics, their hormones, or some other physical characteristics, has not resulted in consistent findings (Nelson, 2005; Schmalleger, 2011). In recent years, studies of brain and aggression have focused more on using fMRI and other brain imaging technologies to map neural systems activated during aggressive actions and thoughts.

Given that in modern military training, video simulations of battlefields are used to train soldiers to fight enemy forces, violent video games have been used to study brain activity and aggression. In a study by Klaus Mathiak and René Weber (2006), 13 young male German participants played a violent video game, 'Tactical Ops: Assault on Terror' and their brain activities were monitored using fMRI. Results show that as compared to non-violent scenes, occurrence of violent scenes had identifiable neural correlates. The general picture that emerges from this and other studies is that:

1 circuits in the hypothalamus and amygdale play an important role in impulsive/reactive aggression;
2 these circuits can be inhibited by activity in the frontal cortex;
3 measures of impulsive/reactive aggression are associated with lower activity in the frontal cortex (Coccaro, McCloskey, Fitzgerald, & Phan, 2007).

There is recognition that the neural correlates of aggression must be considered as part of a wider set of factors, including interactions between environmental conditions, neural circuits, biological signals, and genes (Nelson & Trainor, 2007; Siever, 2008). In the case of individuals who routinely display high levels of impulsive/reactive aggression, intervention through 'mood regulators' and other medications can be useful and necessary. However, such an approach is not useful when considering collective aggression, from gang warfare to nations at war.

Material Factors External to Persons

Material factors have been ascribed a central role in intergroup conflict by theories that assume psychological experiences to be an outcome of material conditions. These theories range from the macro-historic materialist account provided by Karl Marx (1818–1883) (Marx & Engels, 1967[1848]), to the more recent empirically based theories, such as realistic conflict theory (Sherif, 1966) and resource mobilization theory (McCarthy & Zald, 1977). For the purpose of our discussion, the key point we need to derive from Marx is the idea that human consciousness is shaped by relationships within the production process: material conditions shape worldviews. Marx divides the social world into capitalists, who own the means of production, and the proletariat, who sell their labor in the marketplace. Capitalists shape the dominant ideology in society, through their control of education, the media, religion, and other sectors that influence 'how people think'. Although initially the proletariat fails to recognize that they belong to a distinct group with interests that contradict those of the capitalist class, through repeated and increasingly intense clashes between capitalists and the proletariat, there eventually emerges 'class consciousness'. Thus, the material reality of intense class conflict forces people to recognize their class membership, and enter into open class warfare. The outcome is the proletariat revolution, through which the capitalist class is overthrown and a dictatorship of the proletariat is established. Gradually, as people learn to live and work for the collective, the psychology of the people changes. The central government slowly dissolves and disappears, because there is no 'ruling class' and so there is no longer a need for a central authority; given that from a Marxist perspective the function of a central authority in capitalist societies is to represent the interests of the capitalist class. A classless society does not need a central government, because the people rule themselves. In Marx's scheme, the 'way people think and act' inevitably changes as material conditions change. The end result of the historic sequence of changes is also inevitable: class conflict, revolution, dictatorship of the proletariat, dissolution of social classes and evaporation of central governments. Thus, Marx provides a picture of human behavior as malleable, and shaped by external factors.

But are there limits to how much material conditions can change people? Vilfredo Pareto (1848–1923), an Italian researcher, argued for a different kind of inevitability in intergroup relationships, the inevitability of inequality (Pareto, 1935). There would be intergroup conflict and revolutions, Pareto agreed, but the result would be the replacement of one elite by another. Whereas Marx saw history as a series of progressive events, each inevitably leading to the next (feudalism, capitalism, socialism, the classless society), Pareto saw history as an endless cycle, with one elite replacing another. He succinctly described history as the 'graveyard of the aristocracies' (1935, Vol. 3, p. 1430), postulating that every elite makes the mistake of preventing talented non-elite members from rising up through the ranks and joining the elite, with the result that these talented individuals form a counter elite, mobilize the masses, and stage a revolution to topple the existing elite (Pareto's ideas lead us back to the topic of social stratification and hierarchy, which underlie discussions in Chapter 14). However, after the counter-elite topples the old elite, the counter elite establishes itself in a superior position and maintains the same group-based inequalities. In contemporary research, social dominance theory (Sidanius & Pratto, 1999) has shared Pareto's emphasis on continued, universal group-based inequalities. Social dominance theory has gone further, by postulating an evolutionary source for group-based inequalities, and critics have reacted by attacking the theory because it depicts hierarchy and inequality as 'genetically mandated' (Jost, Banaji, & Nosek, 2004, p. 912). Again, we return to the theme of the malleability of behavior: are humans destined always to live in societies characterized by group-based inequalities? Following Marx, some researchers say 'no', while those following Pareto answer 'yes'.

Realistic Conflict Theory

Muzafer Sherif (1906–1988) was a Turkish-American psychologist who conducted brilliant research on norm-formation and conformity to group-established norms, but also made seminal contributions in the area of intergroup relations. Sherif's approach is given the title of 'realistic conflict theory' because he adopts a 'realist' approach in viewing psychological experiences, such as intergroup attitudes, as being shaped by material conditions. For Sherif, how people feel and act toward outgroup members is determined by whether their group is in competition with the outgroup for material resources: If Group A and Group B are in competition for land and water, then they will have negative attitudes toward one another and violent conflict might arise; if Group A and Group B have common material interests, then they will be positively disposed toward one another.

Sherif provided a compelling set of demonstrations of his theory in the context of boys summer camps. The basic design of the study was simple. The researchers acted as camp counselors and welcomed boys to summer camp. The boys were selected to be similar in terms of key demographic characteristics, so that 'natural groupings' (e.g. ethnicity) would interfere as little as possible (all the boys were 11–12-year-old White Christian Americans). During stage one, the boys became acquainted with one another, and some became friends. During stage two, the boys were divided into two groups, making sure that all those who had been identified as forming friendships were assigned to different groups. This was done so that 'friendship patterns' could not account for subsequent findings. During stage three, the two groups engaged in various types of intergroup competition, over both material prizes and prestige. Attitudes against the outgroup became more biased. Negative intergroup feelings intensified and more aggressive leadership emerged in each group. The groups engaged in acts of destruction and violence against each other. Having managed to get the two groups to hate one another, the challenge was now for Sherif to move them back to peaceful relationships again. During stage four, Sherif introduced superordinate goals, goals that both groups wanted to achieve but neither could achieve without the cooperation of the other. For example, a food truck 'broke down' and in order to pull the truck into the camp, the two groups had to cooperate. Through superordinate goals, relationships between the two groups became cooperative again. In a sense, the boys went back to being one group again.

Muzafer Sherif (1906–1988) had the advantage of being born in Izmir, Turkey; this was an advantage in the sense that when he moved to the United States to study social behavior and group dynamics in particular, he looked at the world from the perspective of an outsider. This enabled him to have a distinct viewpoint, one that differed from the traditional white American perspective that dominated social psychology for most of its history. Sherif gave importance to groups and collective processes, and in this way he worked against the individualistic tendency of traditional social psychology. He also gave attention to norms and conformity, because as with many 'outsiders' he recognized the contradiction that exists in American culture between the swagger and rhetoric of non-conformity and independence, and the reality of conformity and adherence to norms.

After completing his studies in the United States and gaining a PhD in social psychology in 1935, Sherif returned to work in Turkey. However, because of political problems with Turkish authorities, he came back to resume an academic career in the United States in 1944. It was soon after his return to America that he met and married Carolyn Sherif (1922–1982), and the two of them collaborated on a number of important research projects. In addition, Carolyn Sherif was a pioneer in the psychology of women.

Muzafer Sherif had wide-ranging research interests, including in the domains of attitude change, but his most important research contributions are in the areas of, first, experimental demonstration of conformity to group established norms and, second, demonstration of the process of intergroup conflict and cooperation. Perhaps Sherif's most lasting contribution will be the concept of superordinate goals, goals that all groups want to achieve, but no group can achieve without the cooperation of other groups. This concept is powerful as both a theoretical concept and as an applied tool, used by practitioners to help manage intergroup conflicts. The concept of superordinate goals has also been influential in education, leading to the applied program 'jigsaw classroom' in which all the members of a team of students have a vital role in the team completing its task. Only when all students contribute can the team complete its collective task.

Cultural Accounts of Intergroup Conflict

Whereas materialist theories argue that psychological experiences are shaped by the material conditions, cultural accounts argue that meaning making is at the heart of intergroup relations. The meaning of material factors, such as land, are themselves cultural constructs. For example, from a materialist perspective groups in the Middle east are fighting over land and other resources, but from a cultural perspective the meaning of the land is key – Jerusalem is not just 'land', it is a cultural carrier (Moghaddam, 2002) with enormous historic significance for Jews and Muslims, as well as of course for Christians. Just as for practicing Christians a cross is much more than two pieces of wood nailed together, and for practicing Muslims the Islamic veil worn by women is not just a piece of cloth. These 'material things' all have significance well beyond their physical characteristics.

Of course, cultural psychologists do not deny the important role of material factors in intergroup relations, but their argument is that it is through collaboratively constructing the social world that people make sense of material factors. Cultural interpretation is at the heart of even the Marxist model of intergroup conflict. Social classes could clash endlessly and no change might come in their relationships. What brings about change, according to Marx, is that the proletariat comes to see themselves as a distinct group with interests that contradict the interests of the capitalist class. In other words, a new identity has to form of the proletariat as a 'class in themselves'. We next turn to consider the most influential psychological theory of intergroup relations since the 1970s, social identity theory (Tajfel & Turner, 1979, 1985).

Identity

In the late 1960s, a curious laboratory experiment was designed by Henri Tajfel and his associates, with unexpected results about the impact of social categorization (Tajfel, 1970; Tajfel, Flament, Billig, & Bundy, 1971). From the 1950s, Tajfel had explored the impact of categorization of non-social stimuli, such as lines of different lengths, and concluded that merely placing items in categories 'A' and 'B' can result in minimization of within group differences, and exaggeration of between group differences (Tajfel, 1959). That is, the members within each category 'A' and 'B' were seen as more alike than they actually were, and the members of the different categories 'A' and 'B' were seen as more different than they actually were. When he turned to study social categorization (i.e. the grouping of people rather than things), Tajfel's team developed the minimal group paradigm: given this term because it was a procedure for forming groups on a minimal basis. During part one of the experiment, participants (British schoolboys) were informed they were members of 'group X' or 'group Y' on the basis of a trivial task (such as dot estimation); in part two, participants allocated points to the members of groups 'X' and 'Y', without knowing their identities, without knowing what the points stood for, without having or expecting to have contact with the persons they allocate points to, and with the understanding that they would not receive any of the points they allocated. In essence, all of the usual functional reasons for showing ingroup bias seemed to be missing from the situation, and yet the findings demonstrate that most people show ingroup favoritism even in this 'minimal' setting.

There are two points worth emphasizing about the findings of the minimal group paradigm. First, there are plenty of 'real world' examples of how people exaggerate the importance of trivial criterion in group life, and use the 'manufactured' difference to differentiate between groups and even discriminate against particular outgroups. For example, consider the Tutsi and Hutu in Ruanda, two groups engaged in violent conflict resulting in over a million fatalities in recent decades. Before the recent atrocities began, Maquet (1961) reported that the height differences between the two groups was emphasized and exaggerated as part of a justification for the superior status enjoyed by the Tutsi.

Tajfel and his associates interpreted the findings of the minimal group paradigm through what became known as social identity theory (Tajfel & Turner, 1979). This theory proposes that people are motivated to achieve a social identity that is positive and distinct: thus, even when we only have a 'trivial' basis on which to differentiate between the ingroup and the outgroup, we will treat this difference as 'important' because it is the only basis on which we can create our desired identity. Social identity theory emerged at the same time as the 'ethnic revival' and the collective mobilization of African-Americans and various other minority movements in the United States and around the world (Moghaddam, 2008a, ch. 5). All these movements relied on a re-defined identity, with new slogans such as 'Black is beautiful', 'women's liberation', and 'gay pride'. The collective minority movements were not restricted to Western societies, but are part of the globalization taking place in the 21st century. We will return to this theme later, when we discuss radicalization and terrorism.

Henri Tajfel (1919–1982) shared with Muzafer Sherif the advantage of coming to social psychology from the perspective of an outsider: he was Jewish and born in Wloclawek, Poland. His university studies in France were cut short by the Second World War, and he fought in the war as a soldier in the French army. He was captured by the Germans and survived a series of prisoner of war camps. He lost many family members in the war and spent the immediate post-war years working for relief organizations helping refugees. After marriage, he moved to live in England and continued his studies in psychology, completing a PhD in 1954. He worked at Durham and Oxford Universities, before being made chair of social psychology at the University of Bristol in 1967.

Tajfel's research on prejudice went against the trend found in psychology after the Second World War, when the focus of most researchers was on personality factors: prejudiced individuals were assumed to have unusual personalities. Typical of this research was *The authoritarian personality* research project (Adorno, Frenkel-Brunswik, Levinson, & Sanford, 1950), which was strongly influenced by Freudian concepts and assumed prejudice to arise out of certain extraordinary personality characteristics. Instead, Tajfel targeted certain common cognitive processes, such as categorization, as being associated with prejudice. By the 1970s, he had moved from exploring the consequences of categorization of things to the categorization of people. Out of this research emerged the so-called 'minimal group paradigm', which shows that intergroup bias can arise out of the categorization of people into arbitrary groups on the basis of trivial criteria.

Tajfel was enormously successful in attracting and motivating a very talented set of students, including Michael Billig, John Turner, Howard Giles, Rupert Brown, and Glynis Breackwell, who went on to further develop social identity theory in different ways. Social identity theory has been tremendously influential in the United States, and has been one of the few examples of European research having an impact on traditional American social psychology. Tajfel continues to be one of the most often cited social psychologists around the world.

Before ending this discussion of social identity theory and its experimental foundations, a few comments on the limitations and potential of this research is needed. On the one hand, the minimal group paradigm does highlight the important point that under certain conditions, even 'trivial' bases for intergroup differences can be socially constructed as 'important' and used as a justification for intergroup bias. Second, social identity theory has focused attention on the tendency for humans to seek distinctiveness, or what in evolutionary terms is 'vacant space', as well as a 'positive identity'. However, in part because of the almost exclusive reliance of the theory on one-hour experimental laboratory experiments, there has been a lack of attention to the 'process' of identity formation.

To be more precise, my identity, 'the person I think I am, how I think I am seen by others …', is continually taking shape and changing through my interactions with others, as well as conversations within myself. For example, in a study of Mapuche adolescents in Chile, Merino and Tileagă (2011) show that a question such as '… how do you see your-self?' (p. 93) leads the participant to provide complex answers that do not fit neatly into categories, and distinguish between facets of group membership, such as feeling like the members of a group but not seeing like them (p. 93). In this study, the research interview itself is treated as a social encounter, one during which the interviewer and the research participant collaboratively influence identity. Similarly, in a study by Naomi Lee (2009) in Venezuela, working-class and affluent Venezuelan women were interviewed about beauti-fication, with identity construction within local moral orders taking place in the process of the research interview. Thus, for example, a working-class Venezuelan participant explained that some wealthy women (incorrectly) think that clothes, cars, cosmetic sur-gery, and other 'external' signs of beautification make a person better than the rest. This participant was positioning herself as enlightened and superior to 'those types of rich women' in moral terms.

Lee's research points to the processes involved in identity construction, and suggest that even in the limited context of Tajfel's minimal group experiment, meaning making is important. This is demonstrated by a study in which the standard minimal group experiment was carried out with British schoolboys under two conditions: in condition one, the criterion for social categorization was trivial (in the context of everyday life), but in condition two the criterion for social categorization was highly important from the perspective of the boys in the study (Moghaddam & Stringer, 1986). It was found that the boys showed ingroup favoritism in both conditions. The authors argued that because in the minimal group experiment the criterion for social categorization is the *only guide for action*, the participants interpret this guide to be important in this context, irrespec-tive of how important a criterion is in other contexts. Thus, irrespective of the 'trivial' or 'important' nature of a criterion in everyday contexts, it is subjectively interpreted as important by the participants in the minimal group experiment because it is the only guide for action.

Subjective Justice

'This is unjust!' 'We are being treated unfairly!' 'Our rights have been violated!' These kinds of statements about justice are routinely made during the process of intergroup conflict. 'Subjective justice', how people feel about the fairness of the treatment received by themselves and others, is at the heart of conflict (Finkel & Moghaddam, 2005). Of course, subjective justice can be very different from formal or blackletter law, the law 'on the books'. At the heart of subjective justice is how people perceive rights, what others owe us (if I have a right to free speech, then others have a duty to let me speak freely), and duties, what we owe others (if I have a duty to teach my class at 10.15am, then I owe it to my students to be prepared and in class on time). However, I will argue that the role of justice in intergroup relations is not easily explained by the available psychological theories.

The major Anglo-Saxon psychological theories have assumed that people strive to see the world as just, that there is a 'justice motive' guiding our behavior (Lerner, 1980). Thus, we tend to 'blame the victim' in all kinds of situations, including when people suffer natural disaster, robbery, rape, and other misfortunes (Hafer & Bègue, 2005). The major reason we 'blame the victim' is assumed to be because in this way we maintain a view of the world as just, thus 'protecting' ourselves – 'It was his fault he was hit by a car, I would not cross the street like that ...'. 'It was her fault she got mugged, I would not put myself in danger like that ...'. People also maintain a view of the world as just by shifting attention from short-term to long-term compensations, such as involved in religious beliefs about the afterlife – 'justice will be served when we die and go to heaven, and the members of that other group die and goes to hell!'

As already discussed in Chapter 14, another major psychological theory that assumes people strive for justice in their relationships and experience anxiety when they believe themselves to be in unjust relationships is equity theory (Walster, Walster, & Berscheid, 1978). According to equity theory, in the course of their social interactions people continuously calculate their 'inputs' (what they put into) and 'outcomes' (what they get out of) their relationships. As long as the ratio of inputs to outcomes for people in a relationship is roughly equal, then the relationship is seen to be just. But it is not only justice outcomes that concern people. The research of Tom Tyler has demonstrated that in addition to distributive justice, the instrumental benefits a person or group derives, people give importance to procedural justice, how they feel they are treated in the procedures leading to the outcome, whether they feel they are respected and their voice is listened to, and the like (Tyler & Huo, 2002). For example, irrespective of whether I receive a traffic violation ticket from a police officer, I come to a sense of justice/injustice because of the way the police officer treated me. She might give me a $100 traffic violation ticket, but I might still feel that I was treated fairly because she showed respect and acted professionally during our interactions.

In assessing how I am treated by a police officer, and how 'fair' my situation is in life generally, I make social comparisons with particular others. For example, my sense of injustice will increase if I feel that a police officer is treating other people in a situation with politeness, but is being rude and unprofessional with me. Most of the research on social comparisons and feelings of relative deprivation has focused on inter-personal relationships (Walker & Smith, 2002). For example, Jose feels deprived when he compares his income to that of Dave's. However, in his seminal study of attitudes toward inequality in England, Runciman (1966) focused also on what he termed 'fraternal deprivation', a person feeling deprived because of her or his group's position in society (pp. 38–40). For example, Jose feels deprived because of what he believes to be the low status of Hispanics as a group in North America. A major research question has been: under what conditions will Jose and others in his group take collective rather than individual action to improve their situation. Experimental evidence suggests that in the North American context, at least, the norms support individual rather than collective action (Wright, Taylor, & Moghaddam, 1990). That is, the cultural system of North America encourages people to try to play out the 'American dream', and the idea that any individual, irrespective of their group characteristics, can make it up the social hierarchy if they work hard and have the requisite talent.

There are also important cross-cultural differences that need to be taken into consideration when studying subjective justice. For example, some cultures have been termed 'honor cultures' because they give highest priority to the role of honor in social relationships, particularly when assessing fairness (Finkel, Harré, & Rodriguez Lopez, 2001). Thus, an unfair outcome is one that 'dishonors' me. Richard Nisbett and his associates have studied what they term a 'culture of honor', which they argue arises in herding societies (Nisbett & Cohen, 1996). Herdsmen live precarious lives, in the sense that their entire wealth is on display in the open, vulnerable to attack. In such a situation, men learn to defend their honor and to react violently to any action that might dishonor them, because putting up with dishonor could signal weakness and open them up to further attack, and the loss of everything they possess. Nisbett and Cohen (1996) found that within the United States, men from traditionally herding regions of the country showed more readiness to react violently to threats to their honor. Also, in reaction to insult, these men, but not men from non-herding regions, showed a marked rise in cortisol and testosterone levels.

Irrationality

A major question underlying psychological research on intergroup conflict is: do humans engaged in intergroup conflict behave rationally? That is, are humans aware of the factors influencing them to fight? The answer is 'no' when we consider a variety of theories, including materialist ones. For example, Marxist theory assumes that the members of different social classes are not initially aware of why there are intergroup conflicts in society, just as evolutionary psychologists assume that the influence of genes is not recognized by people fighting against others with dissimilar genes. Although irrationality at some level is assumed in a variety of theories explaining intergroup conflict, it is the psychodynamic tradition inspired by Sigmund Freud (1856–1939) that takes up this viewpoint most directly.

Freud (1955[1921], 1957[1915]) points out that in all human relationships there are mixed emotions; libidinal ties even between parents and children, and husbands and wives, involve both positive and negative feelings. A challenge in relationships is to displace negative feelings outward, onto targets outside the relationship. When such displacement does not take place and the negative feelings remain within the relationship, their impact can be highly destructive. Consider, for example, a husband and wife who have lived with one another for 25 years and raised two children in a 'loving family', but who are now going through divorce proceedings and fiercely attack one another in and out of law courts. Within the group context, the displacement of negative emotions is just as essential.

Within all human groups, the members experience both negative and positive emotions toward one another. For example, within a basketball team the team members experience rivalries, jealousies, even hatreds, as well as admiration, liking, and other positive sentiments. Despite experiencing some negative sentiments, the team manages to remain cohesive by focusing on the external 'enemy', the opposition team.

The role of the group leader received special attention from Freud, who limited his analysis to groups with leaders. Group members are bound to the group through their identification with the leader. Freud used the examples of the army and the Catholic Church to illustrate his views on group dynamics. An 'illusion' binds people together in both institutions, because both in a church and in an army '... the same illusion holds good of there being a head – in the Catholic Church Christ, in an army its commander-in-chief – who loves all individuals in the group with equal love' (1955[1921], pp. 93–94). Constructive group leadership can inspire a group to achieve superior levels of collaboration and creativity, but group leaders also play a role in displacing negative sentiments onto outgroups, '... every religion is ... a religion of love for those whom it embraces; while cruelty and intolerance towards those who do not belong to it are natural to every religion' (Freud, 1955[1921], p. 98). According to Freud, aggression is not displaced onto outgroup targets randomly, but onto dissimilar outgroups particularly.

The displacement of aggression onto dissimilar others serves to make the ingroup more cohesive and to mobilize support for the group leader. On the one hand, displacement of negative feelings lessens discord within the group. On the other hand, the focus on an 'external enemy' helps to mobilize support for leadership, and diffuse silent dissent. These processes can be highly influential in national and international politics, and can help aggressive leadership mobilize internal support. In some instances, the aggressive rhetoric national leaders employ against one another serves to radicalize both sides, as there is an escalation of threats and no clear path for de-escalation. This kind of irrational 'mutual radicalization' seems to have taken place between the United States and Iran since the 1980s (Konaev & Moghaddam, 2010).

Cultural-Evolutionary Account of Radicalization and Terrorism

The dominant security issues of the 21st century have been associated with radicalization and terrorism, and major conflicts (in Iraq, Afghanistan, among other places) following the tragic terrorist attacks of 9/11. In this section of the chapter, these events are explored through a cultural-evolutionary perspective. This perspective is macro and focuses on processes that are long term and global.

Integral to the cultural-evolutionary perspective is the concept of 'catastrophic evolution', a swift, sharp, and often fatal decline in the numbers of a particular life form (Moghaddam, 2008b). Catastrophic evolution has come about through intergroup contact, particularly since the industrial revolution and the colonization of the non-Western world by Western powers. Catastrophic evolution has been speeded up in the era of globalization, increasing interconnectedness in economies and cultures around the world. An important outcome of colonization and, more recently, globalization, is a decline in diversity. Culture being a relatively 'wooly' concept that is more difficult to define and measure, it is easier to gage the decline in language diversity.

There has been extensive discussion of the decline in diversity in plants and animals (e.g. Baskin, 2002), but far less attention has been given to a decline in diversity in languages and the cultures they 'carry' (Moghaddam, 2008b). Around the time that Columbus arrived in North America, there were approximately 15,000 languages in the world, but roughly 9,000 of those languages have disappeared. It is estimated that by the end of the 21st century, most of the languages alive today will have 'died' (Crystal, 2000). As David Harrison describes in his book *The last speakers* (2010), which is part of the larger literature on 'language death', there are urgent efforts to try to save endangered languages. Hundreds of languages have only a few speakers left and are in serious danger of disappearing forever.

But why should we invest resources into saving endangered languages? There are also arguments to be made in favor of allowing language death to continue, so that more and more people speak the same language. By speaking a common language, people may find that they can communicate better with one another, and so there will be fewer misunderstandings and less likelihood of intergroup conflicts. English has become the common language in science, business, show business, and also diplomacy. This is in large part because for the first time in history, one empire (the British) has been succeeded by another (the American), using the same language (English). The dominance of English, it could be argued, has enabled people in science, business, and other areas to cooperate more effectively with one another. From this perspective, language death has positive outcomes that outweigh the negative ones.

An alternative perspective is that, just as diversity in animals and plants is of great value, diversity in languages is invaluable and improves the survival chances of humans. Languages 'carry' cultures, and particular ways of seeing the world. To some extent, the world looks different in different languages, and the 'collective wisdom' carried in different languages is to some degree different (Deutscher, 2010). This is reflected in the sayings, jokes, and so on, that 'work best' in the original language and in cultural context, and lose their impact when translated. Also, the information conveyed is often different in different languages. For example, if a woman explains in English to her boyfriend 'I spent the evening with a friend,' the rules of English do not force her to indicate the sex of the friend. But in many other languages, such as French, the sex of the friend would necessarily be indicated in the sentence. Thus, from this perspective there are variations in languages, with each language 'carrying' and passing on certain cultures, and there is great value in maintaining this diversity because it makes our world culturally richer and improves our survival chances. The wisdom and values of threatened cultures might prove invaluable to us in the future.

Sudden Contact

Two concepts are particularly useful for better understanding catastrophic evolution. The first is preadaptiveness, '... how prepared a life form is in terms of biological and other characteristics for successful evolution in contact with particular other life forms in a given environment' (Moghaddam, 2008b, p. 96). A second concept is postcontact adaptation speed, how quickly a life form can adapt to successfully compete when first coming into contact with another life form. When a life form with low preadaptativeness and low postcontact adaptation speed comes into 'sudden' contact with a competitor, the chances of its survival are low. The phenomenon of 'invasive species' demonstrates this process in the domain of plants and animals, with thousands of examples around the world of how sudden contact has resulted in the serious decline and sometimes extinction of life forms (Baskin, 2002).

Concluding Comment: The Meeting of Research and Policy

Globalization processes are resulting in societies that are more diverse in terms of ethnicity, religion, language, and other such characteristics (Moghaddam, 2010). As a result, relationships between different ethnic, religious, language, and other such groups have become a central issue in 21st-century societies. By implication, research on intergroup relationships should become a more important topic in psychological science. This implication is being realized, albeit slowly (Taylor & Moghaddam, 1994). Particularly through the influence of European researchers, there is now more psychological research on intergroup relations

(Moghaddam, 2008a). A focus of intergroup research is the policies developed to manage diversity. Such policies are founded on psychological assumptions, many of which have been tested, sometimes directly, through psychological research.

The traditional policy for managing diversity has been assimilation, through which group-based differences 'melt away' and the members of a society become more similar. Minority-assimilation involves minority groups 'melting into' the culture of the majority group; 'melting pot assimilation' involves minority groups and the majority group all changing, 'melting into one another' to create a new culture, a new being – such as 'the American' celebrated by the poet Walt Whitman (1819–1892). This new society would be cohesive, because of the benefits that greater similarity brings, as suggested by the long-established finding in psychology that similarity leads to attraction. In a study involving Algerian, English Canadian, French-Canadian, Greek, Indian and Jewish participants in Canada, we found that group members were more attracted to the members of outgroups they perceived to be more similar to their ingroup (Osbeck, Moghaddam, & Perreault, 1977). Thus, even in multicultural Canada, similarity-attraction is a powerful force in social relations.

But there are practical limitations to how much progress can be made through assimilation policy. Similarity and dissimilarity are social constructions: the criteria we use for similarity can vary across cultures and across situations. Dissimilarity can be 'manufactured' and used to justify intergroup discrimination, even when objectively the dissimilarity is trivial (Tajfel et al., 1971). Physical differences (e.g. skin color) will not 'melt away', and so there is always a potential basis for intergroup discrimination. Because of this and other potential weaknesses in assimilation policy, since the 1970s multiculturalism policy has emerged as a popular alternative (Moghaddam, 2008a).

Multiculturalism was first adopted as official government policy in Canada in 1972, and since then Australia, New Zealand, and a number of other countries have implemented versions of multiculturalism. Although the United States does not have an official policy for managing diversity, or even an official language, multiculturalism has become the de facto policy in public schools in America. The various interpretations of multiculturalism generally have three things in common. First, the highlighting and celebration of group-based differences. Second, the effort to build up pride in heritage cultures. Third, the assumption that pride in ingroup culture will lead people to be open to sharing cultures and better appreciating and accepting others. Unfortunately, these characteristics have in some cases resulted in more problematic intergroup relations, with the result that in 2011, major European leaders in Germany, France and the United Kingdom proclaimed that multiculturalism has not worked.

Critics have pointed out that the celebration of differences has been associated with ethnic stereotypes that are detrimental to some minorities. For example, some young African Americans have been detrimentally influenced by the stereotype that academic work is not for their ingroup, and that any African American who spends a lot of time with books and in libraries is 'acting white' (see Ogbu & Davis, 2003, and the follow-up research of Carter, 2005, and Fryer & Torelli, 2010). Another problematic assumption underlying multiculturalism is that pride and confidence in ingroup will result in greater willingness to share cultures and be open to outgroup members. There are unfortunately many examples in history of groups with high pride and confidence in their own heritage, but negatively disposed to outgroups (e.g. Nazis, religious fanatics, ultra-nationalists).

Shortcomings in assimilation and multiculturalism policies have led to explorations of alternative policies. For example, historians have put forward polyculturalism, which emphasizes the cross-cutting influences of cultures on one another (Prashad, 2001). No culture stands alone, just as no person is an island. Another new policy proposal is omni-culturalism (Moghaddam, 2009), which has two stages: first, children are taught about human commonalities and learn to address the question, 'What is a human being?' Psychological science has an important role to play in answering this question, as there is enormous overlap across humans in their basic characteristics. At a second stage in development, omniculturalism policy requires that attention be given to the distinctiveness of groups. However, in omniculturalism priority always remains with human commonalities. A representative sample of Americans showed solid support for omniculturalism policy (Moghaddam & Breckenridge, 2010), suggesting that there is public support for exploring alternative policies and re-thinking intergroup relations.

References

Adams, J. L., & Harré, R. (2003). Gender positioning. In R. Harré & F. Moghaddam (Eds.), *The self and others*. Westport, CT: Praeger.

Adams, J. S. (1963). Toward an understanding of inequity. *Journal of Abnormal and Social Psychology, 67*, 422–436.

Addis, D. R., Wong, A. T., & Schacter, D. L. (2007). Remembering the past and imagining the future: Common and distinct neural substrates during event construction and elaboration. *Neuropsychologia, 45*(7), 1363–1377.

Adorno, T. W., Frenkel-Brunswik, E., Levinson, D. J., & Sanford, B. W. (1950). *The authoritarian personality*. New York: Harper & Row.

Ainsworth, M. (1978). *Patterns of attachment: A psychological study of the strange situation*. New York: Earlbaum.

Albright, T. D., Jessell, T. M., Kandel, E. R., & Posner, M. I. (2000). Neural science: A century of progress and the mysteries that remain. Review suppl. to *Cell, 100* and *Neuron, 25*, S40.

Allderidge, P. (1979). Hospitals, mad houses, and asylums: Cycles in the care of the insane. *British Journal of Psychiatry, 134*, 321–324.

Allen, W. E., & Chagnon, N. A. (2004). The tragedy of the commons revisited. In Y. T. Lee, C. McCauley, F. M. Moghaddam, & S. Worchel (Eds.), *The psychology of ethnic and cultural conflict* (pp. 23–47). Westport, CT.: Praeger.

Allport, G. W. (1961). *Pattern and growth in personality*. New York: Holt, Rinehart and Winston.

Allport, G. W. (1967). Attitudes. In M. Fishbein (Ed.), *Readings in attitude theory and measurement* (pp. 1–13). New York: Wiley.

Amenomouri, M., Kono, A., Fournier, J., & Winer, G. (1997). A cross-cultural developmental study of directional asymmetries in circle drawing. *Journal of Cross-Cultural Psychology, 28*, 730–742.

Anderson, C. A., Shibuya, A., Ihori, N., Swing, E. L., Bushman, B. J., Sakamoto, A., et al. (2010). Violent video game effects on aggression, empathy, and prosocial behavior in Eastern and Western countries. *Psychological Bulleting, 136*, 151–173.

Archer, J. (2009). Does sexual selection explain human sex differences in aggression? *Behavioral and Brain Sciences, 32*, 249–311.

Argyle, M. (1984). *The psychology of happiness*. London: Methuen.

Argyle, M., & Little, B. R. (1972). Do personality traits apply to social behavior? *Journal for the Theory of Social Behaviour, 2*, 1–33.

Arkes, H. R., & Tetlock, P. E. (2004). Attributions of implicit prejudice, or "Would Jesse Jackson 'fail' the Implicit Association Test?", *Psychological Inquiry, 15*, 257–279.

Asch, S. E. (1987[1952]). *Social psychology*. Oxford: Oxford University Press.

Austin., J. L. (1975). *How to do things with words*. Oxford: Clarendon Press.

Averill, J. (1982). *Anger and aggression: An essay on emotion*. New York: Springer.

Ayer, A. J. (Ed.) (1978). *Logical positivism*. Westport, CT: Greenwood Press.

Baer, J., Kaufman, J. C., & Baumeister, R. (2008). *Are we free? Psychology and free will*. Oxford: OUP.

Baldwin, J.M. (1895). *Mental development in the child and race*. New York: Macmillan.

Baldwin, J.M. (1906). *Thought and things or genetic logic*. London: Library of Philosophy.

Bandura, A. (1973). *Aggression: A social learning analysis*. Englewood Cliffs, NJ: Prentice Hall.

Bandura, A. (1977). *Social learning theory*. Englewood Cliffs, NJ: Prentice Hall.

Bandura, A. (1986). *Social foundations of thought and action*. Englewood Cliffs, NJ: Prentice Hall.

Barkow, J. H., Cosmides, L., & Tooby, J. (1992). *The adapted mind*. Oxford: Oxford University Press.

Bar-On, R., Tranel, D., Denburg, N. L., & Behcara, A. (2005). Exploring the neurological substrate of emotional and social intelligence. In J. T. Cacioppo, & G. G. Bernston (Eds.), *Key readings in social psychology: Social neuroscience* (pp. 223–237). New York: Psychology Press.

Bartlett, F. C. (1916). An experimental study of some problems of perceiving and imagining. *British Journal of Psychology, 8*, 222–266.

Bartlett, F. C. (1932). *Remembering: A study in experimental and social psychology*. Cambridge: Cambridge University Press.

Bartlett, F.C. (1935). 'Remembering', *Scientia, 57*: 221–226.

Barton, R. A. (1998). Visual specialization and brain evolution in primates. *Proceedings of the Royal Society, London, 265B*, 1933–1937.

Baskin, Y. (2002). *A plague of rats and rubber vines*. Washington, DC: Island Press.

Bauer, M., & Gaskell, G. (1999). Towards a paradigm for research on social representations. *Journal for the Theory of Social Behaviour, 29*(2), 163–186.

Bauer, M., & Gaskell, G. (2008). Social representations theory: A progressive research programme for social psychology. *Journal for the Theory of Social Behaviour, 38*(4), 335–353.

Bayne, T., Cleeremans, A., & Wilken, P. (Eds.). (2009). *The Oxford companion to consciousness*. Oxford: Oxford University Press.

Bechara, A., Tranel, D., Damasio, H., & Damasio, A. R. (1996). Failure to respond automatically to anticipated future outcomes following damage to prefrontal cortex. *Cereb. Cortex, 6*, 215–225.

Bekoff, M. (2005). *Wild justice and fair play: Cooperation, forgiveness, and morality in animals*. Chicago, IL: University of Chicago Press.

Bennett, M. R., & Hacker, P. M. S. (2002). The motor system in neuroscience: A history and analysis of conceptual developments. *Progress in Neurobiology, 67*, 1–52.

Bennett, M. R., & Hacker, P. M. S. (2003). *Philosophical foundations of neuroscience*. Oxford: Blackwell.

Ben-Zeʼev, A. (2002). Emotions are not feelings, *Consciousness & Emotion, 3*(2), 81–89.

Berger, P., & Luckman, T. (1966). *The social construction of reality*. Harmondsworth: Penguin.

Bernston, G. G., & Cacioppo, J. T. (2008). The neuroevolution of motivation. In J. Y. Shah, & W. L. Gardner (Eds.), *Handbook of motivation science* (pp. 188–200). New York: Guilford Press.

Berridge, K. C., & Aldridge, J. W. (2008). Decision utility, the brain, and pursuit of hedonic goals. *Social Cognition, 26*(5), 621–646.

Berridge, K. C., & Robinson, T. E. (1998). The role of dopamine in reward: Hedonics, learning, or incentive salience? *Brain Research Reviews, 28*, 308–367.

Berry, J. W., Poortinga, Y. H., Breugelmans, S. M., Chasiotis, A., & Sam, D. L. (2011). *Cross-cultural psychology: Research and applications*. Cambridge: Cambridge University Press.

Billig, M. (1999). *Freudian repression*. Cambridge: Cambridge University Press.

Black, D. W. & Andreasen, N. C. (1994). Schizophrenia, schizophreniform disorder, and delusional paranoid disorder. In J. A. Talbott, R. E. Halas, & S. C. Yudofsky (Eds.), *American Psychiatric Press textbook of psychiatry* (pp. 411–463). Washington, D.C.: American Psychiatric Press.

Blakemore, C., & Cooper, G. F. (1970). Development of the brain depends on visual environment. *Nature, 228*, 477–478.

Bleuler, E. (1911). *Dementia praecox or the group of schizophrenias* (J. Zinkin, & D. C. Lewis, Trans.). New York: International Universities Press, 1950.

Bloom, C. D. (1999). The performance effects of pay dispersion on individuals and organizations. *Academy of Management Journal, 42*, 25–40.

Boesch, E. (1997). The sound of the violin. In M. Cole., Y. Engestrom, & O. Vasquez (Eds.), *Mind, Culture and activity: Seminal papers from the Laboratory of Comparative Human Cognition* (pp. 164–184). Cambridge: Cambridge University Press.

Bowen, M. (1978). *Family therapy in clinical practice*. Northvale, NJ: Jason Aronson Inc.

Bowlby, J. (1978). *The making and breaking of affectional bonds*. London: Tavistock.

Bowlby, J. (1997–8). *Attachment and loss*. Vols 1 – 3. London: Pimlico.

Brenner, W. H. (1999). *Wittgenstein's philosophical investigations*. Albany, NY: SUNY Press.

Brinkmann, S. (2010). *Psychology as a moral science*. New York: Springer.

Brody, N. (2003). Construct validation of the Sternberg Triarchic Abilities Test: Comment and reanalysis. *Intelligence, 31*, 319–329.

Brosnan, S. F. (2010). *An evolutionary perspective on responses to inequity*. Paper presented at the 13th Biennial Conference of the International Society for Justice Research, Banff, Canada.

Brosnan, S. F., & de Waal, F. B. M. (2003). Monkeys reject unequal pay. *Nature, 425*, 297–299.

Brown, A. S., Cohen, P., Harkavy-Friedman, J., & Babulas, V. (2001). Prenatal rubella, premorbid abnormalities, and adult schizophrenia. *Biological Psychiatry, 49*, 473–486.

Brown, R., & Gillman, A. (1960). The pronouns of power and solidarity. *American Anthropologist, 4*, 24–39.

Bruner, J. S. (1983). *In search of mind*. New York: Harper and Row.

Bruner, J. S. (1986). *Actual minds, possible worlds*. Cambridge, MA: Harvard University Press.

Brunner, H. G., Nelen, M., Breakefield, X. O., Ropers, H. H., & van Oost, B. A. (1993). Abnormal behavior associated with a point mutation in the structural gene for monoamine oxidase A. *Science, 268*, 1763–1766.

Bryant, P. E. (1984). Piaget, teachers and psychologists. *Oxford Review of Education, 10*, 251–260.

Buckholtz, J. W., & Meyer-Lindenberg, A. (2008). MAOA and the neurogenetic architecture of human aggression. *Trends in Neurosciences, 31*, 120–129.

Burke, K. (1945). *A grammar of motives*. Englewood Cliffs, NJ: Prentice Hall.

Burke, K. (1969). *A grammar of motives*. Berkeley, CA: University of California Press.

Burton, R. (2000[1621]). *The anatomy of melancholy*. Oxford: Oxford University Press.

Cacioppo, J. T., & Bernston, G. G. (2005). *Social neuroscience: Key readings*. London: Psychology Press.

Cannon, T. D., Rosso, I. M., Hollister, J. M., Bearden, C. E., Sanchez, L. E., & Hadley, T. (2000). A prospective cohort study of genetic and perinatal influences in schizophrenia. *Schizophrenia Bulletin, 26*, 351–366.

Carter, C. S., Mintun, M., Nichols, T., & Cohen, J. D. (1997). Anterior cingulated gyrus dysfunction and selective attention deficits in schizophrenia: 15OH2O PET study during single-trial Stroop task performance. *American Journal of Psychiatry, 154*, 1670–1675.

Carter, P. (2005). *Keep'it real: School success beyond black and white*. New York: Oxford University Press.

Carver, C. F. (2003). The making of a memory mechanism. *Journal of the History of Biology, 36*, 153–195.

Casey, E. S. (2000). *Remembering: Phenomenological study*. Bloomington, IN: Indiana University Press.

Caspi, J., Clay, T., & Moffit, T. (2002). Role of genotype in the cycle of violence in maltreated children. *Science, 197*, 851–854.

Cervo, L., Canetta, A., Calcagno, E., Burbassi, S., Sacchetti, G., Caccia, S., Fracasso, C., Albani, D., Forloni, G., & Invernizzi, R. W. (2005). Genotype-dependent activity of tryptophan hydroxylase-2 determines the response to citalopram in a mouse model of depression. *Journal of Neuroscience, 25*, 8165–8172.

Chagnon, N. (1997). *Yanomamo* (5th ed.). New York: Harcourt Brace.

Chalmers, D. (1996). *The conscious mind*. Oxford: Oxford University Press.

Charlish, A., & Cutting, J. (1995). *Schizophrenia: Understanding and coping with the illness*. London: Thorsons.

Cheung, F. M., Cheung, S. F., Leung, K., Ward, C., & Leung, F. (2003). The English version of the Chinese personality assessment inventory. *Journal of Cross-Cultural Psychology, 34*, 433–452.

Chomsky, N. (1959). Review of B. F. Skinner's *Verbal behaviour*. *Language, 35*, 26–58.

Chua, S. E., & McKenna, P. J. (1995). Schizophrenia: A brain disease? *British Journal of Psychiatry*, *166*, 563–582.

Coccaro, E. F., McCloskey, M. S., Fitzgerald, D. A., & Phan, K. L. (2007). Amygdala and orbitofrontal reactivity to social threat in individuals with impulsive aggression. *Biological Psychiatry*, *62*, 168–178.

Cole, M. (1996). *Cultural psychology: A once and future discipline*. Cambridge, MA: Harvard University Press.

Collins, A., & Perron, P. (1990). *Narrative semiotics and cognitive discourses*. London: Pinter.

Cosmides, L., & Tooby, J. (1995). *The adapted mind: Evolutionary psychology and the generation of culture*. New York: Oxford University Press.

Cosmides, L., & Tooby, J. (1997). The modular nature of intelligence. In B. Scheibel, & J. W. Schop (Eds.), *The origin and evolution of intelligence* (p. 92). Boston, MA: Jones & Bartlett.

Costall, A. (1992). Why British psychology is not social: Frederic Bartlett's promotion of the new academic discipline. *Canadian Psychology/Psychologie canadienne*, *33*(3), 633–639.

Costall, A., & Leudar, I. (2009). *Against theory of mind*. Basingstoke: Palgrave Macmillan.

Crick, F. (1994). *The astonishing hypothesis: The scientific search for the soul*. New York: Scribners.

Crick, F., & Koch, C. (1992). Mind and brain. *Scientific American*, *267*(Sept.).

Crystal, D. (2000). *Language death*. Cambridge: Cambridge University Press.

Csikszentmihalyi, M. (1990). *Flow: The psychology of optimal experience*. New York: Harper and Row.

D'Souza, D. (1995). *The end of racism*. New York: Free Press.

Daanen, P. (2009). Conscious and non-conscious representation in social representations theory: Social representations from the phenomenological point of view. *Culture & Psychology*, *15*, 372–385.

Daly, M., & Wilson, M. (1988). *Homicide*. New York: Aldine de Gruyter.

Damasio, A. R. (2000). *Descartes' error: Emotion, reason, and the human brain*. London: Quiller.

Damasio, A. R. (2010). *Self comes to mind: Constructing the conscious brain*. New York: Pantheon.

Danziger, K. (1990). *Constructing the subject*. Cambridge: Cambridge University Press.

Danziger, K. (2002a). Sealing off the discipline: Wilhelm Wundt and the psychology of memory. In C. D. Green, M. Shore, & T. Teo (Eds.), *The transformation of psychology: Influences of 19th-century philosophy, technology, and natural science* (pp. 45–62). Washington, DC: American Psychological Association.

Danziger, K. (2002b). How old is psychology, particularly concepts of memory? *History and Philosophy of Psychology*, *4*(1), 1–12.

Darwin, C. (1979[1872]). *The expression of emotion in man and animals*. London and New York: St. Martin's Press.

Darwin, C. (1993[1859]). *The origin of species by natural selection or the preservation of favored races in the struggle for life*. New York: Modern Library.

Dawkins, R. (1989). *The selfish gene* (2nd ed.). Oxford: Oxford University Press.

Dawkins, R. (2006[1964]). *The selfish gene*. Oxford: Oxford University Press.

De Waal, F. (1996). *Good natured: The origins of right and wrong in humans and other animals*. Cambridge, MA: Harvard University Press.

Dennett, D. (1969). *Content and consciousness*. London: Routledge and Kegan Paul.

Dennett, D. (1978). *Brainstorms: Philosophical essays on mind and psychology*. Cambridge, MA: Bradford Books/MIT Press.

Dennett, D. (1989). Consciousness. In R. L. Gregory (Ed.). *The Oxford companion to the mind*. Oxford: Oxford University Press.

Dennett, D. (1991). *Consciousness explained*. Boston, MA: Little, Brown.

Dennett, D. (2005). *Sweet dreams: Philosophical obstacles to a science of consciousness*. Cambridge, MA: MIT Press.

Deutscher, G. (2010). *Through the language glass: Why the world looks different in other languages*. New York: Metropolitan.

Dewey, J. (1896). The reflex arc concept in psychology. *Psychological Review, 3*, 357–370.

Dewey, J. (1916). *Democracy and education.* New York: Macmillan.

Dewey, J. (1925). *Experience and nature.* Chicago: Open Court.

Dewey, J. (1934). *Art as experience.* New York: Penguin.

Donald, M. (1991). *Origins of the modern mind.* Cambridge, MA: Harvard University Press.

Donaldson, M. (1978). Children reasoning. In M. Donaldson et al., *Early childhood development and education* (pp. 246–250). New York: Guilford Press.

Donaldson, M., Grieve, R., & Pratt, C. (1983). *Early childhood development and education.* New York: Guilford Press.

Douglas, R. J., & Pribram, K. H. (1969). Distraction and habituation in monkeys with limbic lesions. *Journal of Comparative and Physiological Psychology, 69*(3), 473–480.

DSM IV TR (2004). *Diagnostics and statistical manual of mental disorders IV TR.* Arlington, VA: American Psychiatric Association.

Dudai, Y. (2004). The neurobiology of consolidations, or, how stable is the engram? *Annual Review of Psychology, 55*, 51–86.

Dunbar, R., Barrett, L., & Lycett, J. (2007). *Evolutionary psychology.* Oxford: One World.

Ebbinghaus, H. (1962[1885]). *Memory: A contribution to experimental psychology.* New York: Dover.

Edelman, S., & Vaina, L. M. (2001). *David Marr. International Encyclopedia of Social and Behavioral Sciences.*

Edwards, D., & Potter, J. (1992). *Discursive psychology.* London: SAGE.

Eisenberger, N. I., Way, B. M., Taylor, S. E., Welch, W. T., & Lieberman, D. (2007). Understanding genetic risk for aggression: Clues from the Brain's response to social exclusion. *Biological Psychiatry, 61*, 1100–1108.

Ekman, P. (2003). *Emotions revealed.* London: Weidenfeld and Nicholson.

Emler, N. P., Renwick, S., & Malone, B. (1983). The relationship between moral reasoning and political orientation. *Journal of Personality and Social Psychology, 45*, 1073–1080.

Engelian, A., Yang, Y., Engelian, W., Zonana, J., Stern, E., & Silberweig, D. D. (2002). Physiological mapping of human auditory cortices with silent event-related fMRI technique. *Neuroimage, 16*(4), 944–953.

Ericsson, K. A., & Ward, P. (2007). Capturing the naturally occurring superior performance of experts in the laboratory. *Current Directions in Psychological Science, 16*, 346–350.

Ericsson, K. A., Patel, V. L., & Kintsch, W. (2000). How experts' adaptations to representative task demands account for the expertise effect in memory recall: Comment on Vicente and Wang (1998). *Psychological Review, 107*, 578–592.

Everson, S. (1997). *Aristotle on perception.* Oxford: Clarendon Press.

Eysenck, H. J. (1967). *The biological basis of personality.* Springfield, IL: Thomas.

Eysenck, H. J. (1970). *The structure of personality.* London: Methuen.

Eysenck, H.J. (1985). *Decline and fall of the Freudian empire.* Harmondsworth: Penguin Books.

Fairbairn, W. R. D. (1952). *Psychoanalytic studies of the personality.* New York: Basic Books.

Farr, R. (1996). *The roots of modern social psychology.* Oxford: Blackwell.

Farr, R., & Moscovici, S. (Eds.). (1984). *Social representations.* Cambridge: Cambridge University Press.

Fasel, R., & Spini, D. (2010). Effects of victimization on the belief in a just world in four ex-Yugoslavian countries. *Social Justice Research, 23*, 17–36.

Faulks, S. (1997). *The fatal Englishman.* London: Vintage.

Finkel, N. J., & Moghaddam, F. M. (Eds.). (2005). *The psychology of rights and duties: Empirical contributions and normative commentaries.* Washington, DC: American Psychological Association Press.

Finkel, N. J., Harré, R., & Rodriguez Lopez, J. L. (2001). Commonsense morality across cultures: Notions of fairness, justice, honor and equity. *Discourse Studies, 3*, 5–27.

Flanagan, D. P., & Harrison, P. L. (Eds.). (2005). *Contemporary intellectual assessment: Theories, tests, and issues* (2nd ed.). New York: Guilford Press.

Flynn, J. R. (2007). *What is intelligence? Beyond the Flynn effect.* Cambridge: Cambridge University Press.

Forgas, J. P., Williams, K. D., & Laham, S. M. (2005). Social motivation: Introduction and overview. In J. P. Forgas, K. D. Williams, & S. M. Laham (Eds.), *Social motivation: Conscious and unconscious processes* (pp. 1–17). Cambridge: Cambridge University Press.

Foucault, M. (1965). *Madness and civilization.* New York: Random House.

Freud, A. (1982). *Psychoanalytic psychology of normal development.* London: Hogarth Press.

Freud, S. (1955[1921]). Group psychology and the analysis of the ego. In J. Strachey (Ed. & Trans.), *The standard edition of the complete psychological works of Sigmund Freud* (Vol. 18, pp. 67–143). London: Hogarth Press.

Freud, S. (1957[1915]). Thoughts for the times on war and death. In J. Strachey (Ed. & Trans.), *The standard edition of the complete psychological works of Sigmund Freud* (Vol. 14, pp. 271–302). London: Hogarth Press.

Freud, S. (1961[1930]). Civilization and its discontents. In J. Strachey (Ed. & Trans.), *The standard edition of complete psychological works of Sigmund Freud* (Vol. 21, pp. 64–145). London: Hogarth Press.

Friedman, M., & Rosenman, R. (1974). *Type A behavior and your heart.* New York: Knopf.

Frisby, J. R. (1980). *Seeing: illusion, brain and mind.* Oxford: Oxford University Press.

Frishman, L. J. (2001). Basic visual processes. In E. B. Goldstein (Ed.), *Blackwell Handbook of Perception.* Oxford: Blackwell.

Frishman, L. J. (2001). In E. Goldstein (Ed.). *Handbook of perception* (p. 55). Malden, MA and Oxford: Blackwell.

Fryer, R. G., & Torelli, P. (2010). An empirical analysis of 'acting white'. *Journal of Public Economics, 94,* 380–396.

Gardner, H. (1999). Intelligence reframed: Multiple intelligence in the 21st century. New York: Basic Books.

Gardner, H. (2004). Frames of mind: The theory of multiple intelligences. 20th anniversary edition. New York: Basic Books.

Garfinkel, H. (1967). *Studies in ethnomethodology.* Englewood Cliffs, NJ: Prentice Hall.

Gazzaniga, M. S. (2010). Neuroscience and the correct level of explanation for understanding mind. *Trends in Cognitive Sciences, 14,* 291–292.

Gergen, K. (1985). The social constructionist movement in modern psychology. *American Psychologist, 40,* 266–275.

Gibson, J. J. (1950). *The perception of the visual world.* Boston: Houghton Mifflin.

Gibson, J. J. (1962). Observations on active touch. *Psychological Review, 69,* 477–491.

Gibson, J. J. (1966). *The senses considered as perceptual systems.* Boston, MA: Houghton Mifflin.

Gilligan, C. (1982). *In a different voice.* Cambridge, MA: Harvard University Press.

Gino, F., & Pierce, L. (2009). Dishonesty in the name of equity. *Psychological Science, 20,* 1153–1160.

Giorgi, A., & Giorgi, B. (2008) Phenomenology. In J. A. Smith (Ed.), *Qualitative psychology: A practical guide.* London and Thousand Oaks, CA: SAGE.

Gladkova, A. (2010). Sympathy, compassion and empathy in English and Russian: A linguistic and cultural analysis. *Culture & Psychology, 16,* 267–285.

Glaser, B. G., & Strauss, A. L. (1967). *The discovery of grounded theory.* Chicago, IL: Aldine.

Glăveanu, V. P. (2010). Paradigms in the study of creativity: Introducing the perspective of cultural psychology. *New Ideas in Psychology, 28*(1), 79–93.

Glynn, I. (1999). *Anatomy of thought.* London: Weidenfeld and Nicolson.

Goddard, C., & Wierzbicka, A. (Eds.). (2002). *Meaning and universal grammar: Theory and empirical findings.* Amsterdam: John Benjamins Publishing.

Goffman, E. (1967). *Interaction ritual.* New York: Anchor Books.

Goffman, E. (1968). *Asylums.* Harmondsworth: Penguin.

Goffman, E. (1975). *Frame analysis: An essay on the organization of* experience. Harmondsworth: Penguin.

Goffman, E. (1981). *Forms of talk.* Philadelphia: University of Pennsylvania Press.

Goffman, E. (1990[1969]). *The presentation of self in everyday life.* New York: Doubleday.

Goldstein, E. B. (Ed.). (2001). *Blackwell handbook of perception.* Oxford: Blackwell.

Gopnik, A., & Meltzoff, A. N. (1997). *Words, thoughts and theories.* Cambridge, MA: MIT Press.

Gordon, I. E. (1997). *Theories of visual perception.* Chichester: Wiley.

Gottesman, I. I. (1991). *Schizophrenia genesis: The origins of madness.* New York: Freeman.

Grattan, K. (2008). The dispute over the fate of Terri Sciavo. In F. Moghaddam, R. Harré, & N. Lee (Eds.), *Global conflict resolution through positioning analysis.* New York: Springer.

Green, M. F., Kern, R. S., Braff, D. I., & Mintz, J. (2000). Neurocognitive deficits and functional outcome in schizophrenia: Are we measuring the 'right stuff'? *Schizophrenia Bulletin, 26,* 119–136.

Green, R. G. (1994). Social motivation. In B. Parkinson, & A. M. Colman (Eds.), *Emotion and motivation* (pp. 38–57). London: Longman.

Greenberg, G. (2010). *Manufacturing depression: The secret history of modern disease.* New York: Simon and Schuster.

Greene, J. D., Nystrom, L. E., Engell, A. D., Darley, J. M., & Cohen, J. D. (2004). The neural bases of cognitive conflict and control in moral judgment. *Neuron, 44,* 389–400.

Greene, J., & Haidt, J. (2002). How (and where) does moral judgment work? *Trends in Cognitive Sciences, 6,* 517–523.

Gregory, R. L. (1997). *Mirrors in mind.* London: Penguin.

Gregory, R. L. (1998). *Eye and brain.* Oxford: Oxford University Press.

Greimas, A. J. (1990). On meaning. In F. Collins, & P. Perran (Eds.), *Narrative semiotics and cognitive discourses.* London: Pinter.

Grossman, D. (1995). *On killing: The psychological cost of learning to kill in war and society.* New York: Little, Brown.

Gruber, H. E., & Vanèche, J. J. (1977). *The essential Piaget.* New York: Basic Books.

Habermas, J. (2008). *Between naturalism and religion.* Cambridge: Polity.

Hafer, C. (2000). Do innocent victims threaten the belief in a just world? Evidence from a modified stoop task. *Journal of Personality and Social Psychology, 79,* 165–173.

Hafer, C. L., & Bègue, L. (2005). Experimental research on just-world theory: Problems, developments, and future challenges. *Psychological Bulletin, 131,* 128–167.

Hafer, C. L., Bègue, L., Choma, B. L., & Dempsey, J. L. (2005). Belief in a just world and commitment to long-term deserved outcomes. *Social Justice Research, 18,* 429–444.

Hagins, W. A., Penn, R. D., & Yoshikami, S. (1970). Dark current and retinal current in rods. *Biophysical Journal, 10,* 380–409.

Haier, R. J., Siegel, B. V., Nuechterlein, K. H., Hazlett, E., Wu, J. C., Paek, J., et al. (1988). Cortical glucose metabolic-rate correlates of abstract reasoning and attention studied with positron emission tomography. *Intelligence, 12,* 199–217.

Halbwachs, M. (1992). *On collective memory.* Chicago, IL: Chicago University Press.

Hamer, D. H. (2004). *The God gene.* New York: Doubleday.

Hampton, S. (2009). *Essential Evolutionary Psychology.* London: SAGE.

Harré, R. & Dediać, M. (2012). Maintaining social order in the absence of codes. In A. J. Lock (Ed.), *Discourse and Therapeutic Practice.* Oxford: Oxford University Press.

Harré, R. (1984). Some reflections on the concept of social representations. *Social Research, 51,* 927–938.

Harré, R. (1993). *Social being* (2nd ed.). Oxford: Blackwell.

Harré, R. (2006). *Modeling: Gateway to the unknown.* Amsterdam: Elsevier.

Harré, R. (Ed.). (1986). *The social construction of emotions.* Oxford: Blackwell.

Harré, R., & Moghaddam, F. M. (2003). *The self and others.* Westport, CT: Praeger.

Harré, R., & Rossetti, M. (2010). The right to stand and the right to rule. In F. M. Moghaddam, & R. Harré (Eds.), *Words of conflict, words of war* (pp. 111–123). Santa Barbara, CA: Praeger.

Harré, R., & Secord, P. F. (1972). *The explanation of social behavior.* Oxford: Basil Blackwell.

Harré, R., & van Langenhove, L. (1999). *Positioning theory.* Oxford: Blackwell.

Harrison, K. D. (2010). *The last speakers: The quest to save the world's most endangered languages.* Washington, DC: National Geographic.

Hauser, M. D. (2006). *Moral minds.* New York: HarperCollins.

Healy, D. (1997). *The antidepressant era.* Cambridge, MA: Harvard University Press.

Hearnshaw, L. S. (1974). *Cyril Burt: Psychologist.* Ithaca, NY: Cornell University Press.

Hermans, H. J. M. (2001). The construction of a person position repertoire; method and practice. *Culture and Psychology, 7,* 323–365.

Herzlich, C. (1973). *Health and illness: A social psychological analysis.* London: Academic Press.

Higgins, E. T., & Kruglanski, A. W. (2000). Motivational science: The nature and functions of wanting. In E. T. Higgins, & A.W. Kruglanski (Eds.), *Motivational science: Social and personality perspectives* (pp. 1–20). Philadelphia, PA: Psychology Press.

Hogg, M., & Abrams, D. (1993). Towards a single-process uncertainty-reduction model of social motivation in groups. In M. Hogg, & D. Abrams (Eds.), *Group motivation: Social psychological perspectives* (pp. 173–190). New York: Harvester.

Hollyforde, S., & Whiddett, S. (2002). *The motivation handbook.* London: Chartered Institute of Personnel and Development.

Homans, G. C. (1961). *Social behavior: Its elementary forms.* New York: Harcourt, Brace & World.

Howard, D. V., & Howard, J. H. (in press). Dissociable forms of implicit learning in aging. In M. Naveh-Benjamin, & N. Ohta (Eds.), *Perspectives on human memory and aging.* Philadelphia, PA: Psychology Press.

Hubel, D. H., & Wiesel, T. N. (1959). Receptive fields of single neurons in the cat's striate cortex. *Journal of Physiology, 148,* 574–591.

Huesmann, L. R. (2010). Nailing the coffin shut on doubts that video games stimulate aggression: Comments on Anderson et al. (2010). *Psychological Bulletin, 136,* 179–181.

Hume, D. (1787[1962]). *An enquiry concerning human understanding.* Oxford: Clarendon Press.

Huntington, S. P. (1996). *The clash of civilizations and the remaking of world order.* New York: Simon & Schuster.

Hyman, J. (1991). Visual experience and blindsight. In J. Hyman (Ed.), *Investigating psychology: Sciences of the mind after Wittgenstein* (pp. 166–200). London: Routledge.

International Human Genome Consortium. (2004). Finishing the euchromatic sequence of the human genome. *Nature, 431,* 931–945.

Jablensky, A., Sartorius, N., Ernberg, G., Anker, M., Korten A., Cooper, J. E., Day, R., & Bertelsen, A. (1992). Schizophrenia: Manifestations, incidence and course in different cultures: A World Health Organization ten-country study. *Psychological Medicine Monograph Supplement 20.* Cambridge: Cambridge University Press.

Jaeger, S. (1997). Wolfgang Köhler. In W. G. Bringmann, H. E. Luck, R. Miller, & C. E. Early (Eds.), *A Pictorial History of Psychology* (pp. 277–281). Chicago, IL: Quintessence Publishing.

Jaeggi, S. M., Buschkuehl, M., Jonides, J., & Perrig, W. J. (2008). Improving fluid intelligence with training on working memory. *Proceedings of the National Academy of Science, 105,* 6829–6833.

James, W. (1884). What is an emotion? *Mind, 9,* 188–205.

James, W. (1890). *The principles of psychology.* New York: Holt.

Jasso, G. (2005). Culture and the sense of justice. *Journal of Cross-Cultural Psychology, 36,* 14–47.

Jenkins, J. H., & Barrett, R. J. (2010). *Schizophrenia, culture, and subjectivity: The edge of experience.* Cambridge: Cambridge University Press.

Jensen, A. R. (1998). *The g factor: The science of mental ability.* Westport, CT: Praeger.

Jensen, A. R. (2006). *Clocking the mind: Mental chronometry and individual differences.* Amsterdam: Elsevier.

Jezzard, P., Matthews, P. M., & Smith, S. M. (2001). *Functional MRI: Introduction to methods.* Oxford: Oxford University Press.

Joas, H. (1992). *The creativity of action.* Cambridge: Polity.

Jodelet, D. (1991). *Madness and social representations*. Berkeley: University of California Press and London: Harvester/Wheatsheaf.

Joffe, H. (1999). *Risk and 'the other'*. Cambridge: Cambridge University Press.

Jost, J. T., Banaji, M. R., & Nosek, B. A. (2004). A decade of system justification theory: Accumulated evidence for conscious and unconscious bolstering of the status quo. *Political Psychology, 25*, 881–919.

Jovchelovitch, S. (2007). *Knowledge in context: Representations, communities and culture*. London: Routledge.

Jovchelovitch, S. (2008). Rehabilitation of common sense: Social representations, science and cognitive polyphasia. *Journal for the Theory of Social Behaviour, 38*(4), 431–449.

Jovchelovitch, S., Priego-Hernandez, J., & Glăveanu, V. P. (2010). *Constructing public worlds: Investigating children's representations of the public sphere*. Presented at the 10th International Conference on Social Representations, Tunis.

Jung, C. (1923). *Psychological types* (H. Godwin Baynes, Trans.). New York: Harcourt Brace.

Kalat, J. W. (2005). *Introduction to psychology*. Belmont, CA: Wadsworth Thompson Learning.

Kanazawa, S. (2010). Evolutionary psychology and intelligence research. *American Psychologist, 65*, 279–289.

Karama, S., Ad-Dab'bagh, Y., Haier, R. J., Deary, I. J., Lyttelton, O. C., Lepage, C., & Evans, A. C. (2009). Positive association between cognitive ability and cortical thickness in a representative US sample of healthy 6 to 18 year-olds. *Intelligence, 37*, 145–155.

Kédia, G., Berthoz, S., Wessa, M., Hilton, D., & Martinot, J. L. (2008). An agent harms a victim: A functional magnetic resonance imaging study on specific moral emotions. *Journal of Cognitive Neuroscience, 20*, 1788–1798.

Kelly, A. M. C., & Garavan, H. (2005). Human functional neuroimaging of brain changes associated with practice. *Cerebral Cortex, 15*, 1089–1102.

Kenny, A. J. P. (1963). *Action, emotion and will*. London: Routledge and Kegan Paul.

Kintsch, W. (1995). Introduction. In F. C. Bartlett *Remembering: A study of experimental and social psychology* (pp. xi–xv). Cambridge: Cambridge University Press.

Kitwood, T. M. (1980). *Disclosures to a stranger*. London: Routledge and Kegan Paul.

Kleinginna, R. R., & Kleinginna, A. M. (1981). A categorization of emotion definitions, with suggestions for a consensual definition. *Motivation and Emotions, 5*, 345–379.

Koenig, A. M., & Eagly, A. H. (2005). Stereotype threat in men on a test of social sensitivity. *Sex Roles, 52*, 489–496.

Kohlberg, L. (1963). Moral development and identification. In H. W. Stevenson (Ed.), *Year-book of the National Society for the Study of Children: Part I. Child psychology* (pp. 277–332). Chicago, IL: University of Chicago Press.

Kohlberg, L. (1976). Moral stages and moralization: The cognitive-developmental approach. In T. Lickona (Ed.), *Moral development and behavior* (pp. 31–53). New York: Holt.

Kohlberg, L. (1981). *Philosophy of the moral development*. San Francisco: Harper & Row.

Köhler, W. (1938[1928]). *Gestalt psychology*. New York: Mentes.

Konaev, M., & Moghaddam, F. M. (2010). Mutual radicalization. In F. M. Moghaddam, & R. Harré (Eds.), *Words of conflict, words of war: How the language we use in political processes sparks fighting* (pp. 155–171). Santa Barbara, CA: Praeger Security International.

Kotter, R., & Meyer, N. (1992). The limbic system: A review of its empirical foundation. *Behavioral Brain Research, 52*, 105–127.

Kraepelin, E. (1905). *Lectures on clinical psychiatry* (2nd ed.). London: Baillere, Tindall & Cox.

Kretschmer, E. (1925). *Physique and character: An investigation of the nature of constitution and of the theory of temperament* (W. T. Sprott, Trans.). London: Kegan Paul, Trench, Trubner.

Laing, R. D. (1965). *The divided self*. Baltimore, MD: Penguin.

Lamiell, J.T. (2003). *Beyond individual and group differences: Human individuality, scientific psychology, and William Stern's critical personalism*. Thousand Oaks, CA: Sage.

Lamiell, J. T. (2010). *William Stern.* Lengerich: Pabst.

Langer, C. (1887). *Ueber Gemuthbewgungen,* 3 8. English translation.

Langer, C. G. (1887[1907]). *Les emotions etude psychophysiologique.* (G. Dumas, Trans.) Paris: Alcan.

Langford, D. J., Crager, S. E., Shehzad, Z., Smith, S. B., Sotocinal, S. G., Levenstadt, J. S., et al. (2006). Social modulation of pain as evidence for empathy in mice. *Science, 312,* 1967–1970.

LaPiere, R. T. (1934). Attitudes vs. Actions. *Social Forces, 13,* 230–237.

Lashley, K. S. (1950). In search of the engram. *Symposia of the Society for Experimental Biology, 4,* 454–482.

Lawrie, S. M., & Abukmeil, S. S. (1998). Brain abnormality in schizophrenia: A systematic and quantitative review of volumetric magnetic resonance imaging studies. *British Journal of Psychiatry, 172,* 110–120.

Le Bon, G. (1947). *The crowd.* London: Benn.

Lee, N. (2009). Women's discourse in beauty and class in the Bolivarian Republic of Venezuela. *Culture & Psychology, 15,* 147–167.

Lee, S., & Lee, A. M. (2000). Disordered eating in three communities of China: A comparative study of female high school students in Hong Kong, Shenzhen, and rural Hunan. *International Journal of Eating Disorders, 27,* 317–327.

Lee, Y. T., Jussim, L., & McCauley, C. R. (Eds.). (1995). *Stereotype accuracy: Toward appreciating group differences.* Washington, DC: American Psychological Association Press.

Leite, F. P. (2009). Should IQ, perceptual speed, or both be used to explain response time? *American Journal of Psychology, 122,* 517–526.

León, C. A. (1989). Clinical course and outcome of schizophrenia in Cali, Colombia: a ten-year follow-up study. *Journal of Nervous and Mental Disease, 177,* 593–606.

Lerner, M. J. (1980). *The belief in a just world: A fundamental delusion.* New York: Plenum Press.

Lewin, K. (1935). The conflict between Aritotelian and Galilean modes of thought in contemporary psychology. In K. Lewin (Ed.), *Dynamic theory of personality* (pp. 1–42). New York: McGraw-Hill.

Libet, B. (1999). Do we have free will? *Journal of Consciousness Studies, 6*(8–9), 47–57.

Libet, B., Freeman, A., & Sutherland, K. (Eds.). (2000). *The volitional brain: Toward a neuroscience of free will.* Thoverton: Imprint Academic.

Locke, J. (1700). An essay concerning human understanding.

Lorenz, K. (1961). *On aggression* London: Routledge.

Lorenz, K. (1970). *Studies in animal and human behavior* (R. Martin, Trans.). London: Methuen.

Lorenz, K. (1977). *Behind the mirror.* New York: Harcourt Brace Jovanovich.

Louis, W. R., & Taylor, D. M. (2004). Rights and duties as group norms: Implications of intergroup research for the study of rights and responsibilities. In N. Finkel, & F. M. Moghaddam (Eds.), *The psychology of rights and duties: Empirical contributions and normative commentaries* (pp. 105–134). Washington, DC: American Psychological Association Press.

Luria, A. R. (1979). *The making of mind: a personal account of soviet psychology.* Cambridge, MA: Harvard University Press.

Luria, A. R. (1987). *The mind of a mnemonist: A little book about a vast memory.* Cambridge, MA: Harvard University Press.

Lutz, C. (1988). *Unnatural emotions.* Chicago, IL: Chicago University Press.

Lutz, C. (2001). *Homefront: A military city and the American 20th century.* Boston, MA: Beacon Press.

Lutz, C. (2007). Emotion thought and estrangement. In H. Wulff (Ed.), *The emotions: A cultural reader* (ch. 2). New York: Oxford University Press.

Lutz, C. (2009). *The bases of empire: The global struggle against US military posts.* New York: New York University Press.

Lutz, C., & Collins, J. (1993). *Reading National Geographic.* Chicago, IL: Chicago University Press.

Lutz, C., & Fernandez-Carol, A. (2010). *Carjacked: The culture of the automobile and its effect on our lives*. New York: Palgrave Macmillan.

Lutz, C., & Gutmann, M. (2010). *Breaking ranks: Iraq veterans speak out against the war*. Berkeley: University of California Press.

Lyons, W. (1980). *Emotions*. Cambridge: Cambridge University Press.

Macmillan, M. (2000). *An odd kind of fame: Stories of Phineas Gage*. Cambridge, MA: MIT Press.

Maguire, E. A., Gadian, D. G., Johnsrude, I. S., Good, C. D., Ashburner, J., Frackowiak, R. S., & Frith, C.D. (2000). Navigation-related structural change in the hippocampi of taxi drivers. *Proceedings of the National Academy of Science, 97*, 4398–4403.

Malthus, T. R. (1983). *Essay on the principle of population as it affects the future improvement of society*. London: J. M. Dent.

Manstead, A. S. R. (2008). *Psychology of emotions*. London: SAGE.

Maquet, J. J. (1961). *The premise of inequality in Ruanda: A study of political relations in a central African kingdom*. London: Oxford University Press.

Markman, A. B., & Wood, K. L. (2009). *Tools for innovation*. New York: Oxford University Press.

Marková, I. (2003). *Dialogicality and social representations: The dynamics of mind*. Cambridge: Cambridge University Press.

Marr, D. (1982). *Vision: A computational investigation into the human representation and processing of visual information*. San Francisco, CA: W. H. Freeman.

Marsh, P., Rosser, E., & Harré, R. (1977). *The rules of disorder*. London: Routledge.

Marshall, P. J. (2009). Relating psychology and neuroscience: Taking up the challenges. *Perspectives on Psychological Science, 4*(2), 113–125.

Marx, K., & Engels, F. (1967[1848]). *Communist manifesto*. New York: Pantheon.

Maslow, A. H. (1966). *The psychology of science*. New York: Harper Row.

Maslow, A. H. (1970). *Motivation and personality* (3rd ed.). New York: Longman.

Mathiak, K., & Weber, R. (2006). Toward brain correlates of natural behavior: fMRI during violent video games. *Human Brain Mapping, 27*, 948–956.

McAdams, D. P. (1990). *The person: An introduction to personality psychology*. San Diego, CA and London: Harcourt Brace.

McCarthy, T. D., & Zald, M. N. (1977). Resource mobilization and social movements: A partial theory. *American Journal of Sociology, 82*, 1212–1241.

McCrae, R. R., & Costa, P. T. (2003). *Personality in adulthood* (2nd ed.). New York: Guilford Press.

McGruder, J. (2010). Madness in Zanzibar: An exploration of lived experience. In J. H. Jenkins, & R. J. Barrett (Eds.), *Schizophrenia, culture, and subjectivity: The edge of experience*. Cambridge: Cambridge University Press.

McGuire, P. K., Murray, R. M., & Shah, G. M. S. (1993). Increased blood flow in Broca's area during auditory hallucinations in schizophrenia. *Lancet, 342*, 703–706.

McLeod, P., Plunkett, K., & Rolls, E. T. (1998). *Introduction to connectionist modelling of cognitive processes*. Oxford: Oxford University Press.

Mead, J. H. (1934). *Mind, self, and society*. (C. W. Morris Ed.). Chicago, IL: University of Chicago Press.

Mehta, S., & Farina, A. (1997). Is being "sick" really better? Effect of the disease view of mental disorder on stigma. *Journal of Social and Clinical Psychology, 16*, 405–419.

Melis, A. P., Hare, B., & Tomasello, M. (2006). Chimpanzees recruit the best collaborators. *Science, 311*, 1297–1300.

Meltzoff, A. N., & Moore, M. K. (1977). Imitation of facial and manual gestures by human neonates. *Science, 198*, 75–78.

Meltzoff, A. N., & Moore, M. K. (1994). Imitation, memory, and the representation of persons. *Infant Behavior and Development, 17*, 83–99.

Mendez, M. F. (2006). What frontotemporal dementia reveals about the neurobiological basis of morality. *Medical Hypotheses, 67,* 411–418.

Merino, M. E., & Tileagă, C. (2011). The construction of ethnic minority identity: A discursive psychological approach to ethnic self-definition in action. *Discourse & Society, 22,* 86–101.

Miceli, M., & Castelfranchi, C. (2010). Hope: The power of wish and possibility. *Theory & Psychology, 20,* 251–276.

Michaels, C. F., & Corello, C. (1981). *Direct perception.* Englewood Cliffs, NJ: Prentice Hall.

Middleton, D., & Edwards, D. (1990). Conversational remembering: A social psychological approach. In D. Middleton, & D. Edwards (Eds.), *Collective remembering* (pp. 23–46). London: SAGE.

Midgely, M. (2001). *Science and poetry.* London: Routledge.

Miller, G. A. (1956). The magical number seven, plus or minus two: Some limits on our capacity for processing information. *Psychological Review, 63*(2), 343–355.

Miller, G. A. (2010). Mistreating psychology in the decades of the brain. *Perspectives on Psychological Science, 5*(6), 716–743.

Miller, G. A., Galanter, E., & Pribram, K. (1960). *Plans and the structure of behavior.* New York: Holt, Rinehart & Winston.

Mills, C. W. (1940). Situated actions and vocabularies of motive. *American Sociological Review, 5*(6), 904–913.

Milner, B. (1962). Les troubles de la memorie accompagnant des lesions hippocampiques bilaterales. In P. Passouant (Ed.), *Physiologie de l'hippocampe* (pp. 257–272). Paris: Centre National de la Recherche Scientifique.

Milton, J. (1645). Il penseroso. *The Poems of Mr John Milton.* London: Moseley.

Mischel, W. (1986). *Introduction to personality.* New York: Holt, Rinehart, Winston.

Moerman, D. E. (2002). *Medicine and the "Placebo Effect".* Cambridge: Cambridge University Press.

Moghaddam, F. M. (2002). *The individual and society: A cultural integration.* New York: Worth.

Moghaddam, F. M. (2005). *Great ideas in psychology: A cultural and historical exploration.* Oxford: Oneworld.

Moghaddam, F. M. (2008a). *Multiculturalism and intergroup relations: Psychological implications for democracy in global context.* Washington, DC: American Psychological Association Press.

Moghaddam, F. M. (2008b). *How globalization spurs terrorism.* Westport, CT: Praeger.

Moghaddam, F. M. (2009). Omniculturalism: Policy solutions to fundamentalism in the era of fractured globalization. *Culture & Psychology, 15,* 337–347.

Moghaddam, F. M. (2010). *The new global insecurity.* Santa Barbara, CA: Praeger.

Moghaddam, F. M., & Breckenridge, J. (2010). Homeland security and support for multiculturalism, assimilation, and omniculturalism policies among Americans. *Homeland Security Affairs, 4,* 1–14.

Moghaddam, F. M., & Riley, C. J. (2005). Toward a cultural theory of rights and duties in human development. In N. Finkel, & F. M. Moghaddam (Eds.), *The psychology of rights and duties: Empirical contributions and normative commentaries* (pp. 75–104). Washington, DC: American Psychological Association Press.

Moghaddam, F. M., & Stringer, P. (1986). 'Important' and 'trivial' criteria in the minimal group paradigm. *Journal of Social Psychology, 126,* 345–354.

Moghaddam, F. M., & Vuksanovic, V. (1990). Attitudes and behavior toward human rights across different contexts: The role of right-wing authoritarianism, political ideology, and religiosity. *International Journal of Psychology, 25,* 455–474.

Moll, J., de Oliveira-Souza, R., & Eslinger, P. J. (2003). Morals and the human brain: A working model. *NeuroReport, 14,* 299–305.

Moll, J., Oliviera-Souza, R. de., Bramati, I. E., & Grafman, J. (2005). Functional networks in emotional moral and nonmoral social judgments. In J. T. Cacioppa, & G. E. Berntson (Eds.), *Social neuroscience.* New York and Hove: Psychology Press.

Morris, D. (1967). *The naked ape*. New York: McGraw-Hill.

Morris, I. (1975). *The nobility of failure*. London: Secker and Warburg.

Moscovici, S. (1963). Attitudes and opinions. *Annual Review of Psychology, 14*, 231–260.

Moscovici, S. (1985). *The age of the crowd*. Cambridge: Cambridge University Press.

Moscovici, S. (1997). *Chronique des années égarées*. Paris: Stock.

Moscovici, S. (2000). *Social representations: Explorations in social psychology*. Cambridge: Polity.

Moscovici, S. (2008[1961]). *Psychoanalysis: Its image and its public*. Cambridge: Polity.

Moyal-Sharrock, D. (2004). *Understanding Wittgenstein's on certainty*. London: Palgrave.

Muhlhausler, P., & Harré, R. (1990). *Pronouns and people*. Oxford: Blackwell.

Musick, F. E., & Burns, J. A. (2007). *The auditory system*. London: Pearson, Allyn & Bacon.

Nadel, J., & Butterworth, G. (Eds.). (1999). *Imitation in infancy*. Cambridge: Cambridge University Press.

Nagel, T. (1974). What is it like to be a bat? *Philosophical Review, 83*(4), 435–450.

Nelson, K., & Fivush, R. (2004). The emergence of autobiographical memory: A social cultural developmental theory. *Psychological Review, 111*(2), 486–511.

Nelson, R. J. (Ed.). (2005). *Biology of aggression*. New York: Oxford University Press.

Nelson, R. J., & Trainor, B. C. (2007). Neural mechanisms of aggression. *Nature Reviews: Neuroscience, 8*, 536–546.

Nelson, T. O., & Narens, L. (1990). Metamemory: A theoretical framework and new findings. *The Psychology of Learning and Motivation, 26*, 125–173.

Neubauer, A. C., & Fink, A. (2009). Intelligence and neural efficiency. *Neuroscience and Biobehavioral Reviews, 33*, 1004–1023.

Newell, A., & Simon, H. A. (1972). *Human problem solving*. Englewood Cliffs, NJ: Prentice Hall.

Nigro, G., & Neisser, U. (1983). Point of view in personal memories. *Cognitive Psychology, 15*, 467–482.

Nisbett, R. E. (2009). *Intelligence and how to get it: Why schools and cultures count*. New York: Norton.

Nisbett, R. E., & Cohen, D. (1996). *Culture of honor: Violence and the U.S. South*. Boulder, CO: Westview Press.

Nisbett, R. E., & Miyamoto, Y. (2005). The influence of culture: Holistic vs. analytic perception. *Trends in Cognitive Science, 9*, 467–473.

Noë, A. (2009). Out of our heads: *Why you are not your brain and other lessons from the biology of consciousness*. Hill and Wang: New York.

Nopoulos, P., Flaum, M., & Andreasen, N. C. (1997). Sex differences and brain morphology in schizophrenia. *American Journal of Psychiatry, 154*, 1648–1654.

Nussbaum, N. (2001). *Upheavals of thought: The intelligence of emotions*. Cambridge: Cambridge University Press.

Oatley, K. (1992). *Best laid schemes: The psychology of the emotions*. Cambridge: Cambridge University Press.

Oatley, K., & Jenkins, J. M. (1996). *Understanding emotions*. London: SAGE.

Ogbu, J. O., & Davis, A. (2003). *Black American students in an affluent suburb: A study of academic disengagement*. Oxford: Routledge.

Okada, T., & Nakai, T. (2003). Silent fMRI acquisition methods for large acoustic noise during scan. *Magnetic Resonance in Medical Sciences, 2*(4), 181–187.

Osbeck, L., Moghaddam, F. M., & Perreault, S. (1977). Similarity and attraction among majority and minority groups in a multicultural context. *International Journal of Intercultural Relations, 21*, 113–123.

Pareto, V. (1935). *The mind and society: A treatise on general sociology* (Vols. 1–4). New York: Dover.

Parker, I. (2002). *Critical discursive psychology*. Houndsmills and New York: Palgrave Macmillan.

Parkinson, B. & Colman, A.M. (1994). Introduction. In B. Parkinson, & A.M. Colman (Eds.), *Emotion and motivation* (pp. xi–xvi). London: Longman.

Parrott, W. G. (Ed.). (2007). *Emotions and social psychology.* Philadelphia, PA: Psychology Press.

Parrott, W. G., & Harré, R. (1996). Embarrassment and the threat to character. In R. Harré, & W. G. Parrott (Eds.), *The emotions: Social, cultural, and biological dimensions* (pp. 39–56). Thousand Oaks, CA: SAGE.

Pavlov, I. (1927). *Conditioned reflexes: The investigation of the physiological activity of the cerebral cortex.* London: Oxford University Press.

Piaget, J. (1962). *Play, dreams and imitation in childhood.* New York: Norton.

Pierson, P., & Kacker, J. S. (2010). *Winner-take-all-politics: How Washington made the rich richer – and turned its back on the middle class.* New York: Simon & Schuster.

Polanyi, M. (1958). *Personal knowledge.* Chicago, IL: Chicago University Press.

Potter, J., &Wetherell, M. (1987). *Discourse and social psychology: Beyond attitudes and behavior.* London: SAGE.

Potts, R., & Sloan, C. (2010). *What does it mean to be human?* Washington DC: National Geographic.

Prashad, V. (2001). *Everybody was Kung Fu fighting: Afro-Asian connections and the myth of cultural purity.* Boston, MA: Beacon Press.

Premack, D., & Woodruff, G. (1978). Does the chimpanzee have a theory of mind. *The Behavioral and Brain Sciences, 4,* 515–526.

Propp, V. (1968). *The morphology of the folk tale.* Austin, TX: University of Texas Press.

Quinn, D. M., & Crocker, J. (1999). When ideology hurts: Effects of belief in the protestant ethic and feeling overweight on the psychological well-being of women. *Journal of Personality and Social Psychology, 77,* 402–414.

Randall, C. R., & Mueller, C. W. (1995). Extensions of justice theory: Justice evaluations and employees' reactions in a natural setting. *Social Psychology Quarterly, 58,* 178–194.

Ratner, C. (1997). *Cultural psychology and qualitative methodology.* New York: Plenum Press.

Rest, J., Narvaez, D., Bebeau, M., & Thoma, S. (1999). *Postconventional moral thinking: A Neo-Kohlbergian approach.* Mahwah, NJ: Lawrence Erlbaum.

Reid, T. (2002[1785]). *Essays on the intellectual powers of man.* Edinburgh: Edinburgh University Press, Edinburgh.

Ridley, M. (2003). *Nature via nurture.* New York: Harper Collins.

Roback, A. A. (1927). *The psychology of character with a survey of temperament.* New York: Harcourt and Brace.

Robertson, D., Snarey, J., Ousley, O., Harenski, K., Bowman, F. D., Gilkey, R., & Kilts, C. (2007). The neural processing of moral sensitivity to issues of justice and care. *Neuropsychologia, 45,* 755–766.

Roediger, H. L. III (1997). Review of *Remembering: A study in experimental and social psychology,* Frederic C. Bartlett. *Contemporary Psychology, 42,* 488–492.

Rosenhan, D. L. (1973). On being sane in insane places. *Science, 179,* 250–258.

Rotter, J. B., & Hochreich, D. J. (1975). *Personality.* Glenview, IL: Scott Forsman.

Runciman, W. G. (1966). *Relative deprivation and social justice.* Harmondsworth: Penguin.

Russell, S. J., & Norvig, P. (2009). *Artificial intelligence* (3rd ed.). Upper Saddle Hill, NJ: Prentice Hall.

Rutter, D., & Durkin, K. (1987). Turn-taking in mother-infant interaction: An examination of vocalization and gaze. *Developmental Psychology, 23,* 54–61.

Ryan, M. K., David, B., & Reynolds, K. J. (2004). Who cares? The effect of gender and context on the self and moral reasoning. *Psychology of Women Quarterly, 28,* 246–255.

Ryckman, R. M. (1997). *Theories of personality.* London: Brooks Cole.

Ryle, G. (1949). *The concept of mind.* London: Hutchinson.

Sabat, S. R. (2010). Stern words about the mind-brain problem: Keeping the whole person in mind. *New Ideas in Psychology, 28,* 168–174.

Sabini, J., & Silver, M. (1981). *Morality of everyday life.* Oxford: Oxford University Press.

Sabini, J., & Silver, M. (1998). *Emotion, character and responsibility.* Oxford: Oxford University Press.

Sacks, O. (1983). *Awakenings.* New York: E. P. Dutton.

Sammut, G., & Gaskell, G. (2010). Points of view, social positioning and intercultural relations. *Journal for the Theory of Social Behavior, 40,* 47–64.

Sapolsky, R. M. (2004). Social status and health in humans and other animals. *Annual Review of Anthropology, 33,* 393–418.

Saussure, de, F. (1916[2001]). *Course in general linguistics:* New York: Columbia University Press.

Schachter, S., & Singer, J. F. (1962). Cognitive, social and physiological determinants of emotional state. *Psychological Review, 69*(5), 379–399.

Schacter, D. L., Addis, D. R., & Buckner, R. I. (2007). Remembering the past to imagine the future: The prospective brain. *Nature Reviews. Neuroscience, 8*(9), 657–661.

Schaich Borg, J. S., Hynes, C., Van Horn, J., Grafton, S., & Sinnott-Armstrong, W. (2006). Consequences, actions, and intention as factors in moral judgments: An fMRI investigation. *Journal of Cognitive Neuroscience, 18,* 803–817.

Schank, R., & Abelson, R. (1977). *Scripts, plans, goals and understanding.* Hillsdale, NJ: Erlbaum.

Schmalleger, F. (2011). *Criminology today* (6th ed.). Upper Saddle River, NJ: Pearson/Prentice Hall.

Scott, D., Heitzeg, M. M., Koeppe, R. A., Stohler, C. S., & Zubieta, J-K. (2006). Variations in the human pain stress experience mediated by ventral and dorsal basal ganglia. *Journal of Neuroscience, 26*(42), 10789–10795.

Shami, P., & Stuss, D. T. (1999). Humour appreciation: a role of the right frontal lobe. *Brain, 122,* 657–666.

Shapiro, A. K., & Shapiro, E. (1997). *The Powerful Placebo.* Baltimore: The Johns Hopkins University Press.

Shaver, K. G. (1985). *Attitudes of blame.* New York: Springer.

Sheppard, L. D., & Vernon, P. A. (2008). Intelligence and speed of information-processing: A review of 50 years of research. *Personality and Individual Differences, 44,* 535–551.

Sherif, M. (1966). *Group conflict and cooperation: Their social psychology.* London: Routledge & Kegan Paul.

Sherif, M., & Sherif, C. W. (1956). *An outline of social psychology.* New York: Harper.

Shipton, H. W. (1975). EEG analysis: A history and a prospectus. *Annual Review of Biophysics and Bioengineering, 4,* 1–13.

Shorter, E. (1986). *Paralysis: The rise and fall of a 'hysterical' symptom. Journal of Social History, 19,* 549–582.

Shotter, J. (1975). *Images of man in psychological research.* London: Methuen.

Shweder, R. A. (1991a). *Thinking through cultures.* Cambridge, MA: Harvard University Press.

Shweder, R. A. (1991b). *How to do things with words.* Oxford: Clarendon Press.

Shweder, R. A. (1994) 'You're not sick, you're just in love': Emotion as an interpretative system. In P. Ekman, & R. J. Davidson (Eds.), *The nature of emotions* (pp. 32–44). New York: Oxford University Press.

Shweder, R. A., & Sullivan, M. (1989). The semiotic subject of cultural psychology. In L. Previn (Ed.), *Handbook of personality theory and research.* New York: Guilford.

Sidanius, J., & Pratto, F. (1999). *Social dominance: An intergroup theory of social dominance and oppression.* Cambridge: Cambridge University Press.

Siever, L. J. (2008). Neurobiology of aggression and violence. *American Journal of Psychiatry, 165,* 429–442.

Silverman, D. (1993). *Interpreting qualitative data.* London: SAGE.

Singh, D. (1994). Is thin really beautiful and good? Relationship between EWHR and female attractiveness. *Personality and Individual Differences, 16,* 123–132.

Skinner, B. F. (1948). 'Superstition' in the pigeon. *Journal of Experimental Psychology, 38,* 168–172.

Skinner, B. F. (1974). *About behaviorism.* London: Cape.

Smedslund, J. (1988). *Psychologic.* Berlin and New York: Springer.

Smith, J. A. (Ed.). (2008). *Qualitative psychology: A practical guide*. London and Thousand Oaks: SAGE.

Snyder, S. H. (1976). The dopamine hypothesis in schizophrenia. *American Journal of Psychiatry, 133*, 197–202.

Sousa, R. de (2007). Emotion. *Stanford encyclopedia of philosophy*. The encyclopedia is on-line only (available at: www.plato.stanford.edu).

Stanovich, K. E. (2009). *What intelligence tests miss: The psychology of rational thought*. New Haven, CT: Yale University Press.

Stearns, P. N., & Knapp, M. (1996). Historical perspectives on grief. In R. Harré, & W. G. Parrott (Eds.), *The emotions: Social, cultural, and biological dimensions* (pp. 132–150). Thousand Oaks, CA: SAGE.

Stearns, P. N., & Stearns, C. Z. (1988). *Emotion and social change*. New York: Holmes and Meier.

Stern, W. (1938). *General psychology from a personalist standpoint* (H. D. Spoerl, Trans.). New York: Macmillan.

Sternberg, R. J., & Grigorenko, E. L. (Eds.). (2002). *The general intelligence factor: How general is it?* Mahwah, NJ: Erlbaum.

Sternberg, R. J., & the Rainbow Project Collaborators (2006). The rainbow project: Enhancing the SAT through assessments of analytical, practical, and creative skills. *Intelligence, 34*, 321–350.

Suppes, P., & Han, B. (2000). Brain wave representation of words by superposition of a few sine waves. *Proceedings of the National Academy of Sciences of the USA, 97*, 8738–8743.

Tajfel, H. (1959). Quantitative judgment in social perception. *British Journal of Psychology, 50*, 16–29.

Tajfel, H. (1970). Experiments in intergroup discrimination. *Scientific American, 223*, 96–102.

Tajfel, H. (1978). (Ed.). *Differences between social groups*. London and New York: Academic Press.

Tajfel, H., & Turner, J. C. (1979). An integrative theory of intergroup conflict. In W. G. Austin, & S. Worchel (Eds.), *The social psychology of intergroup relations* (pp. 33–47). Monterey, CA: Brooks/Cole.

Tajfel, H., & Turner, J. C. (1985). The social identity theory of intergroup behavior. In S. Worchel & W. G. Austin (Eds.), *Psychology of intergroup relations* (pp. 7–24). Chicago: Nelson-Hall.

Tajfel, H., Flament, C., Billig, M. G., & Bundy, R. F. (1971). Social categorization and intergroup behavior. *European Journal of Social Psychology, 1*, 149–177.

Tannen, D. (1993). *Framing in discourse*. Oxford: Oxford University Press.

Taylor, D. M., & Moghaddam, F. M. (1994). *Theories of intergroup relations* (2nd ed.). Westport, CT: Praeger.

Taylor, G. (1996). Guilt and remorse. In R. Harré, & W. G. Parrott (Eds.), *The emotions: Social, cultural, and biological dimensions*. Thousand Oaks, CA: SAGE.

Thara, R., Henrietta, M., Joseph, A., Rajkumar, S., & Eaton, W. W. (1994). Ten-year course of schizophrenia. The Madras longitudinal study. *Acta Psychiatrica Scandinavica, 90*, 329–336.

Thomson, J. J. (1986). *Rights, restitution, and risk: Essays in moral theory*. Cambridge, MA: Harvard University Press.

Tinbergen, N. (1969). Ethology. In R. Harré (Ed.), *Scientific Thought: 1900–1960* (pp. 238–268). Oxford: Clarendon Press.

Todorov, T. (1975). *The tell-tale sign*. Lisse: Peter de Ridder Press.

Toga, A. W., & Thompson, P. M. (2005). Genetics of brain structure and intelligence. *Annual Review of Neuroscience, 28*, 1–23.

Tomasello, M. (1999). *The cultural origins of human cognition*. Cambridge, MA: Harvard University Press.

Tomkins, S. S. (1980). Affect as amplification: Some modifications in theory. In R. Plutchik, & H. Kellerman (Eds.), *Emotion: Theory, research, and experience* (pp. 141–164). New York: Academic Press.

Touman, S. E. (1978). The Mozart of psychology. *New York Review of Books*, 51–57.

Turing, A. M. (1950). Computing machinery and intelligence. *Mind NS, 59*, 433–450.

Tyler, T. R., & Huo, Y. J. (2002). *Trust in the law*. New York: Russell Sage Foundation.

Uhlmann, E. L., Brescoll, V. L., & Machery, E. (2010). The motives underlying stereotype-based discrimination against members of stigmatized groups. *Social Justice Research, 23*, 1–16.

Valsiner, J. (2000). *Culture and human development*. Thousand Oaks, CA: SAGE.

Valsiner, J. (2007). *Culture in minds and societies*. Thousand Oaks, CA: SAGE.

Valsiner, J., & Rosa, A. (Eds.). (2007). *The Cambridge handbook of socio-cultural psychology*. New York: Cambridge University Press.

Van den Berghe, P. (1987). *The ethnic phenomenon*. New York: Praeger.

Van Den Bogaert, A., Sleegers, K., De Zutter, S., Heyrman, L., Norrback, K-F., Adolfsson, R., Van Broeckhoven., & Del-Favero, J. (2006). Association with brain-specific tryptophan hydroxylase, tph, with unipolar and bipolar bisorder in a Northern Swedish isolated population. *Archives of General Psychiatry, 63*, 1103–1110.

Van der Vegt, B. J., Lieuwes, N., van de Wall, E. H., Kato, K., Moya-Albiol, L., Martinez-Sanchis, S., de Boer, S. F., & Koolhaas, J. M. (2003). Activation of serotonergic neurotransmission during the performance of aggressive behavior in rats. *Behavioral Neuroscience, 117*, 667–674.

Van Leeuwen, M., Peper, J. S., van den Berg, S. M., Brouwer, R. M., Hulshoff Pol, H. E., Kahn, R. S., & Boomsma, D. (2009). A genetic analysis of brain volumes and IQ in children. *Intelligence, 37*, 181–191.

Von Cranach, M., & Harré, R. (Eds.). (1982). *The analysis of action*. Cambridge: Cambridge University Press.

Von Cranach, M., Doise, W., & Mugny, G. (1992). *Social representations and the social basis of knowledge*. Lewiston, New York: Hogrefe & Huber.

Von Uxkull, J. (1909). *Umwelt und Innenwelt de Tiere*. Berlin: Springer.

Vul, E., Harris, C., Winkielman, P., & Pashler, H. (2009). Puzzlingly high correlations in fMRI studies of emotion, personality, and social cognition. *Perspectives on Psychological Science, 4*, 274–290.

Vygotsky, L. S. (1978a). *Mind in society: The development of higher psychological processes*. Cambridge, MA: Harvard University Press.

Vygotsky, L. S. (1978b). *Thought and language*. Cambridge, MA: MIT Press.

Vygotsky, L. S. (1987). *The collected works of L. S. Vygotsky. Volume 4: The history of the development of higher mental functions*. New York: Plenum Press.

Vygotsky, L. S., & Luria A. (1994). Tool and symbol in child development. In R. van der Veer, & J. Valsiner (Eds.), *The Vygotsky reader*. Oxford: Blackwell.

Wagenmakers, E. J., & Brown, S. (2007). On the linear relation between the mean and the standard deviation of a response time distribution. *Psychological Review, 114*, 830–841.

Wagner, W. (1993). Can representations explain social behavior? A discussion of social representations as rational systems. *Papers on Social Representations, 2*, 236–249.

Wagner, W., & Hayes, N. (2005). *Everyday discourse and common-sense: The theory of social representation*. New York: Palgrave Macmillan.

Wagoner, B. (2011). Meaning construction in remembering: A synthesis of Bartlett and Vygotsky. In J. Stenner, J. Cromby, J. Motzkau, J. Yen, & Y. Haosheng (Eds.), *Theoretical psychology: Global transformations and challenges* (pp. 105–114). Toronto: Captus Press.

Wahba, M., & Bridwell, L. (1976). Maslow reconsidered: A review of research on the need hierarchy theory. *Organizational Behavior and Human Performance, 15*(2), 212–240.

Walker, I., & Smith, H. J. (Eds.). (2002). *Relative deprivation: Specification, development, and integration*. Cambridge: Cambridge University Press.

Walster, E., Walster, G. E., & Berscheid, E. (1978). *Equity: Theory and research*. Boston, MA: Allyn & Bacon.

Watson, J. B. (1913). Psychology as a behaviorist views it. *Psychological Review, 20*, 158–177.

Watson, J. B., & Rayner, R. (1920). Conditioned emotional reactions. *Journal of Experimental Psychology, 3*, 1–14.

Watters, E. (2010). *Crazy like us*. New York: Free Press.

Wegner, D. (2002). *The illusion of conscious will*. Cambridge, MA: MIT Press.

Weiner, B. (1992). *Human motivation: Metaphors, theories, and research*. Newbury Park, CA: SAGE.

Werner, H. (1934). L'Unité des sens. *Journal de Psychologie*, 31, 190–205.

Wertheimer, M. (1938[1923]). Gestalt theory. In W. D. Ellis (Ed. and Trans.), *A source book of Gestalt psychology* (pp. 1–11). London: Routledge.

Wertsch, J. (2002). *Voices of collective remembering*. Cambridge: Cambridge University Press.

White, A. R. (1964). *Attention*. Oxford: Blackwell.

Wierzbicka, A. (1992). *Semantics, culture and cognition*. New York: Oxford University Press.

Wierzbicka, A. (1999). *Emotions across languages and cultures*. Cambridge: Cambridge University Press.

Wierzbicka, A. (2010). Experience, evidence and sense: The hidden cultural legacy of English. Oxford: Oxford University Press.

Wilson, E. (1998). *On human nature*. Cambridge, MA: Harvard University Press.

Wilson, E. O. (1975). *Sociobiology: The new synthesis*. Cambridge, MA: Cambridge University Press.

Wilson, E. O. (1978). *Human nature*. Cambridge, MA: Harvard University Press.

Windelband, W. (1894). *Preludes, articles and speeches*. Tubingen: Mohr.

Winnicott, D. W. (1971). *Playing and reality*. London: Tavistock Publications.

Witelson, S. F., Kigar, D. L., & Harvey, T. (1999). The exceptional brain of Alfred Einstein. *The Lancet*, 353, 2149–2153.

Witkin, H. A., & Goodenough, D. R. (1981). *Cognitive styles: essences and origins*. New York: International Universities Press.

Wittgenstein, L. (1922[2001]). *Tractatus logico-philsophicus*. In D. Pears & B. McGuiness (Eds.). London: Routledge.

Wittgenstein, L. (1953). *Philosophical investigations*. Oxford: Blackwell.

Wittgenstein, L. (1972). *Emotions and life*. Washington, DC: American Psychological Association.

Wittgenstein, L. (1976). *On certainty*. Oxford: Blackwell.

Wood, L. A., & Kroger, R. O. (1986). *Doing discourse analysis*. Thousand Oaks, CA: SAGE.

World Health Organization. (1996). *Schizophrenia and public health*. WHO/MSA/NAM/97.6

Wright, S. C., Taylor, D. M., & Moghaddam, F. M. (1990). Responding to membership in a disadvantaged group: From acceptance to collective protest. *Journal of Personality and Social Psychology*, 58, 994–1003.

Wulff, H. (2007). *The emotions: A cultural reader*. New York: Oxford University Press.

Wundt, W. M. (1916). *Elements of folk psychology* (E. L. Schaub, Trans.). New York: Macmillan.

Yates, F. (1966). *The art of memory*. Chicago, IL: University of Chicago Press.

Young, L. J., Wang, Z., & Insel, T. R. (1998). Neuroendocrine bases of monogamy. *Trends Neurosci*, 21, 71–75.

Young, L., & Saxe, R. (2008). The neural basis of belief encoding and integration in moral judgment. *NeuroImage*, 40, 1912–1920.

Zeigarnik, B. V. (1967). On finished and unfinished tasks. In W. D. Ellis (Ed.), *A sourcebook of Gestalt psychology*. New York: Humanities Press.

Zhang, X., Besaulieu, Sotnikoa, T., Gaitnetdinov, R., & Caron, M. G. (2004). Tryptophan Hydrolase-2 controls brain serotonin synthesis. *Science*, 305, 217.

Zink, C. F., Tong, Y., Chen, O., Bassett, D. S., Stein, J. L., & Meyer-Lindenberg, A. (2008). Know your place: Neural processing of social hierarchy in humans. *Neuron*, 58, 273–283.

Zubin, J., & Spring, B. (1977). Vulnerability: A new view of schizophrenia. *Journal of Abnormal Psychology*, 86, 103–126.

Name Index

Lorenz, K. 46–7, 48, 106, 154, 155, 156, 195, 273–4
Luria, A.R. 39–41, 55–6, 133–5, 136–7
  Vygotsky, L.S. & 174
Lutz, C. 182–3, 184, 187–8

McAdams, D.P. 232
McCrae, R.R. & Costa, P.T. 224, 225, 229, 232
McGruder, J. 249
Malthus, T.R. 270–1
Manstead, A. 183, 193, 195, 202
Marková, I. 176–7
Marr, D. 95–6
Marx, K. 276, 279
Maslow, A. 168, 251
Mehta, S. & Farina, A. 248–9
Merino, M.E. & Tileaga, C. 281
Middleton, D. & Edwards, D. 128–9
Midgely, M. 251–2
Mills, C.W. 166, 171, 176
Milner, B. 124
Moghaddam, F.M. 4, 11, 260, 262, 269, 278, 279–80, 284, 285–6, 287
  & Beckenridge, J. 287
  Finkel, N.J. & 281
  Konaev, M. & 284
  & Riley, C.J. 262
  & Stringer, P. 281
  Taylor, D.M. & 285
  & Vuksanovic, V. 258
Moll, J. et al. 162–3, 265
Moscovici, S. 144, 149, 176, 177, 178
Mühlhäusler, P. & Harré, R. 28
Musick, F.E. & Burns, J.A. 83

Nagel, T. 68
Newell, A. & Simon, H. 50

Nisbett, R.E. 203
  & Cohen, D. 283
  & Miyamoto, Y. 211

Oatley, K. & Jenkins, J. 183, 187, 195

Pareto, V. 276–7
Parkinson, B. & Colman, A.M. 173
Parrott, W.G. & Harré, R. 186–7
Parson, M. 217
Pavlov, I. 105, 111, 122–3, 261
Piaget, J. 99–101, 109, 110, 255, 256
Plato 121
Premack, D. 110
Propp, V. 32

Ratner, C. 144
Reid, T. 59, 60, 79
Ridley, M. 48
Roback, A.A. 219
Rosenhan, D.L. 247, 248
Ryan, M.K. et al. 257
Ryckman, R.M. 217
Ryle, G. 20, 24–6, 66–7, 185

Schachter, S. & Singer, J.F. 194
Schaich Borg, J.S. et al. 266
Shaver, K.G. 11–12
Sheppard, L.D. & Vernon, P.A. 213
Sherif, M. 141–2, 277, 278
Sherrington, C. 122
Shipton, H.W. 38
Shweder, R.A. 10, 143, 149, 202
  & Sullivan, M. 245
Simon, T. 206–7
Singh, D. 157, 158
Skinner, B.F. 112, 123
Smedslund, J. 26
Spearman, C. 207
Stanovich, K.E. 215–16

Stearns, P.N.
  & Knapp, M. 187, 189
  & Stearns, C.Z. 36, 187
Stern, W. 4
Sternberg, R.J. 208, 209
Suppes, P. & Han, B. 41

Tajfel, H. 142, 280
  et al. 279, 286
  & Turner, J.C. 279
Taylor, D.M. & Moghaddam, F.M. 285
Tinbergen, N. 46, 47, 154
Todorov, T. 32
Turing, A. 50, 95

Uhlmann, E.L. et al. 259

Valsiner, J. 150
Van den Berghe, P. 271–2
Van Den Bogaert, A. et al. 53
Vygotsky, L.S. 19, 41, 113, 116–17, 130–3, 136, 137, 140, 161, 174, 175
  & Luria, A. 174

Watson, J.B. 6, 122–3, 261
  & Rayner, R. 123
Weiner, B. 166, 167, 168
Wernicke, C. 39
Wertheimer, M. 85, 86
Wertsch, J. 129
Wierzbicka, A. 14, 22, 36, 65
Wilson, E.O. 48
Winnicott, D.W. 179
Witkin, H.A. & Goodenough, D.R. 223–4
Wittgenstein, L. 9–10, 22, 24, 26, 55, 57, 97, 164, 188–9, 199, 200
Wood, L.A. & Kroger, R.O. 159
Wundt, W.M. 3, 36, 117, 118, 120

Subject Index

mental disorders and treatments
237–9
and culture 247–50
mood disorders 250–1
pseudopatient study 247, 248
whole person approach 251–2
see also schizophrenia
mental images 67
culturally mediated memory
131–2
and emotions 194, 197, 198
and synesthesia 134–5
mental 'speed' and intelligence
213–14, 215–16
mereological fallacy 124, 170
metalanguage 14
mind
as discourse 8–10
theory of 110
'mind-body' ties 141–5
mnemonism 133–5
molecular (M) grammar 12, 13,
14, 39, 45, 51, 251
and organism (O) grammar
framework 37–9
see also grammars of
discourses
mood disorders 250–1
moral reasoning
communal/care-based *vs*
justice-based 256–7
development
moral careers 150–1
stage theory 99, 101, 255–6
neural correlates 264–7
vs non-moral judgments 162–3
positioning theory 33–5, 150
rational and emotional
approaches 265–6
see also justice
motivation 167–9
context of experience 171–3
individual and environmental
factors 169–71
and social representations
173–80
multiculturalism 286–7

narratology
basic principles 29–31
as key aspect 32–3
standard plots 31–2
theory of personality 232
natural selection 46, 47–9, 105–6,
271
nature/nurture debate 46, 227
Necker cube 94

needs hierarchy 168
neo-/pre-frontal cortex
emotions 197
memory and learning 124–5,
136
volume and social group
complexity 49, 156
neural correlates
aggression 275–6
emotion 162–3, 193–5
intelligence 213–15
learning and memory 122–5
moral reasoning 264–7
motivation 168–9
religiosity 159–60
neural efficiency 214
neuroimaging
EEG 41
MRI/fMRI 42–5, 93, 162–3,
168–9, 237
PET 17, 41–2, 93, 214
neuroticism 222–3, 226
neurotransmitters 51–2
dopamine 45, 157, 159–60, 242
glutamate 82
MAOA 273
serotonin 52–4, 159–60

Oedipal theory 104, 233
operant conditioning 111,
112, 123
oral, anal and genital stages
104, 233
organism (O) grammar 12, 13, 14,
45, 110, 130, 131, 251
and molecular (M) grammar
framework 37–9
see also grammars of discourses
oxytocin 157

Paleolithic ancestry 108, 151,
155–6
parent-child relationship 106–7,
233–4, 262–3, 272
parvo- and magno-cellular brain
structures 156
'Pentad' scheme 31–2, 231
perception
brain structures 156
double transduction systems
80–4
hearing 82–4
historical development of study
78–80
hybrid account 76–8
seeing 80–2, 90–1, 93–6
smell and taste 84

perception *cont.*
theories 84–96
computation (Marr) 95–6
ecological (Gibson) 87–91
Gestalt (Köhler) 85–7
hypothesis testing (Gregory)
91–5
touch 84, 89–90
perceptual consciousness 64–5,
72, 73
person
concept of 2, 3, 11, 165
P grammar 11–12, 13, 14, 40,
44, 51, 130, 131, 251
see also grammars of
discourses
personality
and attributes 223–4
body types and endocrine
secretions 230
definitions 217
deviant, origins of 233–4
explanatory formats 226–7
idiographic/nomothetic debate
218–19
and physical health 234
and related concepts 219–20
research methods 225–6
theories
critiques 230–1, 235–6
cultural repertoires 231–2
and descriptions 224–5
dispositional 218, 227–30,
231, 232, 235
trait 226, 231, 232, 235
types 220–3
personality disorder 220
PET scan 17, 41–2, 93, 214
'phi phenomenon' 86
phobias 250
physical health and personality 234
'pickup' (ecological theory of
perception) 89, 91
placebo effect 238
'point of view' concept 151–3
'politeness' 263
polygamy/polygyny 158
polyphasia 176–7
positioning theory 33–5, 150
positron emission tomography
(PET) 17, 41–2, 93, 214
post traumatic stress disorder
(PTSD) 250
potential space, concept of 179–80
practical intelligence 208, 209
pre-frontal cortex *see* neo-/
pre-frontal cortex